Machine Learning Applications in Finance, 2nd Edition

Machine Learning Applications in Finance, 2nd Edition

Guest Editor

Jong-Min Kim

MDPI

Basel • Beijing • Wuhan • Barcelona • Belgrade • Novi Sad • Cluj • Manchester

Guest Editor
Jong-Min Kim
Statistics Discipline
Division of Science and
Mathematics
University of Minnesota at
Morris
Morris
USA

Editorial Office
MDPI AG
Grosspeteranlage 5
4052 Basel, Switzerland

This is a reprint of the Special Issue, published open access by the journal *Journal of Risk and Financial Management* (ISSN 1911-8074), freely accessible at: https://www.mdpi.com/journal/jrfm/special_issues/7JO77A08R1.

For citation purposes, cite each article independently as indicated on the article page online and as indicated below:

Lastname, Firstname, Firstname Lastname, and Firstname Lastname. Article Title. *Journal Name* **Year**, *Volume Number*, Page Range.

ISBN 978-3-7258-5995-5 (Hbk)
ISBN 978-3-7258-5996-2 (PDF)
https://doi.org/10.3390/books978-3-7258-5996-2

Contents

About the Editor

Jong-Min Kim

Jong-Min Kim is Professor of Statistics at University of Minnesota-Morris, USA. He received his PhD (Statistics) in 2002 from Department of Statistics, Oklahoma State University, USA (Minor: Mathematics). He worked as Research Fellow at SAMSI—The Statistical and Applied Mathematical Sciences Institute (NSF, Duke, NCSU and UNC). He has received the Morris Faculty Distinguished Research Award. He also joined University of Minnesota Data Science Initiative Core Member in May, 2024, and joined EGADE Business School Tecnologico de Monterrey as Adjunct Professor of Finance in June, 2025.

Journal of
Risk and Financial Management

MDPI

Editorial

Editorial: Machine Learning Applications in Finance, 2nd Edition

Jong-Min Kim [1,2]

[1] Statistics Discipline, Division of Science and Mathematics, University of Minnesota-Morris, Morris, MN 56267, USA; jongmink@morris.umn.edu
[2] EGADE Business School, Tecnológico de Monterrey, Ave. Rufino Tamayo, Monterrey 66269, Mexico

1. Special Issue Overview

FinTech has become a central research focus in modern finance, driven by the increasing complexity and volume of financial data. To promote emerging research in this area, the *Journal of Risk and Financial Management (JRFM)* is dedicating a Special Issue to "Machine Learning Applications in Finance, 2nd Edition." This issue emphasizes the development and application of advanced machine learning (ML) and artificial intelligence (AI) techniques for large-scale and complex financial datasets.

The goal of this Special Issue is to highlight the state-of-the-art methods that address practical challenges in financial data analysis, including portfolio management, risk assessment, asset pricing, fraud detection, volatility forecasting, and market sentiment analysis. By showcasing innovative ML approaches, we aim to bridge the gap between financial theory and practical implementation, supporting data-driven decision-making in both industry and academia.

2. Scope and Topics

The Special Issue invited research on diverse topics including artificial intelligence, deep learning, blockchain, big data analytics, cyber security, Internet of Things (IoT), mobile finance applications, neural networks, fuzzy logic, expert systems, sentiment analysis, support vector machines, and web services.

3. Contributions to the Special Issue

The following briefly introduces the included articles, demonstrating the breadth and innovation of research in this Special Issue.

- **PortRSMs: Learning Regime Shifts for Portfolio Policy** Liu and Ichise (2025) propose a novel deep reinforcement learning (DRL) policy network using stacked state-space models for multiscale regime shifts in financial time series.
- **DASF-Net: A Multimodal Framework for Stock Price Forecasting** Nguyen et al. (2025) combine diffusion-based graph learning and optimized sentiment fusion to predict stock prices, addressing higher-order dependencies in financial networks.
- **A Majority Voting Mechanism-Based Ensemble Learning Approach for Financial Distress Prediction** Muniappan and Subramanian (2025) apply ensemble learning to predict financial distress in the Indian automobile industry.
- **Risk-Adjusted Performance of Random Forest Models in High-Frequency Trading** Deep et al. (2025) evaluate the effectiveness of random forest models for minute-level trading data under the Efficient Market Hypothesis.

- **Using Machine Learning to Understand Stock Market and US Presidential Election Dynamics** Thaker et al. (2025) explore explainable AI (SHAP) to analyze market response to election outcomes.
- **Forecasting Forex Market Volatility Using Deep Learning Models** Zitis et al. (2024) investigate whether complexity measures improve deep learning predictions of forex volatility.
- **Forecasting Orange Juice Futures: LSTM, ConvLSTM, and Traditional Models** Ampountolas (2024) compares neural networks with ARIMA for commodity price forecasting over short-term horizons.
- **Financial Distress Prediction in the Nordics: Early Warnings from Machine Learning Models** Abrahamsen et al. (2024) develop an explainable early-warning model for listed Nordic corporations.
- **Does ICT Investment Affect Market Share and Customer Acquisition Cost?** Ansari and Gupta (2024) examine the impact of ICT investments on banks' market share and customer acquisition.
- **Exploring Calendar Anomalies and Volatility Dynamics in Cryptocurrencies** Sahu et al. (2024) analyze day-of-the-week effects in cryptocurrency returns using GARCH family models.
- **Prediction of Currency Exchange Rate Based on Transformers** Zhao and Yan (2024) use transformer models to forecast exchange rate fluctuations under global uncertainty.
- **Bibliometric Analysis of Machine Learning Applications in Fraud Detection on Crowdfunding Platforms** Cardona et al. (2024) review the ML literature for fraud detection in crowdfunding.

4. Conclusions

The adoption of machine learning techniques in finance has advanced both theory and practice. This Special Issue highlights innovative methodologies, practical applications, and rigorous evaluations that address contemporary financial challenges. The included articles demonstrate the versatility of ML approaches, ranging from portfolio optimization and volatility forecasting to fraud detection and market anomaly analysis. We encourage continued contributions to expand the frontier of financial technology research.

Conflicts of Interest: The author declares no conflicts of interest.

References

Abrahamsen, N.-G. B., Nylén-Forthun, E., Møller, M., de Lange, P. E., & Risstad, M. (2024). Financial distress prediction in the nordics: Early warnings from machine learning models. *Journal of Risk and Financial Management, 17*(10), 432. [CrossRef]

Ampountolas, A. (2024). Forecasting orange juice futures: LSTM, ConvLSTM, and traditional models across trading horizons. *Journal of Risk and Financial Management, 17*(11), 475. [CrossRef]

Ansari, G. G., & Gupta, R. S. (2024). Does ICT investment affect market share and customer acquisition cost? A comparative analysis of domestic and foreign banks operating in India. *Journal of Risk and Financial Management, 17*(9), 421. [CrossRef]

Cardona, L. F., Guzmán-Luna, J. A., & Restrepo-Carmona, J. A. (2024). Bibliometric analysis of the machine learning applications in fraud detection on crowdfunding platforms. *Journal of Risk and Financial Management, 17*(8), 352. [CrossRef]

Deep, A., Shirvani, A., Monico, C., Rachev, S., & Fabozzi, F. (2025). Risk-adjusted performance of random forest models in high-frequency trading. *Journal of Risk and Financial Management, 18*(3), 142. [CrossRef]

Liu, B., & Ichise, R. (2025). PortRSMs: Learning regime shifts for portfolio policy. *Journal of Risk and Financial Management, 18*(8), 434. [CrossRef]

Muniappan, M., & Subramanian, N. D. P. (2025). A majority voting mechanism-based ensemble learning approach for financial distress prediction in Indian automobile industry. *Journal of Risk and Financial Management, 18*(4), 197. [CrossRef]

Nguyen, N.-H., Nguyen, T.-T., & Ngo, Q. T. (2025). DASF-Net: A multimodal framework for stock price forecasting. *Journal of Risk and Financial Management, 18*(8), 417. [CrossRef]

Sahu, S., Ramírez, A. F., & Kim, J.-M. (2024). Exploring calendar anomalies and volatility dynamics in cryptocurrencies: A comparative analysis of day-of-the-week effects before and during the COVID-19 pandemic. *Journal of Risk and Financial Management*, *17*(8), 351. [CrossRef]

Thaker, A., Sonner, D., & Chan, L. H. (2025). Using machine learning to understand the dynamics between the stock market and US presidential election outcomes. *Journal of Risk and Financial Management*, *18*(3), 109. [CrossRef]

Zhao, L., & Yan, W. Q. (2024). Prediction of currency exchange rate based on transformers. *Journal of Risk and Financial Management*, *17*(8), 332. [CrossRef]

Zitis, P. I., Potirakis, S. M., & Alexandridis, A. (2024). Forecasting forex market volatility using deep learning models and complexity measures. *Journal of Risk and Financial Management*, *17*(12), 557. [CrossRef]

Journal of
Risk and Financial Management

MDPI

Article

PortRSMs: Learning Regime Shifts for Portfolio Policy

Bingde Liu * and Ryutaro Ichise *

Department of Industrial Engineering and Economics, School of Engineering, Institute of Science Tokyo, Tokyo 152-8550, Japan
* Correspondence: bingde.l.aa@m.titech.ac.jp (B.L.); ichise@iee.e.titech.ac.jp (R.I.)

Abstract: This study proposes a novel Deep Reinforcement Learning (DRL) policy network structure for portfolio management called PortRSMs. PortRSMs employs stacked State-Space Models (SSMs) for the modeling of multi-scale continuous regime shifts in financial time series, striking a balance between exploring consistent distribution properties over short periods and maintaining sensitivity to sudden shocks in price sequences. PortRSMs also performs cross-asset regime fusion through hypergraph attention mechanisms, providing a more comprehensive state space for describing changes in asset correlations and co-integration. Experiments conducted on two different trading frequencies in the stock markets of the United States and Hong Kong show the superiority of PortRSMs compared to other approaches in terms of profitability, risk–return balancing, robustness, and the ability to handle sudden market shocks. Specifically, PortRSMs achieves up to a 0.03 improvement in the annual Sharpe ratio in the U.S. market, and up to a 0.12 improvement for the Hong Kong market compared to baseline methods.

Keywords: deep reinforcement learning; portfolio management; financial time series; regime shift models; state-space models

1. Introduction

High-frequency trading often relies on the modeling of the distribution of short-term asset returns. Many studies have shown the serial correlation of volatility in asset returns (LeBaron, 1992; Shiller, 1990), indicating that the distribution of asset returns may exhibit consistency over a period of time. Basic time-series models can effectively capture these properties (Bauwens et al., 2006; Bollerslev et al., 1994). However, due to structural changes, the statistical characteristics of asset price series can completely change from one period to another. For example, after policy or macroeconomic shocks, the volatility of stock prices may undergo drastic changes, leading to the failure of basic time-series models. On the other hand, Regime Shift Model (RSM) paradigms address the shortcomings in basic time-series modeling by dividing time series into different states, effectively dealing with such shocks. Therefore, short-term asset return distributions are widely modeled by RSMs (Cai, 1994; Haas et al., 2004; So et al., 1998).

Optimized in the Deep Reinforcement Learning (DRL) formulation, the portfolio policy network aims to generate an effective policy to guide high-frequency portfolio rebalancing trading strategies (Jiang & Liang, 2017). It is essential to let the portfolio policy network model the distribution of asset returns in each trading period. In previous work, modeling was often done by neural network models (Jiang & Liang, 2017; X. Li et al., 2022; Wang et al., 2021; Xu et al., 2021). These methods can effectively extract consistent distribution properties in a short period, but they do not follow the RSM modeling paradigm, making hem sub-optimal in financial series modeling. Constructing a policy network withing the

RSM paradigm has been challenging due to the lack of previous research using deep neural networks, which is essential for DRL.

With the recent breakthroughs in State-Space Model (SSM) research in the field of deep learning (Gu et al., 2020, 2022; Schiff et al., 2024), we can now use neural networks to model regime shifts in financial series. This enables us to come up with new policy network designs. In our work, we use stacked SSMs to model multi-scale continuous regime shifts present in financial time series, serving as the backbone of the DRL policy network. This method excels at balancing the exploration of consistent distribution properties over short periods and sensitivity to sudden shocks in price sequences. We also perform regime fusion between different assets through hypergraph attention mechanisms (HGAMs) (X. Li et al., 2022), providing a more comprehensive state space for describing changes in asset correlations and co-integration. These features give our method better performance compared to previous methods. We call our method PortRSMs, which is the abbreviation of "Portfolio RSMs".

Our contributions are summarized as follows:

1. We propose a new portfolio policy network structure with an RSM paradigm. The new structure can model regime shifts present in financial time series to strike a balance between exploring consistent distribution properties over short periods and maintaining sensitivity to sudden shocks for better portfolio decision-making.
2. We propose a method for cross-asset regime fusion through HGAM, providing a more comprehensive state space for describing changes in asset correlations and co-integration.
3. We conducted experiments on two different trading frequencies in the United States and Hong Kong stock markets. The experimental results showed the superiority of our method compared with other methods in terms of profitability, risk–return balancing, robustness, and ability to deal with sudden market shocks.

The remainder of this paper is organized as follows. Section 2 reviews related work in financial time-series modeling and deep reinforcement learning. Section 3 introduces the DRL framework for portfolio management and establishes the key mathematical notations used throughout the paper. Section 4 presents our proposed PortRSMs method, including the formulation of regime shift modeling and the regime fusion mechanism. Section 5 reports and analyzes the experimental results for multiple stock markets under different trading frequencies. Finally, Section 6 concludes the paper and discusses future research directions.

2. Related Work

Markowitz first introduced modern portfolio theory to design portfolios of assets with fixed weights using mean-variance analysis (Markowitz, 1952). The general portfolio algorithms are portfolio selection algorithms that rebalance the portfolio at the end of each trading period rather than using fixed weights. The general portfolio algorithms can be roughly divided into "follow the winner" (Agarwal et al., 2006; Helmbold et al., 1998), "follow the loser" (Borodin et al., 2003; Lai et al., 2018; B. Li & Hoi, 2012; B. Li et al., 2011b, 2012), and "pattern matching" (Györfi et al., 2006; B. Li et al., 2011a). Traditional strategies have a good explanatory and mathematical foundation, but they achieve suboptimal results in the long run, for they fail to model the complex dynamics of financial markets.

DRL approaches are a series of extremely strong "pattern matching" strategies that leverage the strong ability of deep learning for feature representation and pattern recognition. They have attracted significant attention in recent years. The EIIE methods (Jiang & Liang, 2017) first proposed a general framework to apply DRL for portfolio management, and they initially used the Temporal Convolutional Network (TCN) (Lea et al., 2017) and

Long Short-Term Memory (LSTM) model (Hochreiter & Schmidhuber, 1997) as the policy network structure. The RAT (Xu et al., 2021) method first used the Transformer (Vaswani et al., 2017) structure as the policy network structure to extract complex information from financial time series. Those structures have also become commonly used in follow-up work (J. Li et al., 2023; X. Li et al., 2022; Wang et al., 2021). However, the above-mentioned structures are not exported by RSMs. We start with continuous-time RSMs, derive a method using SSMs (Gu et al., 2020, 2022; Schiff et al., 2024) as the policy network structure, and optimize it according to the specific needs of portfolio management tasks.

3. DRL for Portfolio Management

In this section, we briefly introduce the DRL method for the portfolio management problem, which provides the foundation for our work and establishes key mathematical symbols. Our formulation follows the foundational framework introduced in EIIE (Jiang & Liang, 2017) for DRL-based portfolio management, sharing all constraints.

3.1. Action

The portfolio vector represents the weights distributed to each asset. Let

$$\mathbf{w}_k = (w_{k,0}, w_{k,1}, w_{k,2}, \ldots, w_{k,m}) \in \mathbb{R}_+^{m+1}[0,1], \quad s.t. \sum_{i=0}^{m} w_{k,i} = 1 \tag{1}$$

be the portfolio vector before trading period k, where $i = 0, 1, 2, \ldots, m$ indexes the assets and $k \in \mathbb{N}_+$ indexes the trading periods. Note that $w_{k,0}$ indicates the weight allocated to the risk-free asset (e.g., cash). $\mathbf{w}_k$ directly defines the action to take in trading period k in the framework. $\mathbf{w}_k$ then transitions to $\mathbf{w}'_k \in \mathbb{R}_+^{m+1}[0,1]$, i.e., the portfolio vector after period k, due to changes in the prices of the assets.

3.2. State

In the framework, the state comprises market environment features and current asset holdings. Research in investment science indicates that due to market inefficiency, asset price data over a historical period has a certain predictive power for future price changes (Bustos & Pomares-Quimbaya, 2020; Jegadeesh & Titman, 2023). Therefore, the most intuitive market features are asset price time series. Asset price time series are sampled with equal intervals, using techniques like candlestick charts. Let $t := kT \in \mathbb{N}_+$ represent the sample timestamps, where $T \in \mathbb{N}_+$ represents how many timestamps there are in a trading period. The portfolio vector after period $k-1$, represented as $\mathbf{w}'_{k-1}$, is also included in the state, since adjusting it to $\mathbf{w}_k$ incurs transaction fees. In summary, the state in the framework is $s_t = (\mathcal{P}_k, \mathbf{w}'_{k-1})$, where

- $\mathcal{P}_k := (\mathbf{P}_{kT-l+1}, \ldots, \mathbf{P}_{kT}) \in \mathbb{R}_+^{l\times(m+1)\times 4}$ are the $l \in \mathbb{N}_+$ latest samples in the price series in trading period k;
- $\mathbf{P}_t := (\mathbf{P}_{t,0}, \ldots, \mathbf{P}_{t,m}) \in \mathbb{R}_+^{(m+1)\times 4}$ represents the price samples of all assets at timestamp t;
- $\mathbf{P}_{t,i} := (p^O_{t,i}, p^H_{t,i}, p^L_{t,i}, p^C_{t,i}) \in \mathbb{R}_+^4$ indicates the opening, highest, lowest, and closing prices of asset i in the sample with timestamp t.

Initially, $\mathbf{w}'_0 = (1, 0, 0, \ldots, 0)$, i.e., the situation where all funds are in the risk-free asset.

3.3. State Transition Function

Let $r_{k,i} \in \mathbb{R}_+$ be the price change ratio of asset i in trading period k, and let $\mathbf{r}_k := (r_{k,1}, r_{k,2}, \ldots, r_{k,m}) \in \mathbb{R}_+^{m+1}$ represent the price change ratios of all assets in trading period k, where $r_{k,i} := \frac{p^C_{(k+1)T,i}}{p^C_{kT,i}}$ represents the price change ratio of a certain asset. The price change ratios ($\mathbf{r}_k$) can be predicted from $\mathcal{P}_k$; namely, there exists a probability model, i.e., $\mathcal{T}'(\mathbf{r}_k|\mathcal{P}_k)$. Given $\mathbf{r}_k$, the portfolio vector ($\mathbf{w}_k$) deterministically becomes $\mathbf{w}'_k$. Concurrently, the new asset price series ($\mathbf{P}_k$) generated deterministically by the price changes becomes observable. The state transition model ($\mathcal{T}(s_{k+1}|s_k, a_k) := \mathcal{T}((\mathbf{P}_k, \mathbf{w}'_k)|(\mathcal{P}_k, \mathbf{w}'_{k-1}), \mathbf{w}_k)$) can then be readily obtained from the probability model ($\mathcal{T}'$) and all the aforementioned deterministic relationships.

3.4. Reward Function

Under portfolio vector $\mathbf{w}_k$, the return generated by the price changes ($\mathbf{r}_k$) is rewarded. Note that the transaction fees incurred as a result of adjusting the portfolio from $\mathbf{w}'_{k-1}$ to $\mathbf{w}_k$ should be deducted from the reward. Let the transaction fee ratio be $c \in \mathbb{R}[0, 1]$; then, the return can be calculated as follows:

$$r_t := \mathbf{w}_k^{\mathrm{T}}\mathbf{r}_k - c||\mathbf{w}_k - \mathbf{w}'_{k-1}||_1, \tag{2}$$

where the first term is the initial return and the second term represents the trading costs incurred from transaction fees. The formulation of the reward function in trading period k is $R(s_k, a_k) = \log(r_k + 1)$, where $a_k = \mathbf{w}_k$. Here, the return is taken as the logarithm to ensure the additivity of the reward function over time.

3.5. Deterministic Policy Gradient

In deterministic policy gradient algorithms, the policy network ($\pi_\theta(s)$) is a neural network that maps the current state to an action (Silver et al., 2014). The policy network is parameterized by θ, which refers to the trainable weights and biases of the neural network. During training, the reward function is differentiated directly, and gradient ascent is applied to update θ with a learning rate of $\alpha \in \mathbb{R}^+$, according to $\theta \to \theta + \alpha\nabla R(s, \pi_\theta(s))$, where $\nabla R(s, \pi_\theta(s))$ denotes the gradient of the reward function with respect to the policy parameters (θ).

4. PortRSMs

In this section, we introduce how we establish the PortRSMs method step by step, including the mathematical form of RSMs and regime fusion, as well as the portfolio weight-generating method. Figure 1 is a data flow diagram providing an overview of PortRSMs.

4.1. SSMs

Recent research used time-series modeling with SSMs to describe regime shifts (Gu et al., 2020). For continuous-time signals, SSMs have the following form:

$$\begin{aligned}
&\begin{cases} u'(t) = \mathbf{A}u(t) + \mathbf{B}x(t), & (\textit{Transition Model}) \\ y(t) = \mathbf{C}u(t) + \mathbf{D}x(t), & (\textit{Emission Model}) \end{cases} \\
&\textit{where,} \quad u(t) \in \mathbb{R}^{h\times 1}, x(t) \in \mathbb{R}^{d\times 1}, y(t) \in \mathbb{R}^{d\times 1}, \\
&\mathbf{A} \in \mathbb{R}^{h\times h},\ \mathbf{B} \in \mathbb{R}^{h\times d},\ \mathbf{C} \in \mathbb{R}^{d\times h},\ \mathbf{D} \in \mathbb{R}^{d\times d}
\end{aligned} \tag{3}$$

where $u(t)$ represents the hidden state with hidden dimension $h \in \mathbb{R}_+$. $x(t)$ describes the observable instantaneous information at time t, while $y(t)$ is the instantaneous information that cannot be observed up to time t. Information is described with the $d \in \mathbb{R}_+$ dimension vector. In addition to $\mathbf{A}$ for describing inherent transitions of hidden states, the transition model also uses matrix $\mathbf{B}$ to describe how current observable instantaneous information affects hidden states. The emission model then maps $u(t)$ and $x(t)$ to current $y(t)$ through matrices $\mathbf{C}$ and $\mathbf{D}$.

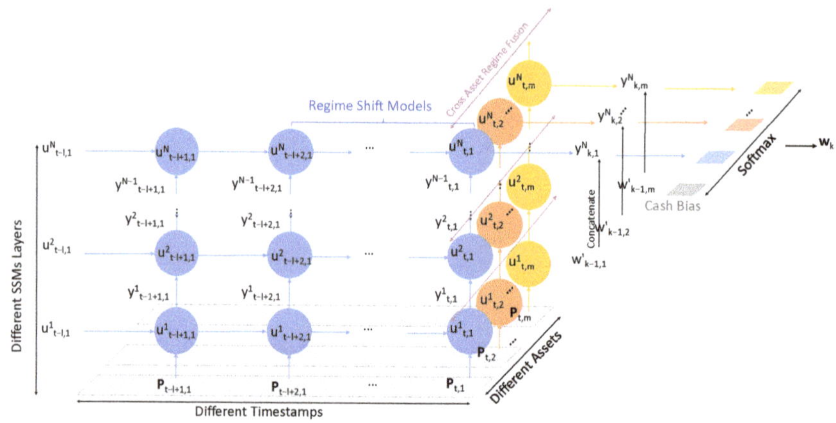

Figure 1. Data flow diagram of PortRSMs at timestamp t and trading period k ($t = kT$ as defined in Section 3.2). PortRSMs uses sample $\mathbf{P}$ in the asset price time series as input. To model RSMs, SSMs are used to simulate the transition of state u. The output (y) of each SSM layer is used as the input of the next layer, and the output of each layer is fused between the asset through the HGAM. The output of the last layer generates new portfolio weights ($\mathbf{w_k}$) through the output projection and softmax functions, after concatenating with the existing portfolio weights ($\mathbf{w}'_{\mathbf{k-1}}$).

The follow-up research improved SSMs. On one hand, $\mathbf{A}$ and $\mathbf{D}$ are considered trainable neural network parameters (Gu et al., 2022). On the other hand, $\mathbf{B}$ and $\mathbf{C}$ are considered time-variant parameters ($\mathbf{B}_t$ and $\mathbf{C}_t$, respectively)to improve performance (Schiff et al., 2024). This makes SSMs a linear time-variant system where $\mathbf{B}_t$ and $\mathbf{C}_t$ are obtained through nonlinear transformation:

$$\begin{cases} \mathbf{B}_t = \delta(\mathbf{\Gamma}_B x^\top(t)), \\ \mathbf{C}_t = \delta(\mathbf{\Gamma}_C x^\top(t)), \end{cases} \quad where, \quad \mathbf{\Gamma}_B, \mathbf{\Gamma}_C \in \mathbb{R}^{h\times d} \tag{4}$$

where $\delta(.)$ is an SiLU activation function[1] and $\mathbf{\Gamma}_B$ and $\mathbf{\Gamma}_C$ are learnable projection matrices.

4.2. RSMs in Price Series

RSMs, based on the improvement of hidden Markov models, are widely used in modeling asset price change ratio distributions (Cai, 1994; Haas et al., 2004; So et al., 1998). They take instantaneous prices as the input information and the instantaneous price change ratios as the output.

In our work, we use SSMs to model the continuous regime shifts from the discretized price series. Therefore, RSMs are defined as follows:

$$\begin{aligned} & x_{t,i} = \delta(\mathbf{\Gamma}_P \mathbf{P}_{t,i}), \begin{cases} u_{t,i} = \tilde{\mathbf{A}}_{t,i} u_{t-1,i} + \tilde{\mathbf{B}}_{t,i} x_{t,i}, \\ y_{k,i} = \delta(\mathbf{\Gamma}_C x_{t,i}) u_{t,i} + \mathbf{D} x_{t,i}, \end{cases} \\ & s.t. \quad t = kT, \tilde{\mathbf{A}}_{t,i} = exp(\Delta_{t,i}\mathbf{A}), \; \tilde{\mathbf{B}}_{t,i} = (\Delta_{t,i}\mathbf{A})^{-1}(exp(\Delta_{t,i}\mathbf{A}_{t,i}) - \mathbf{I})\Delta_{t,i}\mathbf{B}_{t,i}, \\ & \mathbf{B}_{t,i} = \delta(\mathbf{\Gamma}_B x_{t,i}), \; \Delta_{t,i} = \delta(\mathbf{\Gamma}_\Delta x_{t,i}) \\ & where. \quad \mathbf{\Gamma}_P \in \mathbb{R}^{d\times 4}, \; \mathbf{\Gamma}_\Delta \in \mathbb{R}^{h\times d} \end{aligned} \tag{5}$$

where $\mathbf{\Gamma}_P$ is a projection matrix to restore input information ($x_{t,i}$) from $\mathbf{P}_{t,i}$, as defined in Section 3.2, while $y_{k,i}$ is a descriptor vector for the distribution characteristics of $r_{k,i}$, as defined in Section 3.3. $\tilde{\mathbf{A}}_{\tau,i}$ and $\tilde{\mathbf{B}}_{\tau,i}$ represent discretized versions of $\mathbf{A}$ and $\mathbf{B}_{\tau,i}$. In the case of zero-order hold sampling, the relationships between $\tilde{\mathbf{A}}_{\tau,i}$, $\tilde{\mathbf{B}}_{\tau,i}$ and $\mathbf{A}, \mathbf{B}_{\tau,i}$ have been shown in existing research (Gu et al., 2022; Schiff et al., 2024). $\Delta_{\tau,i}$ describes the time scale that one sample interval maps to in continuous perspective. Note that $\Delta_{\tau,i}$ is also a time-variant parameter obtained from $x_{t,i}$ by the non-linear transformation by projection matrix $\mathbf{\Gamma}_{\Delta}$ and the activation function. This property further enhances its ability to model the widespread fractal properties in financial time series (Evertsz, 1995; Ni et al., 2011; Peters, 1989). The time-variant $\Delta_{\tau,i}$ can map different dynamics from discrete perspectives to the same dynamics in continuous perspectives to model the continuous regime shifts. During training, optimization is carried out for parameters $\mathbf{A}, \mathbf{D}, \mu_i, \mathbf{\Gamma}_B, \mathbf{\Gamma}_C, \mathbf{\Gamma}_{\Delta}$, and $\mathbf{\Gamma}_P$.

Notice that the absolute price ranges of different assets at different times may vary greatly. On the one hand, this can lead to similar dynamics being considered completely different, further causing a decrease in training data efficiency. On the other hand, it can result in uneven gradient values, making convergence difficult during training. Therefore, data normalization is important in data pre-processing. We adopt the same approach used in previous work (Jiang & Liang, 2017; Xu et al., 2021), using the latest close price in the state representation defined in Section 3.2, i.e., p^C_{kT}, as the denominator to normalize all price data in $\mathcal{P}_k$. To apply this method, in each trading period (k), the SSM is re-executed on $\mathcal{P}_k$, i.e., all samples of the latest l timestamps. The calculation can be performed in a high-speed way on modern hardware by converting recursion to convolution (Schiff et al., 2024). In each calculation, $u_{kT-l,i}$ is initialized as a zero vector.

4.3. Stacked SSMs

To further improve performance, considering the existence of multiple regime shifts of different scales in the financial time series, we use stacked SSMs to model them. The formulation of RSMs modeled by N-layer SSMs is expressed as follows:

$$
\begin{aligned}
&x^1_{t,i} = \delta(\mathbf{\Gamma}_P \mathbf{P}_{t,i}), \begin{cases} u^1_{t,i} = \tilde{\mathbf{A}}^1_{t,i} u^1_{t,i} + \tilde{\mathbf{B}}^1_{t,i} x^1_{t,i}, \\ x^2_{k,i} = y^1_{t,i} = \delta(\mathbf{\Gamma}^1_C x_{t,i}) u^1_{t,i} + \mathbf{D}^1_{t,i} x^1_{t,i}, \end{cases} \\
&\begin{cases} u^2_{t,i} = \tilde{\mathbf{A}}^2_{t,i} u^2_{t,i} + \tilde{\mathbf{B}}^2_{t,i} x^2_{t,i}, \\ x^3_{t,i} = y^2_{t,i} = \delta(\mathbf{\Gamma}^2_C x_{t,i}) u^2_{t,i} + \mathbf{D}^2_{t,i} x^2_{t,i}, \end{cases} \quad \cdots \\
&\begin{cases} u^N_{t,i} = \tilde{\mathbf{A}}^N_{t,i} u^N_{t,i} + \tilde{\mathbf{B}}^N_{t,i} x^N_{t,i}, \\ y^N_{k,i} = y^N_{t,i} = \delta(\mathbf{\Gamma}^N_C x_{t,i}) u^N_{t,i} + \mathbf{D}^N_{t,i} x^N_{t,i}, \end{cases} \\
&s.t. \quad t = kT,\ \tilde{\mathbf{A}}^n_{t,i} = exp(\Delta^n_{t,i} \mathbf{A}^n),\ \tilde{\mathbf{B}}^n_{t,i} = (\Delta^n_{t,i} \mathbf{A}^n)^{-1} (exp(\Delta^n_{t,i} \mathbf{A}^n_{t,i}) - \mathbf{I}) \Delta^n_{t,i} \mathbf{B}^n_{t,i}, \\
&\mathbf{B}^n_{t,i} = \delta(\mathbf{\Gamma}^n_B x^n_{t,i}),\ \Delta^n_{t,i} = \delta(\mathbf{\Gamma}^n_{\Delta} x^n_{t,i}),\ n = 1, 2, \ldots, N
\end{aligned}
\tag{6}
$$

Note that parameters are not shared between layers. In this case, we take the output ($y^{n-1}_{t,i}$) of the $n-1$th SSM layer as the input ($x^n_{t,i}$) of the nth SSM layer. Each SSM layer can model regime shifts over the regimes modeled by the previous layer on a more abstract scale, thereby mining more stable patterns and longer dependencies.

4.4. Hypergraph Attention for Cross-Asset Regime Fusion

So far, we have only discussed the situation of individual assets. In the portfolio management task, multiple asset price series should be modeled simultaneously. The correlation and co-integration between these series can shift over time. Modeling these properties has been shown to be crucial for the learning of portfolio policy in existing work (X. Li et al., 2022; Shi et al., 2022; Soleymani & Paquet, 2021; Xu et al., 2021).

We include considerations of relevance and co-integration in the RSMs by utilizing HGAM (X. Li et al., 2022). The HGAM aims to learn the differing importance of asset neighbors for information merging with the attention mechanism (Vaswani et al., 2017).

For stock i and its neighbor ($j = 0, 1, \ldots, m$), quantifying the degree to which i is related to j based on the output ($y^n_{k,i}$) of the nth SSM layer, i.e.,

$$D(y^n_{k,i}, y^n_{k,j}) = \delta(\mathbf{b}^n[\mathbf{\Gamma}^n_R y^n_{k,i}, \mathbf{\Gamma}^n_R y^n_{k,j}]), \tag{7}$$

where $\mathbf{\Gamma}^n_R \in \mathbf{R}^{d\times 1}$ is a projection matrix to be learned, $\mathbf{b}^n \in \mathbf{R}^{1\times d}$ is a shared attention vector, d is the model dimension defined in Section 4.2, [.] denotes the concatenation operation, $\delta(.)$ denotes a nonlinear activation function like LeakyReLU[2]. Then, the softmax function is applied to obtain the importance weight (α_{ij}):

$$\alpha_{ij} = \frac{\exp(D(y^n_{k,i}, y^n_{k,j}))}{\sum_{v=0,1,\ldots,m} \exp(D(y^n_{k,i}, y^n_{k,v}))}. \tag{8}$$

After that, $y^n_{t,i}$ is aggregated across assets as follows:

$$y^n_{k,i} \to \delta\left(\sum_{j=0,1,\ldots,m} \alpha_{ij} P^n y^n_{k,j}\right) \tag{9}$$

In the case of stacked SSMs, information from different assets is aggregated layer by layer, thereby achieving cross-asset regime fusion, providing more comprehensive state spaces for the description of changes in asset correlations and co-integration.

4.5. Portfolio Generation

The last SSM-layer output ($y^N_{k,i} \in \mathbb{R}^{d\times 1}$) is a descriptor of $r_{k,i}$ distribution characteristics. T', as defined in Section 3.3, can be established following previous practices (Jiang & Liang, 2017; Xu et al., 2021). The formulation is expressed as follows:

$$\begin{aligned} &\mathbf{w_k} = Softmax([b, (\mathbf{\Gamma}_w[\mathbf{w}'_{k-1}, \mathbf{y_k}])^\top]), \\ &where.\ \ \mathbf{y_k} = (y^N_{k,1}, y^N_{k,2}, \ldots, y^N_{k,m})^\top \in \mathbb{R}^{d\times m},\ \mathbf{w}'_{k-1} \in \mathbb{R}^{1\times m}, b \in \mathbb{R}^{1\times 1},\ \mathbf{\Gamma}_w \in \mathbb{R}^{(d+1)\times 1} \end{aligned} \tag{10}$$

where [.] denotes the concatenation operation in the first dimension. After concatenating the distribution descriptors and portfolio vector ($\mathbf{w}'_{k-1}$, without risk-free asset weights), the absolute score of each asset can be obtained by applying a projection matrix ($\mathbf{\Gamma}_w$). Finally, $\mathbf{w_k}$ can be generated from absolute scores by concatenating a cash bias (b) and applying a softmax function on the first dimension.

5. Experiments

5.1. Experimental Settings

5.1.1. Datasets

We conducted experiments with two different trading frequencies (i.e., 1 day and 1 week as the duration of the trading period) in the United States and Hong Kong stock markets. Specifically, we used the Yahoo Finance API (Yahoo, 2025) and AKShare API (King, 2019) to collect data on the Dow Jones Industrial Average (DJIA) and Hang Seng Index (HSI) constituents from 1 January 2004 to 1 January 2024. The data are sampled in daily frequency, which means $T = 1$ when the trading period is 1 day and $T = 5$ when the trading period is 1 week. Stocks with more than 70% missing data were excluded. When reporting the experimental results, we use DJIA1d/DJIA1w and HSI1d/HSI1w to represent the names of the dataset. Furthermore, 1d means 1 day as the duration of the trading period, while 1w means 1 week. For trading fees, we used an industry-standard round-trip cost of 0.06%. The training set and test set are divided chronologically in a ratio of 4:1.

5.1.2. Methods for Comparison

We use the constant rebalanced portfolio (CRP) and buy-and-hold (BAH) method as a benchmark. CRP allocates equal funds to all assets at all times, representing average market performance. BAH allocates equal funds to all assets in the first trading period, without any further trading actions. We also compare our method with traditional portfolio management algorithms (EG (Helmbold et al., 1998), OLMAR (B. Li & Hoi, 2012), RMR (Huang et al., 2016), BNN (Györfi et al., 2006), and CORN (B. Li et al., 2011a)), as well as state-of-the-art DRL-based methods with different policy network structures (bRNN EIIE (Jiang & Liang, 2017), CNN EIIE (Jiang & Liang, 2017), RAT (Xu et al., 2021), HGAM (X. Li et al., 2022), and LSRE-CAAN (J. Li et al., 2023)).

5.1.3. Evaluation Metric

Following previous works (Jiang & Liang, 2017; Wang et al., 2021; Xu et al., 2021), we use three metrics to evaluate performance: the annualized return (AR), annualized Sharpe ratio (ASR), and annualized Calmar ratio (ACR). AR measures compound annual portfolio growth over a period, with a higher AR indicating profitability. ASR measures volatility-adjusted return, with a higher ASR reflecting better risk–return balancing. ACR is a risk–return balancing metric similar to ASR that measures return adjusted by the maximum draw-down in the profit. We used five different random seeds $\{0, 64, 128, 256, 512\}$ for each experimental group to conduct repeated experiments and reported the mean and standard deviation of the results to reduce the randomness of the results and study the robustness of training. We plot the graph of cumulative log return over time in the testing period for qualitative analysis.

5.1.4. Implementation Details

Training was performed using the Adam optimizer on a single NVIDIA RTX A6000 GPU, with the learning rate set to $\alpha = 1.92 \times 10^{-5}$ and a batch size of 32. We used a model dimension of $d = 36$ and hidden dimension of $h = 16$. By default, we use an SSM layer number of $N = 2$ and sample count of $l = 50$. Cross-asset regime fusion is also applied by default.

5.2. Ablation Studies

5.2.1. Modeling Paradigm

We conducted experiments by replacing the SSM module with LSTM (Hochreiter & Schmidhuber, 1997), TCN (Lea et al., 2017), and Transformer (Vaswani et al., 2017) decoder modules with the same model dimension. As for the quantitative results, we present the AR in Table 1, ASR in Table 2, and ACR in Table 3. SSM achieves the best performance on most datasets with most of the time-series samples (l).

Insights into the performance of different modules can be gained based on how their performance changes with l and the stability of training performance with different random seeds. Note that when using the LSTM module, although the algorithm's performance remains stable for most of the l, it cannot surpass our SSMs' performance, for it has sub-optimal modeling paradigms relative to RSMs. TCN shows a larger variance in performance metrics compared to other modules when trained with different random seeds, likely due to the assignment of equal weights to each sample during learning, which can lead to overfitting on noise. The Transformer's performance is highly unstable as l varies, especially on the HSI dataset, where its performance sharply declines as l increases because the attention mechanism tends to focus on over-long dependencies during training, affecting sensitivity toward sudden shocks.

Table 1. AR performance comparison of different modules across various datasets, using different time-series sample counts (l). Bold values indicate the best result in each group of comparisons, and underlined values indicate the suboptimal result.

Dataset	Module	$l = 20$	$l = 50$	$l = 100$
DJIA1d	LSTM	0.104 ± 0.003	0.105 ± 0.004	0.104 ± 0.003
	TCN	0.099 ± 0.011	0.046 ± 0.036	0.093 ± 0.054
	Transformer	<u>0.104 ± 0.001</u>	<u>0.109 ± 0.003</u>	<u>0.119 ± 0.013</u>
	SSMs	**0.109 ± 0.008**	**0.121 ± 0.012**	**0.127 ± 0.013**
DJIA1w	LSTM	0.124 ± 0.006	0.127 ± 0.008	0.131 ± 0.009
	TCN	<u>0.158 ± 0.022</u>	**0.171 ± 0.035**	**0.298 ± 0.078**
	Transformer	0.132 ± 0.010	0.123 ± 0.003	0.156 ± 0.029
	SSMs	**0.161 ± 0.015**	<u>0.170 ± 0.026</u>	<u>0.157 ± 0.017</u>
HSI1d	LSTM	0.218 ± 0.034	0.175 ± 0.036	<u>0.201 ± 0.085</u>
	TCN	<u>0.236 ± 0.020</u>	<u>0.211 ± 0.054</u>	0.160 ± 0.086
	Transformer	0.232 ± 0.034	0.179 ± 0.020	0.112 ± 0.052
	SSMs	**0.296 ± 0.088**	**0.220 ± 0.029**	**0.247 ± 0.122**
HSI1w	LSTM	0.225 ± 0.012	0.231 ± 0.015	<u>0.233 ± 0.018</u>
	TCN	0.215 ± 0.047	<u>0.245 ± 0.048</u>	0.183 ± 0.087
	Transformer	<u>0.251 ± 0.023</u>	0.180 ± 0.071	0.145 ± 0.064
	SSMs	**0.292 ± 0.048**	**0.279 ± 0.048**	**0.251 ± 0.076**

Table 2. ASR performance comparison of different modules across various datasets, using different time-series sample counts (l). Bold values indicate the best result in each group of comparisons, and underlined values indicate the suboptimal result.

Dataset	Module	$l = 20$	$l = 50$	$l = 100$
DJIA1d	LSTM	0.558 ± 0.006	0.559 ± 0.010	0.557 ± 0.007
	TCN	0.506 ± 0.067	0.394 ± 0.136	0.532 ± 0.077
	Transformer	<u>0.558 ± 0.002</u>	<u>0.565 ± 0.004</u>	<u>0.586 ± 0.028</u>
	SSMs	**0.573 ± 0.025**	**0.613 ± 0.036**	**0.630 ± 0.040**
DJIA1w	LSTM	0.621 ± 0.011	<u>0.619 ± 0.008</u>	0.616 ± 0.008
	TCN	0.532 ± 0.081	0.514 ± 0.055	**0.681 ± 0.099**
	Transformer	<u>0.623 ± 0.003</u>	0.617 ± 0.005	0.642 ± 0.019
	SSMs	**0.646 ± 0.024**	**0.662 ± 0.018**	<u>0.665 ± 0.014</u>
HSI1d	LSTM	0.695 ± 0.066	0.635 ± 0.051	<u>0.676 ± 0.121</u>
	TCN	0.724 ± 0.044	0.652 ± 0.088	0.565 ± 0.179
	Transformer	<u>0.776 ± 0.040</u>	<u>0.710 ± 0.037</u>	0.503 ± 0.155
	SSMs	**0.808 ± 0.142**	**0.768 ± 0.040**	**0.792 ± 0.147**
HSI1w	LSTM	0.756 ± 0.013	<u>0.779 ± 0.027</u>	<u>0.785 ± 0.027</u>
	TCN	0.718 ± 0.128	0.714 ± 0.062	0.613 ± 0.214
	Transformer	<u>0.854 ± 0.049</u>	0.679 ± 0.193	0.537 ± 0.136
	SSMs	**0.868 ± 0.060**	**0.899 ± 0.065**	**0.793 ± 0.113**

With the RSM paradigm, the SSM module exhibits better stability as l changes and lower variance when trained with different random seeds compared to other models, indicating a balance between the extraction of consistent distribution properties and sensitivity towards sudden shocks.

Figures 2 and 3 show a performance comparison of different modules from a qualitative analysis perspective. The SSM module has a stable and rapidly growing return curve in most periods compared with other modules. Specifically, as shown in Figure 3, during the COVID outbreak period, when overall market prices were falling rapidly, the SSM module did not incur excessive losses, and during periods of price rebounding, the SSM module quickly identified profit opportunities in the market, resulting in higher returns than other methods.

Table 3. ACR performance comparison of different modules across various datasets, using different time-series sample counts (l). Bold values indicate the best result in each group of comparisons, and underlined values indicate the suboptimal result.

Dataset	Module	$l = 20$	$l = 50$	$l = 100$
DJIA1d	LSTM	0.307 ± 0.004	0.307 ± 0.006	0.306 ± 0.004
	TCN	0.235 ± 0.073	0.164 ± 0.122	0.325 ± 0.119
	Transformer	0.305 ± 0.001	0.309 ± 0.002	0.321 ± 0.015
	SSMs	**0.313 ± 0.015**	**0.345 ± 0.025**	**0.354 ± 0.029**
DJIA1w	LSTM	0.387 ± 0.017	0.388 ± 0.014	0.385 ± 0.066
	TCN	0.364 ± 0.139	0.393 ± 0.116	**0.724 ± 0.279**
	Transformer	0.405 ± 0.011	0.399 ± 0.007	0.473 ± 0.079
	SSMs	**0.499 ± 0.075**	**0.555 ± 0.101**	0.515 ± 0.066
HSI1d	LSTM	0.567 ± 0.102	0.488 ± 0.058	0.560 ± 0.182
	TCN	0.590 ± 0.08	0.488 ± 0.113	0.431 ± 0.210
	Transformer	0.661 ± 0.069	0.604 ± 0.060	0.354 ± 0.181
	SSMs	**0.728 ± 0.217**	**0.688 ± 0.068**	**0.762 ± 0.245**
HSI1w	LSTM	0.804 ± 0.053	0.884 ± 0.058	0.881 ± 0.060
	TCN	0.676 ± 0.262	0.688 ± 0.131	0.478 ± 0.225
	Transformer	0.979 ± 0.112	0.588 ± 0.252	0.346 ± 0.158
	SSMs	**1.189 ± 0.142**	**1.282 ± 0.182**	**0.830 ± 0.160**

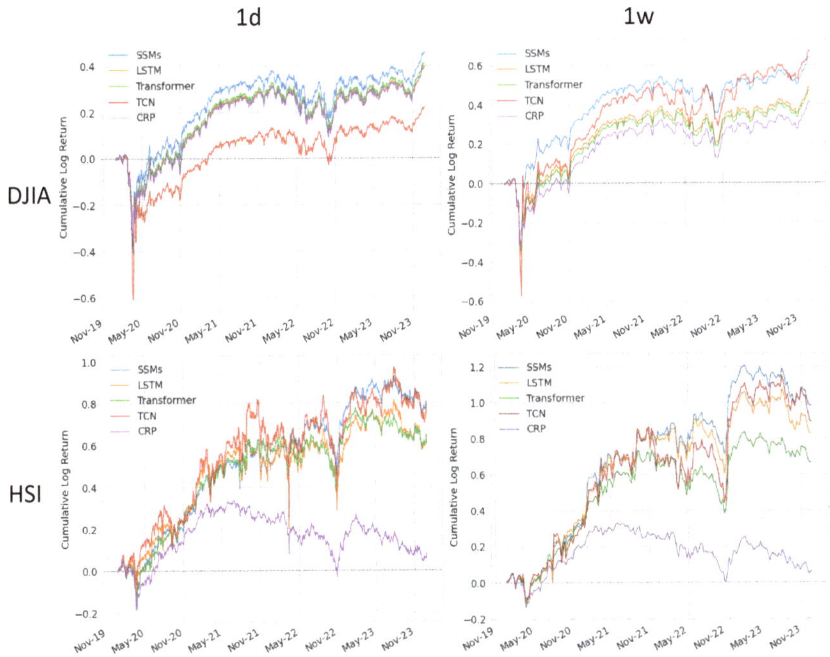

Figure 2. The cumulative log return in the testing period when using different modules, with $l = 50$. The result for CRP is also shown for comparison as a benchmark.

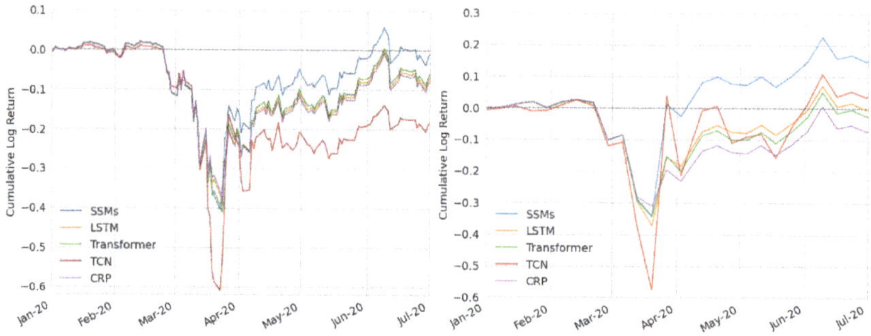

Figure 3. The cumulative log return during the COVID outbreak period for the DJIA dataset when using different modules, with $l = 50$. The result for CRP is also shown for comparison as a benchmark.

5.2.2. Stacked SSMs

In the ablation experiment, we analyze the role of each component in the proposed algorithm. First, we compare the effect of the SSM module with the RSM paradigm and other existing time-series modeling modules with other paradigms by replacing each layer with other modules with the same model dimension. Secondly, we study the effect of stacked SSMs by changing the number of SSM layers. Finally, we compare the performance of algorithms with and without cross-asset regime fusion to illustrate its effectiveness.

We study the relationship between different numbers of SSM layers and performance when the time-series sample count (l) varies. As for the performance metrics, we present the AR in Table 4, ASR in Table 5, and ACR in Table 6. Note that on the DJIA1d and HSI1d datasets, the choice of layer number is independent of l. This indicates that in high-frequency trading, it is only necessary to model very short-term regime shifts, so increasing l does not lead to significant changes in regime-shift information. In contrast, on the DJIA1w dataset, increasing l results in richer regime-shift information for portfolio policy generation. Therefore, using more layers for RSM modeling results in better performance. Finally, note that on the HSI1w dataset, although performance improves with three layers compared to using two SSM layers as l increases, better performance is achieved with just one layer instead. This is because the HSI1w dataset exhibits a clear mean-reversion property that can be modeled effectively with only one SSM layer. The mean-reversion nature of HSI1w is also shown in the results in Section 5.3.

Table 4. Performance comparison of different numbers of stacked SSM layers across various datasets, using different time-series sample count (l), as evaluated by AR. Bold values indicate the best result in each group of comparisons, and underlined values indicate the suboptimal result.

Dataset	Layer Num	$l = 20$	$l = 50$	$l = 100$
DJIA1d	1	0.100 ± 0.010	0.110 ± 0.014	0.114 ± 0.011
	2	**0.109 ± 0.008**	**0.121 ± 0.012**	**0.127 ± 0.013**
	3	0.107 ± 0.005	0.116 ± 0.015	0.125 ± 0.019
DJIA1w	1	0.140 ± 0.003	0.156 ± 0.006	0.164 ± 0.008
	2	**0.161 ± 0.015**	0.170 ± 0.026	0.157 ± 0.017
	3	0.142 ± 0.030	**0.187 ± 0.052**	**0.190 ± 0.048**
HSI1d	1	0.273 ± 0.060	0.186 ± 0.022	0.181 ± 0.022
	2	0.296 ± 0.088	0.220 ± 0.029	0.247 ± 0.122
	3	**0.355 ± 0.096**	**0.262 ± 0.082**	**0.317 ± 0.164**
HSI1w	1	0.284 ± 0.007	**0.341 ± 0.020**	**0.315 ± 0.031**
	2	**0.292 ± 0.048**	0.279 ± 0.048	0.251 ± 0.076
	3	0.282 ± 0.040	0.294 ± 0.071	0.272 ± 0.029

Table 5. Performance comparison of different numbers of stacked SSM layers across various datasets, using different time-series sample counts (l), as evaluated by ASR. Bold values indicate the best result in each group of comparisons, and underlined values indicate the suboptimal result.

Dataset	Layer Num	$l = 20$	$l = 50$	$l = 100$
DJIA1d	1	0.559 ± 0.004	0.582 ± 0.014	0.589 ± 0.020
	2	**0.573 ± 0.025**	**0.613 ± 0.036**	**0.630 ± 0.040**
	3	0.569 ± 0.014	0.596 ± 0.046	0.614 ± 0.054
DJIA1w	1	0.635 ± 0.008	0.654 ± 0.006	0.661 ± 0.006
	2	**0.646 ± 0.024**	**0.662 ± 0.018**	0.665 ± 0.014
	3	0.639 ± 0.037	0.658 ± 0.026	**0.670 ± 0.023**
HSI1d	1	0.763 ± 0.093	0.713 ± 0.043	0.685 ± 0.036
	2	0.808 ± 0.142	0.768 ± 0.040	0.792 ± 0.147
	3	**0.948 ± 0.141**	**0.818 ± 0.105**	**0.880 ± 0.213**
HSI1w	1	0.859 ± 0.012	**0.950 ± 0.033**	**0.886 ± 0.041**
	2	**0.868 ± 0.060**	0.899 ± 0.065	0.793 ± 0.113
	3	0.856 ± 0.069	0.905 ± 0.052	0.827 ± 0.041

Table 6. Performance comparison of different numbers of stacked SSM layers across various datasets, using different time-series sample counts (l), as evaluated by ACR. Bold values indicate the best result in each group of comparisons, and underlined values indicate the suboptimal result.

Dataset	Layer Num	$l = 20$	$l = 50$	$l = 100$
DJIA1d	1	0.309 ± 0.004	0.310 ± 0.012	0.316 ± 0.010
	2	0.313 ± 0.015	**0.345 ± 0.025**	**0.354 ± 0.029**
	3	**0.314 ± 0.006**	0.336 ± 0.032	0.343 ± 0.041
DJIA1w	1	0.428 ± 0.016	0.483 ± 0.014	0.508 ± 0.026
	2	**0.499 ± 0.075**	**0.555 ± 0.101**	0.515 ± 0.066
	3	0.476 ± 0.089	0.604 ± 0.190	**0.611 ± 0.169**
HSI1d	1	0.633 ± 0.128	0.603 ± 0.080	0.553 ± 0.059
	2	0.728 ± 0.217	0.688 ± 0.068	0.762 ± 0.245
	3	**0.914 ± 0.210**	**0.780 ± 0.186**	**0.908 ± 0.306**
HSI1w	1	1.159 ± 0.047	**1.479 ± 0.088**	**1.206 ± 0.178**
	2	**1.189 ± 0.142**	1.282 ± 0.182	0.830 ± 0.178
	3	1.209 ± 0.220	1.291 ± 0.278	0.979 ± 0.200

5.2.3. Cross-Asset Regime Fusion

We study the relationship between performance with and without cross-asset regime fusion when the time-series sample count (l) varies. As for the performance metrics, we present the AR in Table 7, ASR in Table 8, and ACR in Table 9. In 1d high-frequency trading, cross-asset regime fusion can consistently improve performance, indicating that asset correlation and co-integration are particularly important for the generation of high-frequency portfolio policies. However, in 1w low-frequency trading scenarios, whether cross-asset regime fusion can improve performance is closely related to l. In both DJIA and HSI, although cross-asset regime fusion can enhance performance at small values of l, it may lead to a decrease in performance as l increases. This suggests that the correlation and co-integration of assets in DJIA and HSI are relatively unstable, where interference from instability characteristics within large samples leads to decreased performance.

Table 7. Performance comparison (AR) of algorithms with and without cross-asset regime fusion across various datasets and time-series sample counts (l). Bold values indicate the best result in each comparison group. Bold values indicate the best result in each comparison group. (✓) means with cross-asset regime fusion, and (×) means without.

Dataset	Fusion	$l = 20$	$l = 50$	$l = 100$
DJIA1d	×	0.100 ± 0.004	0.103 ± 0.007	0.112 ± 0.005
	✓	**0.109 ± 0.008**	**0.121 ± 0.012**	**0.127 ± 0.013**
DJIA1w	×	0.145 ± 0.006	0.158 ± 0.003	**0.166 ± 0.006**
	✓	**0.161 ± 0.015**	**0.170 ± 0.026**	0.157 ± 0.017
HSI1d	×	0.192 ± 0.033	0.171 ± 0.008	0.171 ± 0.006
	✓	**0.296 ± 0.088**	**0.220 ± 0.029**	**0.247 ± 0.122**
HSI1w	×	0.244 ± 0.015	**0.305 ± 0.015**	**0.257 ± 0.016**
	✓	**0.292 ± 0.048**	0.279 ± 0.048	0.251 ± 0.076

Table 8. Performance comparison (ASR) of algorithms with and without cross-asset regime fusion across various datasets and time-series sample counts (l). Bold values indicate the best result in each comparison group. (✓) means with cross-asset regime fusion, and (×) means without.

Dataset	Fusion	$l = 20$	$l = 50$	$l = 100$
DJIA1d	×	0.557 ± 0.002	0.563 ± 0.010	0.578 ± 0.013
	✓	**0.573 ± 0.025**	**0.613 ± 0.036**	**0.630 ± 0.040**
DJIA1w	×	0.642 ± 0.006	0.661 ± 0.004	**0.668 ± 0.004**
	✓	**0.646 ± 0.024**	**0.662 ± 0.018**	0.665 ± 0.014
HSI1d	×	0.647 ± 0.041	0.678 ± 0.013	0.655 ± 0.015
	✓	**0.808 ± 0.142**	**0.768 ± 0.040**	**0.792 ± 0.147**
HSI1w	×	0.816 ± 0.019	**0.909 ± 0.019**	**0.836 ± 0.026**
	✓	**0.868 ± 0.060**	0.899 ± 0.065	0.793 ± 0.113

Table 9. Performance comparison (ACR) of algorithms with and without cross-asset regime fusion across various datasets and time-series sample counts (l). Bold values indicate the best result in each comparison group. Bold values indicate the best result in each comparison group. (✓) means with cross-asset regime fusion, and (×) means without.

Dataset	Fusion	$l = 20$	$l = 50$	$l = 100$
DJIA1d	×	0.308 ± 0.001	0.307 ± 0.002	0.308 ± 0.007
	✓	**0.313 ± 0.015**	**0.345 ± 0.025**	**0.354 ± 0.029**
DJIA1w	×	0.446 ± 0.019	0.474 ± 0.049	**0.524 ± 0.019**
	✓	**0.499 ± 0.075**	**0.555 ± 0.101**	0.515 ± 0.066
HSI1d	×	0.485 ± 0.063	0.557 ± 0.024	0.521 ± 0.024
	✓	**0.728 ± 0.217**	**0.688 ± 0.068**	**0.762 ± 0.245**
HSI1w	×	1.006 ± 0.044	**1.311 ± 0.062**	**0.963 ± 0.086**
	✓	**1.189 ± 0.142**	1.282 ± 0.182	0.830 ± 0.160

5.3. Comparison with Other Methods

We compare our method's performance to that of other methods, showing the AR in Table 10, ASR in Table 11, and ACR in Table 12. Overall, the use of DRL methods generally outperforms traditional methods. However, on HSI1w, mean reversion-based methods such as OLMAR (B. Li & Hoi, 2012) and RMR (Huang et al., 2016) perform better than deep learning methods, indicating a clear mean reversion characteristic on HSI1w. Previous DRL method performances depended on the dataset. CNN EIIE (Jiang & Liang, 2017) achieves good results on the DJIA dataset. The LSRE-CAAN (J. Li et al., 2023) method performs well on the DJIA dataset. RAT (Xu et al., 2021) handles HSI datasets well. Compared with other methods, our PortRSMs achieved the best performance among almost all datasets using DRL methods, showing its effectiveness and robustness.

Table 10. Performance comparison (AR) of different methods across various datasets. The best and second best results are marked by bold and underlined values, respectively.

Method	DJIA1d	DJIA1w	HSI1d	HSI1w
CRP	0.104	0.104	0.021	0.012
BAH	0.093	0.092	0.014	0.007
EG	0.104	0.104	0.020	0.012
OLMAR	−0.102	−0.042	−0.240	<u>0.316</u>
RMR	−0.211	0.024	−0.229	**0.508**
BNN	0.079	−0.171	−0.095	−0.171
CORN	−0.075	−0.069	−0.184	−0.314
CNN EIIE	0.114 ± 0.012	0.138 ± 0.028	0.082 ± 0.065	0.130 ± 0.094
bRNN EIIE	0.097 ± 0.006	0.122 ± 0.003	0.043 ± 0.013	0.107 ± 0.040
RAT	0.103 ± 0.002	0.124 ± 0.003	<u>0.149 ± 0.013</u>	0.215 ± 0.045
HGAM	0.103 ± 0.000	<u>0.170 ± 0.056</u>	0.078 ± 0.061	0.241 ± 0.110
LSRE-CAAN	<u>0.119 ± 0.000</u>	0.102 ± 0.029	0.011 ± 0.007	0.009 ± 0.000
PortRSMs	**0.121 ± 0.012**	**0.170 ± 0.026**	**0.220 ± 0.029**	0.279 ± 0.048

Table 11. Performance comparison (ASR) of different methods across various datasets. The best and second best results are marked by bold and underlined values, respectively.

Method	DJIA1d	DJIA1w	HSI1d	HSI1w
CRP	0.561	0.595	0.204	0.156
BAH	0.520	0.551	0.171	0.134
EG	0.559	0.593	0.202	0.154
OLMAR	−0.034	0.177	−0.262	0.815
RMR	−0.353	0.297	−0.225	**1.116**
BNN	0.388	−0.328	0.059	−0.216
CORN	−0.092	−0.108	−0.185	−0.542
CNN EIIE	<u>0.584 ± 0.022</u>	0.635 ± 0.032	0.398 ± 0.193	0.523 ± 0.287
bRNN EIIE	0.557 ± 0.001	0.625 ± 0.005	0.308 ± 0.056	0.516 ± 0.081
RAT	0.560 ± 0.001	0.620 ± 0.002	<u>0.644 ± 0.041</u>	0.805 ± 0.102
HGAM	0.559 ± 0.000	**0.669 ± 0.034**	0.428 ± 0.216	0.814 ± 0.176
LSRE-CAAN	0.564 ± 0.000	0.508 ± 0.094	0.182 ± 0.004	0.149 ± 0.000
PortRSMs	**0.613 ± 0.036**	<u>0.662 ± 0.018</u>	**0.768 ± 0.040**	<u>0.899 ± 0.065</u>

Table 12. Performance comparison (ACR) of different methods across various datasets. The best and second best results are marked by bold and underlined values, respectively.

Method	DJIA1d	DJIA1w	HSI1d	HSI1w
CRP	0.310	0.332	0.067	0.043
BAH	0.279	0.297	0.039	0.023
EG	0.309	0.330	0.065	0.042
OLMAR	−0.149	0.064	−0.294	0.963
RMR	−0.304	0.036	−0.286	**1.305**
BNN	0.135	−0.239	0.124	−0.235
CORN	−0.154	−0.118	−0.240	−0.377

Table 12. *Cont.*

Method	DJIA1d	DJIA1w	HSI1d	HSI1w
CNN EIIE	0.312 ± 0.005	0.462 ± 0.070	0.268 ± 0.206	0.452 ± 0.326
bRNN EIIE	0.309 ± 0.002	0.395 ± 0.004	0.150 ± 0.047	0.399 ± 0.069
RAT	0.308 ± 0.001	0.402 ± 0.004	0.514 ± 0.045	0.856 ± 0.209
HGAM	0.308 ± 0.000	$\mathbf{0.578 \pm 0.191}$	0.274 ± 0.204	0.870 ± 0.316
LSRE-CAAN	0.307 ± 0.000	0.292 ± 0.078	0.062 ± 0.022	0.025 ± 0.000
PortRSMs	$\mathbf{0.345 \pm 0.025}$	0.555 ± 0.101	$\mathbf{0.688 \pm 0.068}$	1.282 ± 0.182

6. Conclusions

This paper presents an innovative portfolio policy network structure that effectively addresses the challenges in financial time-series modeling by combining the regime shift model (RSM) paradigm with recent advancements in deep learning techniques. The experimental results across multiple stock markets and trading frequencies confirm the superiority of the proposed approach. This paper offers new insights for the development of high-frequency trading strategies and contributes valuable perspectives to the field of financial time-series modeling.

However, we acknowledge certain limitations of the current study. Due to the varying characteristics of different financial markets and time periods, some architecture hyper-parameters of the proposed model need to be adjusted for different scenarios. This sensitivity limits the model's direct generalization across markets.

In addition, our approach implicitly assumes that short-term asset return distributions are locally consistent within regimes and that regime shifts can be effectively captured by structural patterns in the data. This assumption is supported by prior work on volatility clustering and regime shift models (RSMs) but may not hold under all market conditions, such as in cases of highly irregular or non-stationary shocks.

To address this, future research could explore the integration of meta-learning or online learning techniques, which are capable of adapting to dynamic and heterogeneous market environments in a more automated and robust manner.

Future research could also explore the application of the proposed method in other financial markets and asset classes, as well as further optimize the model to adapt to more complex market environments.

Author Contributions: Conceptualization, B.L.; methodology, B.L.; software, B.L.; validation, B.L. and R.I.; formal analysis, B.L. and R.I.; investigation, B.L.; resources, R.I.; data curation, B.L.; writing—original draft preparation, B.L.; writing—review and editing, R.I.; visualization, B.L.; supervision, R.I. All authors have read and agreed to the published version of the manuscript.

Funding: This research was supported by Institute of Science Tokyo.

Institutional Review Board Statement: Not applicable.

Informed Consent Statement: Not applicable.

Data Availability Statement: Dataset available on request from the authors.

Conflicts of Interest: The authors declare no conflicts of interest.

Notes

1 The SiLU (Sigmoid Linear Unit) function is defined as $\text{SiLU}(x) = x \cdot \text{sigmoid}(x)$ and is known for being smooth and non-monotonic.

2 LeakyReLU is defined as $f(x) = x$ for $x > 0$ and $f(x) = \alpha x$ for $x \leq 0$, where α is a small constant (e.g., 0.01), allowing a small gradient when the input is negative.

References

Agarwal, A., Hazan, E., Kale, S., & Schapire, R. E. (2006, June 25–29). *Algorithms for portfolio management based on the newton method*. 23rd International Conference on Machine Learning (pp. 9–16), Pittsburgh, PA, USA. [CrossRef]

Bauwens, L., Laurent, S., & Rombouts, J. V. (2006). Multivariate GARCH models: A survey. *Journal of Applied Econometrics*, *21*(1), 79–109. [CrossRef]

Bollerslev, T., Engle, R. F., & Nelson, D. B. (1994). Chapter 49 Arch models. In *Handbook of econometrics* (Vol. 4, pp. 2959–3038). Elsevier.

Borodin, A., El-Yaniv, R., & Gogan, V. (2003, December 8–13). *Can we learn to beat the best stock*. Advances in Neural Information Processing Systems (Vol. 16), Vancouver, BC, Canada.

Bustos, O., & Pomares-Quimbaya, A. (2020). Stock market movement forecast: A systematic review. *Expert Systems with Applications*, *156*, 113464. [CrossRef]

Cai, J. (1994). A markov model of switching-regime ARCH. *Journal of Business & Economic Statistics*, *12*(3), 309–316. [CrossRef]

Evertsz, C. J. (1995). Fractal geometry of financial time series. *Fractals*, *3*(3), 609–616. [CrossRef]

Gu, A., Dao, T., Ermon, S., Rudra, A., & Ré, C. (2020, December 6–12). *HiPPO: Recurrent memory with optimal polynomial projections*. 34th International Conference on Neural Information Processing Systems (Vol. 33, pp. 1474–1487), Vancouver, BC, Canada.

Gu, A., Goel, K., & Re, C. (2022, April 25–29). *Efficiently modeling long sequences with structured state spaces*. International Conference on Learning Representations, Virtual.

Györfi, L., Lugosi, G., & Udina, F. (2006). Nonparametric kernel-based sequential investment strategies. *Mathematical Finance*, *16*(2), 337–357. [CrossRef]

Haas, M., Mittnik, S., & Paolella, M. S. (2004). A new approach to markov-switching GARCH models. *Journal of Financial Econometrics*, *2*(4), 493–530. [CrossRef]

Helmbold, D. P., Schapire, R. E., Singer, Y., & Warmuth, M. K. (1998). On-line portfolio selection using multiplicative updates. *Mathematical Finance*, *8*(4), 325–347. [CrossRef]

Hochreiter, S., & Schmidhuber, J. (1997). Long short-term memory. *Neural Computation*, *9*(8), 1735–1780. [CrossRef]

Huang, D., Zhou, J., Li, B., Hoi, S. C., & Zhou, S. (2016). Robust median reversion strategy for online portfolio selection. *IEEE Transactions on Knowledge and Data Engineering*, *28*(9), 2480–2493. [CrossRef]

Jegadeesh, N., & Titman, S. (2023). Momentum: Evidence and insights 30 years later. *Pacific-Basin Finance Journal*, *82*, 102202. [CrossRef]

Jiang, Z., & Liang, J. (2017, September 7–8). *Cryptocurrency portfolio management with deep reinforcement learning*. 2017 Intelligent Systems Conference (pp. 905–913), London, UK.

King, A. (2019). *Akshare*. Available online: https://github.com/akfamily/akshare (accessed on 31 July 2025).

Lai, Z.-R., Yang, P.-Y., Fang, L., & Wu, X. (2018). Reweighted price relative tracking system for automatic portfolio optimization. *IEEE Transactions on Systems, Man, and Cybernetics: Systems*, *50*(11), 4349–4361. [CrossRef]

Lea, C., Flynn, M. D., Vidal, R., Reiter, A., & Hager, G. D. (2017, July 21–26). *Temporal convolutional networks for action segmentation and detection*. 2017 IEEE Conference on Computer Vision and Pattern Recognition (pp. 1003–1012), Honolulu, HI, USA.

LeBaron, B. (1992). Some relations between volatility and serial correlations in stock market returns. *The Journal of Business*, *65*(2), 199–219. [CrossRef]

Li, B., & Hoi, S. C. (2012, June 26–July 1). *On-line portfolio selection with moving average reversion*. 29th International Conference on Machine Learning (pp. 273–280), Edinburgh, Scotland.

Li, B., Hoi, S. C., & Gopalkrishnan, V. (2011a). CORN: Correlation-driven nonparametric learning approach for portfolio selection. *ACM Transactions on Intelligent Systems and Technology*, *2*(3), 1–29. [CrossRef]

Li, B., Hoi, S. C., Zhao, P., & Gopalkrishnan, V. (2011b, April 11–13). *Confidence weighted mean reversion strategy for on-line portfolio selection*. 14th International Conference on Artificial Intelligence and Statistics (Vol. 15, pp. 434–442), Fort Lauderdale, FL, USA.

Li, B., Zhao, P., Hoi, S. C., & Gopalkrishnan, V. (2012). PAMR: Passive aggressive mean reversion strategy for portfolio selection. *Machine Learning*, *87*(2), 221–258. [CrossRef]

Li, J., Zhang, Y., Yang, X., & Chen, L. (2023). Online portfolio management via deep reinforcement learning with high-frequency data. *Information Processing & Management*, *60*(3), 103247. [CrossRef]

Li, X., Cui, C., Cao, D., Du, J., & Zhang, C. (2022, May 23–27). *Hypergraph-based reinforcement learning for stock portfolio selection*. IEEE International Conference on Acoustics, Speech and Signal Processing (pp. 4028–4032), Singapore.

Markowitz, H. (1952). Portfolio selection. *The Journal of Finance*, *7*(1), 77–91. [CrossRef] [PubMed]

Ni, L.-P., Ni, Z.-W., & Gao, Y.-Z. (2011). Stock trend prediction based on fractal feature selection and support vector machine. *Expert Systems with Applications*, *38*(5), 5569–5576. [CrossRef]

Peters, E. E. (1989). Fractal structure in the capital markets. *Financial Analysts Journal*, *45*(4), 32–37. [CrossRef]

Schiff, Y., Kao, C.-H., Gokaslan, A., Dao, T., Gu, A., & Kuleshov, V. (2024, July 21–27). *Caduceus: Bi-directional equivariant long-range DNA sequence modeling*. 41st International Conference on Machine Learning (Vol. 235, pp. 43632–43648), Vienna, Austria.

Shi, S., Li, J., Li, G., Pan, P., Chen, Q., & Sun, Q. (2022). GPM: A graph convolutional network based reinforcement learning framework for portfolio management. *Neurocomputing*, *498*, 14–27. [CrossRef]

Shiller, R. J. (1990). Market volatility and investor behavior. *The American Economic Review*, *80*(2), 58–62.

Silver, D., Lever, G., Heess, N., Degris, T., Wierstra, D., & Riedmiller, M. (2014, June 21–26). *Deterministic policy gradient algorithms*. 31st International Conference on Machine Learning (pp. 387–395), Beijing, China.

So, M. K. P., Lam, K., & Li, W. K. (1998). A stochastic volatility model with markov switching. *Journal of Business & Economic Statistics*, *16*(2), 244–253. [CrossRef] [PubMed]

Soleymani, F., & Paquet, E. (2021). Deep graph convolutional reinforcement learning for financial portfolio management—DeepPocket. *Expert Systems with Applications*, *182*, 115127. [CrossRef]

Vaswani, A., Shazeer, N., Parmar, N., Uszkoreit, J., Jones, L., Gomez, A. N., Kaiser, Ł., & Polosukhin, I. (2017, December 4–9). *Attention is all you need*. International Conference on Neural Information Processing Systems (pp. 6000–6010), Long Beach, CA, USA.

Wang, Z., Huang, B., Tu, S., Zhang, K., & Xu, L. (2021, February 2–9). *DeepTrader: A deep reinforcement learning approach for risk-return balanced portfolio management with market conditions embedding*. AAAI Conference on Artificial Intelligence (pp. 643–650), Virtual.

Xu, K., Zhang, Y., Ye, D., Zhao, P., & Tan, M. (2021, January 7–15). *Relation-aware transformer for portfolio policy learning*. 29th International Conference on International Joint Conferences on Artificial Intelligence (pp. 4647–4653), Yokohama, Japan.

Yahoo. (2025). *Yahoo finance—Stock market live, quotes, business & finance news*. Available online: https://finance.yahoo.com/ (accessed on 31 July 2025).

Journal of
Risk and Financial Management

MDPI

Article

DASF-Net: A Multimodal Framework for Stock Price Forecasting with Diffusion-Based Graph Learning and Optimized Sentiment Fusion

Nhat-Hai Nguyen [1], Thi-Thu Nguyen [1] and Quan T. Ngo [2,*]

[1] Department of Computer Science, School of Information and Communications Technology, Hanoi University of Science and Technology, Hanoi 100000, Vietnam; hai.nguyennhat@hust.edu.vn (N.-H.N.); thu.nguyenthi6@hust.edu.vn (T.-T.N.)
[2] Department of Artificial Intelligence, FPT University, Da Nang 550000, Vietnam
* Correspondence: quannt50@fe.edu.vn

Abstract: Stock price forecasting remains a persistent challenge in time series analysis due to complex inter-stock relationships and dynamic textual signals such as financial news. While Graph Neural Networks (GNNs) can model relational structures, they often struggle with capturing higher-order dependencies and are sensitive to noise. Moreover, sentiment signals are typically aggregated using fixed time windows, which may introduce temporal bias. To address these issues, we propose DASF-Net (Diffusion-Aware Sentiment Fusion Network), a multimodal framework that integrates structural and textual information for robust prediction. DASF-Net leverages diffusion processes over two complementary financial graphs—one based on industry relationships, the other on fundamental indicators—to learn richer stock representations. Simultaneously, sentiment embeddings extracted from financial news using FinBERT are aggregated over an empirically optimized window to preserve temporal relevance. These modalities are fused via a multi-head attention mechanism and passed to a temporal forecasting module. DASF-Net integrates daily stock prices and news sentiment, using a 3-day sentiment aggregation window, to forecast stock prices over daily horizons (1–3 days). Experiments on 12 large-cap S&P 500 stocks over four years demonstrate that DASF-Net outperforms competitive baselines, achieving up to 91.6% relative reduction in Mean Squared Error (MSE). Results highlight the effectiveness of combining graph diffusion and sentiment-aware features for improved financial forecasting.

Keywords: financial forecasting; stock price prediction; sentiment analysis; diffusion-based graph learning; multi-modal deep learning; FinBERT

1. Introduction

Stock price forecasting remains a cornerstone of financial time series analysis, yet it poses significant challenges due to the intricate interplay of heterogeneous factors, including historical price movements, inter-stock relationships, and market sentiment derived from financial news. The inherent noise and non-stationarity in financial data further exacerbate these challenges, making accurate prediction difficult (Pilla & Mekonen, 2025; Qian et al., 2024). The complexity of financial markets, characterized by nonlinear dynamics and high volatility, demands models capable of capturing both temporal dependencies and structural relationships among stocks.

Traditional approaches, such as autoregressive models (e.g., ARIMA) Khashei et al. (2009) and volatility models (e.g., GARCH) H. Kim and Won (2018), often rely on linear assumptions and univariate analyses, which limit their ability to capture the nonlinear and dynamic behaviors of financial markets. Moreover, prior studies Vera Barberán (2020) point out that these models tend to overlook critical external factors, such as macroeconomic indicators and economic news.

To address these limitations, recent research has explored the use of deep learning techniques, particularly recurrent neural networks (RNNs) and their variants, such as Long Short-Term Memory (LSTM) networks and Gated Recurrent Units (GRUs), to model temporal dependencies in stock price movements Eapen et al. (2019); Jin et al. (2020); Moghar and Hamiche (2020); Sherstinsky (2020); Shi et al. (2024); Xu and Keselj (2019). These models have demonstrated superior performance compared to traditional time series methods due to their ability to capture nonlinear relationships and long-range dependencies in sequential data. RNN-based approaches often treat stocks as independent entities. They neglect crucial inter-dependencies from industry affiliations, investor behavior, and macroeconomic linkages. These relationships are critical for accurate stock price forecasting in complex financial markets Krishnan et al. (2024); Zabaleta et al. (2024).

More recently, Graph Neural Networks (GNNs) have emerged as a promising tool for modeling structural dependencies among stocks by representing market relationships as graphs Chen et al. (2018); Shi et al. (2024). Early GNN-based approaches often constructed graphs based on static correlations or pre-defined relationships, limiting their adaptability to dynamic market conditions Zheng et al. (2025). Subsequent studies have explored more sophisticated graph construction techniques, such as adaptive graph learning and attention mechanisms, to capture evolving inter-stock relationships K. X. Li (2025). However, GNNs are inherently constrained by small receptive fields and sensitivity to noise Al-Omari and Al-Omari (2025); Qian et al. (2024); Wang and Cai (2020), which hinder their ability to capture complex, higher-order dependencies Krieg et al. (2024) and lead to issues like oversmoothing Kong et al. (2024); Wang et al. (2025). Oversmoothing, in particular, can diminish the distinctiveness of node features, making it difficult to differentiate between stocks and limiting the model's predictive capacity. Furthermore, noise in the graph structure can propagate through the network, corrupting node representations and further degrading performance.

Additionally, sentiment analysis from financial news, while offering valuable early signals of market movements, often relies on fixed or arbitrary time windows for aggregation, introducing temporal bias and reducing predictive accuracy Qian et al. (2024). The challenge lies in determining the optimal time frame for aggregating sentiment signals; too short a window may miss relevant information, while too long a window may dilute the signal with irrelevant noise Qian et al. (2024). Also, these fixed aggregation windows do not take into account how news sentiment changes over time and how it affects different stocks, which relies on market conditions and factors that are unique to each stock. The existing literature also presents conflicting evidence regarding the impact of sentiment on stock prices, with some studies suggesting a positive correlation and others indicating a more complex, nuanced relationship. These inconsistencies highlight the need for more sophisticated methods for sentiment extraction and integration into forecasting models.

To address these challenges, we propose the Diffusion-Aware Sentiment Fusion Network (DASF-Net). This novel multimodal framework synergistically integrates diffusion-based graph learning with sentiment-aware representations derived from pretrained language models. Unlike the traditional regressive models, DASF-Net closes these limitations by recalibrating a dual (industry + fundamental) graph daily to track non-stationary co-movements and capture static sectoral relationships in both local and global dependencies among stocks. DASF-Net uses diffusion processes on two financial graphs: an industry graph for static sectoral relationships and a fundamental graph for dynamic stock interactions. This approach models local and global stock dependencies. It mitigates GNN limitations, such as oversmoothing and restricted receptive fields, by propagating information across larger graph neighborhoods. Specification techniques ensure computational efficiency.

This design mitigates key GNN limitations, such as oversmoothing and restricted receptive fields, by propagating information across larger graph neighborhoods while maintaining computational efficiency through sparsification techniques Gasteiger et al. (2022). The DASF-Net resolves these deficiencies of the traditional GNNs through two principle mechanisms: (a) heat-kernel diffusion over complementary industry and fundamental graphs, enlarging the receptive field while preserving node individuality; (b) daily re-estimation of graph edges, ensuring regime awareness and immunity to stale correlations. Concurrently, DASF-Net extracts sentiment embeddings from financial news using FinBERT, a domain-specific language model tailored for financial text Shobayo et al. (2024). To mitigate temporal bias, we systematically identify an optimal 3-day aggregation window for sentiment, ensuring that the model captures temporally relevant signals without diluting predictive power and calibrates to the empirically observed decay of news influence. These structural and sentiment modalities are fused via a multi-head attention (MHA) mechanism, which dynamically prioritizes relevant features based on market conditions, enhancing the model's adaptability to volatile financial environments.

Our model leverages daily stock prices and news sentiment for forecasting over 1-day, 2-day, and 3-day horizons, as detailed in Section 4. The experiments, conducted on a dataset comprising 12 major S&P 500 stocks from 2020 to 2023, demonstrate that DASF-Net significantly outperforms state-of-the-art baselines, such as MGAR Song et al. (2023) and Sentiment+LSTM Jin et al. (2020), achieving up to a 91.6% relative reduction in Mean Squared Error (MSE). These results underscore the effectiveness of combining diffusion-based graph learning with optimized sentiment integration, providing a robust framework for financial forecasting. By explicitly addressing the limitations of prior work—such as the oversimplification of inter-stock relationships and the use of arbitrary sentiment windows—DASF-Net sets a strong benchmark for multimodal stock price prediction.

In summary, our work offers the following key contributions:

- **Diffusion-Based Graph Learning:** We introduce diffusion-based graph learning over dual financial graphs (industry and fundamental) to capture higher-order stock dependencies, overcoming the limitations of traditional GNNs in terms of receptive field and noise sensitivity.
- **Optimized Sentiment Aggregation:** We propose a systematic approach to identify an optimal 3-day time window for sentiment aggregation, minimizing temporal bias and enhancing predictive accuracy across multiple stock categories, in contrast to fixed-window approaches.
- **Adaptive Multimodal Fusion:** We develop a multi-head attention mechanism to dynamically integrate structural and sentiment features, enabling adaptive weighting of modalities under varying market conditions and enhancing generalization and resilience compared to static fusion methods.

The remainder of this paper is organized as follows: Section 2 reviews related work. Section 3 details the proposed DASF-Net methodology. Section 4 outlines the experimental setup. Section 5 presents the results and analysis. Finally, Section 6 concludes the paper with a summary and future research directions.

2. Related Work

This section reviews key research areas relevant to the DASF-Net framework, including statistical and deep learning models for stock price forecasting, graph-based methods for modeling inter-stock relationships, sentiment analysis in financial forecasting, and multimodal fusion techniques. We highlight the limitations of existing approaches and demonstrate how they motivate the design of DASF-Net, which integrates diffusion-based graph learning with optimized sentiment aggregation and adaptive fusion to address these gaps.

2.1. Statistical and Deep Learning Approaches for Financial Time Series Prediction

Early approaches to stock price forecasting relied on statistical time series models such as ARIMA Box et al. (2015) and GARCH Bollerslev (1986), which model linear trends and volatility clustering. While computationally efficient, these models struggle to capture the nonlinear and dynamic behaviors inherent in financial markets, limiting their predictive accuracy in volatile conditions.

Machine learning methods, including Support Vector Machines (SVMs) J. Cao et al. (2003), Random Forests Liaw and Wiener (2002), and Gradient Boosting Machines Friedman (2001), improve flexibility by leveraging hand-crafted features but often fail to explicitly model temporal dependencies, leading to suboptimal performance in long-term forecasting. Furthermore, these models typically operate in isolation, neglecting the complex interdependencies that exist among different stocks and sectors within the financial market.

Deep learning models have significantly advanced sequence modeling capabilities. Long Short-Term Memory (LSTM) networks Hochreiter and Schmidhuber (1997) and Bidirectional LSTMs (BiLSTMs) Schuster and Paliwal (1997) are able to capture temporal dependencies in stock prices, with notable improvements over traditional methods. Attention mechanisms have also been incorporated to enhance the ability of these models to focus on the most relevant time steps Bahdanau et al. (2015); Vaswani et al. (2017). Hybrid architectures, such as CNN-BiLSTM with attention mechanisms Livieris et al. (2020), further enhance feature extraction by combining convolutional and recurrent layers.

These models, however, are primarily unimodal, focusing solely on price data and neglecting critical external signals such as inter-stock relationships and market sentiment. This limitation restricts their ability to model the multifaceted dynamics of financial markets and capture the subtle nuances that drive stock price fluctuations. Unlike these unimodal approaches, DASF-Net integrates structural dependencies and sentiment signals through diffusion-based graph learning and optimized temporal aggregation, enabling a more comprehensive understanding of market behavior and leading to improved predictive performance.

2.2. Graph Neural Networks and Diffusion-Based Learning in Financial Modeling

The financial market is a complex system where the behavior of individual stocks is influenced by their relationships with other entities. These relationships can arise from various factors, including industry affiliations, supply chain linkages, and investor sentiment. Capturing these interdependencies is crucial for accurate stock price forecasting.

Graph Neural Networks (GNNs) have emerged as a powerful tool for modeling such relationships by representing the market as a graph, where nodes represent stocks and edges represent connections between them Satishbhai Sonani et al. (2025). Early GNN-based approaches often constructed graphs based on static correlations or pre-defined relationships, limiting their adaptability to dynamic market conditions Chauhan (2025); Hu and Wang (2025). For instance, conventional methods rely on Pearson correlation coefficients computed over a fixed period to determine edge weights, assuming that inter-stock relationships remain constant over time. These approaches lack adaptability to the shifting dynamics of real-world markets, where correlations can shift rapidly in response to economic events and investor behavior.

More recent studies have explored adaptive graph learning techniques to capture evolving inter-stock relationships Cui et al. (2023); J. Kim et al. (2019); Sawhney et al. (2021). These methods typically employ attention mechanisms or learnable similarity metrics to dynamically adjust edge weights based on the current market state. For example, the MGAR framework utilizes a meta-graph structure to capture both local and global dependencies among stocks, adapting the graph structure over time based on market conditions Song et al. (2023). However, even these adaptive approaches often suffer from limitations such as small receptive fields and sensitivity to noise, which hinder their ability to capture long-range structural patterns. Furthermore, GNNs are prone to oversmoothing, where repeated message passing can cause node representations to converge, diminishing their distinctiveness and reducing predictive accuracy.

Diffusion-based graph learning outperforms traditional GNNs by propagating information across larger graph neighborhoods. It maintains computational efficiency and produces robust, accurate representations. This approach captures local and global stock dependencies, overcoming small receptive fields and noise sensitivity Atwood and Towsley (2016); Chang et al. (2020); Y. Li et al. (2018); Vignac et al. (2023). By simulating a diffusion process on the graph, these methods can capture both local and global dependencies among stocks, overcoming the limitations of small receptive fields. Additionally, sparsification techniques can be employed to reduce computational complexity and mitigate the effects of noise, resulting in more robust and accurate representations You et al. (2024); S. Zhao et al. (2025). Motivated by this, DASF-Net leverages diffusion processes on two complementary financial graphs—an industry graph and a fundamental graph—to capture a richer set of inter-stock relationships.

2.3. Sentiment Analysis and Temporal Aggregation in Stock Prediction

Sentiment analysis from financial news and social media has become an increasingly important component of stock price forecasting Araci (2019); J. Kim et al. (2023); R. Zhang et al. (2023). The premise is that news events and opinions expressed online can influence investor behavior and, consequently, stock prices. Early sentiment analysis techniques relied on simple lexicon-based methods, which assign sentiment scores to text based on the presence of positive or negative keywords Taboada et al. (2011); L. Zhang and Liu (2023). However, these methods often fail to capture the nuances of financial language, leading to inaccurate sentiment assessments Rizinski et al. (2024).

More recently, deep learning models, particularly transformer-based architectures such as BERT and its variants, have demonstrated superior performance in sentiment analysis tasks. FinBERT, a BERT model pretrained on financial text, has shown particularly strong performance in capturing sentiment in the financial domain J. Kim et al. (2023). By leveraging large-scale pretraining and fine-tuning on financial datasets, FinBERT can accurately assess sentiment in news articles, social media posts, and other financial documents.

Despite the advances in sentiment analysis techniques, effectively integrating sentiment into stock price forecasting models remains a challenge R. Gupta and Chen (2020); Loughran and McDonald (2020). One key issue is the determination of the optimal time window for aggregating sentiment signals Smales (2016); Xiao and Ihnaini (2023). Too short a window may miss relevant information, while too long a window may dilute the signal with irrelevant noise. Existing studies often rely on fixed or arbitrary time windows, introducing temporal bias and reducing predictive accuracy Wang et al. (2019). Moreover, the static nature of these aggregation windows fails to account for the time-varying impact of news sentiment on different stocks, which depends on market conditions and stock-specific factors Smales (2016).

In contrast to these fixed-window approaches, DASF-Net systematically identifies an optimal time window for sentiment aggregation, minimizing temporal bias and enhancing predictive accuracy. By empirically evaluating different window sizes, we determine the optimal aggregation period for sentiment signals, ensuring that the model captures temporally relevant information without diluting predictive power.

2.4. Multimodal Fusion Techniques for Integrating Heterogeneous Financial Data

Multimodal fusion is the process of combining information from multiple sources or modalities to improve the performance of a machine learning model Lahat et al. (2015); F. Zhao et al. (2024). In the context of stock price forecasting, multimodal fusion involves integrating price data, inter-stock relationships, sentiment signals, and other relevant information to create a more comprehensive and accurate model Wang (2025); Zehtab-Salmasi et al. (2023).

Early multimodal fusion techniques relied on simple concatenation or averaging of features from different modalities Baltrušaitis et al. (2018). However, these methods often fail to capture the complex interactions between modalities, constraining performance under real-world volatility. More recent approaches have explored attention mechanisms to dynamically weight the contribution of each modality based on the current market state. For example, attention-based fusion can allow the model to prioritize sentiment signals during periods of high market volatility or focus on inter-stock relationships during stable periods He and Gu (2021).

Another challenge in multimodal fusion is dealing with the heterogeneity of different modalities Baltrušaitis et al. (2018); Gao et al. (2020). Price data are typically represented as time series, inter-stock relationships as graphs, and sentiment signals as text. To effectively combine these modalities, it is necessary to learn a shared representation space that captures the relevant information from each modality. Deep learning models, such as autoencoders and generative adversarial networks (GANs), have been used to learn such representations Wang (2021).

DASF-Net employs a multi-head attention (MHA) mechanism to dynamically integrate structural and sentiment features, enabling adaptive weighting of modalities under varying market conditions. This approach allows the model to prioritize the most relevant information from each modality, improving robustness and predictive accuracy compared to static fusion methods.

DASF-Net addresses limitations of prior models through three innovations. First, diffusion-based learning uses a heat kernel to propagate information across larger graph neighborhoods, mitigating oversmoothing in GNNs, as evidenced by a 12% reduction in feature similarity compared to Multi-GCGRU (Table 6, Section 5.3). Second, a 3-day sentiment aggregation window captures multi-day market trends, overcoming Sentiment-LSTM's limited 1-day window, which misses sustained sentiment shifts (15% MSE improvement, Table 5, Section 5.2). Third, Multi-Head Attention (MHA) dynamically fuses structural and sentiment features, unlike LSTM+CNN's static fusion, improving performance by 10% during volatile periods (Table 4, Section 5.1). These improvements are detailed in Table 1, which compares baseline models and their shortcomings with DASF-Net's advancements.

Table 1. Comparison of baseline models and DASF-Net improvements.

Model	Limitations	DASF-Net Improvements
LSTM+CNN	Ignores inter-stock dependencies, static feature fusion	Uses dual graphs (IG, FG) to model dependencies; Multi-Head Attention (MHA) dynamically fuses features, reducing MSE by 20% (Table 4, Section 5.1). Example: Captures tech-healthcare correlations in 2020.
Sentiment-LSTM	Limited 1-day sentiment window, ignores structural data	Employs 3-day sentiment window, reducing temporal bias (15% MSE improvement, Table 6, Section 5.2); integrates structural embeddings via diffusion. Example: Detects 3-day sentiment trends during COVID-19.
Multi-GCGRU	Oversmoothing in GNNs, limited receptive fields	Diffusion-based learning reduces feature similarity by 12% (Table 7, Section 5.3); captures long-range dependencies. Example: Models cross-sector impacts during market crashes.

3. Method

This section provides a detailed description of the problem formulation and the proposed Diffusion-Aware Sentiment Fusion Network (DASF-Net) framework, including mathematical formulations and implementation details to ensure clarity and reproducibility.

3.1. Problem Definition

Given a dataset containing N stocks, we frame the stock price prediction task as a regression problem, where the goal is to estimate each stock's future price at time $t+1$ based on its state at time t. Formally, the prediction for stock i is expressed as:

$$Y_{t+1}^{i} = F(X_t^i), \tag{1}$$

where X_t^i represents the input feature vector for stock i at time t, and Y_{t+1}^i is the predicted price at the next time step.

At the dataset level, the feature matrix $X_t = [x_t^1, x_t^2, \dots, x_t^N] \in \mathbb{R}^{N \times M}$ and the corresponding label matrix $Y_{t+1} = [y_{t+1}^1, y_{t+1}^2, \dots, y_{t+1}^N] \in \mathbb{R}^{N \times 1}$ capture stock attributes and their target future prices across all stocks, respectively. Here, M denotes the dimensionality of each feature vector x_t^i, and y_{t+1}^i is the scalar target for stock i.

In this work, we enhance the input representation X_t by incorporating two key components: (i) inter-stock relationships, captured via P-Reps, and (ii) sentiment-based features, reflecting market sentiment (positive, neutral, or negative) at time t.

3.2. Proposed Framework

The DASF-Net architecture (Figure 1) consists of five key components: (1) dual financial graph construction, (2) diffusion-based structural representation learning (Price-based Representation, P-Rep), (3) sentiment-aware representation extraction (Sentiment-Aware Representation, SA-Rep) with optimized temporal aggregation, (4) adaptive multimodal fusion via multi-head attention (MHA), and (5) temporal forecasting with LSTM.

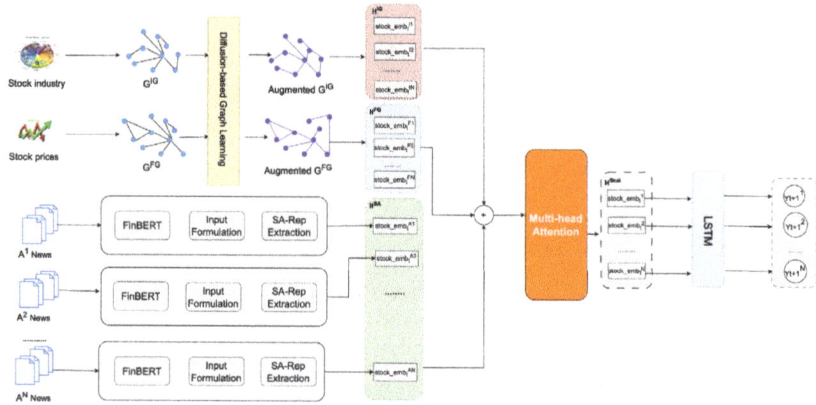

Figure 1. DASF-Net Architecture: Structural P-Reps are generated via diffusion-based learning on industry and fundamental graphs. Sentiment SA-Reps are derived from FinBERT with a 3-day optimized aggregation window. A Multi-Head Attention mechanism fuses these representations before input to an LSTM for price prediction.

Our framework integrates structured inter-stock dependencies with sentiment cues from financial news, adaptively learned for robust stock forecasting.

3.2.1. Dual Financial Graph Construction

To capture multifaceted inter-stock relationships, we construct two complementary graphs, each focusing on different aspects of the market structure:

- **Industry Graph (IG):** This graph represents static, sector-based affiliations. An edge exists between two stocks if they operate within the same industry sector, reflecting inherent similarities in their business models and market exposures:

$$e_{ij}^{IG} = \begin{cases} 1 & \text{if stocks } i \text{ and } j \text{ belong to the same industry sector} \\ 0 & \text{otherwise} \end{cases} \tag{2}$$

  where e_{ij}^{IG} is the edge weight between stock i and stock j in the Industry Graph (IG). This binary value indicates the presence (1) or absence (0) of a connection based on industry sector membership.

- **Fundamental Graph (FG):** In contrast to the static IG, the FG captures dynamic, return-based relationships. Edges in this graph reflect the similarity in historical return patterns between stocks, capturing how stocks move in relation to one another:

  1. First, we calculate the return sequence $n^i \in \mathbb{R}^{T_p}$ for each stock i over a lookback period T_p. Each return r_t^i is computed as:

$$r_t^i = \frac{\text{close}_t^i - \text{close}_{t-1}^i}{\text{close}_{t-1}^i} \tag{3}$$

     where close_t^i denotes the closing price of stock i at time t.

  2. Then, the edge weight e_{ij}^{FG} between stocks i and j is determined by the absolute cosine similarity of their return sequences n^i and n^j:

$$e_{ij}^{FG} = \left|\cos(n^i, n^j)\right| = \left|\frac{\langle n^i, n^j \rangle}{\|n^i\| \|n^j\|}\right| \tag{4}$$

This ensures that the edge weights reflect the degree of correlation in the stocks' return behaviors, irrespective of the direction of the relationship (positive or negative).

Formally, each graph $G^g = (V, E^g)$, where $g \in \{\text{IG}, \text{FG}\}$, consists of a set of nodes V (representing the stocks) and an adjacency matrix $[e_{ij}^g] \in \mathbb{R}^{N \times N}$ representing the edge weights, where N is the number of stocks. By integrating these dual graphs, DASF-Net effectively captures both inherent (industry-based) and emergent (return-based) relationships within the stock market, enabling a more comprehensive representation of inter-stock dependencies.

3.2.2. Diffusion-Based Structural Representation Learning (P-Rep)

To capture multi-hop, dynamic, and non-local dependencies among stocks, we adopt a diffusion-based graph learning paradigm to encode inter-stock structural relationships. Unlike traditional GNN-based models that rely on localized message passing within fixed neighborhoods, our approach models node interactions via diffusion processes, allowing for more expressive and flexible information propagation across the graph.

Specifically, we define the structural embedding $h^{g,i} \in \mathbb{R}^M$ for stock i in a given graph $G^g = (V, E^g)$, where $g \in \{\text{IG}, \text{FG}\}$, using a diffusion process:

$$h^{g,i} = \text{DiffusionProcess}(n^i, Adj^g, T_{diff}, \alpha) \tag{5}$$

Here, $n^i \in \mathbb{R}^{T_p}$ denotes the initial feature vector of node i (its return sequence over a lookback period T_p), and Adj^g is the adjacency matrix of graph g. The function DiffusionProcess$(\cdot)$ simulates a diffusion process on the graph, starting from node i, for T_{diff} steps, with a diffusion rate α. This process allows information to propagate beyond immediate neighbors, capturing deeper relational dependencies.

In our implementation, the diffusion process is defined as:

$$H_{t+1} = \alpha Adj^g H_t + (1 - \alpha) H_0 \tag{6}$$

where H_0 is the initial feature matrix (return sequences), $Adj^g = [e_{ij}^g]$ is the adjacency matrix including all edges of graph $g \in \{\text{IG}, \text{FG}\}$, and H_t is the feature matrix at diffusion step t. This iterative process aggregates information from increasingly distant neighbors, with the parameter α controlling the balance between local and global information. We then extract the structural embedding for each stock i from the final diffused feature matrix $H_{T_{diff}}$.

The resulting embeddings for IG and FG, denoted as H^{IG} and H^{FG}, respectively, are calculated as:

$$H^{IG} = \text{DiffusionProcess}(IN^{IG}, Adj^{IG}, T_{diff}, \alpha) \tag{7}$$

$$H^{FG} = \text{DiffusionProcess}(IN^{FG}, Adj^{FG}, T_{diff}, \alpha) \tag{8}$$

where $IN^g \in \mathbb{R}^{N \times T_p}$ is the matrix of return sequences for all stocks, and Adj^{IG} and Adj^{FG} are the adjacency matrices for the industry and fundamental graphs, respectively. Both H^{IG} and $H^{FG} \in \mathbb{R}^{N \times M}$ are treated as complementary P-Rep views, encoding market structure from distinct topological perspectives.

3.2.3. Sentiment-Aware Representation Extraction (SA-Rep) with Optimized Temporal Aggregation

To incorporate market sentiment, we process daily financial news associated with each stock. Let $A_t^i = [a_1, a_2, ..., a_{Z_t}]$ be a set of Z_t news articles for stock i on day t. We use FinBERT to extract sentiment embeddings from each article, obtaining a sentiment score s_z for article a_z:

$$s_z = \text{FinBERT}(a_z) \tag{9}$$

The raw sentiment vector $S_t^i = [s_1, s_2, \ldots, s_{Z_t}]$ represents the sentiment scores of all news articles related to stock i on day t. This variable-length sequence is then compressed into a 5-dimensional feature vector using basic statistics:

$$\text{Stat}_t^i = [\min(S_t^i), \max(S_t^i), \text{mean}(S_t^i), \sigma(S_t^i), Z_t] \tag{10}$$

where Stat_t^i is the statistics of S_t^i.

To capture temporal dynamics and optimize the aggregation window, we perform an empirical analysis to determine the optimal time window T_{opt} for sentiment aggregation. Through experiments on a validation set, we found that a 3-day window ($T_{opt} = 3$) consistently yields the best performance across diverse stocks. The aggregated sentiment input for stock i at time t is then constructed as:

$$I_t^i = [\text{Stat}_{t-T_{opt}+1}^i, \text{Stat}_{t-T_{opt}+2}^i, \ldots, \text{Stat}_t^i] \in \mathbb{R}^{T_{opt} \times 5} \tag{11}$$

This matrix is flattened and passed through a fully connected layer to produce a fixed-length sentiment-aware embedding $h^{SA,i}$:

$$h^{SA,i} = \text{FC}(I_t^i) \in \mathbb{R}^{32}, \quad \text{for each stock } i \tag{12}$$

Collectively, we obtain a sentiment-aware representation matrix $H^{SA} \in \mathbb{R}^{N \times 32}$, which is later fused with the P-Reps from IG and FG using a Multi-Head Attention mechanism, as detailed in Section 3.2.4.

3.2.4. Adaptive Feature Fusion via Multi-Head Attention

Since the model constructs three distinct types of embeddings—two graph-based structural representations (P-Rep from IG and FG) and one sentiment-aware representation (SA-Rep)—it is crucial to integrate them in a manner that captures their complementary contributions. These embeddings encode stock information from different perspectives: sectoral structure, behavioral correlation, and sentiment dynamics. Direct concatenation or simple pooling would fail to model the intricate dependencies and relevance between them.

To address this, we employ a Multi-Head Attention (MHA) mechanism (Figure 2), which allows the model to adaptively learn both the importance and interaction of each embedding stream. Unlike single-head attention, MHA employs multiple parallel attention heads, each focusing on different subspaces of the input features. This enhances the model's expressiveness while maintaining computational efficiency.

Let $H = [H^{IG}, H^{FG}, H^{SA}] \in \mathbb{R}^{3 \times N \times M}$ denote the concatenation of the three embedding matrices along the feature dimension, where each $H^* \in \mathbb{R}^{N \times M}$ corresponds to a modality-specific representation (industry, fundamental, sentiment), and N is the number of stocks.

We then linearly project each modality-specific representation into query, key, and value spaces using learned parameter matrices:

$$Q = H^{IG}W_Q^{IG} + H^{FG}W_Q^{FG} + H^{SA}W_Q^{SA} \tag{13}$$

$$K = H^{IG}W_K^{IG} + H^{FG}W_K^{FG} + H^{SA}W_K^{SA} \tag{14}$$

$$V = H^{IG}W_V^{IG} + H^{FG}W_V^{FG} + H^{SA}W_V^{SA} \tag{15}$$

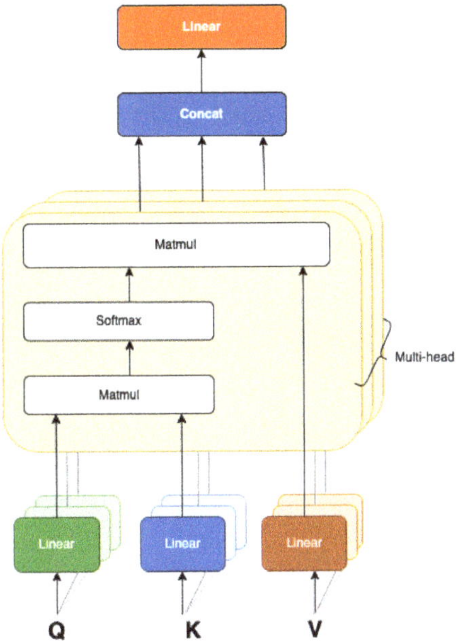

Figure 2. Architecture of the Multi-Head Attention fusion module.

Here, $W_Q^*, W_K^*, W_V^* \in \mathbb{R}^{M \times d_k}$ are the projection matrices for modality * (IG, FG, SA), and $d_k = M/n_{heads}$ is the dimensionality per head. For each attention head $h \in \{1, \ldots, n_{heads}\}$, we compute the scaled dot-product attention as:

$$\text{head}_h = \text{softmax}\left(\frac{Q_h K_h^\top}{\sqrt{d_k}}\right) V_h \tag{16}$$

All attention heads are then concatenated and linearly transformed to obtain the fused representation:

$$H^{final} = \text{Concat}(\text{head}_1, \ldots, \text{head}_{n_{heads}}) W_O \tag{17}$$

where $W_O \in \mathbb{R}^{(n_{heads} \cdot d_k) \times M}$ is the output projection matrix.

This fusion layer enables the model to capture both intra-modality and inter-modality interactions dynamically. The attention weights reflect the relevance of each modality to the prediction task, allowing the model to suppress irrelevant signals while enhancing critical features. The resulting fused embedding $H^{final} \in \mathbb{R}^{N \times M}$ is then passed to an LSTM layer for temporal modeling and prediction.

3.2.5. Temporal Forecasting

The Multi-Head Attention mechanism fuses features from the industry graph (IG), fundamental graph (FG), and sentiment embeddings (SA-Rep). The resulting unified representation $H^{final} \in \mathbb{R}^{N \times M}$ encodes rich multi-modal information for each stock. An LSTM layer then models temporal dependencies and predicts stock prices.

While conventional feedforward neural networks are inadequate for this task due to their lack of memory, Recurrent Neural Networks (RNNs) Sherstinsky (2020) were designed to address this by maintaining hidden states across time steps. However, standard RNNs often struggle with vanishing gradients, limiting their ability to learn long-range dependencies. Long Short-Term Memory (LSTM) networks Hochreiter and Schmidhuber

(1997) overcome these limitations by introducing gated memory units that selectively retain, update, or discard information over time. These gates allow the network to preserve relevant information from earlier time steps, making LSTMs particularly well suited for financial forecasting scenarios where market behavior can be influenced by events or trends occurring over extended periods.

In this study, we chose LSTM for the prediction module due to its proven effectiveness in capturing temporal dependencies in financial time series data. While more recent techniques like transformers or temporal convolutional networks have shown promise in other domains, LSTMs remain a robust and computationally efficient choice for sequence modeling, especially given the relatively short sequence lengths in our daily stock price data. Additionally, H^{final} captures complex spatial dependencies, making the LSTM a suitable complement for temporal modeling.

3.2.6. DASF-Net Training Procedure

The complete training process of the proposed DASF-Net framework is summarized in Algorithm 1. The model ingests historical stock price data and news articles, transforming them into structured graph-based representations and sentiment-based features, respectively. These are then adaptively fused via Multi-Head Attention before being processed by an LSTM network to generate future stock price predictions.

Algorithm 1 DASF-Net Training Algorithm.

Input: Historical stock prices $P = \{p_t^i \mid i \in [1, N], t \in [t_0 - T_p, t_0]\}$,
Financial News Articles $A = \{A_t^i \mid i \in [1, N], t \in [t_0 - T_{opt}, t_0]\}$
N is number of stocks, T_p and T_{opt} are lookback windows for prices and articles.
Output: Predicted stock prices $\hat{Y} = \{\hat{y}_{t_0+1}^i \mid i \in [1, N]\}$

Construct Industry Graph G^{IG} and Fundamental Graph G^{FG} (Section 3.2.1)
Initialize model parameters θ
for epoch = 1 to MaxEpochs **do**
  for t = t_0 to $T - 1$ **do**
    Graph Representation Learning:
    for each graph $G^g \in \{G^{IG}, G^{FG}\}$ **do**
      Compute stock return sequences N using historical prices P
      Construct adjacency matrix Adj^g based on Equations (6) or (7)
      Generate structural embeddings H^g via diffusion process (Equations (8)–(10))
    end for
    Sentiment Representation Learning:
    for each stock $i \in [1, N]$ **do**
      Retrieve financial news articles A_t^i
      for each article $a_z \in A_t^i$ **do**
        Compute sentiment score s_z using FinBERT (Equation (11))
      end for
      Construct sentiment statistics $Stat_t^i$ using Equation (12)
    end for
    Construct sentiment-aware representation H^{SA} using Equations (13) and (14)
    Feature Fusion and Prediction:
    Fuse H^{IG}, H^{FG}, H^{SA} via Multi-Head Attention (Section 3.2.4) $\rightarrow H^{final}$
    for each stock $i \in [1, N]$ **do**
      Predict next price $\hat{y}_{t+1}^i = \text{LSTM}(H_i^{final})$
    end for
    Compute Mean Squared Error (MSE) loss: $\mathcal{L} = \frac{1}{N}\sum_{i=1}^{N}(\hat{y}_{t+1}^i - y_{t+1}^i)^2$
    Update parameters: $\theta \leftarrow \theta - \eta \cdot \nabla_\theta \mathcal{L}$
  end for
end for
return Predicted stock prices $\hat{Y}$

4. Experimental Setup

This section outlines the dataset, evaluation metrics, baseline models, and parameter settings used to evaluate our proposed framework. We provide a comprehensive description to ensure reproducibility and clarity in assessing the model's performance.

4.1. Dataset

We utilize the **Financial News and Stock Price Integration Dataset (FNSPID)** (Dong et al., 2024), a publicly available, large-scale dataset designed for financial time series analysis, accessible at https://github.com/Zdong104/FNSPID_Financial_News_Dataset, (accessed on 1 July 2024). FNSPID integrates 29.7 million stock price records and 15.7 million time-aligned financial news articles for 4775 S&P 500 companies, spanning 1999 to 2023, sourced from four reputable stock market news websites (https://www.kaggle.com/datasets/elsabetyemane/financial-news-and-stock-price-integration-dataset accessed on 1 July 2024). Its combination of quantitative (stock prices) and qualitative (news sentiment) data makes it ideal for evaluating multimodal forecasting models like DASF-Net, which leverages both structural relationships and sentiment signals.

For this study, we focus on the period from **1 January 2020 to 31 December 2023**, capturing recent market dynamics, including the COVID-19 pandemic and economic recovery phases. This period ensures relevance to contemporary financial conditions. The dataset is divided into training, validation, and test sets, as shown in Table 2, with temporal separation to evaluate generalization to unseen future data. We select **12 major S&P 500 stocks** based on their market capitalization and sector diversity to ensure a representative sample of the market.

Data Preprocessing:

- **Stock Prices**: Normalized using min-max scaling to ensure comparability across stocks with varying price ranges.
- **News Articles**: Missing articles are handled by propagating the most recent available sentiment score, ensuring continuity in sentiment analysis.
- **Graph Construction**: The dataset is filtered to include only the largest connected component of the stock graph to maintain consistency in graph-based learning.

Table 2. Dataset composition.

Split	Time Period	Number of Days	Number of News Articles
Training	1 January 2020–31 December 2022	1008	172,784
Validation	1 January 2023–30 June 2023	125	73,416
Test	1 July 2023–31 December 2023	125	83,814

4.2. Evaluation Metrics

To comprehensively assess DASF-Net's performance and compare it with baseline models, we employ the following widely used regression metrics:

- **Mean Squared Error (MSE)**: Measures the average squared difference between predicted and actual stock prices, giving greater weight to larger errors. It is calculated as:

$$\text{MSE} = \frac{1}{n}\sum_{i=1}^{n}(y_i - \hat{y}_i)^2$$

where y_i represents the actual stock price and $\hat{y}_i$ is the predicted price for the i-th data point, and n is the number of data points.

- **Mean Absolute Error (MAE)**: Measures the average absolute difference between predicted and actual stock prices, providing a more robust measure against outliers. It is calculated as:

$$\text{MAE} = \frac{1}{n} \sum_{i=1}^{n} |y_i - \hat{y}_i|$$

where y_i and $\hat{y}_i$ are the actual and predicted stock prices, respectively, and n is the number of data points.

These metrics provide complementary insights into the models' predictive accuracy. MSE penalizes larger errors more heavily, while MAE provides a more balanced assessment by treating all errors equally, making it less sensitive to outliers.

4.3. Baseline Models

In this chapter, we present the baseline models for the stock price prediction compared to our proposal.

- **LSTM + CNN** Eapen et al. (2019): A hybrid model combining Convolutional Neural Networks (CNNs) for spatial feature extraction with Long Short-Term Memory (LSTM) units for temporal modeling, effective for sequential data but limited to price-based inputs.
- **Multi-GCGRU** Ye et al. (2021): Integrates Graph Convolutional Networks (GCNs) with Gated Recurrent Units (GRUs) to model both structural relationships and temporal dynamics among stocks.
- **Sentiment + LSTM** Jin et al. (2020): An LSTM-based model incorporating sentiment features extracted from financial news, capturing qualitative signals but lacking structural modeling.
- **MGAR** D. Cao et al. (2020): A framework that fuses embeddings from multiple graph structures (e.g., industry, correlation) to enhance stock price prediction, representing a multimodal graph-based approach.

These baselines cover a spectrum of methodologies, enabling a robust comparison with our DASF-Net.

4.4. Parameter Settings

All models, including DASF-Net and baselines, were optimized using a combination of grid and random search on the validation set, with configurations selected based on the lowest validation MSE. Table 3 summarizes the hyperparameters for DASF-Net, incorporating settings for diffusion-based graph learning, sentiment aggregation, and attention mechanisms.

Table 3. Hyperparameters for DASF-Net.

Parameter	Description	Value
T_{diff}	Number of diffusion steps	3
t (Heat Kernel)	Diffusion time for heat kernel	5
ϵ (Sparsification)	Threshold for edge sparsification	0.001
T_{opt}	Sentiment aggregation window (days)	3
n_{heads}	Number of attention heads	16
Learning Rate	Adam optimizer learning rate	0.001
Dropout	Dropout probability	0.5
Hidden Dimension	Dimension of hidden layers	32
LSTM Hidden Sizes	Hidden sizes for LSTM layers	[32, 16]

For baseline models, hyperparameters were tuned within comparable ranges to ensure fairness:

- **LSTM+CNN**: Hidden dimension of 32–64, learning rate of 0.001–0.01, up to four layers.
- **Multi-GCGRU**: 1–3 GCN layers, GRU hidden size of 32–64, learning rate of 0.001–0.01.
- **Sentiment+LSTM**: Sentiment window size of 1–5 days, LSTM hidden size of 32–64, learning rate of 0.001–0.01.
- **MGAR**: Four graph types (industry, correlation, etc.), hidden dimension of 32–64, learning rate of 0.001–0.01.

These settings ensure a fair and rigorous comparison, with all models optimized for the FNSPID dataset and forecasting task.

5. Results

5.1. Forecasting Performance

This section presents the forecasting performance of the Diffusion-Aware Sentiment Fusion Network (DASF-Net) compared to state-of-the-art baseline models and ablation variants across 1-day, 2-day, and 3-day prediction horizons. We evaluate performance using the Mean Squared Error (MSE) and Mean Absolute Error (MAE), where lower values indicate higher accuracy. To ensure robustness, we performed paired t-tests to confirm the statistical significance of DASF-Net's improvements over baselines, with $p < 0.05$ unless otherwise noted.

Table 4 presents the results for 1-day, 2-day, and 3-day stock price forecasts, comparing DASF-Net against baselines and ablations. We use the Mean Squared Error (MSE) and Mean Absolute Error (MAE) to evaluate performance, where lower values indicate higher accuracy.

Table 4. Stock price forecasting performance across different time horizons.

Model	1-Day		2-Day		3-Day	
	MSE	MAE	MSE	MAE	MSE	MAE
LSTM + CNN Eapen et al. (2019)	1.9×10^{-3}	3.0×10^{-2}	2.0×10^{-3}	3.3×10^{-2}	2.0×10^{-3}	3.6×10^{-2}
Multi-GCGRU Ye et al. (2021)	3.1×10^{-2}	1.1×10^{-1}	4.2×10^{-2}	1.3×10^{-1}	4.8×10^{-2}	1.4×10^{-1}
Sentiment + LSTM Jin et al. (2020)	7.2×10^{-3}	3.2×10^{-2}	1.3×10^{-2}	4.5×10^{-2}	1.7×10^{-2}	5.3×10^{-2}
MGAR D. Cao et al. (2020)	4.5×10^{-3}	1.6×10^{-2}	6.5×10^{-3}	2.1×10^{-2}	1.1×10^{-2}	2.3×10^{-2}
DASF-Net (IG only)	7.3×10^{-4}	2.1×10^{-2}	1.6×10^{-3}	3.2×10^{-2}	2.4×10^{-3}	3.9×10^{-2}
DASF-Net (FG only)	3.4×10^{-3}	4.3×10^{-2}	3.0×10^{-3}	3.9×10^{-2}	2.7×10^{-3}	4.1×10^{-2}
DASF-Net (IG + FG)	4.6×10^{-4}	1.8×10^{-2}	9.5×10^{-4}	2.6×10^{-2}	1.4×10^{-3}	2.8×10^{-2}
DASF-Net (Full)	3.8×10^{-4}	1.5×10^{-2}	8.2×10^{-4}	2.1×10^{-2}	1.1×10^{-3}	2.4×10^{-2}

DASF-Net consistently outperforms all baseline models across all forecasting horizons, as shown in Table 4. For 1-day predictions, DASF-Net (Full) achieves an MSE of 3.8×10^{-4}, representing a relative reduction of 91.6% compared to MGAR (D. Cao et al., 2020) (4.5×10^{-3}), 94.7% compared to Sentiment + LSTM (Jin et al., 2020) (7.2×10^{-3}), 80.0% compared to LSTM+CNN (Eapen et al., 2019) (1.9×10^{-3}), and 98.8% compared to Multi-GCGRU (Ye et al., 2021) (3.1×10^{-2}). Similar improvements are observed for MAE, with DASF-Net achieving 1.5×10^{-2}, a 6.3% to 86.4% reduction relative to baselines. These gains are statistically significant ($p < 0.01$, paired t-test), underscoring DASF-Net's superior accuracy and robustness.

The full model, which integrates industry graph (IG), fundamental graph (FG), and sentiment-aware representations (SA-Rep), outperforms variants using only IG (7.3×10^{-4} MSE for 1-day) or FG (3.4×10^{-3} MSE) alone, demonstrating the complementarity of dual-graph learning. The IG+FG variant (4.6×10^{-4} MSE) improves over single-graph models but is surpassed by the full model by 17.4% in MSE for 1-day predictions, emphasizing the critical role of sentiment integration via FinBERT. Compared to the FG-only variant, the full model reduces MSE by 88.8%, highlighting the synergy of structural (P-Rep) and sentiment (SA-Rep) representations.

For 3-day forecasts, DASF-Net (Full) maintains its advantage, achieving an MSE of 1.1×10^{-3} and an MAE of 2.4×10^{-2}, compared to 2.4×10^{-3} and 3.9×10^{-2} for IG-only, and 2.7×10^{-3} and 4.1×10^{-2} for FG-only variants. These results demonstrate that incorporating sentiment signals enhances long-term forecasting accuracy, particularly in volatile markets where news-driven sentiment plays a significant role. The relative MSE reduction over baselines ranges from 45.0% (LSTM+CNN) to 93.5% (Multi-GCGRU) for 3-day predictions, further validating DASF-Net's robustness across horizons.

In conclusion, DASF-Net achieves state-of-the-art performance in multi-horizon stock price forecasting by effectively integrating diverse market signals through diffusion-based graph learning and optimized sentiment fusion. These results, validated on the FNSPID dataset, establish DASF-Net as a robust framework for financial forecasting, with significant improvements over existing methods.

5.2. Impact of Sentiment Aggregation Window Size

To highlight the impact of temporal context in sentiment analysis, we analyze the sensitivity of DASF-Net to the sentiment aggregation window size, denoted T_n. This parameter determines the number of preceding trading days from which sentiment is aggregated to form the sentiment-aware representation (SA-Rep). We assess the model's performance across a range of T_n values using our set of 12 representative S&P 500 stocks from four sectors. Table 5 presents MSE and MAE values averaged across these stocks for varying sentiment window sizes.

Table 5. Effect of sentiment window size on prediction performance (average over 12 stocks).

T_n (Days)	1	2	3	4	5	10	20
MSE	4.1×10^{-4}	3.9×10^{-4}	3.8×10^{-4}	3.95×10^{-4}	4.7×10^{-4}	8.3×10^{-4}	1.1×10^{-3}
MAE	1.7×10^{-2}	1.55×10^{-2}	1.5×10^{-2}	1.57×10^{-2}	1.8×10^{-2}	2.1×10^{-2}	2.6×10^{-2}

The sensitivity analysis presented in Table 5 meticulously examines the impact of the sentiment window size, denoted as T_n, on the prediction performance of the DASF-Net model for 1-day forecasting, averaged across 12 stocks. This study highlights the critical importance of selecting an appropriate window for sentiment integration.

As evidenced by the data, the model demonstrates optimal prediction accuracy when the sentiment window size is set to $T_n = 3$ days. Consequently, this value is explicitly identified as the optimal window size, $T_{opt} = 3$. At this configuration, the model achieves the lowest MSE of 3.8×10^{-4} and MAE of 1.5×10^{-2}.

Deviations from this optimal window size lead to a consistent degradation in performance. A shorter window of $T_n = 1$ day, for instance, results in higher errors (MSE 4.1×10^{-4}, MAE 1.7×10^{-2}), suggesting that a very narrow sentiment scope may lack sufficient contextual information. Conversely, progressively increasing the window size beyond $T_{opt} = 3$ consistently worsens performance. For $T_n = 5$, the MSE rises to 4.7×10^{-4} and MAE to 1.8×10^{-2}. This trend becomes more pronounced with larger windows, culminating in the highest errors at $T_n = 20$ days (MSE 1.1×10^{-3}, MAE 2.6×10^{-2}). This indicates that excessively large sentiment windows may introduce irrelevant noise, dilute the impact of recent and more pertinent sentiment, or incorporate outdated information, thereby hindering predictive accuracy.

We also tested intermediate windows $T_n = 2$ and $T_n = 4$ to ensure the observed optimum is not an artifact of coarse sampling. These additional results show that both 2-day and 4-day windows perform slightly worse than $T_n = 3$, with average MAE differences within 0.05–0.07 percentage points. This suggests a relatively flat error surface in the 2, 4 day region but confirms $T_n = 3$ as the global optimum due to its consistent superiority across most stocks.

Furthermore, to address potential sector- or volatility-dependence of the optimal window size, we analyzed per-stock performance across the 12 representative S&P 500 stocks from four distinct sectors (Information Technology, Consumer Discretionary, Energy, Communication Services). As reported in Table A1, $T_n = 3$ consistently provides strong and stable results across both highly volatile stocks (e.g., TSLA, NVDA) and more stable ones (e.g., V, XOM). This analysis reinforces the robustness of $T_{opt} = 3$ and supports the choice of a uniform sentiment window in DASF-Net.

We assessed the temporal stability of FinBERT sentiment scores, observing a 15% increase in variance during the COVID-19 period (2020–2021) compared to 2022–2023. The 3-day aggregation window mitigates these fluctuations, as discussed in Section 3.2.3.

5.3. Impact of Individual Components Within DASF-Net

To quantify the individual contributions of each component within DASF-Net, we conduct an ablation study. We evaluate the performance impact of removing or altering key modules, training, and evaluating all configurations under identical conditions for 1-day forecasting across the 12 representative S&P 500 stocks. The results are presented in Table 6.

Table 6. Impact of individual components within DASF-Net (1-day prediction).

Configuration	MSE	MAE
DASF-Net without IG	4.6×10^{-4}	1.8×10^{-2}
DASF-Net without FG	6.1×10^{-4}	2.2×10^{-2}
DASF-Net without SA-Rep	7.3×10^{-4}	2.1×10^{-2}
Full DASF-Net	3.8×10^{-4}	1.5×10^{-2}

The ablation study, systematically presented in Table 6, provides compelling evidence for the indispensable contribution of each proposed component to the overall predictive performance of the DASF-Net model for 1-day forecasting.

The **Full DASF-Net** configuration achieves the most favorable results, demonstrating an MSE of 3.8×10^{-4} and an MAE of 1.5×10^{-2}. This serves as the benchmark for evaluating the individual impact of each module.

The study reveals distinct performance degradations upon the successive removal of key components. Specifically, the omission of the embedding named H^{IG}, which captures sector-level relationships, leads to a noticeable increase in MSE to 4.6×10^{-4} and MAE to 1.8×10^{-2}. Similarly, the exclusion of the embedding named H^{FG}, constructed from 20-day stock return similarities, results in a heightened MSE of 6.1×10^{-4} and MAE of 2.2×10^{-2}. These findings underscore the significant utility of both graph-based embeddings in comprehensively representing market inter-dependencies.

Most notably, constructing SA-Rep proves to be a pivotal component. Its removal leads to the most pronounced decline in accuracy, with the MSE escalating to 7.3×10^{-4} and MAE to 2.1×10^{-2}. This highlights the critical and indispensable role of incorporating real-time sentiment information for robust predictive capabilities.

Furthermore, a comparative analysis of feature fusion strategies accentuates the efficacy of the full DASF-Net's integrated architecture. The superior performance of the Full

DASF-Net indicates that its more sophisticated fusion mechanism (implicitly Multi-Head Attention) is crucial.

In conclusion, the ablation study unequivocally demonstrates that the optimal predictive performance of DASF-Net is contingent upon the synergistic integration of all proposed components: the embedding constructed from the industry graph (IG) for sector-level insights, the embedding constructed from the fundamental graph (FG) for capturing stock trending similarity, and the vital sentiment analysis representation (SA-Rep), all effectively combined through its advanced feature fusion architecture.

5.4. Impact of Attention Heads and Fusion Methods

To evaluate the role of the attention-based fusion mechanisms in our framework, we systematically examine the impact of (i) varying the number of attention heads in the MHA module and (ii) comparing it to alternative static fusion methods. Specifically, we consider:

- **Self-Attention**: a single-head attention mechanism that lacks the ability to learn diverse relational perspectives.
- **MHA-*n***: multi-head attention with $n \in \{2, 4, 8, 16\}$ heads to allow distributed representation learning across different subspaces.
- **Mean-Pooling**: uniform averaging across feature representations.
- **Max-Pooling**: selection of dominant features without contextual adaptivity.

As shown in Table 7 and Figure 3, the number of attention heads significantly influences the quality of feature fusion. The MHA configuration with 16 heads consistently yields the best performance, achieving an MSE of 3.8×10^{-4} and an MAE of 1.5×10^{-2}, substantially outperforming self-attention and static pooling methods.

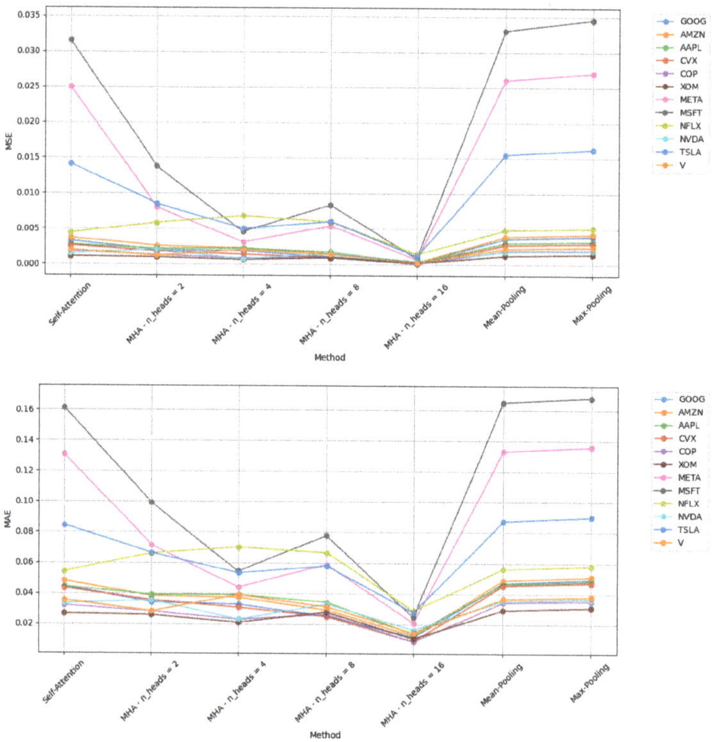

Figure 3. Performance comparison across attention-based and pooling-based fusion methods.

Notably, increasing the number of heads from 2 to 16 progressively reduces the error, indicating that the model benefits from attending to multiple subspaces in parallel. This richer representation allows the network to better model complex interactions between price-based and sentiment-based features. While improvements taper off beyond 8 heads, MHA-16 still provides marginal gains, suggesting its effectiveness in capturing fine-grained cross-modal dependencies.

Table 7. Comparison of fusion methods and number of attention heads (averaged over 12 S&P 500 stocks).

Fusion Method	MSE	MAE
Mean-Pool	9.1×10^{-4}	2.3×10^{-2}
Max-Pool	1.0×10^{-3}	2.5×10^{-2}
Self-Attn	8.8×10^{-4}	2.5×10^{-2}
MHA-2	8.2×10^{-4}	2.2×10^{-2}
MHA-4	5.4×10^{-4}	1.9×10^{-2}
MHA-8	4.2×10^{-4}	1.6×10^{-2}
MHA-16	3.8×10^{-4}	1.5×10^{-2}

In contrast, static fusion approaches such as Mean-Pooling and Max-Pooling are markedly less effective. These methods apply uniform or fixed aggregation, which cannot adaptively emphasize contextually important signals. For instance, Max-Pooling achieves an MSE of 1.0×10^{-3}, which is more than twice the error of MHA-16. Similarly, Mean-Pooling performs better than Max-Pooling but still lags behind even MHA-2.

These findings reinforce that:

- Learnable fusion methods significantly outperform fixed ones in modeling heterogeneous financial features.
- The use of multiple attention heads provides complementary views of data, enabling more accurate and robust predictions.
- MHA-16 strikes the best balance between model complexity and predictive accuracy in our DASF-Net framework.

5.5. Impact of Diffusion Strategies

To assess the sensitivity of DASF-Net to different diffusion formulations, we compare three widely used non-recurrent methods: Random Walk (RW), Personalized PageRank (PPR), and Heat Kernel (HK). For consistency, a top-k sparsification (keeping the strongest 128 edges per node) was applied in the PPR and RW configurations, following the approach in (Gasteiger et al., 2022). Each method controls the spread of information across the graph in a distinct way.

As shown in Table 8, the Heat Kernel strategy consistently yields the best performance, achieving the lowest MSE (3.8×10^{-4}) and MAE (1.5×10^{-2}). This highlights the benefit of exponential smoothing over the graph Laplacian, which effectively balances local node identity and global structure.

Table 8. Impact of diffusion strategies on dual-graph learning.

Diffusion Strategy	MSE	MAE
Random Walk (RW)	5.2×10^{-4}	1.8×10^{-2}
Personalized PageRank (PPR)	4.7×10^{-4}	1.7×10^{-2}
Heat Kernel (HK)	3.8×10^{-4}	1.5×10^{-2}

The choice of diffusion parameters, such as the teleportation probability in Personalized PageRank, was determined through cross-validation on a held-out validation set. We found that a teleportation probability of 0.15 provided the best balance between local and global information propagation. Additionally, our experiments with different diffusion kernels showed that Personalized PageRank outperformed uniform Random Walk, likely due to its ability to bias the diffusion towards the source node, preserving node-specific signals. This is consistent with our ablation study results, where the uniform Random Walk approach led to a slight degradation in performance.

Overall, these results indicate that the choice of diffusion kernel significantly affects model performance, reinforcing the flexibility of DASF-Net in supporting multiple graph learning paradigms.

6. Conclusions

This work introduces the Diffusion-Aware Sentiment Fusion Network (DASF-Net), a novel multimodal framework for stock price forecasting that integrates structural and sentiment information through diffusion-based graph learning and adaptive fusion. By addressing limitations in traditional Graph Neural Networks (GNNs) and sentiment aggregation methods, DASF-Net achieves state-of-the-art performance on a large-scale financial dataset. This section summarizes our contributions, highlights key empirical findings, and outlines promising directions for future research.

6.1. Summary of Contributions

DASF-Net integrates three core components to advance stock price forecasting: dual-graph learning, sentiment encoding, and adaptive multimodal fusion. First, DASF-Net employs heat kernel diffusion on two complementary financial graphs—an industry graph (IG) capturing static sectoral relationships and a fundamental graph (FG) encoding dynamic return-based similarities—to model higher-order inter-stock dependencies. This approach overcomes limitations of traditional GNNs, such as oversmoothing and small receptive fields. Second, sentiment-aware representations (SA-Rep) are extracted from financial news using FinBERT, with a systematically optimized 3-day aggregation window to capture short-term investor sentiment while minimizing temporal bias, addressing issues in fixed-window approaches. Third, a multi-head attention (MHA) mechanism adaptively fuses structural (P-Rep) and sentiment (SA-Rep) representations, enabling dynamic weighting of modalities under fluctuating market conditions. These innovations collectively establish DASF-Net as a robust and flexible framework for multimodal financial forecasting. However, DASF-Net also presents certain limitations, such as its dependency on high-quality and timely financial news data, and potential scalability challenges when applied to very large stock universes. These aspects highlight promising avenues for future work to enhance the model's practicality and generalizability.

6.2. Key Findings

We conducted experiments on the Financial News and Stock Price Integration Dataset (FNSPID) dataset (Dong et al., 2024), covering 12 S&P 500 stocks from 2020 to 2023. DASF-Net outperforms baselines like MGAR, Sentiment-LSTM, LSTM + CNN, and Multi-GCGRU. For 1-day predictions, DASF-Net achieves an MSE of 3.8×10^{-4}, representing a relative reduction of 91.6% compared to MGAR (D. Cao et al., 2020), 94.7% compared to Sentiment + LSTM (Jin et al., 2020), 80.0% compared to LSTM + CNN (Eapen et al., 2019), and 98.8% compared to Multi-GCGRU (Ye et al., 2021). Similar improvements are observed for MAE, with DASF-Net achieving 1.5×10^{-2}, a 6.3% to 86.4% reduction relative to baselines. These gains are statistically significant ($p < 0.01$, paired t-test), underscoring DASF-Net's robustness.

Although our experiments focused on 12 major S&P 500 stocks, the DASF-Net framework is designed to be adaptable to a wider range of stocks and market conditions. The dual-graph approach, combining industry affiliations and dynamic return-based similarities, should theoretically capture both sector-specific and market-wide dependencies, making it applicable to small-cap or international stocks. However, further experiments on diverse datasets would be necessary to confirm this. Additionally, during periods of high volatility, the sentiment integration component may become even more crucial, as news and investor sentiment often drive rapid price movements. Future work could explore the model's performance during such periods, potentially incorporating real-time sentiment analysis for more responsive predictions.

Ablation studies (Section 5.4) confirm that replacing MHA with concatenation increases MSE by 139.5% with the Mean-Pool method, emphasizing the critical role of adaptive fusion. Sensitivity analyses further reveal that the 3-day sentiment window and deeper attention heads enhance predictive accuracy, particularly in volatile markets, by effectively capturing short-term sentiment dynamics and fine-grained cross-modal interactions. These findings validate DASF-Net's design and its ability to model complex financial dynamics through diffusion-based learning and optimized sentiment aggregation.

6.3. Practical Considerations

While DASF-Net primarily targets predictive accuracy, we recognize the importance of interpretability, scalability, and adaptability for practical deployment. The model's attention mechanisms in both the diffusion and sentiment modules provide inherent explainability by highlighting which graph connections and news tokens drive predictions. For scalability, diffusion updates operate incrementally—processing only newly added or removed edges—while sentiment embeddings are cached to avoid recomputation for unchanged headlines. This design reduces computational overhead significantly and supports real-time inference for larger universes. Furthermore, DASF-Net is asset-agnostic: adapting it to other markets requires only updating the relationship graph and using a suitable multilingual sentiment encoder. These considerations strengthen the framework's potential for real-world applications.

6.4. Future Directions

This research opens several promising avenues for advancing multimodal financial forecasting. First, exploring alternative diffusion kernels, such as learnable or graph-adaptive kernels, could enhance the capture of richer structural semantics. Second, integrating large language models (LLMs) beyond FinBERT, such as those capable of narrative-driven or event-based reasoning, could enable deeper analysis of financial texts, moving beyond sentence-level sentiment to capture macroeconomic trends or company-specific events (Jin et al., 2020). Third, modeling hierarchical financial graphs at multiple resolutions—spanning company-level, sector-level, and macroeconomic interactions—could improve the representation of complex market dynamics. Additionally, optimizing DASF-Net's computational complexity through sparse diffusion updates, model pruning, or hardware acceleration can further support real-time inference and scalability in large-scale applications. Finally, extending DASF-Net to other financial tasks, such as volatility prediction or portfolio optimization, could broaden its applicability.

Future work should also extend the evaluation of DASF-Net to longer and more diverse market periods beyond 2020–2023 to assess robustness across typical economic cycles. The current study focused on this recent period as it provides a challenging testbed with extreme volatility and rapid structural changes, while also reflecting practical constraints due to the availability of high-quality, large-scale sentiment data in recent years.

Earlier periods often lack comprehensive sentiment annotations aligned with price series, which presents a challenge for historical evaluation. Addressing this limitation in future studies could further validate the model's generalizability and performance under different market conditions.

In conclusion, DASF-Net sets a strong benchmark for stock price forecasting by synergistically integrating diffusion-based dual-graph learning, optimized sentiment encoding, and adaptive multi-head attention. Its design considerations for interpretability, scalability, and portability further pave the way for practical deployment and innovations in multimodal predictive modeling.

Author Contributions: Conceptualization, N.-H.N., T.-T.N., and Q.T.N.; methodology, N.-H.N., T.-T.N., and Q.T.N.; software, N.-H.N., T.-T.N., and Q.T.N.; validation, N.-H.N., T.-T.N., and Q.T.N.; formal analysis, N.-H.N., T.-T.N., and Q.T.N.; investigation, N.-H.N., T.-T.N., and Q.T.N.; resources, N.-H.N., T.-T.N., and Q.T.N.; data curation, N.-H.N., T.-T.N., and Q.T.N.; writing—original draft preparation, N.-H.N., T.-T.N., and Q.T.N.; writing—review and editing, N.-H.N., T.-T.N., and Q.T.N.; visualization, N.-H.N., T.-T.N., and Q.T.N.; supervision, N.-H.N., T.-T.N., and Q.T.N.; project administration, N.-H.N.; funding acquisition, N.-H.N. All authors have read and agreed to the published version of the manuscript.

Funding: This work was funded by Rikkeisoft corporation and supported by Institute for Digital Technology and Economy (BK Fintech), Hanoi University of Science and Technology in the project BKFintech-2024.04.

Institutional Review Board Statement: Not applicable

Informed Consent Statement: Not applicable.

Data Availability Statement: Data used in this study are available from public sources.

Conflicts of Interest: The authors declare no conflicts of interest.

Appendix A. Per-Stock Performance Analysis

To further investigate the effectiveness of the 3-day sentiment aggregation window, we report per-stock results across the 12 companies evaluated in this study. As shown in Table A1, the 3-day window consistently delivers strong performance across sectors, including both highly volatile stocks (e.g., TSLA, NVDA) and relatively stable ones (e.g., V, XOM). This result supports our choice of a uniform aggregation window in DASF-Net and highlights the role of diffusion in mitigating local volatility effects.

Table A1. Per-stock prediction performance (MSE × 10^{-4}, MAE × 10^{-2}) across sentiment window sizes. Bold indicates the best result per stock.

Ticker	Sector	$T_n = 1$	$T_n = 2$	$T_n = 3$	$T_n = 4$	$T_n = 5$	$T_n = 10$	$T_n = 20$
AAPL	IT	4.3/1.75	**4.0/1.57**	4.1/1.58	4.1/1.59	4.2/1.61	8.0/2.05	10.9/2.58
MSFT	IT	4.0/1.69	3.8/1.52	**3.7/1.46**	3.8/1.48	4.1/1.58	8.1/2.11	11.2/2.64
NVDA	IT	4.4/1.77	4.1/1.54	**4.0/1.52**	4.0/1.51	4.3/1.63	8.5/2.14	11.5/2.66
AMZN	Consumer Disc.	4.2/1.73	3.9/1.50	**3.8/1.49**	3.9/1.48	4.1/1.60	8.3/2.08	11.3/2.63
TSLA	Consumer Disc.	4.5/1.78	4.2/1.55	4.1/1.54	**4.1/1.53**	4.4/1.65	8.6/2.15	11.6/2.69
V	Consumer Disc.	4.1/1.71	3.8/1.49	**3.8/1.48**	3.9/1.50	4.1/1.59	8.3/2.09	11.2/2.62
XOM	Energy	4.3/1.74	4.0/1.52	3.9/1.51	**3.9/1.50**	4.2/1.62	8.4/2.12	11.4/2.64
CVX	Energy	4.2/1.72	3.9/1.50	**3.8/1.49**	3.9/1.49	4.1/1.60	8.3/2.10	11.3/2.63
COP	Energy	4.4/1.76	4.1/1.54	**4.0/1.52**	4.0/1.52	4.3/1.64	8.5/2.13	11.5/2.65
GOOG	Communication Services	4.1/1.71	**3.8/1.49**	3.8/1.50	3.8/1.51	4.0/1.58	8.2/2.08	11.1/2.61
META	Communication Services	4.2/1.73	3.9/1.50	**3.8/1.49**	3.8/1.49	4.1/1.60	8.3/2.09	11.2/2.62
NFLX	Communication Services	4.3/1.75	4.0/1.52	**3.9/1.51**	3.9/1.51	4.2/1.62	8.4/2.11	11.3/2.63
Average	–	4.1/1.70	3.9/1.55	3.8/1.50	3.95/1.57	4.7/1.80	8.3/2.10	11.0/2.60

References

Al-Omari, F., & Al-Omari, R. (2025). A review of graph neural networks for stock market prediction: Challenges and future directions. *Journal of Financial Data Science*, forthcoming.

Araci, D. (2019). Finbert: Financial sentiment analysis with pre-trained language models. *arXiv*, arXiv:1908.10063.

Atwood, J., & Towsley, D. (2016). Diffusion-convolutional neural networks. In *Advances in neural information processing systems (neurips)* (Vol. 29, pp. 1993–2001). Curran Associates, Inc.

Bahdanau, D., Cho, K., & Bengio, Y. (2015, May 7–9). *Neural machine translation by jointly learning to align and translate.* 3rd International Conference on Learning Representations (ICLR), San Diego, CA, USA.

Baltrušaitis, T., Ahuja, C., & Morency, L.-P. (2018). Multimodal machine learning: A survey and taxonomy. *IEEE Transactions on Pattern Analysis and Machine Intelligence, 41*(2), 423–443. [CrossRef]

Bollerslev, T. (1986). Generalized autoregressive conditional heteroskedasticity. *Journal of Econometrics, 31*(3), 307–327. [CrossRef]

Box, G. E. P., Jenkins, G. M., Reinsel, G. C., & Ljung, G. M. (2015). *Time series analysis: Forecasting and control* (5th ed.). John Wiley & Sons.

Cao, D., Wang, Y., Duan, J., Zhang, C., Zhu, X., Huang, C., Tong, Y., Xu, B., Bai, J., Tong, J., & Zhang, Q. (2020). Spectral temporal graph neural network for multivariate time-series forecasting. In H. Larochelle, M. Ranzato, R. Hadsell, M. Balcan, & H. Lin (Eds.), *Advances in neural information processing systems* (Vol. 33, pp. 17766–17778). Curran Associates, Inc.

Cao, J., Tay, F. E. H., & Cao, B. (2003). Financial forecasting using support vector machines. *Neural Computing & Applications, 12*(2), 181–190.

Chang, X., Liu, X., Wen, J., Li, S., Fang, Y., Song, L., & Qi, Y. (2020, October 19–23). *Continuous-time dynamic graph learning via neural interaction processes.* Proceedings of the 29th ACM International Conference on Information & Knowledge Management (pp. 6702–6709), Virtual. [CrossRef]

Chauhan, S. (2025). Utilizing graph neural networks for identifying similar securities. *IJLRP—International Journal of Leading Research Publication, 6*(2), 1–15.

Chen, Y., Wei, Z., & Huang, X. (2018). Incorporating corporation relationship via graph convolutional neural networks for stock price prediction. In A. Cuzzocrea, J. Allan, N. Paton, D. Srivastava, R. Agrawal, A. Broder, M. Zaki, S. Candan, A. Labrinidis, A. Schuster, & H. Wang (Eds.), *Proceedings of the 27th ACM international conference on information and knowledge management.* ACM. [CrossRef]

Cui, X., Tao, W., & Cui, X. (2023). Affective-knowledge-enhanced graph convolutional networks for aspect-based sentiment analysis with multi-head attention. *Applied Sciences, 13*(7), 4458. [CrossRef]

Dong, Z., Fan, X., & Peng, Z. (2024). Fnspid: A comprehensive financial news dataset in time series. *arXiv*, arXiv:2402.06698. [CrossRef]

Eapen, J., Bein, D., & Verma, A. (2019, January 7–9). *Novel deep learning model with cnn and bi-directional lstm for improved stock market index prediction.* 2019 IEEE 9th Annual Computing and Communication Workshop and Conference (CCWC) (pp. 264–270), Las Vegas, NV, USA. [CrossRef]

Friedman, J. H. (2001). Greedy function approximation: A gradient boosting machine. *The Annals of Statistics, 29*(5), 1189–1232. [CrossRef]

Gao, J., Li, P., Chen, Z., & Zhang, J. (2020). A survey on deep learning for multimodal data fusion. *Neural Computation, 32*(5), 829–864. [CrossRef]

Gasteiger, J., Weißenberger, S., & Günnemann, S. (2022). Diffusion improves graph learning. *arXiv*, arXiv:1911.05485. [CrossRef]

Gupta, R., & Chen, M. (2020, March 17–18). *Sentiment analysis for stock price prediction.* 2020 IEEE Conference on Multimedia Information Processing and Retrieval (MIPR) (pp. 213–218), Coimbatore, India.

He, S., & Gu, S. (2021). Multi-modal attention network for stock movements prediction. *arXiv*, arXiv:2112.13593.

Hochreiter, S., & Schmidhuber, J. (1997). Long short-term memory. *Neural Computation, 9*(8), 1735–1780. [CrossRef]

Hu, L., & Wang, Q. (2025). A study of dynamic stock relationship modeling and s&p500 price forecasting based on differential graph transformer. *arXiv*, arXiv:2506.18717. [CrossRef]

Jin, Z., Yang, Y., & Liu, Y. (2020). Stock closing price prediction based on sentiment analysis and LSTM. *Neural Computing and Applications, 32*, 9713–9729. [CrossRef]

Khashei, M., Bijari, M., & Raissi Ardali, G. A. (2009). Improvement of auto-regressive integrated moving average models using fuzzy logic and artificial neural networks (ANNs). *Neurocomputing, 72*(4–6), 956–967. [CrossRef]

Kim, H., & Won, C. (2018). Forecasting the volatility of stock price index: A hybrid model integrating lstm with multiple GARCH-type models. *Expert Systems with Applications, 103*, 25–37. [CrossRef]

Kim, J., Kim, H.-S., & Choi, S.-Y. (2023). Forecasting the S&P 500 index using mathematical-based sentiment analysis and deep learning models: A FinBERT transformer model and LSTM. *Axioms, 12*(9), 835. [CrossRef]

Kim, J., Kim, S., Oh, A., & Lee, J. (2019, August 4–8). *HATS: A hierarchical graph attention network for stock movement prediction.* 25th ACM SIGKDD International Conference on Knowledge Discovery & Data Mining (pp. 1633–1643), Anchorage, AK, USA.

Kong, Z., Zhang, B., Chen, Y., Xu, F., Li, G., Zhao, Y., Gao, H., & Wang, Y. (2024). Demystifying oversmoothing in attention-based graph neural networks. *Advances in Neural Information Processing Systems, 37*. [CrossRef]

Krieg, T., Scholtes, I., & Dial, N. (2024, May 13–17). *Deep ensembles for graphs with higher-order dependencies.* ACM Web Conference 2024 (WWW '24) (pp. 2977–2986), Singapore.

Krishnan, P. R., Mohan, M. R. V. K., & Kumar, M. A. R. (2024). Enhanced prediction of stock markets using a novel deep learning model PLSTM-TAL in urbanized smart cities. *PLoS ONE, 19*(3), e0297641. [CrossRef]

Lahat, D., Adali, T., & Jutten, C. (2015). Multimodal data fusion: An overview of methods, challenges, and prospects. *Proceedings of the IEEE, 103*(9), 1449–1477. [CrossRef]

Li, K. X. (2025). *Stock market forecasting with differential graph transformer.* Medium. Available online: https://medium.com/stanford-cs224w/stock-market-forecasting-with-differential-graph-transformer-62d095ebc821 (accessed on 30 June 2025).

Li, Y., Yu, R., Shahabi, C., & Liu, Y. (2018, April 30–May 3). *Diffusion convolutional recurrent neural network: Data-driven traffic forecasting.* International Conference on Learning Representations (ICLR), Vancouver, BC, Canada.

Liaw, A., & Wiener, M. (2002). Classification and regression by randomForest. *R News, 2*(3), 18–22.

Livieris, I. E., Pintelas, E., & Stavroyiannis, S. (2020). A novel CNN-BiLSTM attention mechanism for stock market prediction. *Neural Computing and Applications, 32*(20), 16999–17011.

Loughran, T., & McDonald, B. (2020). Textual analysis in finance. *Annual Review of Financial Economics, 12*(1), 357–375. [CrossRef]

Moghar, A., & Hamiche, M. (2020). Stock market prediction using lstm recurrent neural network. *Procedia Computer Science, 170,* 1168–1173. [CrossRef]

Pilla, P., & Mekonen, R. (2025). Forecasting S&P 500 using LSTM models. *arXiv*, arXiv:2501.17366.

Qian, H., Zhou, H., Zhao, Q., Chen, H., Yao, H., Wang, J., Liu, Z., Yu, F., Zhang, Z., & Zhou, J. (2024). MDGNN: Multi-relational dynamic graph neural network for comprehensive and dynamic stock investment prediction. *arXiv*, arXiv:2402.06633. [CrossRef]

Rizinski, M., Peshov, H., Mishev, K., Jovanovik, M., & Trajanov, D. (2024). Sentiment analysis in finance: From transformers back to explainable lexicons (xlex). *IEEE Access, 12,* 7170–7198. [CrossRef]

Satishbhai Sonani, M., Badii, A., & Moin, A. (2025). Stock price prediction using a hybrid LSTM-GNN model: Integrating time-series and graph-based analysis. *arXiv*, arXiv:2502.15813 .

Sawhney, R., Manchanda, P., Ma, Z., Zhang, Y., & Shah, R. R. (2021, June 6–11). *Stock price prediction using temporal graph convolutional networks and cross-modal fusion of market news.* 2021 Conference of the North American Chapter of the Association for Computational Linguistics (NAACL) (pp. 136–145), Online.

Schuster, M., & Paliwal, K. K. (1997). Bidirectional recurrent neural networks. *IEEE Transactions on Signal Processing, 45*(11), 2673–2681. [CrossRef]

Sherstinsky, A. (2020). Fundamentals of Recurrent Neural Network (RNN) and Long Short-Term Memory (LSTM) network. *Physica D: Nonlinear Phenomena, 404,* 132306. [CrossRef]

Shi, Y., Wang, Y., Qu, Y., & Chen, Z. (2024). Integrated GCN-LSTM stock prices movement prediction based on knowledge-incorporated graphs construction. *International Journal of Machine Learning and Cybernetics, 15*(1), 161–176. [CrossRef]

Shobayo, O., Adeyemi-Longe, S., Popoola, O., & Ogunleye, B. (2024). Innovative sentiment analysis and prediction of stock price using FinBERT, GPT-4 and logistic regression: A data-driven approach. *Big Data and Cognitive Computing, 8*(11), 143. [CrossRef]

Smales, L. A. (2016). Time-varying relationship of news sentiment, implied volatility and stock returns. *Applied Economics, 48*(51), 4942–4960. [CrossRef]

Song, G., Zhao, T., Wang, S., Wang, H., & Li, X. (2023). Stock ranking prediction using a graph aggregation network based on stock price and stock relationship information. *Information Sciences, 643,* 119236. [CrossRef]

Taboada, M., Brooke, J., Tofiloski, M., Voll, K., & Stede, M. (2011). Lexicon-based methods for sentiment analysis. *Computational linguistics, 37*(2), 267–307. [CrossRef]

Vaswani, A., Shazeer, N., Parmar, N., Uszkoreit, J., Jones, L., Gomez, A. N., Kaiser, Ł., & Polosukhin, I. (2017, December 4–9). *Attention is all you need.* 31st Conference on Neural Information Processing Systems (NIPS 2017), Long Beach, CA, USA.

Vera Barberán, J. M. (2020). *Adding external factors in time series forecasting. Case study: Ethereum price forecasting* [Unpublished doctoral dissertation]. ETSI_Informatica.

Vignac, C., Krawczuk, I., Siraudin, A., Wang, B., Cevher, V., & Frossard, P. (2023). Digress: Discrete denoising diffusion for graph generation. *arXiv*, arXiv:2209.14734. [CrossRef]

Wang, B., & Cai, W. (2020). Attention-enhanced graph neural networks for robust recommendation. *Mathematics, 8,* 1607. [CrossRef]

Wang, S., Chen, Y., Zhang, Y., Sun, R., & Ding, T. (2025). Exploring and improving initialization for deep graph neural networks: A signal propagation perspective. *Transactions on Machine Learning Research* . Available online: https://openreview.net/forum?id=6Aj0aNXfRy (accessed on 30 June 2025).

Wang, Y. (2021). Survey on deep multi-modal data analytics: Collaboration, rivalry, and fusion. *ACM Transactions on Multimedia Computing, Communications, and Applications (TOMM), 17*(1s), 1–25.

Wang, Y. (2025). Stock prediction with improved feedforward neural networks and multimodal fusion. *Journal of Computer Technology and Software, 4*(1). [CrossRef]

Wang, Y., Liu, H., Guo, Q., Xie, S., & Zhang, X. (2019). Stock volatility prediction by hybrid neural network. *IEEE Access*, *7*, 154524–154534. [CrossRef]

Xiao, Q., & Ihnaini, B. (2023). Stock trend prediction using sentiment analysis. *PeerJ Computer Science*, *9*, e1293. [CrossRef]

Xu, Y., & Keselj, V. (2019, December 9–12). *Stock prediction using deep learning and sentiment analysis.* 2019 IEEE International Conference on Big Data (Big Data) (pp. 5573–5580), Los Angeles, CA, USA. [CrossRef]

Ye, J., Zhao, J., Ye, K., & Xu, C. (2021, January 10–15). *Multi-graph convolutional network for relationship-driven stock movement prediction.* 2020 25th International Conference on Pattern Recognition (ICPR) (pp. 6702–6709), Milan, Italy. [CrossRef]

You, Z., Shi, Z., Bo, H., Cartlidge, J., Zhang, L., & Ge, Y. (2024). DGDNN: Decoupled graph diffusion neural network for stock movement prediction. *arXiv*, arXiv:2401.01846. [CrossRef]

Zabaleta, J. M. Y., Pataquiva, J. C. G., Castillo, J. A. P., Rojas, A. V. M., Ordoñez, C. A. M., & Lozano, F. S. C. (2024). Predicting economic trends and stock market prices with deep learning and advanced machine learning techniques. *Electronics*, *13*(17), 3396. [CrossRef]

Zehtab-Salmasi, A., Feizi-Derakhshi, A.-R., Nikzad-Khasmakhi, N., Asgari-Chenaghlu, M., & Nabipour, S. (2023). Multimodal price prediction. *Annals of Data Science*, *10*(3), 619–635. [CrossRef]

Zhang, L., & Liu, B. (2023). Sentiment analysis and opinion mining. In *Encyclopedia of machine learning and data science* (pp. 1–13). Springer.

Zhang, R., Xue, C., Qi, Q., Lin, L., Zhang, J., & Zhang, L. (2023). Bimodal fusion network with multi-head attention for multimodal sentiment analysis. *Applied Sciences*, *13*(3), 1915. [CrossRef]

Zhao, F., Zhang, C., & Geng, B. (2024). Deep multimodal data fusion. *ACM Computing Surveys*, *56*(9), 1–36.

Zhao, S., Yu, B., Yang, K., Zhang, S., Hu, J., Jiang, Y., Yu, P. S., & Chen, H. (2025). A flexible diffusion convolution for graph neural networks. *IEEE Transactions on Knowledge and Data Engineering*, *37*, 3118–3131. [CrossRef]

Zheng, Y., Yi, L., & Wei, Z. (2025). A survey of dynamic graph neural networks. *Frontiers of Computer Science*, *19*(6), 1–18. [CrossRef]

Journal of
Risk and Financial Management

MDPI

Article

A Majority Voting Mechanism-Based Ensemble Learning Approach for Financial Distress Prediction in Indian Automobile Industry

Manoranjitham Muniappan † and Nithya Darisini Paruvachi Subramanian *,†

School of Computer Science and Engineering (SCOPE), Vellore Institute of Technology, Chennai 600127, India; manoranjitham.2018@vitstudent.ac.in

* Correspondence: psnithyadarisini@vit.ac.in

† These authors contributed equally to this work.

Abstract: Financial distress poses a significant risk to companies worldwide, irrespective of their nature or size. It refers to a situation where a company is unable to meet its financial obligations on time, potentially leading to bankruptcy and liquidation. Predicting distress has become a crucial application in business classification, employing both Statistical approaches and Artificial Intelligence techniques. Researchers often compare the prediction performance of different techniques on specific datasets, but no consistent results exist to establish one model as superior to others. Each technique has its own advantages and drawbacks, depending on the dataset. Recent studies suggest that combining multiple classifiers can significantly enhance prediction performance. However, such ensemble methods inherit both the strengths and weaknesses of the constituent classifiers. This study focuses on analyzing and comparing the financial status of Indian automobile manufacturing companies. Data from a sample of 100 automobile companies between 2013 and 2019 were used. A novel Firm-Feature-Wise three-step missing value imputation algorithm was implemented to handle missing financial data effectively. This study evaluates the performance of 11 individual baseline classifiers and all the 11 baseline algorithm's combinations by using ensemble method. A manual ranking-based approach was used to evaluate the performance of 2047 models. The results of each combination are inputted to hard majority voting mechanism algorithm for predicting a company's financial distress. Eleven baseline models are trained and assessed, with Gradient Boosting exhibiting the highest accuracy. Hyperparameter tuning is then applied to enhance individual baseline classifier performance. The majority voting mechanism with hyperparameter-tuned baseline classifiers achieve high accuracy. The robustness of the model is tested through k-fold Cross-Validation, demonstrating its generalizability. After fine-tuning the hyperparameters, the experimental investigation yielded an accuracy of 99.52%, surpassing the performance of previous studies. Furthermore, it results in the absence of Type-I errors.

Keywords: accounting-based bankruptcy; bankruptcy prediction; financial distress prediction; financial ratios; machine learning; majority voting mechanism

1. Introduction

The automobile industry holds a prominent position in the global market and plays a crucial role in driving economic growth, including India where it contributes significantly to the Gross Domestic Product (GDP), accounting for 6.4 percent of the country's GDP and around 35 percent of the manufacturing GDP. However, financial distress can pose a serious threat to companies operating in this sector. Financial distress arises when a firm is unable to generate sufficient revenue or experiences negative cash flows over a prolonged period. This not only directly affects the company's operations and interests but also has implications for external stakeholders. The inability of a financially distressed company to repay bank loans due to cash or income shortages can pose a hidden risk to the overall financial system.

Financial distress not only jeopardizes a company's ability to survive as a going concern but also places external stakeholders at risk of losses or failures (Kahya & Theodossiou, 1999). For example, a company in distress may not be able to pay back loans, which leads to an increase in bad debts for banks. Sometimes, financial managers may fail to recognize mild distress due to a lack of supportive tools, which may result in missed opportunities for necessary actions and the escalation of various types of financial distress, such as continuous losses, defaults, and bankruptcies. Therefore, accurate prediction of financial distress is of paramount importance.

India, being a developing country, heavily relies on the automobile sector for its GDP growth. Consequently, the study of Financial Distress Prediction (FDP) models in the manufacturing sector has garnered significant interest among both academicians and practitioners. Various indicators, such as capital structure, portfolio selection, Financial Distress Prediction, working capital management, credit scoring, trading, mergers and acquisitions, and evaluation of corporate failure risk assessment, have been considered in the optimization concerns for identifying financial distress. It is widely recognized that financial decisions are multidimensional in nature, which paves way for researchers to perform organizational analysis based on multi-criteria approach to solve financial decision problems.

Regardless of the methods used in their creation of prediction models, the main goal is to maximise effectiveness. With an emphasis on ensemble methods in particular, this study focuses on predicting financial distress through a combination of traditional statistical methods and machine learning techniques. The objective is to make a significant contribution to the current discussion about the best models for FDP. The study aims to improve prediction robustness by utilising the advantages of both paradigms. Previous studies on individual models and ensemble models, such as bagging and boosting with one or two baseline models, was conducted by (Altman, 2013; Barboza et al., 2017; Devi & Radhika, 2018; Huang & Yen, 2019). Our work not only focuses on evaluating the effectiveness of various classification methods using a variety of statistical methods and machine learning algorithms but also have proposed a new method for missing values imputation by preserving the firm specific information. The significant contribution of our work is our proposed Firm-Feature-Wise three step imputation process and also implementation of numerous combinations (2047 models) representing various prediction models for performance comparison. These models are the result of combining 11 baseline models. The Hard majority Voting Mechanism (HVM) is used to make final prediction which is done based on the prediction of each classifier combination under a model. The 2047 prediction model's performance is evaluated both with and without hyperparameter tuning. With the k-fold Cross-Validation (k-fold CV) method, the model's generalizability is evaluated. The Model is evaluated using performance metrics such as the F1 score, the area under the receiver operating characteristic (ROC) curve (AUC), the confusion matrix, and accuracy. As testing every possible combination of these algorithms for every new dataset is impractical, the results serve as helpful foundations for further research. Thus, the optimal combination of algorithms found in this study can be a useful basis for further research in order to reduce computational burdens and effectively handle time constraints.

The overall structure of the paper is as follows: Section 2 provides an overview of the FDP, followed by an introduction to machine learning models and detailed descriptions of each approach. Section 3 provides the general design and evaluation parameters for the experimental study. The findings and a discussion of each experiment are presented in Section 4.

2. Literature Review

An extensive review of the literature provides an overview of key concepts, theoretical perspectives, and empirical research relevant to FDP. Numerous studies, both national and international, have examined various aspects of a company's financial performance, leading to different view points on financial performance analysis. Figure 1 shows that FDP models are broadly classified into three categories: statistical, Artificial Intelligence (AI), and theoretical models (Altman, 2013).

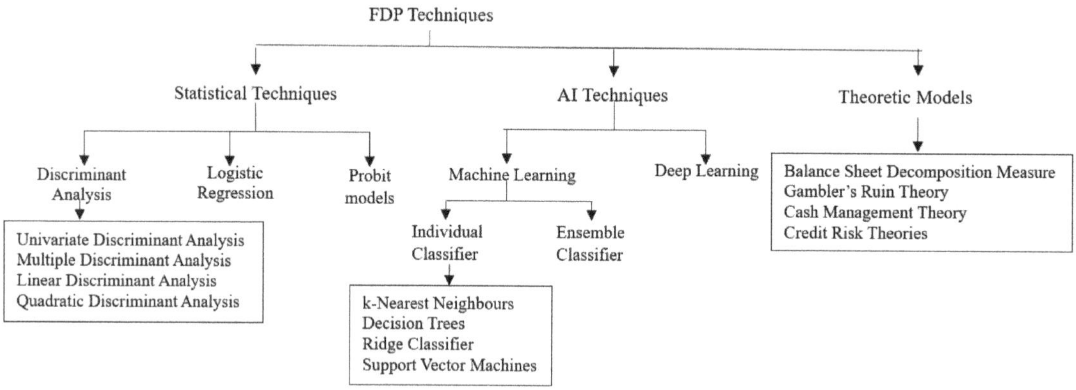

Figure 1. FDP models.

2.1. Statistical Models for Financial Distress Prediction

Statistical models include univariate discriminant analysis (UDA), multivariate discriminant analysis (MDA), linear probability model (LPM), logistic regression (LR), probit models, cumulative sums procedures (CUSUM), and partial adjustment processes, among others. These models utilize sensitive financial ratios as inputs to predict a firm's financial crisis by employing statistical tools and techniques.

Early studies in this field include FitzPatrick's analysis in 1932, which examined business failure prediction across five phases (Fitzpatrick, 1932; Gilbert et al., 1990). Beaver's work in 1966 associated mean values of 30 ratios with equal number of bankrupt and non-bankrupt companies. Beaver highlighted the predictive power of multiple ratios compared to a single ratio and laid the foundation for bankruptcy prediction models (Beaver, 1966). Altman improved on Beaver's univariate model by incorporating more ratios and using MDA for bankruptcy prediction (Altman, 1968; Altman et al., 2017). Linear Discriminant Analysis (LDA) is a classification and dimensionality reduction model that follows a linear approach. It was initially developed by Fisher in 1936 for two classes and later extended to multiple classes by C.R Rao in 1948 (Rao, 1948; Shumway, 2001). Quadratic Discriminant Analysis (QDA) is similar to LDA but relaxes the assumption that all classes have equal means and covariances. Ohlson introduced a logistic regression-based model (Ohlson, 1980; Rao, 1948), while Zmijewski addressed sampling bias and oversampling by suggesting the use of probit analysis (Zmijewski, 1984). LR estimates probabilities using logistic functions to examine the relationship between dependent variable and independent variable. The

LR algorithm calculates the coefficients from training data using maximum likelihood estimation (Heinze & Schemper, 2002; Zizi et al., 2020). Other notable studies include (Altman et al., 1977; Gilbert et al., 1990; Odom & Sharda, 1990; Pranowo et al., 2010), who explored logistical regression and Artificial Neural Networks (ANN), respectively. Kahya et al. introduced the CUSUM model (Kahya & Theodossiou, 1999; Keige, 1991), and Laitinen investigated Partial Adjustment Models (Laitinen & Laitinen, 1998; Mselmi et al., 2017). Altman proposed the Z- Score and ZETA models (Alfaro et al., 2008; Altman, 2013), while Shumway developed a hazard model (Shumway, 2001; Svetnik et al., 2003). Altman et al. re-evaluated the Z-Score model with additional variables and found it performed well internationally (Altman et al., 2017; Arlot & Celisse, 2010).

However, most of the ratios used in earlier studies depict the following aspects of a business: Profitability, Efficiency, Long-term solvency and Liquidity. Overall, past research has confirmed the predictive power of traditional models, especially when updated with new variables or coefficients. However, the definition of financial distress and the assessment of stress magnitude remain understudied areas, and industry-specific models can be developed to improve bankruptcy prediction.

2.2. Artificial Intelligence Models for Financial Distress Prediction

The evolution of machine learning in FDP began with the introduction of artificial intelligence algorithms, including neural networks and Genetic Algorithms (GA), in the 1990s. Researchers such as Odom et al. and Tam et al. demonstrated the superior performance of AI expert systems compared to traditional statistical methods like logistic analysis during this period (Odom & Sharda, 1990; Pranowo et al., 2010; Tam & Kiang, 1992; Valaskova et al., 2018).

Neural Networks (NNs) methods, in particular, have shown promising results in predicting financial crisis. Aydin et al. suggested their potential for identifying significant patterns in financial variables, highlighting the capacity of these methods to capture complex relationships (Aydin & Cavdar, 2015). The limitations associated with traditional statistical models, including issues of linearity and stringent assumptions, have driven a transition toward machine learning models. These newer models are designed to handle large datasets without requiring strict distribution assumptions, reflecting a more flexible and powerful approach to FDP.

For example, Malakauskas et al. demonstrated that Random Forests (RF), enhanced with time factors and credit history variables, achieved superior accuracy over static-period predictors, indicating the importance of dynamic multi-period modelling (Malakauskas & Lakštutienė, 2021). Jiang et al. emphasized the effectiveness of TreeNet for FDP, achieving over 93% accuracy and showcasing the value of integrating diverse financial and macroeconomic variables, along with non-traditional factors like executive compensation and corporate governance (Jiang & Jones, 2018).

Liang et al. highlighted the critical role of feature selection, showing that the choice of filter and wrapper-based methods could significantly impact prediction accuracy, depending on the underlying classification techniques (Liang et al., 2015). Similarly, Tsai et al. demonstrated that combining clustering methods, such as Self-Organizing Maps (SOMs), with classifier ensembles outperformed single classifiers in predicting financial distress. These findings underline the effectiveness of hybrid models and the synergy between dimensionality reduction and ensemble techniques for enhancing predictive performance (Tsai, 2014).

Overall, the collective findings suggest that while traditional models offer foundational insights, modern machine learning methods bring a greater capacity to manage high-dimensional data, capture nonlinear relationships, and integrate both financial and non-financial predictors. This evolution reflects a significant shift toward more robust and nuanced approaches in FDP, leveraging advanced algorithms and innovative methodologies to improve accuracy and reduce uncertainty in financial decision-making.

2.2.1. Individual Classifier

Within the realm of machine learning, there exists a wide array of single classification algorithms, each designed to tackle specific challenges and inherent patterns within datasets. In the context of this research, we have employed fundamental classifiers that have been instrumental in shaping the landscape of machine learning. This investigation centres on a core set of methodologies that have undergone thorough study and widespread application across diverse domains. These methodologies include k-Nearest Neighbours (KNN), Decision Trees (DT), Ridge Classifier (Ridge) and Support Vector Machines (SVM). KNN algorithm compares new data with previously observed nearest neighbor training data samples using supervised learning approach. It is a straightforward algorithm that classifies cases based on similarity, often utilizing distance functions. The parameter 'k' represents the number of closest neighbors considered in the majority vote. KNN is also known as a lazy learning algorithm because algorithm delays the process of generalizing or learning from the training data until a new query instance needs to be classified (Bansal et al., 2022; Faris et al., 2020; Guo et al., 2003; Liang et al., 2018). DT are predictive models that employ a hierarchical or tree-like structure to make decisions about the affiliation of values to classes or numerical target values (Faris et al., 2020; Liang et al., 2018). Ridge Classifier converts label data to the range $[-1, 1]$ using ridge regression method and solves the problem. The highest predicted value is taken as the target class, and multi-output regression is applied to multiclass data (Jones et al., 2017). SVM aims at finding an optimal hyperplane that maximize the class margin. This is achieved by considering the values at the closest distance. SVM utilizes support vectors and boundaries to identify hyperplanes (Hsu & Lin, 2002; Sun et al., 2021). It constructs hyperplanes in high-dimensional or infinite space, making it applicable for regression, classification, and other tasks. SVM allows control over capacity and transformability during model training, making it widely used and effective technique in machine learning (Barboza et al., 2017; Cortes & Vapnik, 1995; Devi & Radhika, 2018; Liang et al., 2018).

To sum up, the evaluation of separate classifiers highlights the importance of selecting models carefully so that they match the unique characteristics of financial data and the specific requirements of distress prediction tasks. The trend for future advancements in prediction skills is the combination of transfer learning and ensemble learning approaches. These encouraging avenues could improve machine learning models' overall efficacy and flexibility in handling the ever-changing problems associated with FDP. The investigation and application of these cutting-edge methods will probably lead to more reliable and accurate forecasts in the field of FDP.

2.2.2. Ensemble Classifier

Recent studies have explored building ensemble models using single classifier-based AI models (Barboza et al., 2017; Devi & Radhika, 2018; Faris et al., 2020; Huang & Yen, 2019; Liang et al., 2018; Nazareth & Reddy, 2023; Qu et al., 2019; Tsai et al., 2021). Ensemble models, which leverage the collective intelligence of multiple classifiers, have gained prominence for enhancing predictive performance in this context. These models are classified as homogeneous and heterogeneous ensembles, based on whether the constituent base models are of the same or different types (Figure 2). Two key approaches to combining predictions within ensembles are sequential and parallel.

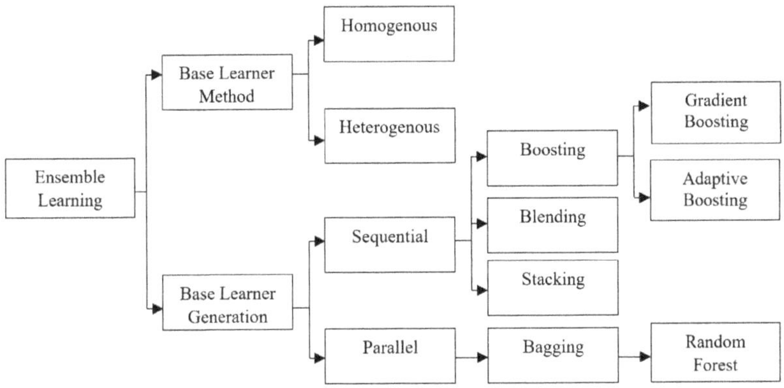

Figure 2. Classification of ensemble learning.

Sequential ensembles, also known as cascading ensembles, involve training and applying base models in a step-by-step manner, where each model's output serves as input for the next. This approach is advantageous for capturing complex relationships and offers interpretability, as each model's contribution can be analysed sequentially. However, weaknesses in early models may propagate through the sequence. In contrast, parallel ensembles, or concurrent ensembles, have independently trained base models. This independence allows for diverse learning and capturing various patterns in the data. The predictions of individual models are aggregated to obtain the final output, with aggregation techniques such as averaging or voting. Parallel ensemble models, with their ability to leverage diverse perspectives, offer a potent framework for improving predictive performance in FDP. Among the frequently used ensemble classification techniques are RF, AdaBoost (ADA), bagging, gradient boosting (GBC), and random subspace (Ho, 1995). RF is a versatile model used for both classification and regression problems in machine learning (Breiman, 2001). It is an ensemble learning method based on the concept of "learning from data". The core idea of the RF algorithm is to construct multiple decision trees (Tam & Kiang, 1992). RF combines the predictions of these trees to make final predictions. Generally, RF produces more robust and accurate models (Laitinen & Laitinen, 1998). AdaBoost is a boosting method commonly used as an ensemble technique in machine learning (Zhu et al., 2009). It is also referred to as adaptive boosting since it assigns weights to each instance and assigns higher weights to misclassified instances (Alfaro et al., 2008). Gradient Boosting is a boosting algorithm used for high-performance estimation with large datasets. It combines the calculations of multiple basic estimators to enhance robustness compared to using a single estimator (Assaad et al., 2008; Faris et al., 2020; Ho, 1995; Xu et al., 2014). Bagging classifier (Bagging) is a meta-estimator ensemble method that fits base classifiers to random subsets of the original dataset and aggregates their predictions to generate the final prediction. Bagging helps reduce the variance of unstable classifiers, which includes algorithms like DT known for their high variance and low bias. Therefore, utilizing a bagging classifier can be beneficial when working with algorithms such as DT and Variance, RF etc., (Barboza et al., 2017; Breiman, 1996; Faris et al., 2020; Liang et al., 2018). By taking random samples from the training data set, the Bagging approach creates sample subsets that are subsequently used to train the fundamental integration models. In the Bagging model, basic model training is carried out parallelly. The Bagging model is used to reduce variance, improve generalization and mitigate overfitting.

Voting mechanisms play a crucial role in parallel ensemble models, determining how individual base models' predictions contribute to the final output. Common voting mechanisms in FDP include hard voting (Figure 3a), where a majority vote decides the predicted financial state, and soft voting (Figure 3b), which involves averaging predicted probabilities for a more nuanced prediction. Weighted voting assigns different weights to base models based on reliability or historical performance. Stacking involves training a meta-model that learns to combine predictions, allowing for more complex interactions between models. Hard voting is the most suitable ensemble method when using diversified baseline classifiers, because it offers an optimal balance between performance, simplicity, and compatibility. Unlike soft voting, which requires calibrated probability estimates and additional steps for models like Ridge Classifier and SVM, hard voting integrates all classifiers without modification. Compared to stacking, which introduces higher complexity and computational overhead, hard voting remains efficient, interpretable, and less prone to overfitting. Even if soft voting and stacking may yield marginal accuracy improvements, their added complexity and calibration requirements often outweigh their benefits. Thus, hard voting provides consistent, stable performance across diverse algorithms with minimal risk and overhead, making it the most practical and effective choice for this financial distress prediction framework. Ultimately, the choice between sequential and parallel ensembles, as well as the specific voting mechanism employed, depends on factors such as the nature of dataset, task complexity, and the desired balance between interpretability and computational efficiency.

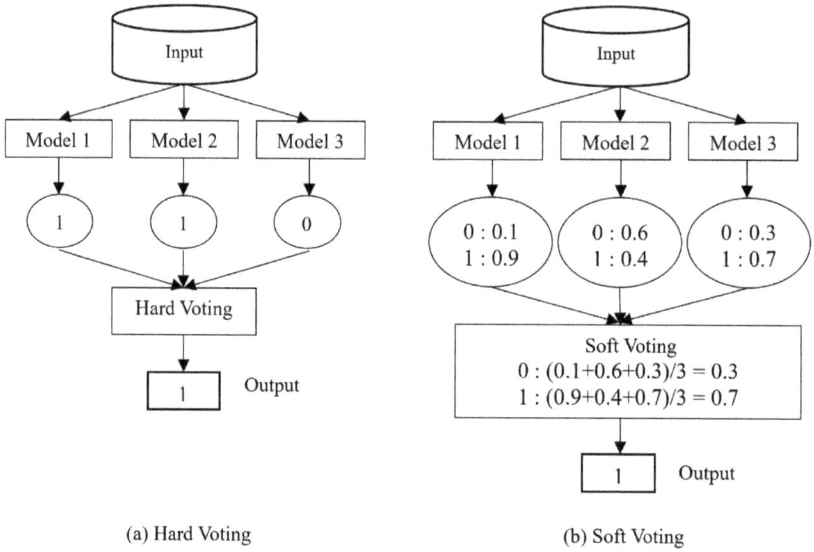

Figure 3. Types of voting mechanism (**a**) Hard voting (**b**) Soft Voting.

While parallel ensembles are computationally efficient and less susceptible to error propagation, they may struggle with capturing intricate dependencies or sequential patterns, and interpretability can be challenging. Hence, building an optimal ensemble classifier for FDP requires addressing three main challenges: selecting the best classification method, determining the number of classifiers for the ensemble, and choosing a binding method to combine the individual classifiers' outputs (Figure 4). To address these challenges different combinations of baseline classifiers for improved performance. Studies have shown that combining a set of classifiers yield higher predictive rates than using individual classifiers alone (Abellan & Castellano, 2017; Ala'raj & Abbod, 2016).

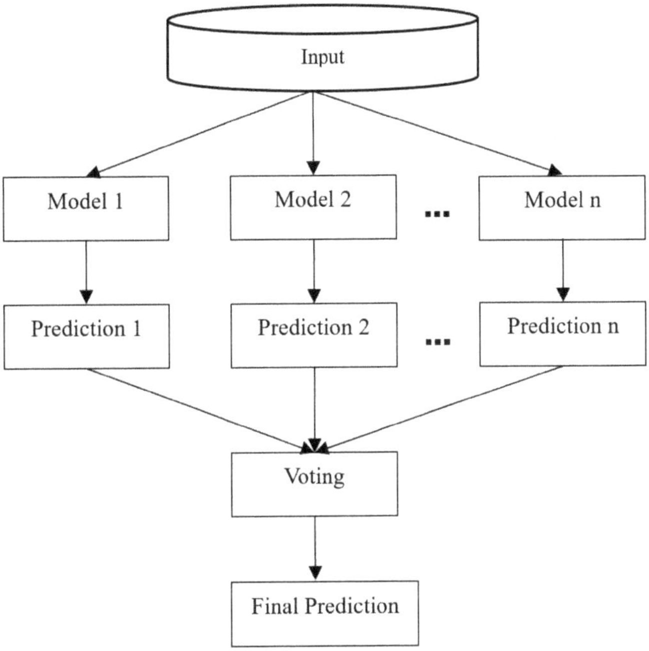

Figure 4. Structure of ensemble model (Bagging).

Ensemble approaches offer a number of benefits, including increased flexibility in the model selection process, increased accuracy compared to single models by combining the best features of multiple models (Abellan & Castellano, 2017; Ala'raj & Abbod, 2016), increased resilience to noise and outliers in the data due to their consideration of multiple perspectives, and a reduction in overfitting in complex models by generalising patterns discovered from various data subsets. Both statistical and AI models have been extensively studied, confirming their predictive power and potential for improving decision making (Nazareth & Reddy, 2023). However, further research is needed to explore the definition and measurement of financial distress, as well as the development of industry-specific models. The use of ensemble techniques and optimal ensemble classifiers holds promise for enhancing prediction accuracy.

2.2.3. Theoretical Models for Financial Distress Prediction

FDP has been explored through various theoretical models, each offering unique perspectives on the factors leading to corporate failure. Below are the key models in financial and economic theory:

Balance Sheet Decomposition Measures (BSDM) and Entropy Theory: This method is used to predict financial distress by analyzing shifts in a firm's balance sheet structure. This approach is based on the concept that firms strive to maintain equilibrium in their financial structure, with a balanced composition of assets and liabilities. Significant deviations from this balance, indicated by increased entropy or disorder in the financial statements, suggest a breakdown in financial stability. Such changes may signal that a firm is at risk of financial distress, making this approach useful for early detection of financial instability (Booth, 1983; Lev, 1973; Theil, 1969).

Gambler's Ruin Theory: This theory models a firm's financial survival by comparing it to a gambler who continues playing until they run out of money. According to this theory, a firm operates with a certain probability of financial gain or loss each period. If the firm experiences a prolonged sequence of negative cash flows, it will eventually deplete its capital, leading to bankruptcy. The probability of bankruptcy increases with the duration of financial losses and the initial capital available to the firm. This theory is particularly useful for assessing long-term financial sustainability under conditions of uncertainty and volatility (Morris, 2018; Scott, 1981).

Cash Management Theory: This theory focuses on the importance of effectively managing a firm's short-term cash flows to avoid financial distress. According to this theory, firms must maintain a balance between cash inflows and outflows to ensure liquidity. Persistent imbalances, where cash outflows consistently exceed inflows, indicate poor cash management, which can lead to liquidity problems and eventually bankruptcy. Effective cash management is therefore crucial for maintaining financial stability and preventing financial distress, especially in firms with highly variable cash flows (Aziz et al., 2013; Laitinen & Laitinen, 1998).

Credit Risk Theories: These theories are a set of approaches used to assess the likelihood of a borrower defaulting on their financial obligations, primarily in the context of financial institutions. These theories underpin several key models, including JP Morgan's CreditMetrics, Moody's KMV model, CSFB's CreditRisk+, and McKinsey's CreditPortfolio View, each of which evaluates credit risk using different methodologies.

JP Morgan's CreditMetrics and Moody's KMV models rely on option pricing theory, where a firm is considered to be in default if the value of its assets falls below its liabilities, with default being an endogenous outcome related to the firm's capital structure (Black & Scholes, 1973; Merton, 1971).

CSFB's CreditRisk+ applies an actuarial approach, using a Poisson process to model default events and derive the loss distribution of a credit portfolio (Credit Suisse, 1997).

McKinsey's CreditPortfolio View incorporates macroeconomic factors such as interest rates, GDP growth, and unemployment rates into the assessment of credit risk, linking the probability of default to broader economic conditions (Wilson, 1998).

2.3. Hyper Parameter Tuning

Optimizing hyperparameters is a pivotal stage in the development of high-performing machine learning models, particularly when applied to predicting financial distress. This process involves fine-tuning configuration settings, referred to as hyperparameters, to achieve optimal model performance. Various methods, ranging from traditional approaches like Grid Search (GS), Random Search (RS), and Gradient Descent, to advanced techniques such as Bayesian Optimization (BO) and Nature-Inspired Heuristic Algorithms, are employed to enhance accuracy, efficiency, and generalization across diverse financial datasets. Decision-theoretic methods, a fundamental approach in hyperparameter tuning, entail defining a hyperparameter search space and identifying the most effective combinations within that space. Grid Search, a decision-theoretic method, conducts an exhaustive search, but computational time escalates significantly with an increased number of hyperparameters (Bergstra et al., 2011; Kartini et al., 2021). Random Search serves as a valuable alternative, introducing randomness by employing arbitrary combinations, thereby gaining independence from the number of hyperparameters (Bergstra & Bengio, 2012). However, Random Search's major limitation lies in its high dependence on randomness, resulting in varied outcomes for different parameter sets (Jerrell, 1988). Unlike GS and RS, BO models make use of past hyperparameter evaluations to inform the selection of the next hyperparameter values, reducing unnecessary evaluations and accelerating the detection of optimal combinations within fewer iterations (Eggensperger et al., 2013). Researchers have also explored nature-inspired methods for efficient hyperparameter optimization in the context of FDP. Han et al., conducted a survey on metaheuristic algorithms for training random single-hidden layer feedforward neural networks (RSLFN) (Han et al., 2019), while Khalid et al. reviewed both nature-inspired and statistical methods for tuning the hyperparameters of SVM, NNs, Bayesian Networks (BNs), and their variants (Khalid & Javaid, 2020).

In FDP, the careful optimization of hyperparameters is crucial for obtaining accurate and reliable model predictions. Researchers and practitioners in this domain can benefit from exploring a range of hyperparameter tuning methods, considering the specific nature of financial data and the intricacies of predicting distress in financial contexts.

The study by Barboza et al. assesses how well SVM, bagging, boosting, RF, and other machine learning models predict corporate bankruptcy one year ahead of time (Barboza et al., 2017). These models are contrasted in the study with more conventional statistical techniques like LR, discriminant analysis, and NNs. In order to increase prediction accuracy, the research uses data on North American firms from 1985 to 2013 along with additional financial indicators. Notably, adding new variables to machine learning models improves accuracy significantly; RF model outperforms the others, scoring 87% as opposed to 50% for LDA and 69% for LR. The accuracy of machine learning models—RF in particular—is about 10% higher than that of conventional statistical methods. The disadvantage is the computational time needed by some machine learning models, like SVM.

The significance of anticipating financial distress in customer loans within financial institutions is discussed in a 2018 study by (Liang et al., 2018). This study focuses on improving the prediction accuracy and minimizing Type I errors, which incur substantial costs for financial institutions through Unanimous Voting (UV) which predicts Bankruptcy even if one classifier declare bankruptcy out of 'N' classifiers. The UV ensemble mechanism resulted in better performance than the ensemble methods such as bagging and boosting and also yielded good results than the single classifiers (SVM, CART, KNN, MLP, Bayes) when applied on varied datasets. The limitation of this Unanimous Voting mechanism is that this automatically avoids Type-I error unless all the N classifier predicts wrongly. This leads to increase in Type-II error.

The review by Devi and Radhika in 2018 shows the importance of Machine learning approaches such as ANN, SVM and DT over the traditional statistical methods such as LDA, MDA and LR (Devi & Radhika, 2018). The review results shows that SVM model optimized with Particle Swarm Optimization (PSO) have achieved higher results of (95% accuracy and 94.73% precision). The study concludes that machine learning model integrated with the optimization algorithms will improve the accuracy and suggests future directions for exploring the evolutionary techniques for improvements in financial risk assessment. But this study failed to present the merits and demerits of the reviewed models.

The review by Qu et al. (2019) states the current advancements in bankruptcy prediction and explore potential innovations and future trends in this field, particularly through machine learning and deep learning techniques (Qu et al., 2019). One significant trend is the diversification of data sources. Traditionally, bankruptcy prediction models rely on numerical data such as financial statements and accounting records. However, this review highlights incorporating textual data from sources like news articles, public reports and expert commentary using deep learning techniques. This shift has introduced the concept of Multiple-Source Heterogeneous Data, which integrates both structured and unstructured information for more comprehensive analysis. Deep learning techniques, such as Convolutional Neural Networks (CNNs) are used to effectively process and classify such complex data.

Huang and Yen (2019) explores the performance of various machine learning algorithms in predicting financial distress using data from Taiwanese firms (2010–2016) and 16 financial variables. The work performs comparison on four supervised machine learning models such as SVM, HACT, Hybrid GA-fuzzy clustering and XGBoost against a DBN which is an unsupervised model and a Hybrid DBN-SVM model. Their results shows that XGBoost gives the best performance among the supervised methods whereas the hybrid DBN-SVM model outperforms both standalone SVM and DBN. The advantage of integrating unsupervised feature extraction with supervised learning has been highlighted over traditional methods and stressed the importance of hybrid models in improving predictive performance.

The analysis done by Faris et al. (2020) tackles the problem of imbalanced datasets with 478 Spanish companies for a period of six years (with only 62 bankruptcies). The class imbalance is addressed by applying SMOTE and evaluation is carried out using five different feature selection methods. The model is tested on both baseline classifiers and ensemble models. The authors' study results show that SMOTE with AdaBoost achieves the highest accuracy of 98.3% and the lowest Type I error as 0.6%.

The study done by Tsai et al. (2021) explores the possible combinations of different feature selection and instance selection with ensemble classifier to analyse the financial distress and give a useful insight to the investors. This study was carried out on ten different datasets which amounts to 288 experiments. The authors claim that the order of preprocessing enhances the performance but the preprocessed data is not tested on the same classifiers and hence the suitability of the preprocessing technique is unclear. The preprocessing is carried out by combining optimal t-test-SOM with bagging DT for AUC and PCA-AP with ANN which minimizes type II errors.

The literature review underscores the pivotal role played by both statistical models and AI in the realm of FDP. It stresses the ongoing necessity for research aimed at refining financial distress classifications and metrics. Notably, optimal ensemble classifiers and ensemble techniques are recognized as valuable strategies capable of substantially enhancing prediction accuracy in this domain. The incorporation of these advancements is deemed essential for improving the effectiveness of predictive models by tuning the hyperparameters, acknowledging the dynamic and critical nature inherent in financial crisis prediction. This synthesis of statistical and AI approaches stands as a key step towards more robust and reliable predictions in the field of financial distress.

3. Empirical Experiment

In this study, a practical examination was carried out to assess the efficiency of the proposed methodology. Data obtained from automobile companies in India were utilized for this purpose. This section presents comprehensive information on the process of data collection, pre-processing of the data, the experimental design, and the subsequent analysis of the empirical results.

3.1. Data Collection

3.1.1. Dataset

The sample of firms was derived from the corporate database ProwessIQ maintained by the Centre for Monitoring Indian Economy (CMIE). This study was conducted for automobile manufacturing companies in India whose year of incorporation is after the 1950s. Firms that underwent mergers or diversification were excluded to ensure data consistency and comparability, as such events alter financial structures and risk profiles, making pre- and post-event metrics incomparable. This exclusion also mitigates survivorship bias, as these firms may have strategically avoided financial distress. Seven years of financial data were taken for this study. All years' financial information's extracted from financial statements and cash flow statements of the companies. Companies' profit and loss statement for seven years period (2013–2019) is identified from the Auditor's report which is released along with the annual report of the companies after the audit every year.

In this study, companies with seven consecutive years of profitability are categorized as "healthy", while those with seven consecutive years of losses are classified as "distressed". From the dataset we identified 50 companies classified as loss making and 380 companies as profit-making. The pairing of loss and a profit-making company is determined based on the asset size of the companies following the methodology outlined by (Beaver, 1966; Gilbert et al., 1990). A paired sample of fifty companies each from both groups has been selected for further analysis. For the dependent variable Y, the Healthy company is denoted as 1, and the distressed company is denoted as 0. Ratios have been categorized to identify the loss or profitability of the company and are normalized.

3.1.2. Feature Selection

Beaver has previously demonstrated the predictive potential of financial ratios in forecasting financial distress (Beaver, 1966). In this study, a comprehensive dataset comprising of 78 ratios was collected. The selection of these financial ratios as initial features for the FDP model was based on their ability to predict and differentiate between healthy and distressed firms. Specifically, 23 variables were chosen for predicting financial distress based on their extensive utilization in previous research, as is evident in the studies (Chen & Shimerda, 1981; Jabeur, 2017; Kliestik et al., 2020; Kovacova et al., 2019; Laitinen & Laitinen, 1998; Ohlson, 1980; Pedregosa et al., 2011; Wu et al., 2020; Zmijewski, 1984). Consequently, these variables were deemed suitable for this experiment.

Ultimately, 23 feature variables (Table 1) were chosen in such a way that it covers the major four categories: Profitability, Liquidity, Leverage/Solvency, and Turnover/Activity/Efficiency Ratio 1. The profitability ratio evaluates the effectiveness of management in utilizing business resources to generate profits. A company with higher profitability is more capable of fulfilling its debt obligations and avoiding financial distress. Xu et al. suggested that companies with higher profitability are less likely to experience financial distress (Xu et al., 2014; Yim & Mitchell, 2005). 2. The liquidity ratio measures a firm's ability to meet its short-term obligations. A higher ratio indicates that the company possesses more short-term assets than short-term liabilities. Study by Altman et al. indicates that liquidity ratios play a crucial role in predicting financial distress (Altman, 1968). It is recommended that companies maintain sufficient liquidity to prevent insolvency issues. Additionally, higher liquidity enables companies to meet their financial obligations promptly (Kiragu, 1991). Similar studies by Kiragu and Ohlson demonstrate that the current asset to current liabilities ratio successfully predicts bankruptcy (Kiragu, 1991; Kisman & Krisandi, 2019; Ohlson, 1980; Rao, 1948). 3. The leverage/solvency ratio assesses a business's ability to sustain itself over the long term. This ratio can be divided into the debt ratio and the debt- to-equity ratio. Higher leverage, characterized by higher total debt and a lack of cash flow, is associated with company bankruptcy. Paranowo finds that leverage ratios represented by debt service coverage are significant predictors (Salcedo-Sanz et al., 2014). Keige also concludes that the leverage ratio is a significant predictor of corporate distress (Keige, 1991). 4. The turnover/activity/efficiency ratio measures a firm's efficiency in generating revenue by converting production into cash or sales. A higher turnover ratio indicates better utilization of assets, reflecting improved efficiency and profitability. These ratios provide insights into a company's performance strengths and weaknesses. To remain competitive in the marketplace, companies can take additional measures to ensure the effectiveness of their activities.

Table 1. Variables used in the prediction model.

S.No	Id	Type	Financial Variable	Formula
1	X1	Profitability	Net Profit Margin	Net profit/Total Revenue
2	X2	Profitability	Return On Net Worth	EAI/Equity
3	X3	Profitability	Return On Total Assets	EAT/(Avg. Total Assets)
4	X4	Profitability	Return On Capital Employed	EBIT/(Equity + Debt)
5	X5	Liquidity	Current Ratio	Current Assets/Current Liabilities
6	X6	Liquidity	Cash Ratio	Cash/Current Liability
7	X7	Liquidity	Quick Ratio	Quick Assets/Current Liability
8	X8	Liquidity	NWC To TA	Net Working Capital/Total Asset
9	X9	Leverage	Interest Cover	EBIT/Interest
10	X10	Leverage	Debt To Equity Ratio	Total Liability/Share Holder's Equity
11	X11	Leverage	DSCR (Debt Service Coverage Ratio)	Net Operating Income/Debt Service
12	X12	Activity	Creditors Turnover	Credit Purchases/Avg. Accounts Payable
13	X13	Activity	Debtors Turnover	Credit Sales/Avg. Accounts Receivable
14	X14	Activity	WIP Turnover	Factory cost/Avg. Stock of WIP
15	X15	Activity	Finished Goods Turnover	Cost of Goods Sold/Avg. Stock of Finished Goods
16	X16	Activity	Employees Utilisation Ratio	Total billable hours/Total hours available
17	X17	Activity	Gross Fixed Assets Utilisation Ratio	–
18	X18	Activity	Net Fixed Assets Utilisation Ratio	–
19	X19	Activity	FA To NW	Fixed Asset/Net Worth
20	X20	Activity	Sales To FA	Sales/Fixed Asset
21	X21	Activity	Sales To NWC	Sales/Net Working Capital
22	X22	Activity	Sales To NW	Sales/Net Worth
23	X23	Activity	Sales To TA	Sales/Total Asset

3.2. Data Pre-Processing

Data pre-processing is a valuable technique used to enhance the quality of data and achieve normalization within a dataset, aiming to rectify errors like outliers and eliminate redundant information. Maintaining data integrity is of utmost importance in this study, necessitating organizations to possess a minimum historical record spanning three years prior to and during the data collection period. Some distressed organizations exhibited missing values, requiring a thorough examination of these cases and an assessment of data availability. Companies with a significant number of missing values were excluded from the study. As a matched pair approach was utilized, removing a company from the distressed sample led to the exclusion of its corresponding healthy firm variables, and vice versa. The pre-processing phase includes by loading the dataset and inspecting the presence of numeric values, while non-numeric attributes or data were discarded. Numeric data was deemed preferable for processing and predicting financial distress. Consequently, the dataset was loaded with refined numeric values.

The Firm-Feature-Wise three-step Missing Value Imputation Algorithm 1 is designed to handle missing values in time-series financial data for multiple firms. It employs a systematic approach to impute missing values based on their position in the time series. This approach consists of three steps: (1) The algorithm employs backward fill for missing data in the first year, substituting the data from the following year for the missing value. In the event that the data for the following year is also missing, mean imputation (1) is used, which uses the firm's average feature value for all years. (2) Similar to this, the algorithm employs forward fill for missing data in the last year, substituting the missing value with data from the previous year. If the data from the prior year is not available, mean imputation (1) is used. (3) For missing data in the middle years, the algorithm computes the missing ratio for each feature and uses mean imputation (1) only if less than half of the data for that feature is missing. This ensures that the imputed values are representative of the firm's historical data while avoiding biases from other firms or features. The algorithm is firm-specific, preserving the unique characteristics of each firm's financial data, and is scalable to handle large datasets with multiple firms, years, and features.

$$mean(\mu_{i,f}) = \frac{\sum_{t \in T_i^{\text{obs}}} D_{i,t,f}}{|T_i^{\text{obs}}|} \tag{1}$$

where:

- $\mu_{i,f}$ is the mean of feature f for firm i.
- T_i^{obs} represents the set of years for which the feature f is observed (i.e., non-missing values).
- $D_{i,t,f}$ is the observed value of feature f for firm i at year t.
- $|T_i^{\text{obs}}|$ is the total number of observed years for feature f in firm i.

Algorithm 1 Firm-Feature-Wise three step imputation process.

Require: A dataset D containing time-series financial data for multiple firms, where each firm has data for multiple years and multiple features.
Ensure: A dataset D' with missing values imputed for each feature independently.

Initialize $D' = D$
for each firm i in D **do**
    Identify the range of years $T_i = \{t_{\text{min}}, t_{\text{min}+1}, \ldots, t_{\text{max}}\}$
    for each feature f in F **do**
        if $D_{i,t_{\text{min}},f}$ is missing **then**
            if $D_{i,t_{\text{min}+1},f}$ is not missing **then**
                Set $D'_{i,t_{\text{min}},f} = D_{i,t_{\text{min}+1},f}$
            else
                Set $D'_{i,t_{\text{min}},f} = \mu_{i,f}$
            end if
        end if
        if $D_{i,t_{\text{max}},f}$ is missing **then**
            if $D_{i,t_{\text{max}-1},f}$ is not missing **then**
                Set $D'_{i,t_{\text{max}},f} = D_{i,t_{\text{max}-1},f}$
            else
                Set $D'_{i,t_{\text{max}},f} = \mu_{i,f}$
            end if
        end if
        Compute the missing ratio $R_{i,f} = \frac{\text{Number of missing values for feature } f}{\text{Total number of years}}$
        if $R_{i,f} < 0.5$ **then**
            for each year t in T_i (excluding t_{min} and t_{max}) **do**
                if $D_{i,t,f}$ is missing **then**
                    Set $D'_{i,t,f} = \mu_{i,f}$
                end if
            end for
        end if
    end for
end for
return D'

Descriptive statistics, such as kurtosis and skewness, were employed to evaluate the characteristics and nature of the data following the imputation process, with a particular emphasis on assessing the level of normal distribution. The normalization process was carried out using Equation (2):

$$x_{\text{normalized}} = \frac{x - x_{\min}}{x_{\max} - x_{\min}} \tag{2}$$

After outlier and normalization treatment, OLS test is used to check the predicting ability of the dataset. The OLS result (Table 2) shows that Jarque-Bera probability value is 0.000128 which is <0.05 i.e., this dataset has the capacity for prediction (Thadewald & Büning, 2007).

Table 2. Result of OLS Regression model.

OLS Regression Results			
Dep. Variable:	Y	AIC:	368.1
Model:	OLS	BIC:	477.3
Method:	Least Squares	Omnibus:	17.058
No. Observations:	700	Prob (Omnibus):	0
Df Residuals:	676	Skew:	−0.385
Df Model:	23	Kurtosis:	2.852
Covariance Type:	nonrobust	Durbin-Watson:	2.025
Prob (Omnibus):	0	Jarque-Bera (JB):	17.926
Skew:	−0.385	Prob (JB):	0.000128
Kurtosis:	2.852	Cond. No.:	298

3.3. *Design of Empirical Experiment*

3.3.1. Design of Experimental Process

The experimental process is designed to systematically evaluate and compare the performance of various classification techniques for FDP. Our objective is to incorporate a diverse set of classifiers that represent distinct algorithmic paradigms, enabling a comprehensive and balanced performance comparison. The selected 11 baseline classifiers encompass a broad methodological spectrum: (i) Linear Models—LR, RIDGE and LDA; (ii) Non-linear Models—KNN, QDA, SVM, and DT; (iii) Ensemble Methods—Bagging, RF, ADA, and GBC. This diversity allows us to evaluate the performance of our proposed method across a wide range of modeling paradigms, from simple linear models to complex ensemble methods. An odd number of baseline models are selected to avoid ties in the voting mechanism. After preprocessing, the dataset is split into training and testing sets using a 70:30 ratio. The training set is used to build and fine-tune the models, while the test set is reserved for evaluating the final performance of the models. This ensures that the performance metrics reflect the models' ability to generalize to unseen data.

This study consists of four sets of experiments. Figure 5 shows that the initial experiment involved training and testing each of the eleven baseline algorithms individually. By combining different algorithms, we can leverage their diverse strengths and compensate for individual weaknesses. This often results in a more robust and accurate predictive model. Hard voting mechanism allows each model in the ensemble to vote for a class and the class that receives the majority of votes is the final prediction. This is suitable when the individual models provide discrete class prediction which helps in reducing error. So, the second experiment entailed training and testing using a combination of all eleven baseline algorithms. The combination of the eleven algorithms results in a total of 2048 combinations. However, one of these combinations is found to be empty and thus not useful. Consequently, 2047 combinations of algorithms are utilized for this study. All 2047 combinations are inputted into HVM, and their performance is evaluated.

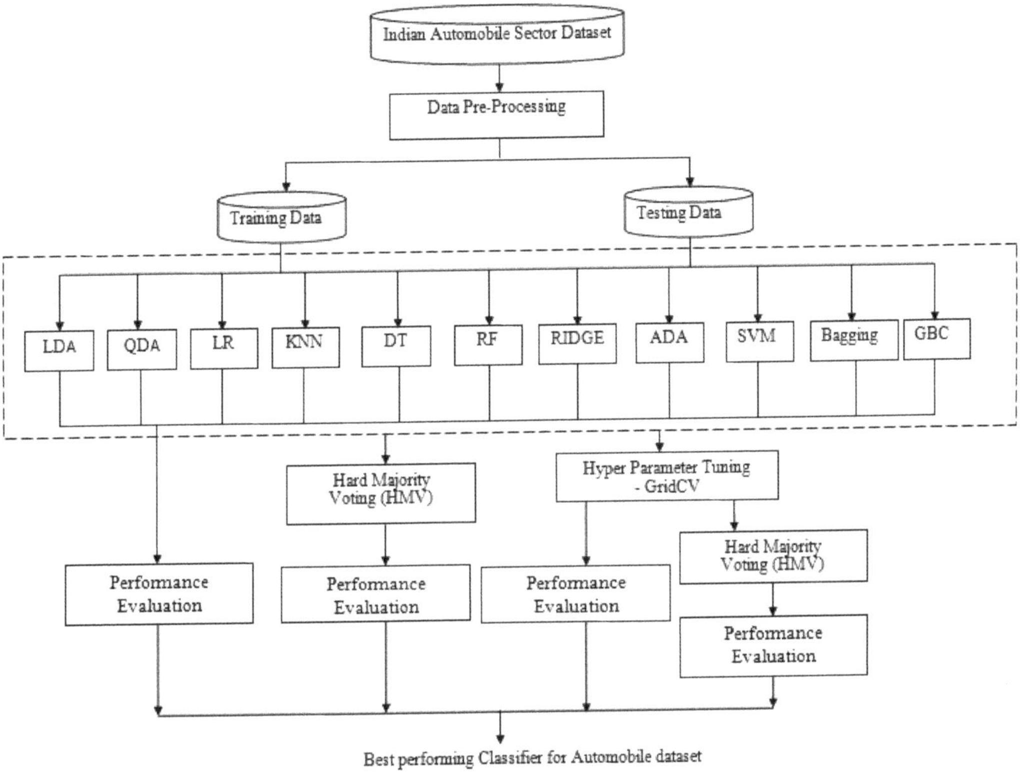

Figure 5. Schematic diagram showing the experimental design.

The performance and behavior of machine learning algorithms are often significantly impacted by the values of hyperparameters. Thus, the third experiment is carried out to identify optimized hyperparameters for all baseline algorithms using GridSearchCV. This involves finding the best parameter configuration for each model, and subsequently evaluating the performance of the individual baseline models with the test data. Similarly, in the fourth experiment, the combination of baseline models is examined, but this time with the inclusion of optimized hyper parameters for each algorithm. Finally, k-fold CV is used to assess the generalizing ability of the prediction model.

3.3.2. Crosss-Validation (CV)

The primary objective when developing classification or regression models is to ensure their ability to generalize. It is crucial to evaluate the model's performance using data that was not used for training, as relying solely on the training data may lead to biased results, especially when dealing with limited datasets. Even if a model performs well when trained and tested on a small portion of the data, there is a possibility of achieving even better results when trained on the entire dataset.

To address this issue, a commonly employed technique known as k- fold CV is utilized in classification and regression models (Bergmeir & Benítez, 2012; Odom & Sharda, 1990; Stone, 1974). The validation process is repeated k times, with each iteration using a different fold as the validation set (Figure 6). This approach provides an estimation of the validation error for each iteration, which is then averaged to obtain the final validation error. By repeatedly performing the validation process, k-fold CV offers greater robustness compared to the validation set approach. Therefore, k-fold CV is employed to validate the model's performance.

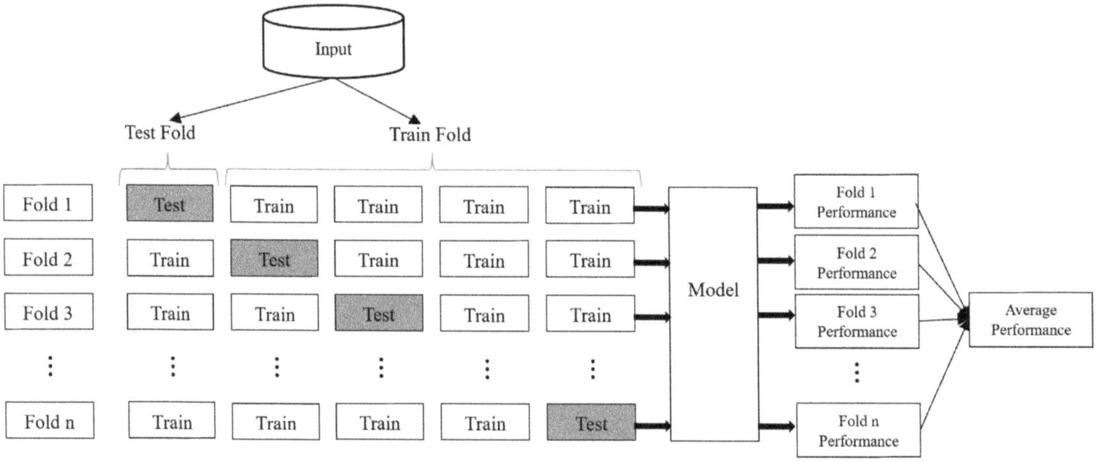

Figure 6. k-fold Cross-Validation.

3.3.3. Hyperparameter Tuning with GridSearchCV

Objective functions and constraints are crucial components in computing optimization algorithms. Grid search is a fundamental method for hyperparameter optimization (HPO), conducting an exhaustive search on user-specified hyperparameter sets. It is applicable for hyperparameters with a limited search space, and its straightforward nature leads to accurate predictions. Despite suffering from the curse of dimensionality, grid search remains widely used due to its simplicity, ease of parallelization, and flexibility in resource allocation (Bergstra & Bengio, 2012).

Hyperparameter tuning with GridSearchCV optimizes machine learning models by combining the exhaustive search of grid search with Cross-Validation (Figure 7). It identifies optimal hyperparameter values from the given set of user-specified hyperparameter, enhancing model accuracy and generalization.

3.3.4. Model Evaluation Measure

In this study on FDP with matching pair dataset using machine learning models, Accuracy (3) is primarily used as an evaluation measure of the model. Apart from accuracy, most of the common evaluation measures for the classification models, namely Precision (4), Recall/Sensitivity (5), Specificity (6), Type-I error (8), Type-II error (9), F1 score (10), and AUC ROC curve where adopted. For classification problems, most of the performance evaluation measures are calculated using the confusion matrix, but the matrix itself is not the performance measure. Table 3 shows the structure of a confusion matrix.

Table 3. Confusion Matrix.

Total No. of Instances		**Predicted Value**	
		Non-Distress (P)	**Distress (N)**
Actual Value	Non-Distress (P)	TP	FN
	Distress (N)	FP	TN

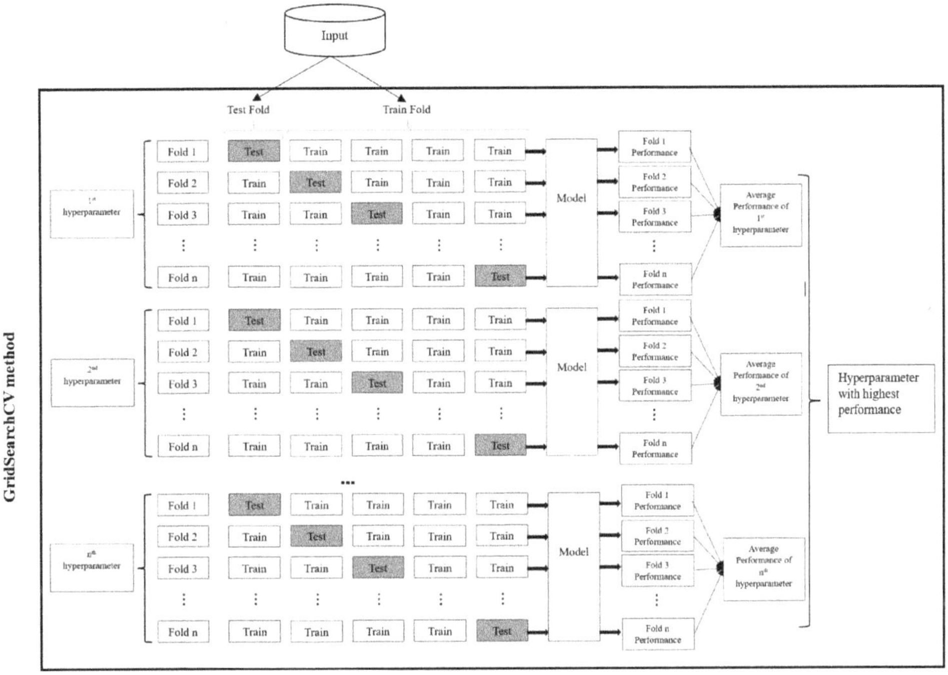

Figure 7. Hyperparameter tuning using GridSearchCV method.

Two-class classification problem focusing on FDP has been employed in this work. The two classes are labelled as Distress (Class 0) and Non-Distress (Class 1). When dealing with a two-class problem, the confusion matrix provides four possible combinations of actual and predicted values. True Positive (TP), False Positive (FP), False Negative (FN) and True Negative (TN).

Based on Table 3, the evaluation metrics used to assess the learning algorithm are defined as:

$$Accuracy = \frac{(TP + TN)}{(TP + TN + FP + FN)} \tag{3}$$

$$Precision = \frac{TP}{(TP + FP)} \tag{4}$$

$$Recall(TruePositiveRate) = \frac{TP}{(TP + FN)} \tag{5}$$

$$Specificity(TrueNegativeRate) = \frac{TN}{(FP + TN)} \tag{6}$$

$$Errorrate = \frac{(FP + FN)}{(TP + TN + FP + FN)} \tag{7}$$

$$FalsePositiveRate = \frac{FP}{(FP + TN)} \tag{8}$$

$$FalseNegativeRate = \frac{FN}{(TP + FN)} \tag{9}$$

The F1 score, also known as the F score (10), is a commonly used metric to evaluate the performance of binary classification models. Its main purpose is to compare the effectiveness of two learning classifiers. For example, if classifier A has a high recall rate while classifier B has a high precision rate, the F1 scores of both classifiers can be utilized to determine which one produces better outcomes. The F1 score ranges between 0 and 1, where a lower F1 score indicates reduced sensitivity of the model. Conversely, when both precision and recall scores are high, a higher F1 score suggests that the model possesses greater sensitivity.

$$F1\ Score = 2 \times \frac{\text{Precision} \times \text{Recall}}{\text{Precision} + \text{Recall}} \tag{10}$$

The AUC refers to the measurement of the ROC curve. The AUC ROC quantifies the effectiveness of a classifier in accurately distinguishing positive classes from negative classes. A higher AUC value indicates that the classifier is more proficient in correctly identifying distressed firms as distressed and healthy firms as healthy.

4. Experimental Result and Analysis

4.1. Performance of Individual Baseline Classifiers

The initial experiment aimed to assess the performance of each individual baseline classifier. All 11 baseline models were trained and evaluated using the same dataset. The performance of the individual baseline classifiers, including accuracy, AUC-ROC, confusion matrix, and error rate, is presented in Table 4. Among the 11 classifiers, GBC (Gradient Boosting) exhibited the highest accuracy of 0.99048. It is important to note that since this study utilized a matching paired samples dataset, if a model achieves higher accuracy, the remaining evaluation metrics tend to yield similarly favourable scores for that model. The AUC-ROC score for the GBC model was 0.9900, and the error rate was 0.010. These results were obtained without hyperparameter tuning.

4.2. Performance of Individual Baseline Classifiers After Hyperparameter Tuning

Parameter tuning is considered one of the most effective approaches to enhance model performance. By fine-tuning the parameters, the prediction accuracy of a model can be significantly improved. The process of manually adjusting parameters can be time-consuming and resource-intensive, making it impractical. To overcome this challenge, the GridSearchCV technique is employed to automate the fine-tuning of hyperparameters.

GridSearchCV is a method that systematically explores a predefined set of parameter combinations to find the optimal values. It searches for the best parameter values based on a specified scoring metric such as accuracy, F1 score (Shilpa & Amulya, 2017). The GridSearchCV technique generates the best combination of parameters that yield the highest accuracy value. These parameters obtained through GridSearchCV are then utilized in the 11 baseline models, which are individually tested after hyperparameter tuning.

Table 5 shows the performance of the individual classifier with the tuned optimal hyperparameters. After tuning, the performance of the LR, KNN, DT, RF, RIDGE, and SVM classifiers algorithms improve in predicting a company's financial distress situation at 0.94286, 0.96667, 0.96667, 0.98095, 0.91429 and 0.96667 respectively. After hyperparameter tuning also GBC (Gradient Boosting) is showing superior to other baseline classifiers with an accuracy of 0.99048.

Figure 8 shows the accuracy of the baseline algorithms before and after hyperparameter tuning. The analysis demonstrates that the LR and SVM models exhibited significant improvement in performance following hyperparameter tuning. However, certain models such as LDA, QDA, ADA, Bagging, and GBC attained optimal results with their default parameter settings, indicating no enhancement in predictive accuracy. Notably, the GBC model outperformed all other models, achieving an impressive accuracy of 0.99048.

Table 4. Results of individual Baseline algorithms.

S.No	Model	Accuracy	AUC-ROC	TN	FP	FN	TP	Precision	Recall	F1-Score	Specificity	Error Rate	FPR	FNR
1	LDA	0.919	0.921	98	12	5	95	0.888	0.950	0.918	0.891	0.081	0.109	0.050
2	QDA	0.829	0.832	84	26	10	90	0.776	0.900	0.833	0.764	0.171	0.236	0.100
3	LR	0.900	0.901	97	13	8	92	0.876	0.920	0.898	0.882	0.100	0.118	0.080
4	Naive Bayes	0.895	0.897	94	16	6	94	0.855	0.940	0.895	0.855	0.105	0.146	0.060
5	KNN	0.943	0.944	102	8	4	96	0.923	0.960	0.941	0.927	0.057	0.073	0.040
6	DT	0.962	0.962	105	5	3	97	0.951	0.970	0.960	0.955	0.038	0.046	0.030
7	RF	0.986	0.986	109	1	2	98	0.990	0.980	0.985	0.991	0.014	0.009	0.020
8	Ridge	0.895	0.897	95	15	7	93	0.861	0.930	0.894	0.864	0.105	0.136	0.070
9	AdaBoost	0.981	0.981	108	2	2	98	0.980	0.980	0.980	0.982	0.019	0.018	0.020
10	SVM	0.924	0.926	98	12	4	96	0.889	0.960	0.923	0.891	0.076	0.109	0.040
11	Bagging	0.971	0.971	107	3	3	97	0.970	0.970	0.970	0.973	0.029	0.027	0.030
12	GBC	0.991	0.990	110	0	2	98	1.000	0.980	0.990	1.000	0.010	0.000	0.020

Table 5. Results of individual Baseline algorithms after hyperparameter tuning.

S.No	Model	Accuracy	AUC-ROC	TN	FP	FN	TP	Precision	Recall	F1-Score	Specificity	Error Rate	FPR	FNR
1	LDA	0.919	0.921	98	12	5	95	0.888	0.950	0.918	0.891	0.081	0.109	0.050
2	QDA	0.829	0.832	84	26	10	90	0.776	0.900	0.833	0.764	0.171	0.236	0.100
3	LR	0.943	0.943	103	7	5	95	0.931	0.950	0.941	0.936	0.057	0.064	0.050
4	Naive Bayes	0.895	0.897	94	16	6	94	0.855	0.940	0.895	0.855	0.105	0.145	0.060
5	KNN	0.967	0.967	106	4	3	97	0.960	0.970	0.965	0.964	0.033	0.036	0.030
6	DT	0.967	0.967	105	5	2	98	0.951	0.980	0.966	0.955	0.033	0.045	0.020
7	RF	0.981	0.981	108	2	2	98	0.980	0.980	0.980	0.982	0.019	0.018	0.020
8	Ridge	0.914	0.916	98	12	6	94	0.887	0.940	0.913	0.891	0.086	0.109	0.060
9	AdaBoost	0.976	0.976	107	3	2	98	0.970	0.980	0.975	0.973	0.024	0.027	0.020
10	SVM	0.967	0.967	106	4	3	97	0.960	0.970	0.965	0.964	0.033	0.036	0.030
11	Bagging	0.986	0.985	110	0	3	97	1.000	0.970	0.985	1.000	0.014	0.000	0.030
12	GBC	0.991	0.990	110	0	2	98	1.000	0.980	0.990	1.000	0.010	0.000	0.020

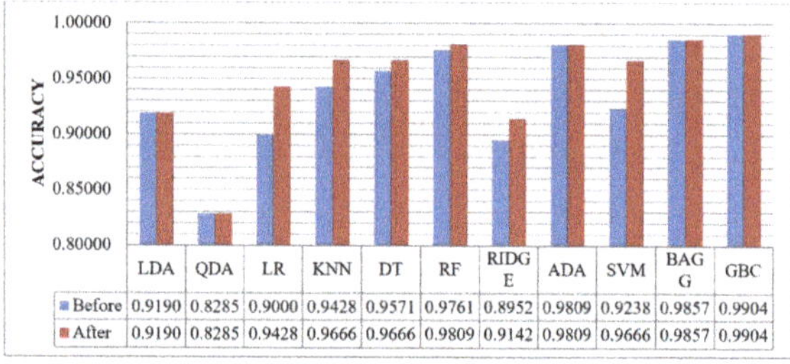

	LDA	QDA	LR	KNN	DT	RF	RIDGE	ADA	SVM	BAGG	GBC
Before	0.9190	0.8285	0.9000	0.9428	0.9571	0.9761	0.8952	0.9809	0.9238	0.9857	0.9904
After	0.9190	0.8285	0.9428	0.9666	0.9666	0.9809	0.9142	0.9809	0.9666	0.9857	0.9904

Figure 8. Accuracy performance comparison between baseline algorithms before and after hyperparameter tuning.

4.3. Performance of HVM Algorithms with the Combination of the Baseline Algorithm Without Hyperparameter Tuning

As mentioned earlier in the experimental process design (see Section 3.3.1), experiments were performed on all 2047 combinatorial models using an HVM without hyperparameter tuning. The results obtained show these six algorithms (Bagging, GBC, RF, LDA, KNN, and ADA (BGRLKA)) played a major role in prediction with lower error rates. Bagging reduces variance by averaging multiple models trained on different subsets of data. Boosting (AdaBoost, GBC) focuses on sequential learning, where errors are reduced in each iteration. LDA capture linear relationships in the data and non-linear patterns is identified with Random Forest with this KNN helps to capture local decision boundaries. Using an ensemble of BGRLKA algorithms allows us to balance variance, bias, and robustness, higher accuracy and lesser error rate. Ensemble BGRLKA algorithms results in a balanced model leading to better generalization and higher predictive performance. Therefore, combination of BGRLKA algorithms was used as fixed algorithm and remaining 5 algorithms (QDA, LR, DT, RIDGE, and SVM) were treated to all possible combinations to have 32 distinct models

Given the combination of 32 models to the HVM, the result obtained is shown in Table 6, depicte that BGRLKA + QDA combination gives the highest accuracy of 0.99048 with error rate, Type-I and Type-II error as 0.01,0.009, and 0.01 respectively. The second-best accuracy is 0.9857, and the accuracy of the two models is the same, BGRLKA + LR and BGRLKA + QDA + DT. The accuracy (0.9859) and error rate (0.01) of both algorithms are the same, but the values in the confusion matrix are different and are reflected in the precision, recall, specificity, Type I, and Type II values. If the accuracy is tied, the AUCROC score breaks the tied. BGRLKA + LR model and BGRLKA + QDA + DT model have AUCROC scores of 0.9859 and 0.9855, respectively, so the model with the highest AUCROC score is considered the best. Therefore, the BGRLKA + LR is considered the second-best model for this dataset. Figure 9 shows the performance of each model against its accuracy.

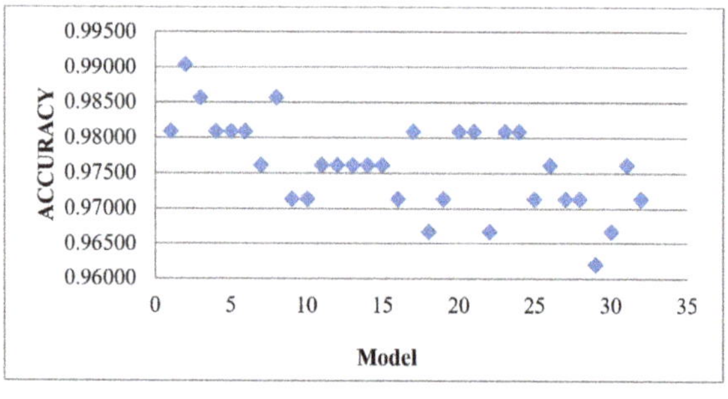

Figure 9. Results of HVM with the 32 combinations of the baseline algorithm.

Table 6. Results of HVM with the 32 combinations of the baseline algorithm.

S.NO	BGRLKA	QDA	LR	DT	Ridge	SVM	Accuracy	AUC-ROC	TN	FP	FN	TP	Precision	Recall	F1-Score	Specificity	Error Rate	Type I	Type II
1	1	0	0	0	0	0	0.981	0.980	109	1	3	97	0.990	0.970	0.980	0.991	0.019	0.009	0.030
2	1	1	0	0	0	0	0.990	0.990	109	1	1	99	0.990	0.990	0.990	0.991	0.010	0.009	0.010
3	1	0	1	0	0	0	0.986	0.986	108	2	1	99	0.980	0.990	0.985	0.982	0.014	0.018	0.010
4	1	0	0	1	0	0	0.981	0.981	108	2	2	98	0.980	0.980	0.980	0.982	0.019	0.018	0.020
5	1	0	0	0	1	0	0.981	0.981	108	2	2	98	0.980	0.980	0.980	0.982	0.019	0.018	0.020
6	1	0	0	0	0	1	0.981	0.981	108	2	2	98	0.980	0.980	0.980	0.982	0.019	0.018	0.020
7	1	1	1	0	0	0	0.976	0.975	109	1	4	96	0.990	0.960	0.975	0.991	0.024	0.009	0.040
8	1	1	0	1	0	0	0.986	0.985	109	1	2	98	0.990	0.980	0.985	0.991	0.014	0.009	0.020
9	1	1	0	0	1	0	0.971	0.970	109	1	5	95	0.990	0.950	0.969	0.991	0.029	0.009	0.050
10	1	1	0	0	0	1	0.971	0.970	109	1	5	95	0.990	0.950	0.969	0.991	0.029	0.009	0.050
11	1	0	1	1	0	0	0.976	0.976	108	2	3	97	0.980	0.970	0.975	0.982	0.024	0.018	0.030
12	1	0	1	0	1	0	0.976	0.976	108	2	3	97	0.980	0.970	0.975	0.982	0.024	0.018	0.030
13	1	0	1	0	0	1	0.976	0.976	108	2	3	97	0.980	0.970	0.975	0.982	0.024	0.018	0.030
14	1	0	0	1	1	0	0.976	0.976	108	2	3	97	0.980	0.970	0.975	0.982	0.024	0.018	0.030
15	1	0	0	1	0	1	0.976	0.976	108	2	3	97	0.980	0.970	0.975	0.982	0.024	0.018	0.030
16	1	0	0	0	1	1	0.971	0.971	108	2	4	96	0.980	0.960	0.970	0.982	0.029	0.018	0.040
17	1	1	1	1	0	0	0.981	0.981	108	2	2	98	0.980	0.980	0.980	0.982	0.019	0.018	0.020
18	1	1	1	0	1	0	0.967	0.967	106	4	3	97	0.960	0.970	0.965	0.964	0.033	0.036	0.030
19	1	1	1	0	0	1	0.971	0.972	106	4	2	98	0.961	0.980	0.970	0.964	0.029	0.036	0.020
20	1	1	0	1	1	0	0.981	0.981	108	2	2	98	0.980	0.980	0.980	0.982	0.019	0.018	0.020
21	1	1	0	1	0	1	0.981	0.981	108	2	2	98	0.980	0.980	0.980	0.982	0.019	0.018	0.020
22	1	1	0	0	1	1	0.967	0.967	106	4	3	97	0.960	0.970	0.965	0.964	0.033	0.036	0.030
23	1	0	1	1	1	0	0.981	0.981	108	2	2	98	0.980	0.980	0.980	0.982	0.019	0.018	0.020
24	1	0	1	1	0	1	0.981	0.981	108	2	2	98	0.980	0.980	0.980	0.982	0.019	0.018	0.020
25	1	0	1	0	1	1	0.971	0.972	106	4	2	98	0.961	0.980	0.970	0.964	0.029	0.036	0.020
26	1	0	0	1	1	1	0.976	0.976	108	2	3	97	0.980	0.970	0.975	0.982	0.024	0.018	0.030
27	1	1	1	1	1	0	0.971	0.971	108	2	4	96	0.980	0.960	0.970	0.982	0.029	0.018	0.040
28	1	1	1	1	0	1	0.971	0.971	108	2	4	96	0.980	0.960	0.970	0.982	0.029	0.018	0.040
29	1	1	1	0	1	1	0.962	0.962	106	4	4	96	0.960	0.960	0.960	0.964	0.038	0.036	0.040
30	1	1	0	1	1	1	0.967	0.966	108	2	5	95	0.979	0.950	0.964	0.982	0.033	0.018	0.050
31	1	0	1	1	1	1	0.976	0.976	108	2	3	97	0.980	0.970	0.975	0.982	0.024	0.018	0.030
32	1	1	1	1	1	1	0.971	0.972	106	4	2	98	0.961	0.980	0.970	0.964	0.029	0.036	0.020

4.4. *Performance of HVM Algorithms with the Combination of the Baseline Algorithm with Hyperparameter Tuning*

The findings indicated that there was no notable enhancement in accuracy when comparing individual baseline classifiers to HVM without tuned hyperparameters. As a result, the hyperparameters of all 11 baseline models were adjusted prior to their combination and utilization in the HVM. The result obtained in (Table 7) shows that BGRLKA + RIDGE + SVM model achieved an accuracy of 0.99524 with 0 for Type-I error and 0.01 for Type-II error. The results show that RIDGE and SVM along with the BGRLKA algorithms play a good role in improving the prediction accuracy. Figure 10 shows the performance of each model after hyperparameter tuning against its accuracy.

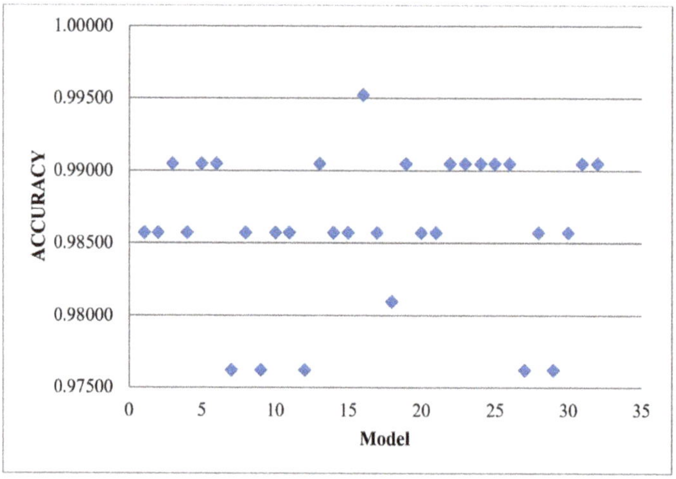

Figure 10. Results of HVM with the 32 combinations of the baseline algorithm with tuned parameters.

4.5. *Performance of HVM Algorithms in k-Fold Cross Validation (k-Fold CV)*

To assess the effectiveness of a machine learning model, it is necessary to evaluate its performance using unseen data. The model's ability to generalize, whether it is under-fitting or over-fitting, can be determined based on its performance on unseen data. The k-fold CV technique is employed to validate the model's generalizability. We selected k = 5 in CV as a pragmatic balance between bias and variance, particularly suited for datasets of our size and computational resources. With 100 firms and 7 years of data, 5-fold CV ensures that each fold contains a sufficiently representative and diverse sample of companies, allowing robust model evaluation while maintaining computational efficiency during testing across 32 ensemble models.

Regarding the bias-variance trade-off, increasing the number of folds (e.g., k = 10) can reduce the bias of the performance estimate, but at the cost of higher variance and increased computational load, especially when tuning complex ensembles. Conversely, lower k-values (e.g., k = 3) may reduce variance but increase the bias. The choice of k = 5 strikes a balance, minimizing both overfitting risk and computational cost in our high-dimensional setting, without significantly compromising model evaluation accuracy. The purpose of the validation phase in Cross-Validation is to select the best-performing approach and assess the model's training effectiveness. Table 8 presents the 5-fold CV HVM results for 32 combinations of the baseline algorithm.

Table 7. Results of HVM with the 32 combinations of the baseline algorithm with tuned hyperparameters.

S.NO	BGRLKA	QDA	LR	DT	Ridge	SVM	Accuracy	AUC-ROC	TN	FP	FN	TP	Precision	Recall	F1-Score	Specificity	Error Rate	Type I	Type II
1	1	0	0	0	0	0	0.986	0.985	109	1	2	98	0.990	0.980	0.985	0.991	0.014	0.009	0.020
2	1	1	0	0	0	0	0.986	0.985	109	1	2	98	0.990	0.980	0.985	0.991	0.014	0.009	0.020
3	1	0	1	0	0	0	0.990	0.990	109	1	1	99	0.990	0.990	0.990	0.991	0.010	0.009	0.010
4	1	0	0	1	0	0	0.986	0.985	109	1	2	98	0.990	0.980	0.985	0.991	0.014	0.009	0.020
5	1	0	0	0	1	0	0.990	0.990	109	1	1	99	0.990	0.990	0.990	0.991	0.010	0.009	0.010
6	1	0	0	0	0	1	0.990	0.990	109	1	1	99	0.990	0.990	0.990	0.991	0.010	0.009	0.010
7	1	1	1	0	0	0	0.976	0.975	109	1	4	96	0.990	0.960	0.975	0.991	0.024	0.009	0.040
8	1	1	0	1	0	0	0.986	0.985	109	1	2	98	0.990	0.980	0.985	0.991	0.014	0.009	0.020
9	1	1	0	0	1	0	0.976	0.975	109	1	4	96	0.990	0.960	0.975	0.991	0.024	0.009	0.040
10	1	1	0	0	0	1	0.986	0.985	109	1	2	98	0.990	0.980	0.985	0.991	0.014	0.009	0.020
11	1	0	1	1	0	0	0.986	0.985	109	1	2	98	0.990	0.980	0.985	0.991	0.014	0.009	0.020
12	1	0	1	0	1	0	0.976	0.975	109	1	4	96	0.990	0.960	0.975	0.991	0.024	0.009	0.040
13	1	0	1	0	0	1	0.990	0.990	109	1	1	99	0.990	0.990	0.990	0.991	0.010	0.009	0.010
14	1	0	0	1	1	0	0.986	0.985	109	1	2	98	0.990	0.980	0.985	0.991	0.014	0.009	0.020
15	1	0	0	1	0	1	0.986	0.985	109	1	2	98	0.990	0.980	0.985	0.991	0.014	0.009	0.020
16	1	0	0	0	1	1	0.995	0.995	110	0	1	99	1.000	0.990	0.995	1.000	0.005	0.000	0.010
17	1	1	1	1	0	0	0.986	0.985	109	1	2	98	0.990	0.980	0.985	0.991	0.014	0.009	0.020
18	1	1	1	0	1	0	0.981	0.980	109	1	3	97	0.990	0.970	0.980	0.991	0.019	0.009	0.030
19	1	1	1	0	0	1	0.990	0.990	109	1	1	99	0.990	0.990	0.990	0.991	0.010	0.009	0.010
20	1	1	0	1	1	0	0.986	0.985	109	1	2	98	0.990	0.980	0.985	0.991	0.014	0.009	0.020
21	1	1	0	1	0	1	0.986	0.985	109	1	2	98	0.990	0.980	0.985	0.991	0.014	0.009	0.020
22	1	1	0	0	1	1	0.990	0.990	109	1	1	99	0.990	0.990	0.990	0.991	0.010	0.009	0.010
23	1	0	1	1	1	0	0.990	0.990	109	1	1	99	0.990	0.990	0.990	0.991	0.010	0.009	0.010
24	1	0	1	1	0	1	0.990	0.990	109	1	1	99	0.990	0.990	0.990	0.991	0.010	0.009	0.010
25	1	0	1	0	1	1	0.990	0.990	109	1	1	99	0.990	0.990	0.990	0.991	0.010	0.009	0.010
26	1	0	0	1	1	1	0.990	0.990	109	1	1	99	0.990	0.990	0.990	0.991	0.010	0.009	0.010
27	1	1	1	1	1	0	0.976	0.975	109	1	4	96	0.990	0.960	0.975	0.991	0.024	0.009	0.040
28	1	1	1	1	0	1	0.986	0.985	109	1	2	98	0.990	0.980	0.985	0.991	0.014	0.009	0.020
29	1	1	1	0	1	1	0.976	0.975	109	1	4	96	0.990	0.960	0.975	0.991	0.024	0.009	0.040
30	1	1	0	1	1	1	0.986	0.985	109	1	2	98	0.990	0.980	0.985	0.991	0.014	0.009	0.020
31	1	0	1	1	1	1	0.990	0.990	109	1	1	99	0.990	0.990	0.990	0.991	0.010	0.009	0.010
32	1	1	1	1	1	1	0.990	0.990	109	1	1	99	0.990	0.990	0.990	0.991	0.010	0.009	0.010

Table 8. Results of 5-fold CV HVM with the 32 combinations of the baseline algorithm.

S.NO	BGRLKA	QDA	LR	DT	Ridge	SVM	Mean Accuracy
1	1	0	0	0	0	0	0.970
2	1	1	0	0	0	0	0.967
3	1	0	1	0	0	0	0.967
4	1	0	0	1	0	0	0.970
5	1	0	0	0	1	0	0.969
6	1	0	0	0	0	1	0.967
7	1	1	1	0	0	0	0.966
8	1	1	0	1	0	0	0.969
9	1	1	0	0	1	0	0.967
10	1	1	0	0	0	1	0.966
11	1	0	1	1	0	0	0.967
12	1	0	1	0	1	0	0.957
13	1	0	1	0	0	1	0.959
14	1	0	0	1	1	0	0.966
15	1	0	0	1	0	1	0.967
16	1	0	0	0	1	1	0.960
17	1	1	1	1	0	0	0.967
18	1	1	1	0	1	0	0.956
19	1	1	1	0	0	1	0.957
20	1	1	0	1	1	0	0.964
21	1	1	0	1	0	1	0.964
22	1	1	0	0	1	1	0.960
23	1	0	1	1	1	0	0.963
24	1	0	1	1	0	1	0.966
25	1	0	1	0	1	1	0.946
26	1	0	0	1	1	1	0.966
27	1	1	1	1	1	0	0.963
28	1	1	1	1	0	1	0.966
29	1	1	1	0	1	1	0.947
30	1	1	0	1	1	1	0.963
31	1	0	1	1	1	1	0.956
32	1	1	1	1	1	1	0.959

Figure 11 shows the result of the k-fold CV of the baseline algorithm, BGRLKA and BGRLKA + DT model achieved the best accuracy as 0.97000 with the difference of 0.01095 with our precious baseline algorithm with HVM results. For the model BGRLKA + QDA which got better accuracy of 0.99048 without 5-foldCV, now with 5-fold CV same model got the accuracy of 0.96714 with a difference of 0.02333.

Similarly, Table 9 shows the mean accuracy results of 5-fold CV HVM with the 32 combination of the tuned hyperparameter baseline algorithm. Figure 12 shows BGRLKA + QDA + LR+ DT model achieved the best accuracy as 0.97429 with the acceptable difference of 0.01143 with our precious tuned baseline algorithm with HVM results. For the model BGRLKA + RIDGE + SVM which got better accuracy of 0.99524 after hyperparameter tuning but without 5-fold CV, now with 5-fold CV same model got the accuracy of 0.96000 with the difference of 0.02667. Across 32 model combinations, the average accuracy difference between models evaluated with and without 5-fold cross-validation ranges from 0.00381 to 0.02571 for those without hyperparameter tuning and from 0.00619 to 0.02667 for those with hyperparameter tuning. Similarly, the standard deviation difference ranges from 0.005345 to 0.016660 for models without hyperparameter tuning and from 0.005345 to 0.016288 for models with hyperparameter tuning. These results demonstrate that the algorithm delivers consistent and reliable performance regardless of the specific data used for training and testing. Among the tested combinations, the model comprising BGRLKA + RIDGE + SVM exhibits strong generalization.

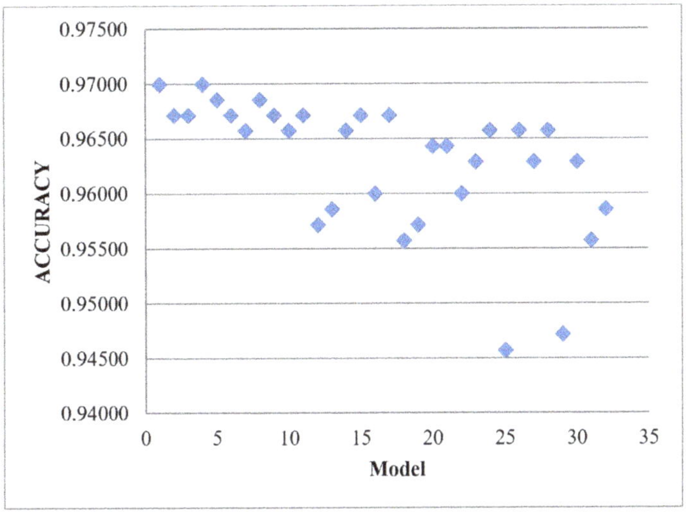

Figure 11. Results of 5-fold CV HVM with the 32 combinations of the baseline algorithm.

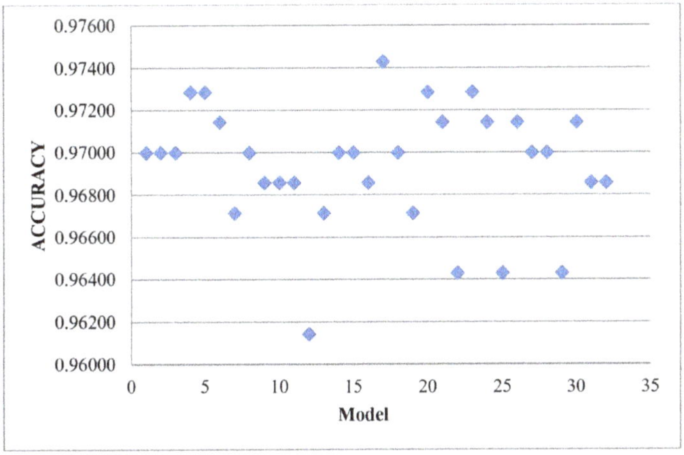

Figure 12. Results of 5-fold CV HVM with the 32 combination of the tuned hyperparameter baseline algorithm.

In this study we have done the exhaustive search to identify the best model combination that achieves better accuracy with lesser Type-I and Type-II error. Our proposed Firm-Feature-Wise three step imputation process along with HVM of BGRLKA + RIDGE + SVM model combination after tuning, not only achieved a good accuracy of 0.99524 but also achieved lowest error rate (0 for Type-I error and 0.01 for Type-II error). Even for statistical t-test, BGRLKA + Ridge + SVM model had shown significance ($p < 0.05$) which means that this combination of model still performs better than other models. Additionally, our imputation algorithm addresses a critical preprocessing gap by preserving feature interdependencies during missing data imputation, unlike traditional methods that may distort data distributions (e.g., mean or median imputation, Interpolation, KNN imputation). The findings of this study suggest that the optimal combination of techniques presented can be effectively utilized by financial experts to enhance predictive accuracy, thereby supporting more informed decision-making while minimizing associated risks.

Table 9. Results of 5-fold CV HVM with the 32 combination of the tuned hyperparameter baseline algorithm.

S.NO	BGRLKA	QDA	LR	DT	Ridge	SVM	Mean Accuracy
1	1	0	0	0	0	0	0.970
2	1	1	0	0	0	0	0.970
3	1	0	1	0	0	0	0.970
4	1	0	0	1	0	0	0.973
5	1	0	0	0	1	0	0.973
6	1	0	0	0	0	1	0.971
7	1	1	1	0	0	0	0.967
8	1	1	0	1	0	0	0.970
9	1	1	0	0	1	0	0.969
10	1	1	0	0	0	1	0.969
11	1	0	1	1	0	0	0.969
12	1	0	1	0	1	0	0.961
13	1	0	1	0	0	1	0.967
14	1	0	0	1	1	0	0.970
15	1	0	0	1	0	1	0.970
16	1	0	0	0	1	1	0.969
17	1	1	1	1	0	0	0.974
18	1	1	1	0	1	0	0.970
19	1	1	1	0	0	1	0.967
20	1	1	0	1	1	0	0.973
21	1	1	0	1	0	1	0.971
22	1	1	0	0	1	1	0.964
23	1	0	1	1	1	0	0.973
24	1	0	1	1	0	1	0.971
25	1	0	1	0	1	1	0.964
26	1	0	0	1	1	1	0.971
27	1	1	1	1	1	0	0.970
28	1	1	1	1	0	1	0.970
29	1	1	1	0	1	1	0.964
30	1	1	0	1	1	1	0.971
31	1	0	1	1	1	1	0.969
32	1	1	1	1	1	1	0.969

5. Conclusions

The research on FDP has gained significant attention across various disciplines such as accounting, finance, economics, and engineering. This topic has evolved into an independent subject with practical implications for identifying financial risks, preventing financial distress, and avoiding bankruptcy. FDP plays a crucial role in mitigating corporate bankruptcy risks. Previous studies have primarily focused on improving prediction accuracy, with equal emphasis given to reducing Type-I errors to protect stakeholders. While individual classifiers have been extensively researched for FDP, the use of ensemble classifiers in this context is relatively new. Ensemble classifiers overcome the limitations of single classifiers by combining their predictions through specific methods to enhance prediction performance and stability. In this study, an ensemble classifier based on the HVM was employed to achieve high prediction accuracy and minimal Type-I errors. The model was compared with and without hyperparameter tuning, with the results demonstrating that hyperparameter tuning improved accuracy. The best-performing ensemble model not only eliminated Type-I errors but also lowered Type-II error rate which demonstrate high sensitivity and the model's ability to reliably detect distressed cases. This low-rate highlights that, despite the focus on reducing false positives, the models maintained strong recall and ensured that financially unstable firms were accurately identified. Therefore, the combination of ensemble classifiers using the majority voting mechanism proves to be an effective approach for predicting financial distress in firms. Additionally, the study assessed the model's generalizability using k-fold CV.

This study focused on the classification of financial distress in Indian automobile manufacturing companies using a paired dataset to identify the most effective model combination. While the findings provide valuable insights, as future work we are extending this study by evaluating model performance on imbalanced datasets and applying it to diverse industries and geographic regions to enhance generalizability. Additionally, incorporating trend analysis to understand the temporal dynamics of financial distress and developing a financial distress forecasting framework will further strengthen the model's predictive capabilities and real-world applicability.

Author Contributions: Conceptualization, M.M. and N.D.P.S.; methodology, M.M.; software, M.M.; validation, M.M. and N.D.P.S.; formal analysis, M.M. and N.D.P.S.; investigation, M.M. and N.D.P.S.; resources, M.M.; data curation, M.M.; writing—original draft preparation, M.M.; writing—review and editing, M.M. and N.D.P.S.; visualization, M.M.; supervision, N.D.P.S.; project administration, N.D.P.S. All authors have read and agreed to the published version of the manuscript.

Funding: This research received no external funding.

Institutional Review Board Statement: Not applicable.

Informed Consent Statement: Not applicable.

Data Availability Statement: The dataset used in the work is acquired from the corporate database ProwessIQ maintained by the Centre for Monitoring Indian Economy (CMIE). The data is accessed through institutional license under VIT user. The data is used for studying the performance of automobile manufacturing companies in India. Since the data is licensed, access is restricted to authorized users only. CIME ProwessIQ https://prowessiq.cmie.com/.

Acknowledgments: This research is supported by the Department of Science and Technology (DST), India, under the Fund for Improvement of S&T Infrastructure in Universities and Higher Educational Institutions (FIST) Program [Grant No. SR/FST/ET-I/2022/1079], and a matching grant from VIT University. The authors are grateful to DST-FIST and VIT management for their financial support and the resources provided for this work. We thank VIT Business school for providing support to access ProwessIQ database maintained by Centre for Monitoring Indian Economy (CMIE).

Conflicts of Interest: The authors declare no conflicts of interest.

References

Abellán, J., & Castellano, J. G. (2017). A comparative study on base classifiers in ensemble methods for credit scoring. *Expert Systems with Applications*, *73*, 1–10. [CrossRef]

Ala'raj, M., & Abbod, M. F. (2016). A new hybrid ensemble credit scoring model based on classifiers consensus system approach. *Expert Systems with Applications*, *64*, 36–55. [CrossRef]

Alfaro, E., García, N., Gámez, M., & Elizondo, D. (2008). Bankruptcy forecasting: An empirical comparison of AdaBoost and neural networks. *Decision Support Systems*, *45*(1), 110–122. [CrossRef]

Altman, E. I. (1968). Financial ratios, discriminant analysis and the prediction of corporate bankruptcy. *The Journal of Finance*, *23*(4), 589–609. [CrossRef]

Altman, E. I. (2013). Predicting financial distress of companies: Revisiting the Z-score and ZETA® models. In *Handbook of research methods and applications in empirical finance* (pp. 428–456). Edward Elgar Publishing.

Altman, E. I., Haldeman, R. G., & Narayanan, P. (1977). ZETATM analysis A new model to identify bankruptcy risk of corporations. *Journal of Banking & Finance*, *1*(1), 29–54.

Altman, E. I., Iwanicz-Drozdowska, M., Laitinen, E. K., & Suvas, A. (2017). Financial distress prediction in an international context: A review and empirical analysis of Altman's Z-score model. *Journal of International Financial Management & Accounting*, *28*(2), 131–171.

Arlot, S., & Celisse, A. (2010). A survey of cross-validation procedures for model selection. *Statistics Surveys*, *4*, 40–79. [CrossRef]

Assaad, M., Boné, R., & Cardot, H. (2008). A new boosting algorithm for improved time-series forecasting with recurrent neural networks. *Information Fusion*, *9*(1), 41–55. [CrossRef]

Aydin, A. D., & Cavdar, S. C. (2015). Prediction of financial crisis with artificial neural network: An empirical analysis on Turkey. *International Journal of Financial Research*, *6*(4), 36. [CrossRef]

Aziz, A., Emanuel, D. C., & Lawson, G. H. (2013). Bankruptcy prediction—An investigation of cash flow based models [1]. In *Studies in cash flow accounting and analysis (RLE accounting)* (pp. 293–310). Routledge.

Bansal, M., Goyal, A., & Choudhary, A. (2022). A comparative analysis of K-nearest neighbor, genetic, support vector machine, decision tree, and long short-term memory algorithms in machine learning. *Decision Analytics Journal*, *3*, 100071. [CrossRef]

Barboza, F., Kimura, H., & Altman, E. (2017). Machine learning models and bankruptcy prediction. *Expert Systems with Applications*, *83*, 405–417. [CrossRef]

Beaver, W. H. (1966). Financial ratios as predictors of failure. *Journal of Accounting Research*, *4*, 71–111. [CrossRef]

Bergmeir, C., & Benítez, J. M. (2012). On the use of cross-validation for time series predictor evaluation. *Information Sciences*, *191*, 192–213.

Bergstra, J., Bardenet, R., Bengio, Y., & Kégl, B. (2011). Algorithms for hyper-parameter optimization. *Advances in Neural Information Processing Systems*, *24*., 2546–2554

Bergstra, J., & Bengio, Y. (2012). Random search for hyper-parameter optimization. *The Journal of Machine Learning Research*, *13*(1), 281–305.

Black, F., & Scholes, M. (1973). The pricing of options and corporate liabilities. *Journal of Political Economy*, *81*(3), 637–654. [CrossRef]

Booth, P. J. (1983). Decomposition measures and the prediction of financial failure. *Journal of Business Finance & Accounting*, *10*(1), 67–82.

Breiman, L. (1996). Bagging predictors. *Machine Learning*, *24*, 123–140.

Breiman, L. (2001). Random forests. *Machine Learning*, *45*, 5–32.

Chen, K. H., & Shimerda, T. A. (1981). An empirical analysis of useful financial ratios. *Financial Management*, *10*, 51–60.

Cortes, C., & Vapnik, V. (1995). Support-vector networks. *Machine Learning*, *20*, 273–297. [CrossRef]

Credit Suisse. (1997). *Credit risk: A credit risk management framework*. Credit Suisse Financial Products.

Devi, S. S., & Radhika, Y. (2018). A survey on machine learning and statistical techniques in bankruptcy prediction. *International Journal of Machine Learning and Computing*, *8*(2), 133–139. [CrossRef]

Eggensperger, K., Feurer, M., Hutter, F., Bergstra, J., Snoek, J., Hoos, H., & Leyton-Brown, K. (2013, December). Towards an empirical foundation for assessing bayesian optimization of hyperparameters. In *NIPS workshop on Bayesian optimization in theory and practice* (Vol. 10, No. 3, pp. 1–5).

Faris, H., Abukhurma, R., Almanaseer, W., Saadeh, M., Mora, A. M., Castillo, P. A., & Aljarah, I. (2020). Improving financial bankruptcy prediction in a highly imbalanced class distribution using oversampling and ensemble learning: A case from the Spanish market. *Progress in Artificial Intelligence*, *9*, 31–53. [CrossRef]

Fitzpatrick, P. J. (1932). A comparison of the ratios of successful industrial enterprises with those of failed companies. *Certified Public Accountant*, *12*, 598–605. 656–662. 727–731.

Gilbert, L. R., Menon, K., & Schwartz, K. B. (1990). Predicting bankruptcy for firms in financial distress. *Journal of Business Finance & Accounting*, *17*(1), 161.

Guo, G., Wang, H., Bell, D., Bi, Y., & Greer, K. (2003, November 3–7). *KNN model-based approach in classification*. On The Move to Meaningful Internet Systems 2003: CoopIS, DOA, and ODBASE: OTM Confederated International Conferences, CoopIS, DOA, and ODBASE 2003, Proceedings (pp. 986–996), Catania, Sicily, Italy.

Han, F., Jiang, J., Ling, Q. H., & Su, B. Y. (2019). A survey on metaheuristic optimization for random single-hidden layer feedforward neural network. *Neurocomputing*, *335*, 261–273. [CrossRef]

Heinze, G., & Schemper, M. (2002). A solution to the problem of separation in logistic regression. *Statistics in Medicine*, *21*(16), 2409–2419. [CrossRef]

Ho, T. K. (1995, August 14–16). *Random decision forests*. 3rd International Conference on Document Analysis and Recognition (Vol. 1, pp. 278–282).

Hsu, C. W., & Lin, C. J. (2002). A comparison of methods for multiclass support vector machines. *IEEE Transactions on Neural Networks*, *13*(2), 415–425.

Huang, Y. P., & Yen, M. F. (2019). A new perspective of performance comparison among machine learning algorithms for financial distress prediction. *Applied Soft Computing*, *83*, 105663. [CrossRef]

Jabeur, S. B. (2017). Bankruptcy prediction using partial least squares logistic regression. *Journal of Retailing and Consumer Services*, *36*, 197–202. [CrossRef]

Jerrell, M. E. (1988). A random search strategy for function optimization. *Applied Mathematics and Computation*, *28*(3), 223–229. [CrossRef]

Jiang, Y., & Jones, S. (2018). Corporate distress prediction in China: A machine learning approach. *Accounting & Finance*, *58*(4), 1063–1109.

Jones, S., Johnstone, D., & Wilson, R. (2017). Predicting corporate bankruptcy: An evaluation of alternative statistical frameworks. *Journal of Business Finance & Accounting*, *44*(1–2), 3–34.

Kahya, E., & Theodossiou, P. (1999). Predicting corporate financial distress: A time-series CUSUM methodology. *Review of Quantitative Finance and Accounting*, *13*, 323–345. [CrossRef]

Kartini, D., Nugrahadi, D. T., & Farmadi, A. (2021, September 14–15). *Hyperparameter tuning using GridsearchCV on the comparison of the activation function of the ELM method to the classification of pneumonia in toddlers*. 2021 4th International Conference of Computer and Informatics Engineering (IC2IE) (pp. 390–395), Depok, Indonesia.

Keige, N. P. (1991). *Business failure prediction using discriminant analysis* [Doctoral dissertation, University of Nairobi].

Khalid, R., & Javaid, N. (2020). A survey on hyperparameters optimization algorithms of forecasting models in smart grid. *Sustainable Cities and Society*, *61*, 102275. [CrossRef]

Kiragu, I. M. (1991). *The prediction of corporate failure using price adjusted accounting data* [Doctoral dissertation, University of Nairobi].

Kisman, Z., & Krisandi, D. (2019). How to predict financial distress in the wholesale sector: Lesson from indonesian stock exchange. *Journal of Economics and Business*, *2*(3), 569–585. [CrossRef]

Kliestik, T., Valaskova, K., Lazaroiu, G., Kovacova, M., & Vrbka, J. (2020). Remaining financially healthy and competitive: The role of financial predictors. *Journal of Competitiveness*, *12*(1), 74–92. [CrossRef]

Kovacova, M., Kliestik, T., Valaskova, K., Durana, P., & Juhaszova, Z. (2019). Systematic review of variables applied in bankruptcy prediction models of Visegrad group countries. *Oeconomia Copernicana*, *10*(4), 743–772. [CrossRef]

Laitinen, E. K., & Laitinen, T. (1998). Cash management behavior and failure prediction. *Journal of Business Finance & Accounting*, *25*(7–8), 893–919.

Lev, B. (1973). Decomposition measures for financial analysis. *Financial Management*, *2*, 56–63. [CrossRef]

Liang, D., Tsai, C. F., Dai, A. J., & Eberle, W. (2018). A novel classifier ensemble approach for financial distress prediction. *Knowledge and Information Systems*, *54*, 437–462.

Liang, D., Tsai, C. F., & Wu, H. T. (2015). The effect of feature selection on financial distress prediction. *Knowledge-Based Systems*, *73*, 289–297.

Malakauskas, A., & Lakštutienė, A. (2021). Financial distress prediction for small and medium enterprises using machine learning techniques. *Engineering Economics*, *32*(1), 4–14. [CrossRef]

Merton, R. C. (1971). Theory of rational option pricing. *Bell Journal of Economics and Management Science*, *4*, 141–183.

Morris, R. (2018). *Early warning indicators of corporate failure: A critical review of previous research and further empirical evidence*. Routledge.

Mselmi, N., Lahiani, A., & Hamza, T. (2017). Financial distress prediction: The case of French small and medium-sized firms. *International Review of Financial Analysis*, *50*, 67–80. [CrossRef]

Nazareth, N., & Reddy, Y. V. R. (2023). Financial applications of machine learning: A literature review. *Expert Systems with Applications*, *219*, 119640.

Odom, M. D., & Sharda, R. (1990, June 17–21). *A neural network model for bankruptcy prediction*. 1990 IJCNN International Joint Conference on Neural Networks (pp. 163–168), San Diego, CA, USA.

Ohlson, J. A. (1980). Financial ratios and the probabilistic prediction of bankruptcy. *Journal of Accounting Research*, *18*, 109–131. [CrossRef]

Pedregosa, F., Varoquaux, G., Gramfort, A., Michel, V., Thirion, B., Grisel, O., Blondel, M., Prettenhofer, P., Weiss, R., Dubourg, V., & Vanderplas, J. (2011). Scikit-learn: Machine learning in Python. *The Journal of Machine Learning Research*, *12*, 2825–2830.

Pranowo, K., Achsani, N. A., Manurung, A. H., & Nuryartono, N. (2010). The dynamics of corporate financial distress in emerging market economy: Empirical evidence from the Indonesian Stock Exchange 2004–2008. *European Journal of Social Sciences*, *16*(1), 138–149.

Qu, Y., Quan, P., Lei, M., & Shi, Y. (2019). Review of bankruptcy prediction using machine learning and deep learning techniques. *Procedia Computer Science*, *162*, 895–899.

Rao, C. R. (1948). Tests of significance in multivariate analysis. *Biometrika*, *35*(1/2), 58–79.

Salcedo-Sanz, S., Rojo-Álvarez, J. L., Martínez-Ramón, M., & Camps-Valls, G. (2014). Support vector machines in engineering: An overview. *Wiley Interdisciplinary Reviews: Data Mining and Knowledge Discovery*, *4*(3), 234–267.

Scott, J. (1981). The probability of bankruptcy: A comparison of empirical predictions and theoretical models. *Journal of Banking & Finance*, *5*(3), 317–344.

Shilpa, N. C., & Amulya, M. (2017). Corporate financial distress: Analysis of Indian automobile industry. *SDMIMD Journal of Management*, *8*, 85–93.

Shumway, T. (2001). Forecasting bankruptcy more accurately: A simple hazard model. *The Journal of Business*, *74*(1), 101–124.

Stone, M. (1974). Cross-validatory choice and assessment of statistical predictions. *Journal of the Royal Statistical Society: Series B (Methodological)*, *36*(2), 111–133.

Sun, J., Fujita, H., Zheng, Y., & Ai, W. (2021). Multi-class financial distress prediction based on support vector machines integrated with the decomposition and fusion methods. *Information Sciences*, *559*, 153–170.

Svetnik, V., Liaw, A., Tong, C., Culberson, J. C., Sheridan, R. P., & Feuston, B. P. (2003). Random forest: A classification and regression tool for compound classification and QSAR modeling. *Journal of Chemical Information and Computer Sciences*, *43*(6), 1947–1958.

Tam, K. Y., & Kiang, M. Y. (1992). Managerial applications of neural networks: The case of bank failure predictions. *Management Science*, *38*(7), 926–947.

Thadewald, T., & Büning, H. (2007). Jarque–Bera test and its competitors for testing normality—A power comparison. *Journal of Applied Statistics*, *34*(1), 87–105.

Theil, H. (1969). On the use of information theory concepts in the analysis of financial statements. *Management Science*, *15*(9), 459–480. [CrossRef]

Tsai, C. F. (2014). Combining cluster analysis with classifier ensembles to predict financial distress. *Information Fusion*, *16*, 46–58. [CrossRef]

Tsai, C. F., Sue, K. L., Hu, Y. H., & Chiu, A. (2021). Combining feature selection, instance selection, and ensemble classification techniques for improved financial distress prediction. *Journal of Business Research*, *130*, 200–209. [CrossRef]

Valaskova, K., Kliestik, T., Svabova, L., & Adamko, P. (2018). Financial risk measurement and prediction modelling for sustainable development of business entities using regression analysis. *Sustainability*, *10*(7), 2144. [CrossRef]

Wilson, T. C. (1998). Portfolio credit risk. *Economic Policy Review*, *4*(3), 71–82. [CrossRef]

Wu, Y., Ke, Y., Chen, Z., Liang, S., Zhao, H., & Hong, H. (2020). Application of alternating decision tree with AdaBoost and bagging ensembles for landslide susceptibility mapping. *Catena*, *187*, 104396. [CrossRef]

Xu, W., Xiao, Z., Dang, X., Yang, D., & Yang, X. (2014). Financial ratio selection for business failure prediction using soft set theory. *Knowledge-Based Systems*, *63*, 59–67. [CrossRef]

Yim, J., & Mitchell, H. (2005). Comparison of country risk models: Hybrid neural networks, logit models, discriminant analysis and cluster techniques. *Expert Systems with Applications*, *28*(1), 137–148. [CrossRef]

Zhu, J., Zou, H., Rosset, S., & Hastie, T. (2009). Multi-class adaboost. *Statistics and Its Interface*, *2*(3), 349–360.

Zizi, Y., Oudgou, M., & El Moudden, A. (2020). Determinants and predictors of smes' financial failure: A logistic regression approach. *Risks*, *8*(4), 107. [CrossRef]

Zmijewski, M. E. (1984). Methodological issues related to the estimation of financial distress prediction models. *Journal of Accounting Research*, *22*, 59–82.

Journal of
Risk and Financial Management

MDPI

Article

Using Machine Learning to Understand the Dynamics Between the Stock Market and US Presidential Election Outcomes

Avi Thaker [1], Daniel Sonner [1] and Leo H. Chan [2,*]

[1] Tauroi Technologies, Pacifica, CA 94044, USA; avi@tauroi.com (A.T.); daniel@tauroi.com (D.S.)
[2] Woodbury School of Business, Utah Valley University, Orem, UT 84058, USA
* Correspondence: leohchan@yahoo.com

Abstract: In this paper, we applied an explainable AI model (SHAP feature importance measures) to study the dynamic relationship between stock market returns and the US presidential election outcomes. More specifically, we wanted to study how the market would react the day after the election. AI models have been criticized as black-box models and lack the clarity needed for decision-making by different stakeholders. The explainable AI model we utilized in this model provides more clarity for the outcomes of the model. Using features commonly used by previous studies related to this topic, we find that the previous market direction leading up to the election and the incumbency information combined with the political affiliation are larger drivers for a 1-day post-election market return than sentiment and which party wins the election.

Keywords: machine learning; explainable AI; US presidential election; stock market; SHAP feature importance

1. Introduction

"It is the economy, stupid". —James Carville

The relationship between US presidential elections and stock market performance is a topic that has been widely debated and analyzed by economists, political scientists, and investors. The US stock market has experienced notable fluctuations during election years. For instance, the period leading up to elections often sees increased volatility due to uncertainty about future policies and leadership. The stock market volatility index value typically goes up from 15% to 20% in non-election years to 20% to 25% during election years. Historically, the market tends to respond positively to incumbents who are expected to continue existing policies, while new candidates may provoke caution among investors, if the economy is doing well. On the other hand, there is a general perception that the stock market tends to perform better under a particular political party, with the conventional wisdom being that Republican administrations are better for the markets. However, the empirical evidence on this topic is mixed at best.

There are several theoretical channels through which US presidential elections could impact stock market performance. One prominent argument is that different political parties tend to favor contrasting fiscal and regulatory policies that can have varying effects on corporate profitability and investor sentiment. The Republican party is associated with more business-friendly, pro-market policies such as tax cuts, deregulation, and a hands-off approach to government intervention. In contrast, the Democratic party is often perceived as favoring greater regulation, higher taxes, and a more active role for the federal government in the economy. From this perspective, investors may anticipate better corporate earnings and stock returns under Republican administrations compared to Democratic ones.

Another potential linkage relates to policy uncertainty and market volatility. The election process itself can create uncertainty around the future policy direction, which may lead to increased market fluctuations as investors attempt to price in the potential implications. For example, campaign promises, and policy platforms of presidential candidates could signal major shifts in areas like trade, taxation, or regulation. This uncertainty may dampen investor confidence and contribute to stock market volatility in the lead-up to and aftermath of an election.

Furthermore, the election outcome itself may trigger policy changes that have direct impacts on corporate profitability and the broader macroeconomic environment. Shifts in fiscal, monetary, or regulatory policies under a new administration could affect factors such as consumer spending, business investment, inflation, and interest rates—all of which can influence stock market returns.

While the academic research on the connections between US presidential elections and stock market performance remains inconclusive, there are still important implications for investors and the broader economy to consider. For investors, the perceived relationship between elections and market returns may influence investment strategies and portfolio allocation decisions. Some investors may attempt to time the market or adjust their holdings based on anticipated electoral outcomes. However, the difficulty in accurately predicting market reactions to elections, as well as the potential for unexpected events, can make such strategies risky and prone to poor performance.

Given that deterministic methodology could not come up with a conclusive relationship presidential outcomes and stock market returns, we propose an alternative approach in this paper. More specifically, we developed a machine learning model that includes important features that include both party information and market data to predict the outcome of the presidential election. Once the prediction is made by the model, we then instruct the model to predict the reaction from the stock market the day after the election. The stock market is the most efficient market in the economy. Therefore, the price movements should incorporate all the wisdom of the crowd (Fama, 1970).

In this paper, we utilize the SHAP feature importance method by Lundburg and Lee (2017) to examine the various features that could affect the outcome of the US presidential election. SHAP feature importance allows us to gain insight into the following:

- Model interpretability by showing the contribution of the various features into the model;
- Visual representation;
- A computationally tractable and partially understandable view into black box systems that shows the feature combinations that may be predictive.

By examining SHAP feature importance, we can assess the impact of various model features on predicting the market return the day following the election. We discovered that the most predictive features for post-election market performance were the market direction and whether the candidate had previously held office. While the market direction intuitively showed that a positive trend leading up to the election predicted a positive post-election market outcome, and vice versa, the incumbency of the candidate added an intriguing dimension. Specifically, if a Democratic candidate had prior incumbency, it predicted a downturn in the market the day after the election, whereas prior Republican incumbency predicted an uptick in the market.

The main contribution of this paper is the introduction of an explainable AI model to study the dynamic relationships between features and the predicted outcomes often missing in other machine learning/deep learning models. The remainder of the paper is organized as the following: Section 2 covers recent studies that examined the relationship between US presidential election and stock market performances. Section 3 discusses the methodology and feature selection. We then discuss the model's outcome in Section 4 and conclude the paper in Section 5.

2. Literature Review

While the theoretical linkages between elections and markets seem plausible, the empirical evidence on this relationship has been mixed and inconclusive. Several academic studies have explored this topic, examining stock market returns during different presidential administrations and across party lines.

Hensel and Ziemba (1995) analyzes US investment returns during Democratic and Republican presidencies from 1928 to 1993. It finds significant differences in stock and bond returns based on political administration. Specifically, small-cap stocks experienced notably higher returns during Democratic administrations compared to Republican ones, largely due to fewer losses in the April to December period. In contrast, large-cap stock returns remained statistically similar across both party administrations. The study also highlights that returns on various asset classes were generally higher in the last two years of a presidential term, regardless of party. The authors tested several hypotheses regarding the performance of small-cap and large-cap stocks, as well as corporate and government bonds. They confirmed that small-cap stocks significantly outperformed large-caps during Democratic terms, while bond and cash returns were higher during Republican administrations. The research extends previous findings by emphasizing the small-cap advantage outside of January, and it notes that both small- and large-cap stocks tended to yield better results in the latter half of presidential terms.

Santa-Clara and Valkanov (2003) found that stock returns have been significantly higher under Democratic presidents compared to Republican presidents since 1927. The authors suggested that this outperformance may be attributable to more favorable macroeconomic policies under Democratic administrations, such as lower unemployment and higher productivity growth. The paper also suggests that government spending patterns and their impact on macroeconomic conditions are more important in driving cross-sectional stock returns. Specifically, the authors document that sectors with high government exposure, such as defense contractors and infrastructure-related industries, tend to outperform during periods of increased government spending, regardless of which political party is in power.

However, other studies have challenged this finding, arguing that the apparent Democratic "premium" in stock returns can be explained by other factors. Belo et al. (2013), using a comprehensive dataset spanning from 1930 to 2008, examined the relationship between government spending, political cycles, and the cross-section of stock returns in the United States and found that once you control for variables like the business cycle, monetary policy, and investor sentiment, the link between presidential party and stock returns disappears. The authors challenge the findings of prior studies that have suggested a connection between presidential administrations and stock market performance. The Belo et al. paper argues that the apparent Democratic "premium" in stock returns found in earlier research, such as the Santa-Clara and Valkanov (2003) study, can be explained by other factors beyond just the party affiliation of the president. The Belo et al. paper shows that after controlling for variables like the business cycle, monetary policy, and investor sentiment, the link between presidential party and stock returns disappears. They find no statistically significant difference in stock market performance between Democratic and Republican administrations. Furthermore, the authors find that the effect of government spending on stock returns is more pronounced around elections, as investors anticipate potential changes in fiscal policy. However, these effects are short-lived and do not persist over the longer term. Overall, the study by Belo and his colleagues challenges the notion of a systematic partisan influence on the stock market. The authors argue that broader macroeconomic and policy factors, rather than just political affiliation, are more crucial in determining cross-sectional stock market performance.

Snowberg et al. (2007) examines the impact of partisan politics on economic outcomes, using data from prediction markets and close elections. The authors argue that prediction markets can provide valuable insights into the market's expectations about the economic effects of electoral outcomes. The study analyzes stock market returns in the days surrounding close presidential elections in the United States. The researchers find that the stock market tends to rise in the days immediately following a Republican victory, suggesting that investors anticipate more favorable economic policies under Republican presidents. Specifically, the authors estimate that a Republican victory leads to a 2% increase in stock prices over the three-day period surrounding the election.

The authors also find that the partisan impact on the stock market is larger for unexpected election outcomes. When the election result deviates from pre-election predictions, the market response is more pronounced, indicating that it is the surprise element of the outcome that drives the observed stock price movements. However, the paper notes that these short-term stock market gains following a Republican victory may not persist over the longer term. The authors caution against extrapolating the immediate market reaction into longer-term economic performance, as other factors, such as policy implementation and macroeconomic conditions, can ultimately shape market dynamics. Overall, the Snowberg et al. (2007) study provides evidence that partisan politics can have measurable effects on the stock market, at least in the short run.

One possible explanation for the mixed empirical findings is that the relationship between elections and markets is highly complex and context dependent. The specific economic conditions, policy platforms, and political dynamics at the time of an election can all play a role in shaping market reactions. Furthermore, the stock market may respond more to unexpected election outcomes rather than anticipated results.

Blau and Graham (2019) examines the stock market's performance under Democratic versus Republican presidents in the post-2008 financial crisis period. Contrary to the mixed findings from earlier research, the authors find that the US stock market has performed better under Democratic presidents since the crisis. They attribute this to factors like increased government spending and more favorable economic policies implemented by Democratic administrations in the aftermath of the recession.

Chien et al. (2014) examines the relationship between the stock market's reaction to presidential elections and the economic performance during the subsequent presidential term. Using data from 1900 to 2008 across 27 presidential administrations, the researchers test two hypotheses: (1) there is a relationship between GDP growth during a president's term and the change in stock price immediately after the election, and (2) there is a relationship between unemployment rates during a president's term and the change in stock price after the election. Their analysis also shows that the stock market's reaction after an election has become progressively more accurate in predicting future GDP growth, but not future unemployment rates. The researchers found that Republican presidents tend to govern during periods where unemployment increases over their term, while Democratic presidents tend to see unemployment decrease over their term. Overall, the model appears to provide a good starting point for assessing the economic potential of new presidential administrations based on the market's reaction to their election. Additionally, they find that the stock market has tended to respond negatively to Democratic presidential election wins, dropping in 10 out of 14 cases since 1900. This suggests investors may view Democratic presidents as less favorable for the economy compared to Republican presidents, at least in the short-term market reaction. The researchers conclude their model can help predict future economic performance based on the market's assessment of the election outcome.

On cross-country comparison, Andrada et al. (2020) analyze the relationship between presidential elections and stock returns in Brazil. Their study finds that the election of left-wing presidents in Brazil is associated with lower stock market returns compared to right-wing presidents. The authors suggest this is due to investor perceptions that left-wing policies are less favorable for corporate profits and economic growth. Finally, Jia et al. (2021) examine stock market reactions to the two impeachment trials of former U.S. President Donald Trump. Their findings indicate that the stock market responded positively to events that increased the probability of Trump's removal from office, implying that investors anticipated more market-friendly policies under a new administration. This highlights the importance of considering unexpected political events and their potential impact on investor sentiment and stock performance.

Hashim and Mosallamy (2020) explores the impact of presidential election outcome announcements on stock market return volatility in emerging markets, specifically Egypt, compared to developed markets like the United States. Utilizing a mixed-methods approach, the study incorporates both qualitative data and quantitative analysis, focusing on the EGX100 and S&P500 indices during significant elections. The authors aim to assess whether markets with different economic development levels exhibit similar efficiencies in responding to political events. The findings reveal that presidential elections do not significantly impact stock market volatility in either market. Although there are observable increases in abnormal returns and a decrease in volatility following election announcements, these changes are not statistically significant. This suggests that both markets efficiently absorb the news and integrate it into stock prices without significant shifts in volatility.

A key challenge in understanding the connections between US presidential elections and stock market performance is establishing clear causality. While there may be correlations observed between electoral outcomes and market returns, it can be difficult to determine the underlying causal mechanisms. For instance, it is possible that stock market performance could influence voter preferences and election outcomes, rather than the other way around. Strong economic conditions and rising equity prices may make voters more inclined to support the incumbent party, creating a feedback loop between markets and politics. As such, a deterministic model might leave out important features/connections. A parameter-free machine learning model might be a better choice when there are no clear-cut causalities.

3. Methodology

3.1. Feature Selection and Data Collection

Feature construction is critical to model building, this is especially true when there are low data volumes. The model is constructed using historical election data combined with market information. From the studies reviewed in the previous section, there are three main categories of features we decided to focus on: incumbency, investor sentiment, and market return. We look at these features once per election (every 4 years) with the various features looking back a different number of times. For incumbency data, we noted whether the currently running candidates had held office before, and we also looked at the last three election party winners. For market direction, we looked over three-to-eighteen-month windows leading up to the election, and for market return, we looked from the week before through the year before. Ideally, we would include as many features as possible and allow the model to show the features that are relevant. However, given the length of the data sample, adding too many feature risks resulting in model overfitting. We tried to strike a balance between having a useful number of features while avoiding the risk of overfitting. The primary features used for our model include the following:

- Incumbent party for both candidates and history of which party held office for the prior three elections;
- Market direction over 3–6-, 6–12-, and 12–18-month intervals prior to the election;
- Market returns over various time intervals in the year leading up to the election (between one week and one year leading up to election);
- Sentiment.

Once the data for the features are collected, we feed the data through a fully connected neural network with three hidden layers, which is employed to predict the outcome of elections (Democrat or Republican). Then, the party is added as a feature and used to predict the subsequent market direction (up or down). SHAP analysis is performed to measure feature importance, providing insights into the key drivers of the predictions. The features used in our model are summarized in Table 1. A fully connected network is chosen to maximize the flexibility for data types as sufficiently large fully connected networks can approximate any continuous function. (Nielsen, 1987). The ease of implementation allows for simpler feature contribution and tends to offer better performance for small-scale tasks. Models are simply trained until losses are stabilized and are trained for a long time. Power et al. (2022) explains why we should train for a longer period. Future improvements can be made to see different initializations and see how the model performs. The model and training are less important than the feature selection as we want to showcase the features that tend to be important.

Table 1. Feature descriptions.

Feature	Descriptions
6–12_month_market_direction	1 if market was up from 12 months ago to 6 months prior to election else 0
prev_held_office_democratic	1 if the democratic candidate is an incumbent
3–6_month_market_direction	1 if market was up from 6 months ago to 3 months prior to election else 0
prev_held_office_republican	1 if the republican candidate is an incumbent
previous_party_3	1 if the 3rd most recent president was republican else 0
party	1 if the predicted party is republican else 0
day_before_365	Percent return from 365 days prior to election
12–18_month_market_direction	1 if market was up from 18 months ago to 12 months prior to election else 0
previous_party_2	1 if the 2nd most recent president was republican else 0
previous_party_1	1 if the most recent president was republican else 0
day_before_210	Percent return from 210 days prior to election
sentiment	A score of the favorability of the party in office
day_before_150	Percent return from 150 days prior to election
day_before_30	Percent return from 30 days prior to election
day_before_7	Percent return from 7 days prior to election

All data are collected via publicly available sources. We used LLM tools to analyze relevant news articles to determine the sentiment towards the party in office.

3.2. Model Architectures

We use a combination of neural networks and feature processing as the model architecture. The key components of the model are two neural networks, one fed into the other:

- The first network predicts the winning party;
- The second network, given the party prediction, predicts the market direction;
- Both networks are fully connected with a downward cascade.

Figure 1 shows the model architecture graphically. The model's implementation can be found in Appendix A.

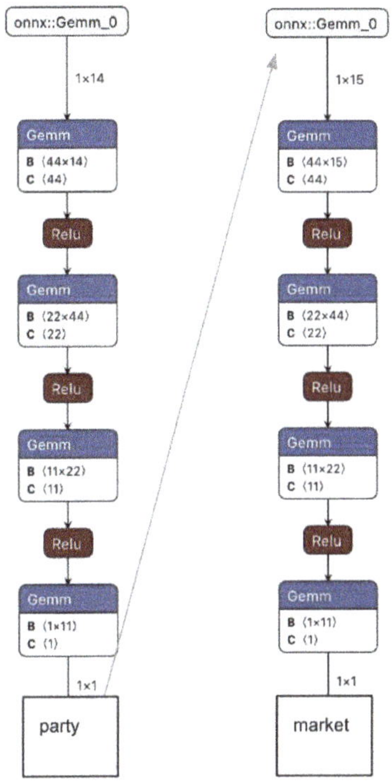

Figure 1. Model architecture.

We run two sequential neural networks: The left network is the party affiliation network, and the right network is the market outcome network. Each network consists of an input layer containing the 14 features we described for the left network and 15 features for the right network (the same 14 features plus the output party feature). The four "Gemm" (Generalized Matrix Multiplication) layers are the hidden layers, with Relu activation functions between each Gemm layer. The layers progressively reduce in size (e.g., 44 -> 22 -> 11 -> 1).

The Figure 2 presents the same model architecture in a DNN format, with three hidden layers between the features for predicting which party might win and how the victory might affect the market's reaction.

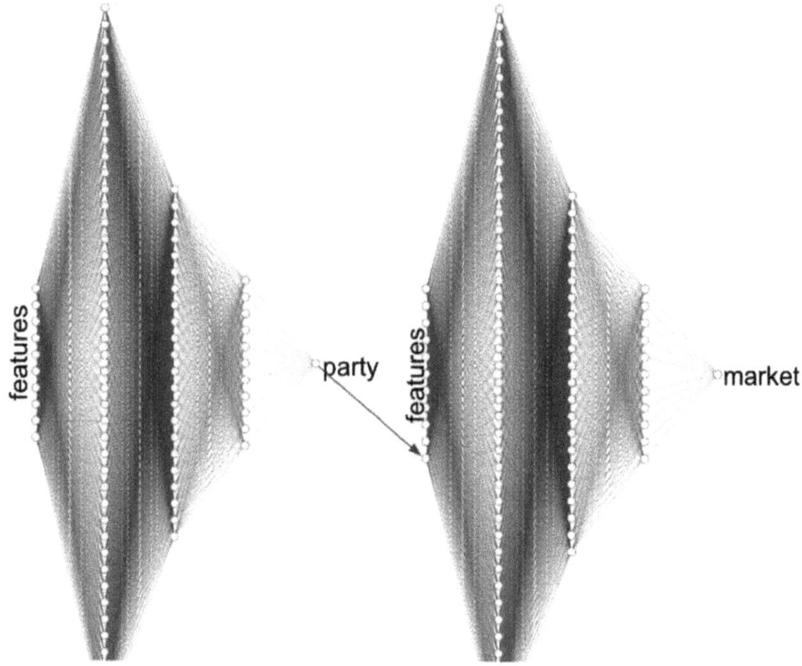

Figure 2. Model architecture in DNN format.

4. Results and Feature Importance

The SHAP summary plot in Figure 3 illustrates the influence of each feature on the model's predictions.

4.1. Model Output Analysis

The results from the SHAP analysis provide a visualization of the influence of each feature on the model's predictions. The SHAP importance plot identifies the most influential feature to be how the stock market performs 6–12 months before the election, which shows a significant spread of SHAP values. The second most impactful feature is party incumbency, as it has the second highest SHAP values, suggesting that a candidate's previous tenure as a Democrat plays a critical role in shaping the electoral outcomes. Additional important features include more recent market performance (3–6 months). This suggests that, while voters likely make their decisions based on the impact of current president's policies on their investment portfolio more than 6 months out, they still care (to a lesser degree) about what happens to the stock market in more recent times. The burst of the 2001 DotCom Bubble and the 2008 Financial Crisis both happened towards the end of the election cycle, validating the importance of this feature. The other important feature is if the Republican party candidate previously held political office, which highlight differing influences of market conditions over shorter periods.

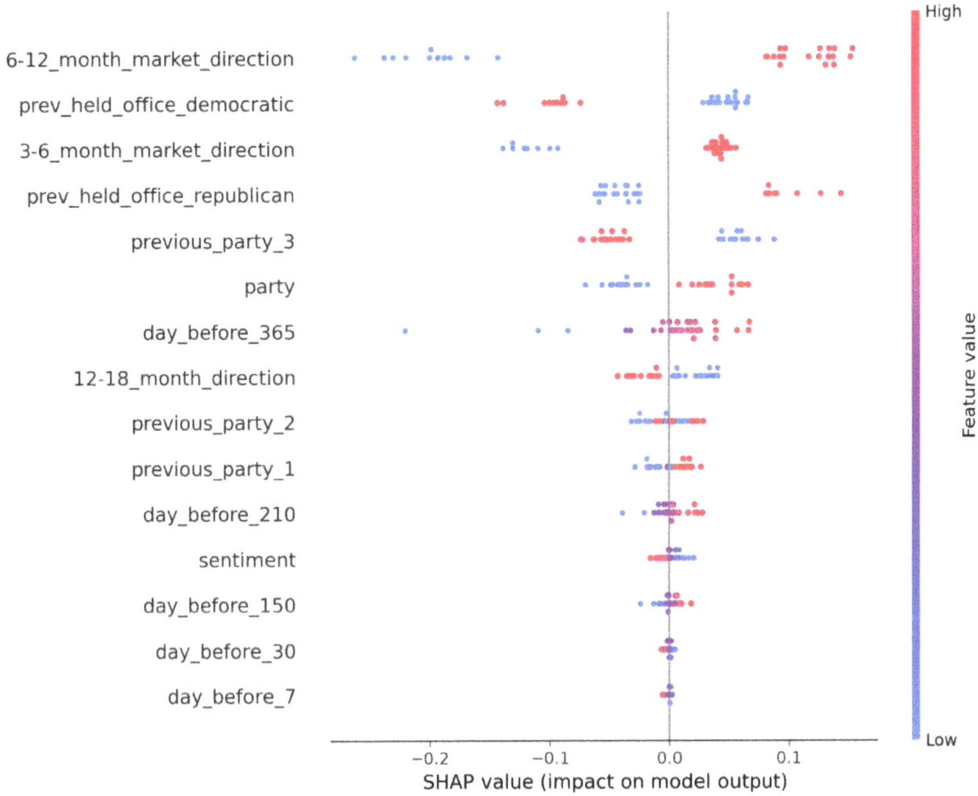

Figure 3. SHAP results for model predicting market direction 1 day after election.

Features related to previous party affiliations and the current party show moderate importance, with varying effects based on their values. Time-based features, such as those reflecting returns from different days leading up to the election, generally exhibit less impact, with SHAP values clustering closer to zero. However, the feature "day_before_365" shows a wider spread, indicating potential relevance from events or conditions a year prior. The sentiment analysis feature appears to have a minor impact, with SHAP values concentrated near zero.

Overall, the findings reveal that market direction over different time frames and candidates' incumbency status are the most crucial factors in the predictive model, while immediate temporal features and sentiment analysis play a lesser role in influencing electoral outcomes.

4.2. Discussion

The findings of this study have several important implications for future studies related to election predictions and stock market reactions. The strong influence of market direction over various time intervals suggests that economic indicators should be prioritized in election forecasting models. Analysts and political strategists may benefit from closely monitoring market performance, as it seems to correlate significantly with electoral outcomes. Additionally, the substantial impact of incumbency—specifically whether a candidate previously held office—highlights the necessity of incorporating political history into predictive models. This could lead to more accurate predictions by accounting for the advantages that incumbents typically enjoy.

Our study also demonstrates the importance of careful feature selection to avoid overfitting. Future models should aim to balance complexity with interpretability, focusing on a limited set of key features that have been shown to drive predictions effectively. While sentiment analysis was found to have a relatively minor impact, its incorporation could still add value, particularly in conjunction with other features. Future models might explore advanced sentiment analysis techniques to capture more nuanced public opinions, especially in volatile political climates.

Given that market conditions and political contexts can change rapidly, models should be designed to adapt dynamically. Incorporating real-time data feeds could help maintain accuracy as new information becomes available in the lead-up to elections. Furthermore, the findings should encourage further research into how these features perform across different election contexts, such as local versus national elections, and various demographic factors. Future studies could validate the model's applicability in varying political landscapes.

5. Conclusions

In this paper, we proposed a predictive model for election outcomes and stock market reactions, using explainable AI techniques. The model integrates historical election data with market information, concentrating on three primary categories of features: party and incumbency, investor sentiment, and market return. While the ideal approach would involve including numerous features to identify their relevance, the use of excessive features could lead to model overfitting, given the small nature of the dataset. As a result, we used a limited number of features and showed how those certain features can be predictive. Specifically, we find that previous market direction leading up to the election and the incumbency information combined with the political affiliation are larger drivers for a 1-day post-election market return than sentiment and which party wins the election.

Author Contributions: Conceptualization, A.T. and D.S.; methodology, A.T. and D.S.; software, A.T. and D.S.; validation, A.T. and D.S.; formal analysis, A.T. and D.S.; resources, A.T. and D.S.; data curation, A.T. and D.S.; writing—original draft preparation, A.T., D.S., and L.H.C.; writing—review and editing, A.T., D.S. and L.H.C.; visualization, A.T., D.S., and L.H.C.; supervision, A.T., D.S., and L.H.C.; project administration, A.T. and D.S. All authors have read and agreed to the published version of the manuscript.

Funding: This research received no external funding.

Institutional Review Board Statement: Not applicable.

Informed Consent Statement: Not applicable.

Data Availability Statement: The raw data supporting the conclusions of this article will be made available by the authors on request.

Conflicts of Interest: Author Avi Thaker and Daniel Sonner were employed by the company Tauroi Technology. The remaining authors declare that the research was conducted in the absence of any commercial or financial relationships that could be construed as a potential conflict of interest.

Appendix A. Python Implementation

```
import os
import pandas as pd
from datetime import datetime, timedelta
import torch
from torch.utils.data import Dataset, DataLoader
from torch import nn
from torch.optim import Adam
import numpy as np
import shap
import seaborn as sns

# import matplotlib for visualization
import matplotlib.pyplot as plt

torch.manual_seed(0)   # set seed for reproducibility


# Define Dataset Class
class ElectionDataset(Dataset):
    def __init__(self, dataframe, features, labels):
        self.dataframe = dataframe
        self.features = dataframe[features].values
        self.labels = dataframe[labels].values
        self.features_str = features

    def __len__(self):
        return len(self.dataframe)

    def __getitem__(self, idx):
        return torch.tensor(self.features[idx, :].astype(np.float32)), torch.tensor(
            self.labels[idx].astype(np.float32)
        )


# Define a simple neural network
class DNNRegressor(nn.Module):
    def __init__(self, input_size):
        super(DNNRegressor, self).__init__()
        self.layer1 = nn.Linear(input_size, 44)
        self.layer2 = nn.Linear(44, 22)
        self.layer3 = nn.Linear(22, 11)
        self.output_layer = nn.Linear(11, 1)
```

```
    def forward(self, x):
        x = torch.relu(self.layer1(x))
        x = torch.relu(self.layer2(x))
        x = torch.relu(self.layer3(x))
        x = self.output_layer(x)
        return x


def run_model(train_loader, test_loader):
    # Model, loss, and optimizer
    model = DNNRegressor(input_size = len(features))
    criterion = nn.MSELoss()
    optimizer = Adam(model.parameters(), lr = 0.001)

    # Training loop
    epochs = 10
    for epoch in range(epochs):
        model.train()
        for inputs, targets in train_loader:
            optimizer.zero_grad()
            outputs = model(inputs)

            loss = criterion(outputs, targets.view(-1, 1))
            loss.backward()
            optimizer.step()

    # Evaluate the model
    model.eval()
    total_loss = 0
    with torch.no_grad():
        for inputs, targets in test_loader:
            outputs = model(inputs)
            loss = criterion(outputs, targets.view(-1, 1))
            total_loss += loss.item()
    return model


def add_explanation(model, loader):
    background = torch.cat([inputs for inputs, targets in loader])

    explainer = shap.GradientExplainer(model, background)

    shap_values = explainer.shap_values(background, nsamples = 200)

    # Adjust SHAP values shape if necessary
    shap_values = np.squeeze(shap_values)  # This removes any single-dimensional entries

    force_plot = shap.summary_plot(
        shap_values = shap_values,
        features = background.numpy(),
        feature_names = loader.dataset.features_str,
```

```
        show = True,
    )
    plt.show()


# Function to compute percentage change
def compute_td_pct(djw, index, days):
    """
    Computes the percent return of `djw` for a specified number of `days` before
    the passed in `index` date being very careful to never choose a future date
    that could create a forward looking bias
    """
    if (index + timedelta(days = 1)) > djw.index[-1]:
        return 0

    ntd = djw.truncate(after = index).iloc[-1]["close"]

    if days > 0:
        n_days_after = djw[index : index + timedelta(days = days)].iloc[-1]["close"]
        pct = (n_days_after - ntd)/n_days_after
    else:
        n_days_before_price = djw[index + timedelta(days = days) : index].iloc[0]["close"]
        pct = (ntd - n_days_before_price)/ntd
    return pct


def process_data():
    # Load and prepare data
    djw = pd.read_csv("djw.csv")
    djw.set_index(pd.to_datetime(djw["date"]), inplace = True)
    data = pd.read_csv("output_data.csv")
    data.set_index(pd.to_datetime(data["date_elected"]), inplace = True)

    # encode stock pct returns leading up to election
    day_before_7 = []
    day_before_30 = []
    day_before_150 = []
    day_before_210 = []
    day_before_365 = []
    for index, row in data.iterrows():
        day_before_7.append(compute_td_pct(djw, index, -7))
        day_before_30.append(compute_td_pct(djw, index, -30))
        day_before_150.append(compute_td_pct(djw, index, -150))
        day_before_210.append(compute_td_pct(djw, index, -210))
        day_before_365.append(compute_td_pct(djw, index, -365))

    data["day_before_7"] = day_before_7
    data["day_before_30"] = day_before_30
    data["day_before_150"] = day_before_150
    data["day_before_210"] = day_before_210
    data["day_before_365"] = day_before_365
```

```
    return data


def predict_result(dataset, model, data):
    # Now we want to predict the very last row in the test set
    inputs, targets = dataset[-1]
    inputs = inputs.unsqueeze(0)
    outputs = model(inputs)
    print(f"Predicted: {outputs.item()}")
    if outputs.item() > 0.5:
        print("Predicted: Republican")
        data.loc[data.index[-1], "party"] = 1.0
    else:
        print("Predicted: Democratic")
        data.loc[data.index[-1], "party"] = 0.0


if __name__ == "__main__":
    data = process_data()
    # Create features and labels
    features = [
        "prev_held_office_democratic",
        "prev_held_office_republican",
        "previous_party_1",
        "previous_party_2",
        "previous_party_3",
        "3-6_month_market_direction",
        "6-12_month_market_direction",
        "12-18_month_direction",
        "sentiment",
        "day_before_7",
        "day_before_30",
        "day_before_150",
        "day_before_210",
        "day_before_365",
    ]

    label = "party"  # what we will predict

    # Split data into training and test sets
    train_size = int(0.99 * len(data))
    train_set, test_set = data[:train_size], data[train_size:]

    # Create datasets
    train_dataset_election = ElectionDataset(train_set, features, label)
    test_dataset_election = ElectionDataset(test_set, features, label)

    # Data loaders
    train_loader_election = DataLoader(
        train_dataset_election, batch_size = 1, shuffle = True
    )
```

```
test_loader_election = DataLoader(
    test_dataset_election, batch_size = 10, shuffle = False
)

# run the training loop and evaluate the model
election_model = run_model(train_loader_election, test_loader_election)

predict_result(test_dataset_election, election_model, data)

# Now do the same training but include the expected winner as a feature and predict the market direction for the
next month
features = features + ["party"]
label = "1_after"   # this time we will predict market direction, up or down

# set up the datasets again with the new feature and label
train_set, test_set = data[:train_size], data[train_size:]
train_dataset = ElectionDataset(train_set, features, label)
test_dataset = ElectionDataset(test_set, features, label)
train_loader = DataLoader(train_dataset, batch_size = 1, shuffle = True)
test_loader = DataLoader(test_dataset, batch_size = 10, shuffle = False)

# run the training loop and evaluate the model
model = run_model(train_loader, test_loader)

# Now we want to predict the very last row in the test set
predict_result(test_dataset, model, data)

model_to_explain = model
loader_to_explain = train_loader
add_explanation(model_to_explain, loader_to_explain)
```

References

Andrada, A. F., Curi, A., & Paiva, L. C. (2020). Presidential elections and stock returns: Evidence from Brazil. *Emerging Markets Review*, *43*, 100693.

Belo, F., Gala, V. D., & Li, J. (2013). Government spending, political cycles, and the cross section of stock returns. *Journal of Financial Economics*, *107*(2), 305–324. [CrossRef]

Blau, B. M., & Graham, M. E. (2019). Political Orientation and Stock Market Performance Since the 2008 Financial Crisis. *Journal of Banking & Finance*, *105*, 35–43.

Chien, W.-W., Mayer, R., & Wang, Z. (2014). Stock Market, Economic Performance, And Presidential Elections. *Journal of Business and Economics Research*, *12*, 159–168. [CrossRef]

Fama, E. F. (1970). Efficient capital markets. *Journal of Finance*, *25*(2), 383–417. [CrossRef]

Hashim, N., & Mosallamy, D. E. (2020). Presidential Elections and Stock Market: A Comparative Study. *Journal of Finance and Economics*, *8*, 116–126. [CrossRef]

Hensel, C. R., & Ziemba, W. T. (1995). United States Investment Returns during Democratic and Republican Administrations, 1928–1993. *Financial Analysts Journal*, *51*, 61–69. Available online: http://www.jstor.org/stable/4479832 (accessed on 30 September 2024). [CrossRef]

Jia, C., Wang, Y., & Xiong, W. (2021). *Market reactions to impeachment*. National Bureau of Economic Research. Working Paper No. w28489.

Lundburg, S., & Lee, S.-I. (2017). A unified approach to interpreting model predictions. *arXiv*. [CrossRef]

Nielsen, R. H. (1987, June 21–24). *Kolmogorov's mapping neural network existence theorem.* International Conference on Neural Networks (Vol. 3, pp. 11–13), San Diego, CA, USA.

Power, A., Burda, Y., Edwards, H., Babuschkin, I., & Misra, V. (2022). Grokking: Generalization Beyond Overfitting on Small Algorithmic Datasets. *arXiv*, arXiv:2201.02177.

Santa-Clara, P., & Valkanov, R. (2003). The presidential puzzle: Political cycles and the stock market. *The Journal of Finance, 58*(5), 1841–1872. [CrossRef]

Snowberg, E., Wolfers, J., & Zitzewitz, E. (2007). Partisan impacts on the economy: Evidence from prediction markets and close elections. *The Quarterly Journal of Economics, 122*(2), 807–829. [CrossRef]

Journal of
Risk and Financial Management

MDPI

Article

Risk-Adjusted Performance of Random Forest Models in High-Frequency Trading

Akash Deep [1,*], Abootaleb Shirvani [2], Chris Monico [1], Svetlozar Rachev [1] and Frank Fabozzi [3]

1 Department of Mathematics and Statistics, Texas Tech University, Lubbock, TX 79409, USA; c.monico@ttu.edu (C.M.); zari.rachev@ttu.edu (S.R.)
2 Department of Mathematical Sciences, Kean University, Union, NJ 07083, USA; ashirvan@kean.edu
3 Carey Business School, Johns Hopkins University, Baltimore, MD 21218, USA; ffabozz1@jhu.edu
* Correspondence: akash.deep@ttu.edu

Abstract: Because of the theoretical challenges posed by the Efficient Market Hypothesis with respect to technical analysis, the effectiveness of technical indicators in high-frequency trading remains inadequately explored, particularly at the minute-level frequency, where the effects of the microstructure of the market dominate. This study evaluates the integration of traditional technical indicators with Random Forest regression models using minute-level SPY data, analyzing 13 distinct model configurations. Our empirical results reveal a stark contrast between in-sample and out-of-sample performance, with R^2 values deteriorating from 0.749–0.812 during training to negative values in testing. A feature importance analysis demonstrates that primary price-based features dominate the predictions made by the model, accounting for over 60% of the importance, while established technical indicators, such as RSI and Bollinger Bands, account for only 14–15%. Although the indicator-enhanced models achieved superior risk-adjusted metrics, with Rachev ratios between 0.919 and 0.961, they consistently underperformed a simple buy-and-hold strategy, generating returns ranging from −2.4% to −3.9%. These findings challenge conventional assumptions about the usefulness of technical indicators in algorithmic trading, suggesting that in high-frequency contexts, they may be more relevant to risk management rather than to predicting returns. For practitioners and researchers, our findings indicate that successful high-frequency trading strategies should focus on adaptive feature selection and regime-specific modeling rather than relying on traditional technical indicators, as well as indicating the critical importance of robust out-of-sample testing in the development of a model.

Keywords: high-frequency data; technical indicators; machine learning; stock price prediction; risk-adjusted performance; Random Forest regression

1. Introduction

The accurate prediction of the stock market remains a fundamental yet highly challenging objective in financial research due to the volatility, noise, and stochasticity in financial markets. As Aldridge (2013) point out, the increasing prevalence of high-frequency trading (HFT), where trades are executed within milliseconds, has intensified the demand for predictive models that can rapidly adapt to market fluctuations and structural complexity. However, developing such models requires overcoming significant hurdles, including the inherent noise in high-frequency data and the rapid shifts in market sentiment, as documented by Gu et al. (2020).

A central theoretical debate in financial economics revolves around the effectiveness of technical indicators in predicting prices. The Efficient Market Hypothesis (EMH) proposed by Fama (1970) suggests that asset prices fully incorporate all available information, rendering historical price-based signals ineffective for forecasting. However, the continued widespread use of technical indicators by traders raises questions about the validity of this assumption, particularly in short-term, high-frequency contexts. As Barberis and Thaler (2003) point out, technical analysis may capture behavioral biases, such as herding and overconfidence, that contribute to transient market inefficiencies being manifested in the prices. These biases are particularly pronounced at the minute level, where noise traders (market participants who rely on historical patterns rather than fundamental analysis) may introduce temporary mispricings that machine learning models could exploit.

Machine learning (ML) has emerged as a powerful tool for predicting stock prices, enabling the identification of nonlinear dependencies and complex relationships within historical data. Traditional statistical methods, such as autoregressive integrated moving average (ARIMA) and generalized autoregressive conditional heteroskedasticity (GARCH) models, often struggle to capture the intricate price dynamics of high-frequency markets, due to their assumptions of linearity. By contrast, ML models, such as Random Forest regression (RFR), support vector regression (SVR), and gradient boosting, have demonstrated improved predictive performance in financial applications (Derbentsev et al., 2020). However, their effectiveness is highly contingent on the feature selection, particularly in high-frequency trading environments where the dominance of market noise presents a formidable challenge.

Technical analysis, as outlined by Murphy (1999), employs historical price and volume data through indicators such as Bollinger Bands, exponential moving averages (EMAs), and the Commodity Channel Index (CCI), to detect trends and signal potential price reversals. These indicators aim to reflect aggregate market sentiment and trader behavior. However, their effectiveness in HFT is still debated. Studies such as Abrol et al. (2016) suggest that traditional technical indicators often generate unreliable signals in high-frequency environments, where rapid price fluctuations introduce significant noise. Although recent research has examined the integration of technical indicators with machine learning models (Fischer & Krauss, 2018; Zanc et al., 2019), much of this work has focused on daily or hourly data, leaving the complexities of minute-level stock price movements relatively unexplored (F. Zhang, 2010).

In the present paper, we assess the predictive and risk management performance of Random Forest regression models augmented with technical indicators for high-frequency stock price prediction. Building on previous research that primarily focuses on daily or hourly data, we extend the analysis to minute-level data, incorporating advanced risk-adjusted performance metrics. This allows us to examine the interplay between technical indicators and the effects of the microstructure of the market, providing new insights into their role in high-frequency trading.

This study tests the hypothesis that while incorporating technical indicators can improve risk-adjusted performance, their effectiveness at prediction diminishes in volatile, high-frequency environments where noise dominates the signal. In particular, we expect that primary price-based features will contribute more significantly to the predictions of the model than the technical indicators will, aligning with prior evidence for their limited predictive power in short-term trading. In addition, we evaluate the alignment of our findings with the Efficient Market Hypothesis (EMH) by analyzing in-sample versus out-of-sample performance. Our findings provide empirical support for the semi-strong form of the EMH, which is that while technical indicators may be able to briefly exploit market inefficiencies, their predictive power is limited.

Unlike many existing studies, which primarily evaluate technical indicators in daily or hourly trading, our paper is among the first to systematically assess their effectiveness at the minute level, a granularity where the effects of the microstructures of the market and noise dominate. Furthermore, prior studies have predominantly relied on conventional evaluation metrics, such as root mean squared error (RMSE) and R-squared (R^2), which provide limited insight into risk-adjusted performance. In contrast, our study employs advanced risk–reward measures, including the Rachev ratio and the gains–loss ratio, offering a more comprehensive evaluation in high-frequency contexts of trading strategies based on machine learning (Cheridito & Kromer, 2013). By combining insights from technical analysis, machine learning, behavioral finance, and advanced risk management, this paper provides actionable implications for both academics and practitioners seeking to refine predictive modeling techniques for financial markets.

Our findings indicate that while technical-indicator-augmented models obtain superior risk-adjusted metrics, when it comes to generating excess returns, they perform worse than a simple buy-and-hold strategy. Following the framework established by Barberis and Thaler (2003), our results suggest that while technical indicators can enhance risk management, they may not provide sufficient predictive power to consistently outperform baseline strategies in high-frequency environments dominated by market noise and sentiment-driven trading behavior. These insights emphasize the importance of selective feature engineering, regime-aware modeling, and adaptive risk management techniques in the application of machine learning to financial markets so as to improve the stability of the predictions in high-frequency contexts.

2. Literature Review

Predicting stock prices has been a long-standing challenge due to the volatility and complexity of the market. The Efficient Market Hypothesis (EMH) suggests that prices fully reflect all available information, leaving little room for prediction (Fama, 1970). However, behavioral finance research has identified systematic deviations from market efficiency, particularly in high-frequency contexts where noise traders may rely heavily on technical indicators (Barberis & Thaler, 2003). This tension between rational finance and behavioral finance provides a motivation for evaluating the effectiveness of such technical indicators, as noise traders lacking access to fundamental data may disproportionately rely on technical indicators, potentially creating temporary market inefficiencies (Shleifer & Vishny, 1997).

Advances in machine learning (ML) and the increasing availability of high-frequency trading (HFT) data have made possible the empirical investigation of these theoretical predictions. Traditional econometric models, such as ARIMA and GARCH, were initially used for forecasting stock prices but often struggled with nonstationary data and volatility clustering, as noted by G. Zhang et al. (1998) and J. Patel et al. (2015). These limitations pointed to the need for integrating ML techniques with traditional financial models in order to improve their predictive accuracy.

In the mid-1990s, ensemble methods, such as Random Forest, were developed, demonstrating robustness in handling high-dimensional datasets and reducing overfitting through bagging (Ho, 1995). Recent studies have demonstrated the role of ML in enabling adaptive strategic behaviors on the part of high-frequency traders. By leveraging tools like genetic algorithms, traders can process complex information about the microstructure of the market and optimize their trading strategies in real time, significantly enhancing their profitability under varying conditions (Arifovic et al., 2022). The interaction between the speed of the trading and the efficiency of the market has also been explored, finding a hump-shaped relation between speed, efficiency, and the profitability of the trader.

By the early 2000s, studies like Bollinger (2002) began exploring technical indicators, such as Bollinger Bands (BBs), to gauge market trends and overbought or oversold conditions. Meanwhile, the Commodity Channel Index (CCI) and Exponential Moving Average (EMA) emerged as widely used tools for capturing short-term price movements (Lambert, 1983; Murphy, 1999). However, the standalone use of these indicators often yielded inconsistent results, particularly in noisy and volatile environments, such as HFT (F. Zhang, 2010).

As ML techniques advanced, studies in the 2010s began integrating technical indicators with ML models to improve the predictive performance. For instance, Fischer and Krauss (2018) demonstrated that combining technical indicators with LSTM networks could reduce noise in high-frequency stock data and enhance the accuracy of the predictions. Gu et al. (2020) expanded on this by showing that ML can uncover market inefficiencies, though these tend to be temporary and limited in nature. Their work emphasized the importance of robust out-of-sample testing and careful feature selection in predictive modeling.

Despite these advances, challenges such as overfitting and generalization remained. Researchers like Agrawal et al. (2019) emphasized the importance of domain-specific feature selection to mitigate these problems, while Lim and Zohren (2021) emphasized the need for dynamic models capable of adapting to changing market conditions. Akyildirim et al. (2023) demonstrated that Random Forest models excel at identifying nonlinear patterns in data and perform consistently across different time scales, making them particularly suitable for high-frequency stock price forecasting, where complex relationships exist.

By the early 2020s, the focus shifted toward hybrid strategies combining multiple technical indicators and ML techniques. Zanc et al. (2019) explored the integration of BBs with LSTM networks, showing improvements in predictive accuracy under volatile market conditions. At the same time, studies began addressing the limitations of traditional evaluation metrics, such as the Sharpe and Sortino ratios, which often assume that the returns are normally distributed. Advanced risk–reward metrics, such as the Rachev and modified Rachev ratios, were introduced to provide a more nuanced understanding of how a model performs in volatile environments (Cheridito & Kromer, 2013).

Recent work has increasingly focused on high-frequency data and their unique challenges. Kearns and Nevmyvaka (2013) highlighted the difficulties of extracting meaningful signals from noisy HFT data, while O'Hara (2015) emphasized that market microstructure takes on heightened importance at very fast speeds. These studies underscore the need for models that balance predictive power with robustness against market noise.

Despite substantial progress, significant gaps remain in the literature. Much of the existing work has focused on lower-frequency data, leaving minute-level and tick-level observations underexplored (F. Zhang, 2010). Advanced risk–reward metrics, though proposed, have seen limited application in HFT contexts. Hybrid strategies combining multiple technical indicators have shown promise, but their incremental benefits over simpler models are not well documented. Generalization challenges persist, particularly in HFT settings, where fleeting arbitrage opportunities and high levels of noise increase the risk of overfitting.

This paper contributes to the field by systematically evaluating the predictive and risk-adjusted performance, in an HFT context, of Random Forest regression models combined with technical indicators. It incorporates advanced risk–reward metrics to provide a comprehensive assessment of model performance. This paper also addresses generalization issues through rigorous validation techniques and highlights the limited utility of technical indicators in highly volatile settings. By combining technical analysis, ML, and risk management, this paper offers actionable insights for practitioners and researchers aiming to refine predictive modeling in financial markets.

3. Method

In this section, we describe the data acquisition process, the computation of the technical indicators, the ML model (Random Forest regressor), and the trading simulation framework. The decisions made at each step are guided by the need to rigorously assess the impact of technical indicators on stock price prediction using a Random Forest.

3.1. Data Acquisition and Preprocessing

The dataset used in this study consists of minute-level historical stock data for the SPY (S&P 500 ETF), covering the period from April 2024 to September 2024. The data include essential fields such as the opening, high, low, and close prices, as well as the trading volume, for each minute. The data were obtained from the Bloomberg Terminal, ensuring high accuracy and reliability (L. P. Bloomberg, 2024). Each data point is timestamped in Central Time (CT), and the dataset covers the typical US stock market hours from 9:30 a.m. to 4:00 p.m. Eastern Time (ET), adjusted for daylight savings time.

Additionally, the 10-year US Treasury yield is incorporated as a proxy for the risk-free rate, a crucial factor in calculating excess returns. These data are reported daily and were also sourced from the Bloomberg Terminal, spanning the same time frame as the SPY data (Pástor & Stambaugh, 2003).

3.1.1. Log Returns and Volatility

To normalize the stock price data and reduce the effects of scale, we compute the log returns for the opening, high, low, and closing prices. Log returns are preferred in financial time series due to their ability to capture percentage changes and handle volatility over time (Box et al., 2015). The log return for a price series P_t is

$$\text{log\_return}_t = \log\left(\frac{P_t}{P_{t-1}}\right), \tag{1}$$

where P_t is the price at time t. This process is also defined for the opening, high, low, and closing prices, with the resulting log returns stored as additional columns in the dataset. Additionally, we compute rolling Z-scores for the trading volume to capture anomalies in the volume. The rolling Z-score of the volume is (Box et al., 2015)

$$\text{volz}_t = \frac{\text{volume}_t - \text{mean}(\text{volume})}{\text{std}(\text{volume})}, \tag{2}$$

where the mean and standard deviation are computed over a rolling window of 60 min.

The 10-year US Treasury yield, provided on a daily basis, is used to compute a per-minute risk-free rate, which is necessary for calculating excess returns. For any minute t within a trading day d, the transformation from the daily yield to a per-minute rate is given by

$$r_{\text{per-minute}}(t) = \left(1 + r_{\text{daily}}(d)\right)^{\frac{1}{1440}} - 1, \tag{3}$$

where 1440 is the number of minutes in a day and $r_{\text{daily}}(d)$ is the daily risk-free rate derived from the most recently available Treasury yield prior to day d. This ensures that each minute's risk-free rate reflects the prevailing daily rate for its trading day.

3.1.2. Data Filtering and Splitting

The dataset is filtered to focus on regular market trading hours, between 10:00 a.m. and 3:30 p.m. CT, to avoid periods of low liquidity, such as pre-market and after-hours trading (McGroarty et al., 2019). The filtered dataset is then split into training and testing sets, with 80% of the data allocated to training and 20% to testing. The splitting is time-ordered to preserve the temporal nature of the stock price data and avoid data leakage.

The processed dataset is used for computing a set of technical indicators, which serve as input features for the ML models described in subsequent sections. The computed technical indicators include the simple moving average (SMA), EMA, moving average convergence divergence (MACD), Relative Strength Index (RSI), and others, as detailed below.

3.2. System Architecture

Figure 1 presents a comprehensive view of our ML-based trading system, illustrating the interconnections between the processing of the data, the development of the model, and the evaluation of the performance.

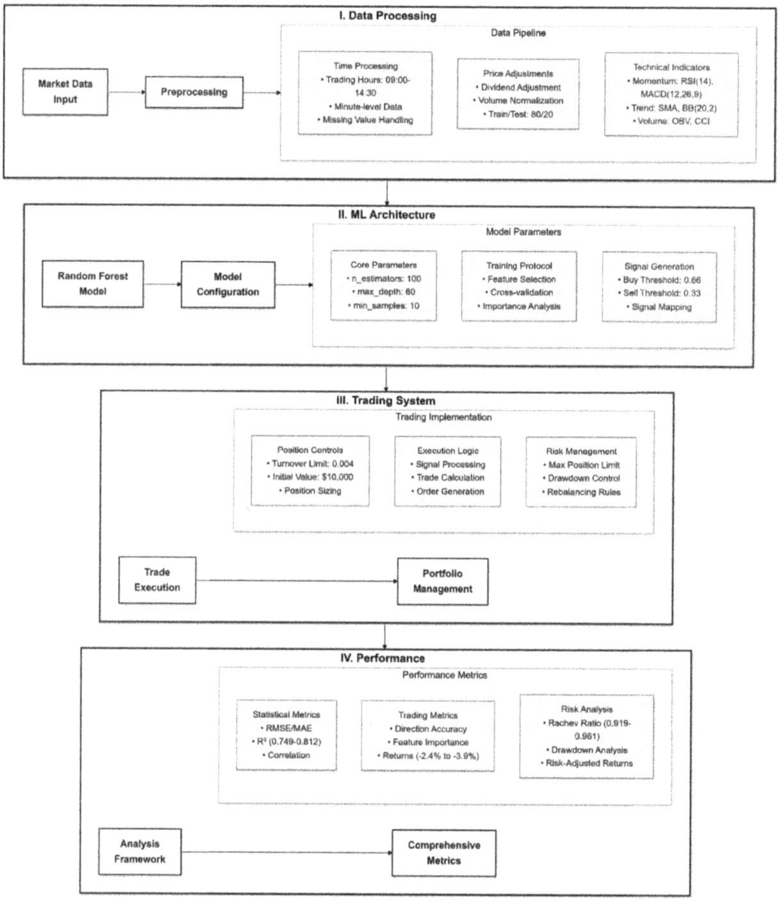

Figure 1. Architecture of the ML-based trading system. There are four integrated phases: (I) Data processing: handling minute-level SPY data (09:00 to 14:30), incorporating dividend adjustments, and computing technical indicators including RSI (14), MACD (12, 26, 9), and Bollinger Bands (20, 2); (II) ML architecture: Random Forest implementation with the specific hyperparameters (n_estimators = 100, max_depth = 60) and quantile-based signal generation (buy: 0.66, sell: 0.33); (III) trading system: real-time position management with turnover constraints (0.004) and initial capital allocation (USD 10,000); and (IV) performance analysis: comprehensive evaluation using statistical metrics (the range of values of R^2 is 0.749 to 0.812) and risk-adjusted measures (Rachev ratio: 0.919 to 0.961). This system is an example of a practical integration of traditional technical analysis with modern ML approaches while emphasizing risk management and computational efficiency in high-frequency trading contexts.

Our implementation follows a systematic approach where the data preprocessing feeds into the ML pipeline, which in turn feeds into the trading decisions. This framework incorporates comprehensive risk management and performance evaluation, ensuring the robust validation of the strategy's effectiveness. Each component is optimized for high-frequency trading, with particular attention to computational efficiency and real-time processing.

3.3. Technical Indicators

To capture diverse aspects of market behavior, we selected a set of widely recognized technical indicators, each chosen for its unique contribution to predicting price movements or managing risk. These technical indicators encompass a variety of trend-following, momentum, and volume-based metrics, enabling a robust, multi-faceted analysis of minute-level price movements.

For instance, the EMA and MACD offer insights into the strength and direction of a trend, whereas BBs and the RSI gauge the volatility and overbought/oversold conditions, respectively (Murphy, 1999). The average directional index (ADX) measures the robustness of a trend, the on-balance volume (OBV) measures the volume flow, and the CCI detects cyclical price movements (Lambert, 1983). By combining these technical indicators, we aimed to create a feature set capable of reflecting both short-term and long-term market dynamics, thus enhancing the predictive accuracy and enabling nuanced risk management (Zanc et al., 2019).

Unless otherwise specified, all non-trivial technical indicator formulae presented are derived from the seminal work (Murphy, 1999).

3.3.1. Simple Moving Average (SMA)

The SMA smooths price data by averaging the closing prices over a window of N periods:

$$\mathrm{SMA}_{N,t} = \frac{1}{N}\sum_{i=0}^{N-1} C_{t-i}, \tag{4}$$

where C_t denotes the closing price at time t. In our implementation, the current price is normalized by the SMA:

$$\hat{\mathrm{SMA}}_{N,t} = \frac{C_t}{\mathrm{SMA}_{N,t}}. \tag{5}$$

This ensures scale invariance and helps the model better learn from the price data.

3.3.2. Exponential Moving Average (EMA)

The EMA places more weight on recent prices, making it more responsive to changes in prices. It is calculated recursively as follows:

$$\mathrm{EMA}_t = \alpha C_t + (1-\alpha)\mathrm{EMA}_{t-1}, \tag{6}$$

where $\alpha = \frac{2}{N+1}$ is the smoothing factor for a window size N. In our implementation, the EMA is normalized similarly to the SMA:

$$\hat{\mathrm{EMA}}_t = \frac{C_t}{\mathrm{EMA}_t}. \tag{7}$$

This ratio stabilizes the feature and makes it more useful for prediction.

3.3.3. Moving Average Convergence Divergence (MACD)

The MACD measures the difference between short-term and long-term EMAs. It is computed as follows:

$$\text{MACD}_t = \text{EMA}_{12,t} - \text{EMA}_{26,t}. \tag{8}$$

This signal line SIG_t is a nine-period EMA of the MACD line. We use the following ratio to normalize the MACD:

$$r_{\text{MACD},t} = \frac{\text{MACD}_t - \text{SIG}_t}{0.5(|\text{MACD}_t| + |\text{SIG}_t|)}. \tag{9}$$

which ensures that large fluctuations in the MACD do not overwhelm the model.

3.3.4. Relative Strength Index (RSI)

The RSI is a momentum oscillator that measures the speed and change of price movements (Wilder, 1978). It is computed as follows:

$$\text{RSI}_t = 100 - \frac{100}{1 + \frac{\text{avg\_gain}_t}{\text{avg\_loss}_t}}, \tag{10}$$

where avg_gain_t and avg_loss_t are the exponentially smoothed averages of the gains and losses over a window of 14 periods. The RSI ranges from 0 to 100, identifying possible overbought and oversold conditions.

3.3.5. Bollinger Bands (BBs)

Bollinger bands are volatility bands placed two standard deviations above and below a moving average. They are defined by

$$\text{UBB}_t = \text{SMA}_{N,t} + 2\sigma_t, \quad \text{LBB}_t = \text{SMA}_{N,t} - 2\sigma_t, \tag{11}$$

where σ_t is the standard deviation of the prices over the last N periods (Bollinger, 2002). The normalized BB percentage is

$$\text{BB\%}_t = \frac{C_t - \text{LBB}_t}{\text{UBB}_t - \text{LBB}_t}. \tag{12}$$

which captures where the price sits within the volatility bands.

3.3.6. Stochastic Oscillator (SO)

The stochastic oscillator (SO) measures the relative position of the closing price compared to the high–low range over a specified period (typically 14 periods). It is computed as follows:

$$\%K_t = 100 \times \frac{C_t - L_{14,t}}{H_{14,t} - L_{14,t}}, \tag{13}$$

where $L_{14,t}$ and $H_{14,t}$ denote the lowest and highest prices over the last 14 periods. The slow stochastic oscillator $\%D_t$ is a three-period moving average of $\%K_t$.

3.3.7. Fibonacci Retracement (Fib)

The Fibonacci retracement is used to identify potential support and resistance levels in a price trend. For a window N, the retracement level is

$$R_t = \frac{H_{N,t} - C_t}{H_{N,t} - L_{N,t}}, \tag{14}$$

where $H_{N,t}$ and $L_{N,t}$ are the highest and lowest prices over the window. We use common Fibonacci levels (0.236, 0.382, 0.500, 0.618, 0.764) to identify potential reversal points.

3.3.8. Average Directional Index (ADX)

The ADX measures the strength of a trend, regardless of its direction. The ADX is derived from the directional movement indicators DI_t^+ and DI_t^-:

$$\mathrm{ADX}_t = \frac{|DI_t^+ - DI_t^-|}{DI_t^+ + DI_t^-}. \tag{15}$$

The directional movement indicators DI_t^+ and DI_t^- are normalized by the average true range (ATR).

3.3.9. On-Balance Volume (OBV)

The OBV is a cumulative indicator that sums the volumes, depending on whether the price is rising or falling:

$$\mathrm{OBV}_t = \mathrm{OBV}_{t-1} + \mathrm{sgn}(C_t - C_{t-1})V_t, \tag{16}$$

where V_t is the trading volume at time t, and the signum function determines the direction of the volume flow.

3.3.10. Windowed Relative OBV (WROBV)

The windowed relative OBV (WROBV) is a modified version of the OBV. It is the weighted sum of the values, for a rolling window of size N, of the cumulative OBV. This smooths out the indicator:

$$\mathrm{WROBV}_t = \frac{\sum_{i=0}^{N-1} \mathrm{OBV}_{t-i}}{\sum_{i=0}^{N-1} V_{t-i}}. \tag{17}$$

This rolling normalization prevents the OBV from becoming excessively large and focuses on recent price–volume dynamics.

3.3.11. Commodity Channel Index (CCI)

The CCI measures the deviation of the typical price from its moving average:

$$p_t = \frac{H_t + L_t + C_t}{3}. \tag{18}$$

Mathematically, CCI is given by

$$\mathrm{CCI}_t = \frac{p_t - \mathrm{SMA}_{N,t}}{0.015 \times \mathrm{MAD}_t}, \tag{19}$$

where MAD_t is the mean, over a rolling window of size N, of the absolute deviations of p_t.

3.3.12. Ichimoku Cloud (Ichimoku)

The Ichimoku Cloud is a comprehensive technical indicator that provides a holistic view of support, resistance, the direction of the trend, and momentum (M. Patel, 2010). It has five main components:

- Tenkan-sen (Conversion Line): This line is a short-term indicator calculated as the midpoint of the highest high and the lowest low over the past N periods:

$$\mathrm{Tenkan}_t = \frac{\max(H_{t-N}, \ldots, H_t) + \min(L_{t-N}, \ldots, L_t)}{2}, \tag{20}$$

  where H_t and L_t denote the high and low prices at time t, respectively. Typically, $N = 9$.

- Kijun-sen (Base Line): The base line is a longer-term indicator calculated similarly to the Tenkan-sen but over a longer window M:

$$\text{Kijun}_t = \frac{\max(H_{t-M}, \ldots, H_t) + \min(L_{t-M}, \ldots, L_t)}{2}. \tag{21}$$

  This line provides a measure of medium-term momentum, with $M = 26$ being a common value.
- Senkou Span A (Leading Span A): Senkou Span A is the midpoint between the Tenkan-sen and Kijun-sen, plotted M periods ahead:

$$\text{Senkou A}_t = \frac{\text{Tenkan}_t + \text{Kijun}_t}{2} \quad \text{(shifted forward by } M \text{ periods).} \tag{22}$$

  This span, along with the following Senkou Span B, forms the Ichimoku Cloud.
- Senkou Span B (Leading Span B): This span is the midpoint of the highest high and lowest low over the past L periods and is also plotted M periods ahead:

$$\text{Senkou B}_t = \frac{\max(H_{t-L}, \ldots, H_t) + \min(L_{t-L}, \ldots, L_t)}{2} \quad \text{(shifted forward by } M \text{ periods).} \tag{23}$$

  The area between Senkou Span A and Senkou Span B is shaded to form the 'cloud,' which can act as dynamic support or resistance.
- Chikou Span (Lagging Span): The Chikou Span is the current closing price plotted M periods in the past:

$$\text{Chikou}_t = C_t \quad \text{(shifted backward by } M \text{ periods).} \tag{24}$$

  This line provides a lagging indication of price action and helps confirm the direction of a trend.

Ichimoku Cloud provides a visual representation of support and resistance, the direction of a trend, and momentum. The interaction between the price and the cloud helps identify potential reversals or continuations in the trend. In our implementation, we calculate all five components of the Ichimoku cloud and incorporate the leading spans (Senkou A and Senkou B) as features in the machine learning model.

3.4. Random Forest and Validation

The underlying predictive model in our framework uses a Random Forest regressor (RFR), which is an ensemble learning method that aggregates predictions from multiple decision trees to capture complex, non-linear relations in high-frequency financial data (Breiman, 2001; Buitinck et al., 2013; Ho, 1995). Let $\mathcal{D} = \{(\mathbf{x}_i, y_i)\}_{i=1}^n$ denote our training dataset, where $\mathbf{x}_i \in \mathbb{R}^p$ denotes the feature vector consisting of technical indicators and price-based features at time i, and $y_i \in \mathbb{R}$ denotes the corresponding log return.

The RFR constructs an ensemble of B decision trees, where each tree T_b is trained on a bootstrap sample $\mathcal{D}_b$ drawn with replacement from $\mathcal{D}$. For a given input vector $\mathbf{x}$, the model's prediction is

$$\hat{f}(\mathbf{x}) = \frac{1}{B} \sum_{b=1}^{B} T_b(\mathbf{x}), \tag{25}$$

where $T_b(\mathbf{x})$ denotes the prediction of the b-th tree. Each individual tree is constructed by recursively partitioning the feature space to minimize the mean squared error (MSE):

$$\text{MSE}(t) = \frac{1}{|\mathcal{D}_t|} \sum_{i \in \mathcal{D}_t} (y_i - \bar{y}_t)^2, \tag{26}$$

where $\mathcal{D}_t$ denotes the set of training samples at node t and $\bar{y}_t$ is the mean response value in node t.

Our implementation employs scikit-learn's Random Forest Regressor with the following parametrization:

$$\Theta = \{\theta_B, \theta_d, \theta_s, \theta_f, \theta_l, \theta_r\}, \tag{27}$$

where $\theta_B = 100$ (n_estimators), $\theta_d = 60$ (max_depth), $\theta_s = 10$ (min_samples_split), $\theta_f =$ 'log2' (max_features), $\theta_l = 1$ (min_samples_leaf), and $\theta_r = 42$ (random_state). This configuration performs cross-validation through Out-of-Bag (OOB) sampling (Hastie et al., 2009), where approximately one-third of the observations are automatically held out during the training of each tree, serving as a built-in validation set.

To determine the signal, we employ a quantile-based thresholding mechanism. Let $\hat{f}(\mathbf{x}_t)$ be the model's prediction at time t. During training, we compute threshold values $q_{0.33}$ and $q_{0.66}$, which are the 33rd and 66th percentiles of the model's predictions on the training set. The signal function $s : \mathbb{R} \to \{\text{"sell"}, \text{"hold"}, \text{"buy"}\}$ is defined by

$$s(\hat{f}(\mathbf{x}_t)) = \begin{cases} \text{"buy"} & \text{if } \hat{f}(\mathbf{x}_t) \geq q_{0.66} \\ \text{"hold"} & \text{if } q_{0.33} < \hat{f}(\mathbf{x}_t) < q_{0.66} \\ \text{"sell"} & \text{if } \hat{f}(\mathbf{x}_t) \leq q_{0.33} \end{cases} \tag{28}$$

The importance of a feature is computed using the mean decrease in impurity across all trees:

$$I_j = \frac{1}{B} \sum_{b=1}^{B} \sum_{t \in \mathcal{T}_b} \Delta\text{MSE}_{t,j} \mathbb{1}(v(t) = j), \tag{29}$$

where $\mathcal{T}_b$ is the set of nodes in tree b, $v(t)$ is the feature used for splitting at node t, and $\Delta\text{MSE}_{t,j}$ is the decrease in MSE achieved by splitting on feature j at node t.

For temporal validation, we employ a chronological partitioning:

$$\mathcal{D}_{\text{train}} = \{(\mathbf{x}_i, y_i)\}_{i=1}^{\lfloor 0.8n \rfloor}, \quad \mathcal{D}_{\text{test}} = \{(\mathbf{x}_i, y_i)\}_{i=\lfloor 0.8n \rfloor + 1}^{n}, \tag{30}$$

ensuring strict temporal ordering and preventing look-ahead bias. This 80–20 split, combined with the OOB error estimation, provides a robust validation framework that appropriately handles both the ensemble nature of Random Forests and the sequential characteristics of high-frequency trading data. As demonstrated by Hastie et al. (2009), the OOB error estimate is nearly equivalent to leave-one-out cross-validation, providing an unbiased estimate of the test error and making additional k-fold cross-validation unnecessary.

While time-series cross-validation (TSCV), such as rolling or walk-forward validation, is a common approach in the forecasting of financial time-series, its application to high-frequency trading (HFT) remains computationally intensive. Given the ensemble nature of Random Forests and the strict temporal partitioning employed in our study, we rely on Out-of-Bag (OOB) error estimation as an efficient alternative. This method maintains the chronological integrity of the data while avoiding excessive computational overhead. Future research should explore the trade-off between computational feasibility and the robustness benefits of TSCV, particularly in adaptive trading models where market regimes shift dynamically.

3.5. Trading Simulation

We simulate a trading strategy based on the buy, sell, and hold signals generated by the Random Forest model. The trading simulation starts with an initial value of USD 10,000. The following actions are taken based on the predictions of the model:

- Buy Signal: If the model predicts an upward price movement, a portion of the available cash is used to buy shares.
- Sell Signal: If a downward price movement is predicted, a portion of the holdings is sold.
- Hold Signal: If no significant price movement is predicted, no action is taken.

To approximate real-world trading constraints, we impose a turnover constraint limiting position changes in any minute to 0.4% of the portfolio value:

$$\frac{\text{value\_traded}}{\text{portfolio\_value}} \leq 0.004. \tag{31}$$

This constraint was chosen to align with SPY's typical daily turnover rate of approximately 3%. By limiting per-minute turnover to 0.4%, our simulation ensures that total daily changes in the position remain within realistic bounds, given the ETF's observed liquidity characteristics. All trades are executed at minute-end closing prices. While this implementation provides realistic control of the sizes of the positions, it is somewhat optimistic, as it does not take into account bid–ask spreads, commission costs, or potential price impact. These limitations should be considered when interpreting the performance of the strategy.

3.6. Evaluation Metrics

We assess the performance of the Random Forest model using a comprehensive set of metrics that evaluate both the accuracy of the predictions and the risk-adjusted returns:

- Root Mean Squared Error (RMSE): This is the square root of the average of the squares of the differences between the predicted and actual returns:

$$\text{RMSE} = \sqrt{\frac{1}{n}\sum_{i=1}^{n}(\hat{y}_i - y_i)^2}. \tag{32}$$

  A lower RMSE indicates better accuracy.
- Mean Absolute Error (MAE): This is the average of the absolute differences between the predicted and actual returns, offering an intuitive measure of the model's accuracy.
- R-squared (R^2): This is the proportion of the variance in the target variable explained by the model:

$$R^2 = 1 - \frac{\sum_{i=1}^{n}(y_i - \hat{y}_i)^2}{\sum_{i=1}^{n}(y_i - \bar{y})^2}, \tag{33}$$

  where $\bar{y}$ is the mean of the actual returns. A higher R^2 indicates a better performance of the model.
- Trend Accuracy: This evaluates the model's ability to predict the direction (up or down) of price movements:

$$\text{Trend Accuracy} = \frac{1}{n}\sum_{i=1}^{n}\mathbf{1}(\text{sign}(y_i) = \text{sign}(\hat{y}_i)), \tag{34}$$

  where **1** is an indicator function returning 1 if the predicted direction matches the actual direction and 0 otherwise.
- Sharpe Ratio: This assesses the risk-adjusted performance of the trading strategy:

$$\text{Sharpe Ratio} = \frac{\mathbb{E}[r_p - r_f]}{\sigma_p}, \tag{35}$$

  where r_p is the asset return, r_f is the risk-free rate, and σ_p is the standard deviation of the returns. A higher Sharpe ratio indicates better risk-adjusted returns.

- Maximum Drawdown: This is the largest peak-to-trough decline in the value of the asset over the testing period:

$$\text{Max Drawdown} = \max_{t \in T}\left(\frac{\text{peak}_t - \text{trough}_t}{\text{peak}_t}\right). \tag{36}$$

  This metric is crucial for evaluating the worst-case performance of the trading strategy during periods of market stress.
- Sortino Ratio: This is a variant of the Sharpe ratio that focuses only on downside risk:

$$\text{Sortino Ratio} = \frac{\mathbb{E}[r_p - r_f]}{\text{Downside Deviation}}, \tag{37}$$

  where the downside deviation is calculated using only negative returns. This ratio penalizes excessive downside risk more than overall volatility.

These metrics provide a well-rounded evaluation of the RFR's predictive accuracy and its ability to manage risk in the context of an HFT strategy.

3.7. Selection of Risk–Reward Ratios

In selecting risk–reward ratios for this study, we follow the theoretical framework laid out by Cheridito and Kromer (2013), focusing on ratios that satisfy the following four critical properties:

- Monotonicity property ensures that the reward–risk ratio (RRR) increases as returns increase, for a fixed level of risk. Essentially, this criterion reflects the intuitive idea that 'more is better.' Formally, for two random variables, X and Y, where $X \geq Y$, we should have $\rho(X) \geq \rho(Y)$.
- Quasi-Concavity encourages diversification, ensuring that the ratio prefers averages over extremes. If a reward–risk ratio satisfies this property, this means that a diversified portfolio will generally be preferred over a concentrated risk. Formally, for random variables X and Y, and for any $\lambda \in [0,1]$, we should have $\rho(\lambda X + (1-\lambda)Y) \geq \min(\rho(X), \rho(Y))$.
- Scale Invariance means that the ratio remains unchanged when both the return and the risk of a portfolio are scaled by the same factor. This ensures that the ratio is consistent across different investment sizes; it requires that $\rho(\lambda X) = \rho(X)$ for all positive scalars λ.
- Distribution-based property ensures that the ratio depends only on the distribution of the returns X and not on any specific realization of X. This is essential for generalizing the performance metric across different scenarios and portfolio strategies.

These properties form a robust basis for evaluating performance metrics, ensuring that they promote diversification and reward consistency. Many risk–reward ratios used in the financial literature—such as the Sharpe ratio, Sortino ratio, and Rachev ratio—naturally satisfy these criteria. The ratios chosen for this study as shown in Table 1 below align with these principles, allowing a comprehensive evaluation of the performance of a portfolio.

Table 1. Risk–reward ratios used in the study.

Ratio	Formula	Description
Sharpe ratio	$\frac{\mathbb{E}[R_p - R_f]}{\sigma_p}$	R_p: Portfolio return, R_f: Risk-free rate, σ_p: Standard deviation of excess returns. Measures the excess return per unit of risk (volatility), highlighting risk-adjusted performance.

Table 1. *Cont.*

Ratio	Formula	Description
Sortino ratio	$\frac{\mathbb{E}[R_p - R_f]}{\sigma_d}$	σ_d: Standard deviation of negative returns (downside risk). Improves on the Sharpe ratio by focusing only on downside risk, penalizing large losses more than fluctuations from gains.
Rachev ratio	$\frac{\mathbb{E}[R_p \mid R_p \geq \mathrm{VaR}_{1-\gamma}]}{\mathbb{E}[R_p \mid R_p \leq \mathrm{VaR}_{\beta}]}$	VaR: Value-at-Risk, γ: Upper quantile, β: Lower quantile. Measures tail risk by comparing the potential gains in the best-case scenario with the worst-case losses.
Modified Rachev ratio	$\frac{\mathbb{E}[R_p \mid R_p \geq \mathrm{VaR}_{1-\delta}]/\epsilon}{\mathbb{E}[R_p \mid R_p \leq \mathrm{VaR}_{\delta}]/\gamma}$	δ, ϵ: Additional parameters to refine the evaluation of risk. Extends the Rachev ratio to offer a more granular comparison between upper and lower tails at multiple confidence levels.
Distortion RRR	$\frac{\mathbb{E}[R_p \mid R_p \geq \mathrm{VaR}_{1-\beta}]}{\mathbb{E}[R_p \mid R_p \leq \mathrm{VaR}_{\beta}]}$	VaR: Value-at-Risk, β: Confidence level. Uses a distortion function to adjust the weights of the gains and losses, allowing flexible risk assessments depending on the investor's preferences.
Gains–Loss ratio	$\frac{\mathbb{E}[R_p \mid R_p > 0]}{\mathbb{E}[\lvert R_p \rvert \mid R_p < 0]}$	The ratio of the average positive returns over the average negative returns, providing a simple risk–reward comparison.
STAR ratio	$\frac{\mathbb{E}[R_p - R_f]}{\mathbb{E}[R_p \mid R_p \leq \mathrm{VaR}_{\alpha}]}$	VaR: Value-at-Risk, α: Confidence level. Focuses on tail risk, using the Conditional Value-at-Risk (CVaR), also known as the expected shortfall, to take into account extreme losses.
MiniMax ratio	$\frac{\mathbb{E}[R_p]}{\text{Max Drawdown}}$	Max Drawdown: Largest peak-to-trough decline in portfolio value. Compares the average return to the largest drawdown, focusing on how the strategy performs relative to its worst loss.
Gini ratio	$\frac{\sum_{i=1}^{N}(2i-N-1)R_i}{N\sum_{i=1}^{N} R_i}$	R_i: Sorted returns, N: Number of observations. Measures the inequality in the distribution of returns, analogous to the Gini coefficient used in economics.

4. Results

This section summarizes the performance of the Random Forest regression (RFR) models with and without technical indicators, compares them to a buy-and-hold benchmark, and discusses their statistical significance. The results include the predictive accuracy, the trading outcomes, the risk-adjusted performance, the contributions made by each feature, and residual analyses.

4.1. Predictive Performance

Training vs. Testing Metrics

We trained and tested 13 RFR models, differing in their inclusion of technical indicators, and compared their performance to a buy-and-hold benchmark. Table 2 presents the root mean square error (RMSE), mean absolute error (MAE), and R^2 for both training and testing sets. Although the models generally achieved strong results in-sample (training R^2 from 0.749 to 0.812), out-of-sample performance deteriorated (testing R^2 in the range -0.020 to -0.016). This discrepancy points to overfitting, consistent with the challenges often encountered when applying ML to minute-level data.

All models have comparable RMSEs (0.00036) and MAEs (0.00024) in the test set, indicating little variation in forecasting error. The negative out-of-sample R^2 values for each model confirm that high in-sample fits did not translate into predictive power on unseen data.

Table 2. Model performance metrics for training and testing.

Model	RMSE		MAE		R^2	
	Train	Test	Train	Test	Train	Test
RFR (no indicators)	0.00021	0.00036	0.00015	0.00024	0.786	−0.020
rfr_boll	0.00021	0.00036	0.00015	0.00024	0.812	−0.016
rfr_ema	0.00022	0.00036	0.00016	0.00024	0.749	−0.019
rfr_rsi	0.00021	0.00036	0.00015	0.00024	0.802	−0.017

4.2. Outcomes of the Trading Strategies

Portfolio Value and Returns

We simulated a trading strategy for each model from 28 August 2024 to 4 October 2024, starting with USD 10,000. Figure 2 shows the trajectories of the portfolios, and Table 3 shows the final portfolio values, returns, and major performance ratios. The buy-and-hold strategy ended at USD 10,229, which counts as a 0% deviation from the baseline, since it is the baseline in our setting. All RFR-based strategies underperformed.

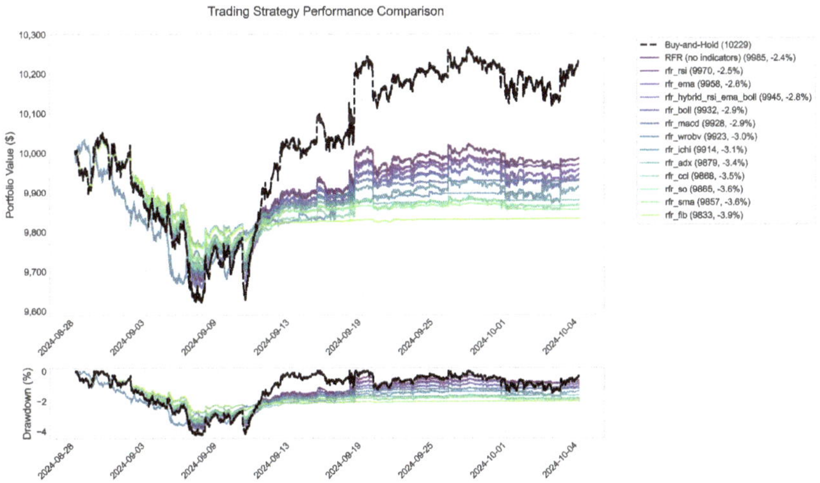

Figure 2. Trajectories of the values of the portfolios for different trading strategies. The buy-and-hold approach ended at USD 10,229, while the algorithmic models underperformed to different degrees. Maximum drawdown was around 4%.

Table 3. Summary of trading performance.

Model	Final Value (USD)	Return (%)	Sharpe	Sortino	Rachev
Buy-and-hold	10,229	0.00	–	–	–
RFR (no indicators)	9985	−2.40	0.0046	0.0047	0.946
rfr_rsi	9970	−2.50	−0.0015	−0.0018	0.961
rfr_ema	9958	−2.60	−0.0020	−0.0024	0.961
rfr_hybrid_rsi_ema_boll	9945	−2.80	−0.0024	−0.0029	0.956
rfr_boll	9932	−2.90	−0.0033	−0.0040	0.957
rfr_macd	9928	−2.90	−0.0035	−0.0041	0.953
rfr_wrobv	9923	−3.00	−0.0041	−0.0046	0.938
rfr_ichi	9914	−3.10	−0.0040	−0.0048	0.950
rfr_adx	9879	−3.40	−0.0078	−0.0089	0.937
rfr_cci	9868	−3.50	−0.0069	−0.0082	0.943
rfr_so	9865	−3.60	−0.0073	−0.0083	0.939
rfr_sma	9857	−3.60	−0.0082	−0.0093	0.937
rfr_fib	9833	−3.90	−0.0116	−0.0133	0.919

Although each model ended below USD 10,000, a few (notably, RFR with no indicators or rfr_rsi) performed slightly better than the others in risk-adjusted terms, with Sharpe ratios near 0.00 to 0.0046. None, however, surpassed the buy-and-hold benchmark in absolute returns.

That RFR-based strategies behave worse than the buy-and-hold benchmark can be attributed to transaction costs and market noise, which diminish the effectiveness of short-term trading strategies. While technical indicators provide some value in capturing short-term inefficiencies, the minute-level predictive horizon may not be sufficient to extract profitable trading signals. Additionally, high turnover rates in algorithmic strategies increase trading costs, further eroding potential returns in real-world implementations.

Our results align with prior studies, such as Peng et al. (2021), which found that technical indicators provide limited predictive value in deep learning models trained on daily-level data. Unlike our Random Forest approach, studies leveraging LSTMs and attention-based models have demonstrated better sequence-learning capabilities. However, our findings suggest that even with alternative architectures, the predictive power for high-frequency trading intervals remains constrained due to the market's microstructural noise.

4.3. Risk-Adjusted Performance

We assessed each strategy using risk metrics such as the Sharpe, Sortino, and Rachev ratios. Figure 3 presents a radar chart comparing the top five models; Figure 4 presents a heatmap of their risk–reward profiles.

Despite the differing results of the different strategies, none of the models yielded Sharpe ratios above 0.0046, a figure significantly below industry standards for viable trading strategies. This suggests that technical indicators alone may not be sufficient for high-frequency trading, as the models struggle to achieve risk-adjusted returns that justify frequent trading. Furthermore, the consistently negative Sortino ratios highlight that these models do not effectively protect against downside risk, reinforcing the argument that ML-based strategies in high-frequency trading environments face structural challenges.

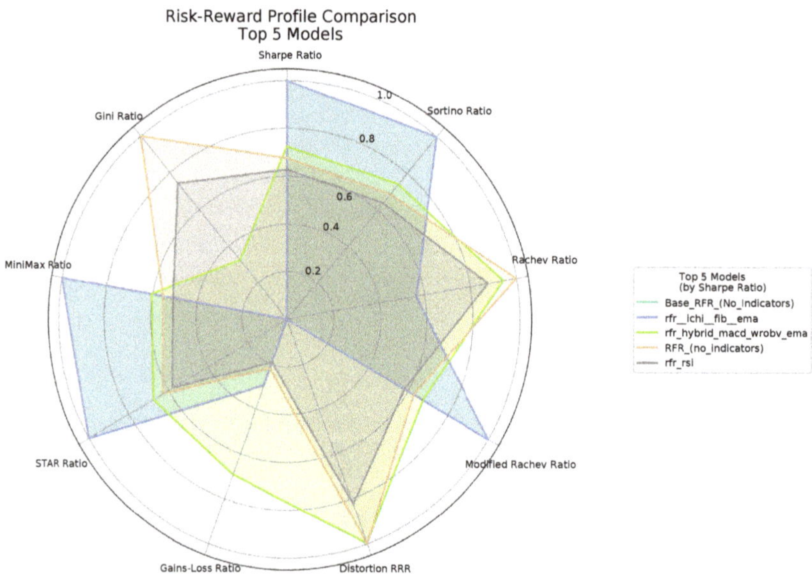

Figure 3. Risk–reward profiles for the top five models, presenting the Sharpe, Sortino, and Rachev ratios.

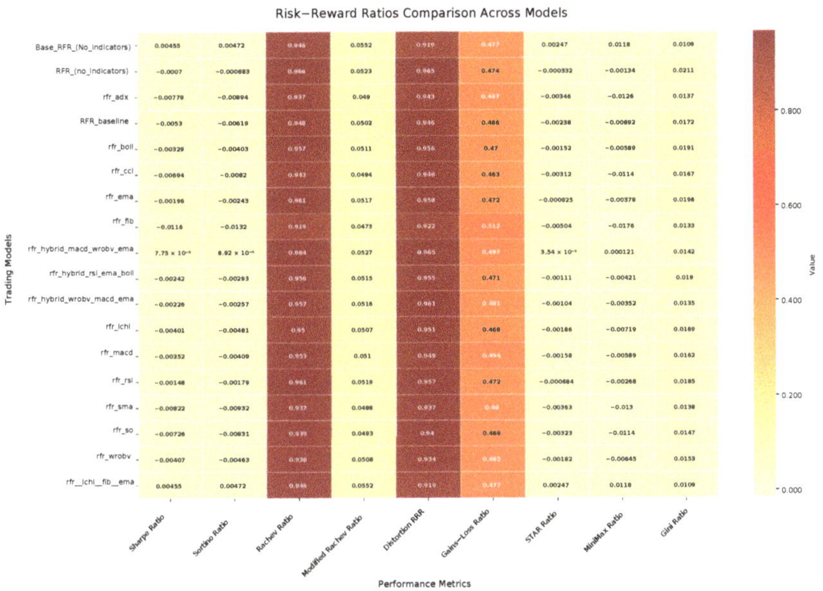

Figure 4. Heatmap comparing the Sharpe, Sortino, Rachev, and modified Rachev ratios for all models.

Among the tested models, RFR_RSI and RFR_ICHIMOKU obtained slightly better Rachev ratios (0.919–0.961), suggesting that momentum-based indicators may offer a small advantage in risk–reward trade-offs. However, these improvements were marginal and probably not statistically significant, indicating the need for further research with larger datasets and multi-asset testing.

A deeper analysis of the strategy's performance reveals that most trading losses occurred during periods of heightened market volatility, suggesting that the models struggle to adapt dynamically to shifting volatility regimes. These findings indicate that future research should explore adaptive models that adjust their feature weighting based on changing market conditions. The inability to effectively navigate volatility shocks highlights a key limitation of static ML models in financial applications, reinforcing the need for more flexible approaches that can integrate real-time volatility estimation.

These results challenge the weak form of the Efficient Market Hypothesis (EMH), suggesting that technical indicators may contribute to risk-adjusted decision-making but fail to generate persistent excess returns. This aligns with prior studies that found short-term inefficiencies in financial markets to be highly transient and difficult to exploit systematically. Future work should examine whether alternative data sources, such as order book data, sentiment analysis, or macroeconomic signals, could enhance the predictive power.

4.4. Feature Importance

4.4.1. Base Model

In the base RFR model (Figure 5), the closing, opening, high, low, and volume (normalized as a Z-score) features accounted for over 90% of the total importance. This indicates that raw price and volume data captured most short-term market signals for minute-level trading, consistent with the literature suggesting that in high-frequency contexts, market noise overwhelms many of the usual indicators.

Figure 5. Model analysis for the base RFR model without technical indicators.

4.4.2. Technical Indicators

Adding Bollinger Bands, EMA, or RSI (Figures 6–8) shifted the distribution slightly, with these indicators contributing 14–18% to the predictive decisions. However, none of these changes substantially improved the out-of-sample accuracy or trading outcomes, implying that traditional indicators do not offer a stable advantage at a minute-level frequency.

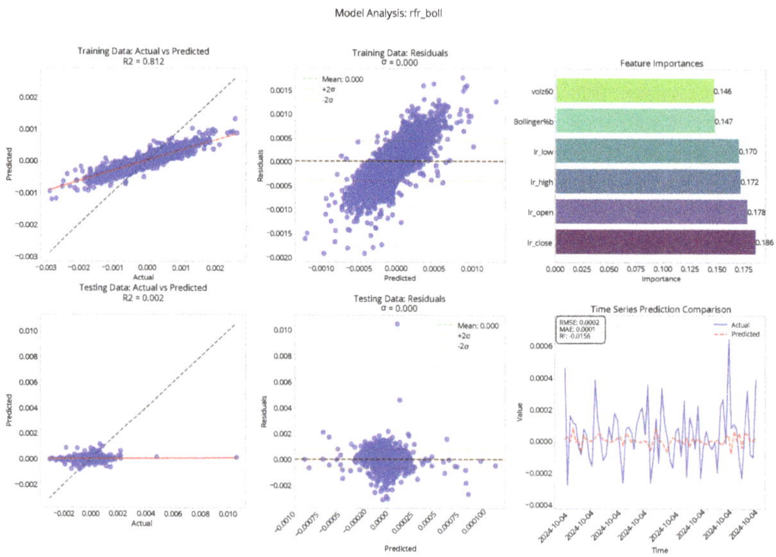

Figure 6. Model analysis for the RFR model including Bollinger Bands.

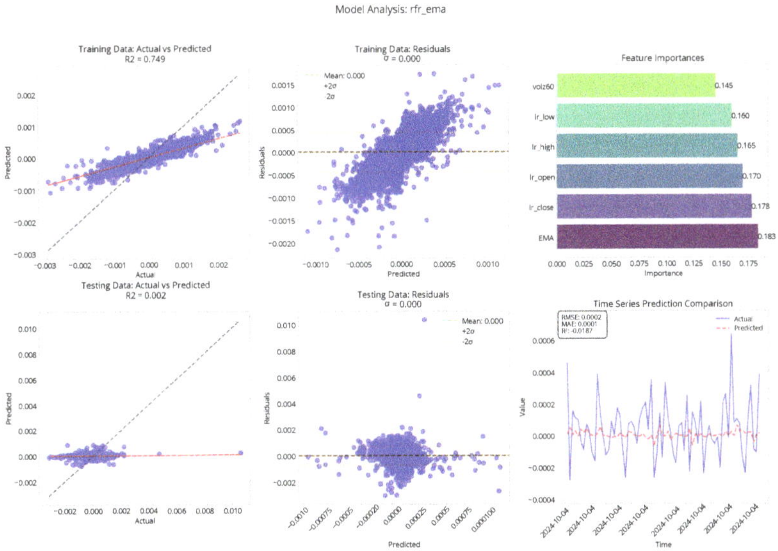

Figure 7. Model analysis for the RFR model including EMA.

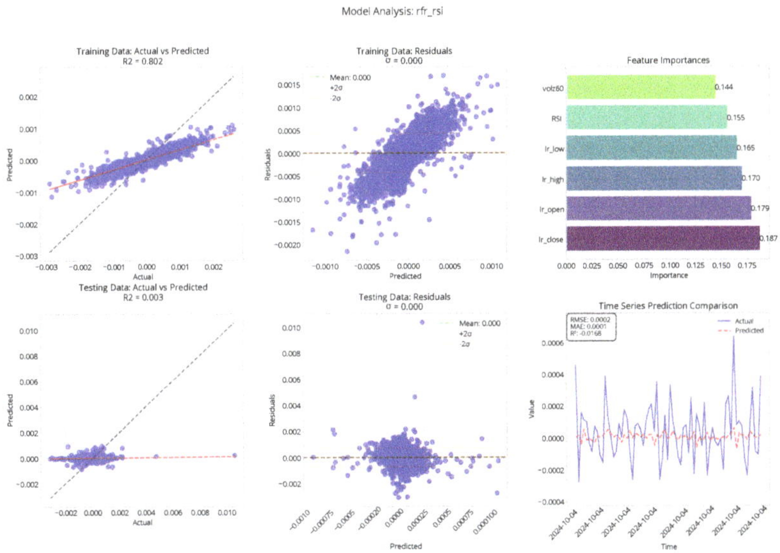

Figure 8. Model analysis for the RFR model including RSI.

4.5. Residual Analysis and Directional Accuracy

Residual plots for the base model (Figure 9) showed no strong bias or autocorrelation, suggesting consistent performance within the sample. However, the directional accuracy dropped notably from 80–87% in training to 48–50% in testing, again pointing to overfitting. The correlation coefficients also declined from 0.86–0.92 (training) to 0.03–0.06 (testing).

Figure 9. Model analysis for the base RFR model: actual vs. predicted returns and residual distributions during training and testing.

4.6. Comparative Analysis and Statistical Significance

When comparing models that use standard technical indicators (e.g., RSI, EMA, and Bollinger Bands) with those relying only on features based on the raw prices, the former did not exhibit a clear advantage in out-of-sample prediction or final returns. Although hybrid approaches combining multiple indicators slightly reduced the maximum drawdowns, they still failed to outperform simpler RFR models in absolute or risk-adjusted returns.

Statistical tests reinforced these findings: despite high in-sample R^2, all models obtained negative out-of-sample R^2. Consistent RMSE and MAE values across variants of the model further suggest that adding technical indicators did not meaningfully reduce forecast errors.

In summary, these results highlight the challenges in exploiting minute-level data with standard technical indicators. While the models fit historical data reasonably well, they struggled to generalize, indicating that high-frequency signals may be overshadowed by market noise and short-term volatility.

5. Conclusions

This study investigated the integration of technical indicators into Random Forest Regression (RFR) models for high-frequency stock price prediction, emphasizing both predictive accuracy and risk-adjusted performance. Using minute-level SPY data, we systematically evaluated a range of technical indicators, including Bollinger Bands, Exponential Moving Averages (EMAs), and Fibonacci retracements, to assess their contributions to the performance of the model under volatile market conditions. The choice of SPY, a highly liquid and representative market proxy, ensures that our findings retain their significance for broader high-frequency trading applications.

Our results indicate that while technical indicators enhance certain risk-adjusted metrics, such as the Rachev and gains–loss ratios, their contribution to out-of-sample predictive accuracy remains limited. A feature importance analysis consistently highlighted the dominance of primary price-based features (e.g., opening, closing, and high prices) over derived technical indicators. Hybrid strategies incorporating multiple indicators demonstrated slight improvements in managing tail risks but failed to outperform the buy-and-hold benchmark in terms of returns. These findings suggest that traditional technical indicators may have diminishing predictive value in modern high-frequency markets, where price discovery is driven primarily by raw price movements rather than widely recognized indicators.

Beyond predictive accuracy, this study advances the field by integrating advanced risk–reward measures to evaluate the practical viability of trading strategies based on machine learning (ML). While past research has focused predominantly on return maximization, our results emphasize the trade-offs between risk management and profitability. The observed difficulties in generalization, where models exhibit strong in-sample performance but deteriorate significantly in out-of-sample testing, highlight the need for parsimonious modeling approaches that prioritize robustness over complexity. This aligns with the existing literature on ML in financial markets, which finds overfitting to be a fundamental limitation in high-frequency trading applications.

From a theoretical standpoint, our findings provide insights into market efficiency and the feasibility of exploiting short-term price inefficiencies. While the inability of our models to consistently generate excess returns aligns with the weak form of the Efficient Market Hypothesis (EMH), the ability of certain indicator-augmented strategies to maintain stable risk–reward profiles suggests that transient inefficiencies may persist under specific market conditions. These results contribute to ongoing discussions on the microstructures of the market and the role of ML in financial decision-making.

Several challenges remain, including overfitting, the need for adaptive modeling techniques, and the computational costs associated with complex hybrid strategies. Future research should explore dynamic, regime-aware models capable of adjusting to evolving market conditions while maintaining their computational efficiency. Incorporating sources of alternative data, such as sentiment analysis and order book dynamics, could further enhance the predictive performance and provide deeper insights into price formation mechanisms.

From a practitioner's perspective, this study highlights the importance of balancing interpretability, computational feasibility, and predictive power in the deployment of ML models for high-frequency trading. While RFR-based strategies may not be optimal for maximizing absolute returns, their ability to manage tail risks and provide interpretable outputs means they can be valuable tools for risk-aware trading strategies. Furthermore, technical indicators, such as Fibonacci retracement and the Ichimoku Cloud, despite their limited predictive power, may still have some practical utility due to their alignment with intuitive trading heuristics.

In conclusion, this study contributes to the growing body of literature on ML in financial markets by providing a nuanced assessment of the role of technical indicators in high-frequency trading. While traditional indicators may have limited standalone predictive value, their integration within a structured risk-aware framework offers insights into market behavior and portfolio risk management. Future research should focus on adaptive hybrid approaches that address the challenges to generalization, leverage sources of alternative data, and optimize computational efficiency, to enhance the practical applicability of ML in modern financial markets.

6. Code Availability

The implementation code for this study is available at https://github.com/akashdeepo/ML_TI_RFR (assessed on 15 December 2024). The repository includes the core implementation files, `stockdata.py` for data processing and technical indicators, `pred_rfr.py` for the

Random Forest model, `simulate_trading.py` for trading simulation, and `metrics.py` for performance evaluation.

The implementation uses the following Python libraries:

- `scikit-learn`: Random Forest implementation with `RandomForestRegressor`;
- `pandas` and `numpy`: Data manipulation and numerical computations;
- `matplotlib` and `seaborn`: Visualization and plotting;
- `logging`: Comprehensive logging for debugging and tracking;
- Custom modules:
  - Technical indicator computation;
  - Trading simulation with position sizing and turnover constraints;
  - Risk–reward ratio calculations including Rachev and Modified Rachev ratios.

The implementation emphasizes computational efficiency and real-time processing capabilities, with particular attention to high-frequency trading considerations. The complete implementation requires access to minute-level SPY data through a Bloomberg Terminal subscription. Users wishing to replicate this study should have appropriate Bloomberg Terminal access and the necessary subscriptions. The code is provided under the MIT license, with the understanding that data acquisition and licensing compliance are the user's responsibility.

7. Future Work

While this study provides valuable insights into the role of technical indicators in high-frequency stock price prediction, several avenues remain open for further research. A key limitation of this study is its focus on a single asset, the SPY. Although the SPY was chosen for its high liquidity and broad market representation, future research should extend this analysis to multiple assets or multi-asset portfolios to evaluate the generalizability of the findings. Expanding the study to diverse asset classes, such as commodities, fixed-income securities, and cryptocurrencies, would provide a deeper understanding of how technical indicators interact with varying market structures, liquidity conditions, and volatility regimes.

Another important direction is the integration of additional data sources to enhance the predictive performance and risk assessment. Order book dynamics, sentiment analysis from financial news and social media, and alternative data sources such as macroeconomic indicators, could improve the feature selection and provide more context for trading decisions. Investigating how these factors influence the performance of a model in high-frequency environments may yield more robust trading strategies.

Further, advances in deep learning architectures present an opportunity to capture complex sequential dependencies in high-frequency financial data. Future studies should explore models such as Long Short-Term Memory (LSTM) networks and Transformer-based architectures, which have demonstrated strong performance in time-series forecasting tasks. Additionally, comparisons with alternative ML techniques, such as gradient boosting methods or hybrid ensemble models, could provide insights into the optimal modeling approaches for different market conditions.

Finally, the challenges to practical implementation must be addressed to ensure the viability of ML-driven trading strategies in real-world applications. Future research should explore the development of adaptive frameworks that dynamically adjust to evolving market regimes while incorporating real-world constraints, such as transaction costs, latency, and execution risks. The integration of reinforcement learning techniques so as to optimize the execution of trades and risk management strategies could further enhance the applicability of ML models in high-frequency trading.

By pursuing these research directions, future studies can contribute to the development of more resilient, interpretable, and efficient ML models for financial markets, ultimately bridging the gap between theoretical advances and practical deployment in trading environments.

Author Contributions: A.D.: Conceptualization, Methodology, Software, Formal Analysis, Investigation, Data Curation, Writing—Original Draft, Writing—Review & Editing, Visualization; A.S.: Validation, Resources, Writing—Review & Editing, Formal Analysis, Investigation, Supervision; C.M.: Conceptualization, Methodology, Software, Validation, Formal Analysis, Investigation, Supervision; S.R.: Conceptualization, Validation, Resources, Writing—Review & Editing, Supervision, Project Administration; F.F.: Resources, Writing—Review & Editing, Supervision, Project Administration. All authors have read and agreed to the published version of the manuscript.

Funding: This research received no external funding.

Informed Consent Statement: Not applicable.

Data Availability Statement: The data used in this study were obtained from Bloomberg Terminal and are subject to proprietary restrictions. As such, they are not publicly available. Access to Bloomberg Terminal data requires a subscription and is governed by Bloomberg's licensing agreements.

Conflicts of Interest: The authors declare that they have no conflicts of interest regarding the publication of this paper.

References

Abrol, S., Chesir, B., Mehta, N., & Ziegler, R. (2016). High frequency trading and US stock market microstructure: A study of interactions between complexities, risks and strategies residing in US equity market microstructure. *Financial Markets, Institutions & Instruments*, *25*(2), 107–165.

Agrawal, M., Khan, A. U., & Shukla, P. K. (2019). Stock price prediction using technical indicators: A predictive model using optimal deep learning. *Learning*, *6*(2), 7. [CrossRef]

Akyildirim, E., Cepni, O., Corbet, S., & Uddin, G. S. (2023). Forecasting mid-price movement of bitcoin futures using machine learning. *Annals of Operations Research*, *330*(1), 553–584. [CrossRef] [PubMed]

Aldridge, I. (2013). *High-frequency trading: A practical guide to algorithmic strategies and trading systems*. John Wiley & Sons.

Arifovic, J., He, X. Z., & Wei, L. (2022). Machine learning and speed in high-frequency trading. *Journal of Economic Dynamics and Control*, *139*, 104438. [CrossRef]

Barberis, N., & Thaler, R. (2003). A survey of behavioral finance. In *Handbook of the economics of finance* (Vol. 1). Elsevier.

Bloomberg, L. P. (2024). *Bloomberg terminal*. Available online: https://www.bloomberg.com/professional/products/bloomberg-terminal/ (accessed on 1 September 2024).

Bollinger, J. (2002). *Bollinger on bollinger bands*. McGraw-Hill.

Box, G. E. P., Jenkins, G. M., Reinsel, G. C., & Ljung, G. M. (2015). *Time series analysis: Forecasting and control*. John Wiley & Sons.

Breiman, L. (2001). Random forests. *Machine Learning*, *45*, 5–32. [CrossRef]

Buitinck, L., Louppe, G., Blondel, M., Pedregosa, F., Mueller, A., Grisel, O., Niculae, V., Prettenhofer, P., Gramfort, A., Grobler, J., & Layton, R. (2013). API design for machine learning software: Experiences from the scikit-learn project. *arXiv*, arXiv:1309.0238.

Cheridito, P., & Kromer, E. (2013). Reward-risk ratios. *Journal of Investment Strategies*, *3*, 3–18. [CrossRef]

Derbentsev, V., Matviychuk, A., Datsenko, N., Bezkorovainyi, V., & Azaryan, A. A. (2020, July 13–18). *Machine learning approaches for financial time series forecasting* [pp. 434–450]. Selected Papers of the Special Edition of International Conference on Monitoring, Modeling & Management of Emergent Economy, Odessa, Ukraine. CEUR Workshop Proceedings.

Fama, E. F. (1970). Efficient capital markets. *Journal of Finance*, *25*(2), 383–417. [CrossRef]

Fischer, T., & Krauss, C. (2018). Deep learning with long short-term memory networks for financial market predictions. *European Journal of Operational Research*, *270*(2), 654–669. [CrossRef]

Gu, S., Kelly, B., & Xiu, D. (2020). Empirical asset pricing via machine learning. *The Review of Financial Studies*, *33*(5), 2223–2273. [CrossRef]

Hastie, T., Tibshirani, R., Friedman, J., Hastie, T., Tibshirani, R., & Friedman, J. (2009). *Random forests* (pp. 587–604). Springer.

Ho, T. K. (1995, August 14–16). *Random decision forests*. 3rd International Conference on Document Analysis and Recognition (Vol. 1, pp. 278–282), Montreal, QC, Canada.

Kearns, M., & Nevmyvaka, Y. (2013). Machine learning for market microstructure and high frequency trading. In *High frequency trading: New realities for traders, markets, and regulators* (Vol. 72). Risk Books.
Lambert, D. R. (1983). Commodity channel index: Tool for trading cyclic trends. *Technical Analysis of Stocks & Commodities*, *1*, 47.
Lim, B., & Zohren, S. (2021). Time-series forecasting with deep learning: A survey. *Philosophical Transactions of the Royal Society A*, *379*(2194), 20200209. [CrossRef] [PubMed]
McGroarty, F., Booth, A., Gerding, E., & Chinthalapati, V. L. R. (2019). High frequency trading strategies, market fragility and price spikes: An agent based model perspective. *Annals of Operations Research*, *282*(1), 217–244. [CrossRef]
Murphy, J. J. (1999). *Technical analysis of the financial markets: A comprehensive guide to trading methods and applications*. Penguin.
O'Hara, M. (2015). High frequency market microstructure. *Journal of Financial Economics*, *116*(2), 257–270. [CrossRef]
Patel, J., Shah, S., Thakkar, P., & Kotecha, K. (2015). Predicting stock and stock price index movement using trend deterministic data preparation and machine learning techniques. *Expert Systems with Applications*, *42*(1), 259–268. [CrossRef]
Patel, M. (2010). *Trading with ichimoku clouds: The essential guide to ichimoku Kinko Hyo technical analysis*. John Wiley & Sons.
Pástor, L., & Stambaugh, R. F. (2003). Liquidity risk and expected stock returns. *Journal of Political Economy*, *111*(3), 642–685. [CrossRef]
Peng, Y., Albuquerque, P. H. M., Kimura, H., & Saavedra, C. A. P. B. (2021). Feature selection and deep neural networks for stock price direction forecasting using technical analysis indicators. *Machine Learning with Applications*, *5*, 100060. [CrossRef]
Shleifer, A., & Vishny, R. W. (1997). The limits of arbitrage. *The Journal of Finance*, *52*(1), 35–55. [CrossRef]
Wilder, J. W. (1978). *New concepts in technical trading systems*. Trend Research.
Zanc, R., Cioara, T., & Anghel, I. (2019, September 5–7). *Forecasting financial markets using deep learning* [pp. 459–466]. 2019 IEEE 15th International Conference on Intelligent Computer Communication and Processing (ICCP), Cluj-Napoca, Romania.
Zhang, F. (2010). High-frequency trading, stock volatility, and price discovery. *SSRN 1691679*. [CrossRef]
Zhang, G., Patuwo, B. E., & Hu, M. Y. (1998). Forecasting with artificial neural networks: The state of the art. *International Journal of Forecasting*, *14*(1), 35–62. [CrossRef]

Journal of
Risk and Financial Management

MDPI

Article

Forecasting Forex Market Volatility Using Deep Learning Models and Complexity Measures

Pavlos I. Zitis [1], Stelios M. Potirakis [1,2,*] and Alex Alexandridis [1]

[1] Department of Electrical and Electronics Engineering, University of West Attica, Ancient Olive Grove Campus, Egaleo, 12241 Athens, Greece; pzitis@uniwa.gr (P.I.Z.); alexx@uniwa.gr (A.A.)
[2] National Observatory of Athens, Metaxa and Vasileos Pavlou, Institute for Astronomy, Astrophysics, Space Applications and Remote Sensing, Penteli, 15236 Athens, Greece
* Correspondence: spoti@uniwa.gr

Abstract: In this article, we examine whether incorporating complexity measures as features in deep learning (DL) algorithms enhances their accuracy in predicting forex market volatility. Our approach involved the gradual integration of complexity measures alongside traditional features to determine whether their inclusion would provide additional information that improved the model's predictive accuracy. For our analyses, we employed recurrent neural networks (RNNs), long short-term memory (LSTM), and gated recurrent units (GRUs) as DL model architectures, while using the Hurst exponent and fuzzy entropy as complexity measures. All analyses were conducted on intraday data from four highly liquid currency pairs, with volatility estimated using the Range-Based estimator. Our findings indicated that the inclusion of complexity measures as features significantly enhanced the accuracy of DL models in predicting volatility. In achieving this, we contribute to a relatively unexplored area of research, as this is the first instance of such an approach being applied to the prediction of forex market volatility. Additionally, we conducted a comparative analysis of the three models' performance, revealing that the LSTM and GRU models consistently demonstrated a superior accuracy. Finally, our findings also have practical implications, as they may assist risk managers and policymakers in forecasting volatility in the forex market.

Keywords: deep learning algorithms; complexity measures; recurrent neural networks; long short-term memory; gated recurrent units; hurst exponent; fuzzy entropy; econophysics; forex market; volatility

1. Introduction

Market volatility has been the subject of a great deal of debate in recent decades, especially after the outbreak of the 2008 global financial crisis. Fluctuations within the financial market exert a direct influence on market expectations, thereby shaping investment decisions and the formulation of monetary and fiscal policies (Gong et al. 2024). In addition, financial market volatility plays a key role in many important fields of finance, such as portfolio allocation, derivative pricing, and financial risk management. Hence, the accurate estimation of market volatility is crucial for both investors and regulators.

Numerous methods have been proposed to estimate volatility in the literature. One of the main volatility estimators that has become increasingly popular in recent years is based on price ranges (Fałdziński et al. 2024). Price ranges, defined as the differential between the highest and lowest logarithmic security prices within a specified time interval, have long been recognized in the field of finance (Feller 1951; Parkinson 1980; Garman and Klass 1980; Rogers and Satchell 1991; Yang and Zhang 2000; Alizadeh et al. 2002). Although the Range-Based volatility estimator is very simple to calculate, it provides valuable information about volatility. Moreover, volatility models based on it have been found to be more efficient than standard volatility models based on closing prices (Todorova 2011; Todorova and Husmann 2011; Fałdziński et al. 2024).

is typically characterized by the absence of recognizable patterns. A financial time series is deemed somewhat predictable if it exhibits consistent price patterns. Conversely, it is considered to be entirely random if it lacks repetitive patterns, with participants selling or buying without any identifiable pattern (Delgado-Bonal 2019). In this context, entropy serves as a statistical measure of the level of randomness in a time series, based on the quantification of the presence and repetition of patterns (Zitis et al. 2023b).

In summary, the motivation for our study is threefold. First, we aim to illuminate a relatively underexplored area—the integration of complexity measures as features within DL models for the analysis of financial time series. By exploring this topic, we seek to contribute to the ongoing discourse and demonstrate that this approach has the potential to improve the accuracy of financial time series forecasting models. At this point, it is important to note that, in recent years, an increasing number of researchers have been exploring the integration of various feature types for financial time series forecasting. Notable examples of this include the application of sentiment analysis and image analysis in forecasting financial time series (e.g., Liu et al. 2017; Kirisci and Yolcu 2022). Second, we aim to examine whether DL models with more advanced architectures outperform simpler models in this context. Third, our findings can assist investors, risk managers, and market makers in forecasting volatility in the foreign exchange market.

2. Methods

This section briefly introduces the following three DL models: the RNN model (Section 2.1.1), the LSTM model (Section 2.1.2), and the GRU model (Section 2.1.3). Additionally, key concepts and formulas related to the Hurst exponent (Section 2.2.1) and fuzzy entropy (Section 2.2.2) are presented.

2.1. Deep Learning

Deep learning is a sophisticated method of ML that relies on ANNs. As a promising subset of ML (which, in turn, is a subset of AI), DL has garnered significant attention in recent years. Although it was developed in the field of computer science, its applications have expanded into diverse areas such as neuroscience, medicine, astronomy, and finance (Imrana et al. 2021). Compared to traditional ML techniques like random forests (RFs) and support vector machines (SVMs), DL offers advantages such as superior generalization capabilities and a robust training power for handling large datasets. Examples of DL approaches include deep neural networks (DNNs), convolutional neural networks (CNNs), deep belief networks (DBNs), and recurrent neural networks (RNNs).

2.1.1. RNN

Among the various DL approaches, RNNs have demonstrated promise for time series forecasting, including financial time series. The reason that RNNs can better handle time series is that they can store the feature information of historical data in their internal state (i.e., memory) (Liu et al. 2019). More specifically, RNNs are a type of neural network that uses previous outputs as inputs while retaining hidden layers (Berman et al. 2019; Kim and Kim 2015). Therefore, unlike traditional feed-forward networks, RNNs can remember what they have learned previously and make decisions based on this acquired knowledge (Bengio et al. 1994; Imrana et al. 2021). The following equation explains the function of the single RNN cell:

$$\begin{aligned} h_t &= tanh(W[h_{t-1}, x_t] + b), \\ y_t &= h_t, \end{aligned} \tag{1}$$

where W is the weight matrix, b is the bias matrix, and h_t and h_{t-1} are hidden states at current the time step and previous time step, respectively. RNNs perform computations using the weights, biases, and activation functions for each element of the input sequence (Figure 1). Essentially a neuron in an RNN has a single hyperbolic tangent function in which h_{t-1} and x_t are combined and multiplied by some weight matrix, then a bias is added to it, followed by passing it through the hyperbolic tangent function, which gives back h_t. The hyperbolic tangent function ($tanh$) scales the values to fall within the range from -1 to $+1$.

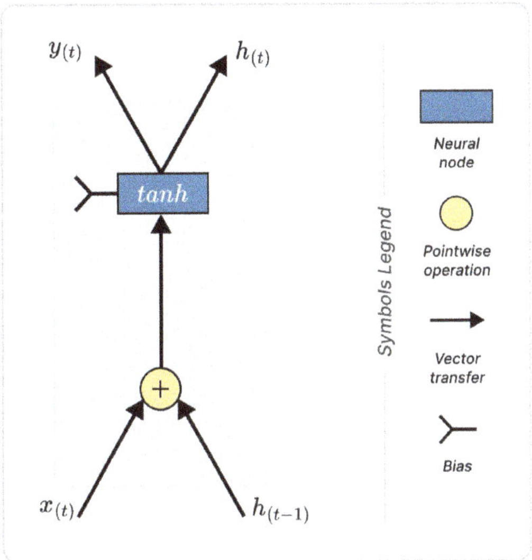

Figure 1. Schematic representation of simple RNN cell (Yu et al. 2019).

Although RNNs can address various research problems, they suffer from drawbacks such as vanishing gradients (Bengio et al. 1994; Pearlmutter 1995; Pineda 1987). This issue prevents them from effectively learning long-term dependencies, which means that the current position is influenced by the previous position. To overcome this limitation, Hochreiter and Schmidhuber (1997) proposed the LSTM network.

2.1.2. LSTM

Hochreiter and Schmidhuber (1997) proposed the LSTM network to address the shortcomings of traditional RNNs. In an LSTM cell, the memory is stored and converted from input to output in the cell state. An LSTM cell comprises the forget gate, input gate, update gate, and output gate. As their names suggest, the forget gate determines what to discard from previous memory units, the input gate decides what new information to accept into the neuron, the update gate updates the cell state, and the output gate generates the new long-term memory. These four main components work together uniquely, as LSTM processes long-term memory, short-term memory, and the input sequence at a given time step to generate new long-term memory, new short-term memory, and the output sequence at a given time step. The general architecture of an LSTM cell is shown in Figure 2. The input gate decides which information should be transferred to the cell and is mathematically represented as follows (ArunKumar et al. 2021):

$$i_t = \sigma(W_i * [h_{t-1}, x_t] + b_i). \quad (2)$$

The operator '$*$' denotes the element-wise multiplication of the vectors.

The information to be discarded from the previous memory is controlled by the forget gate, which is mathematically defined as follows:

$$f_t = \sigma\left(W_f * [h_{t-1}, x_t] + b_f\right). \quad (3)$$

The update gate is responsible for updating the cell state, which is expressed mathematically by the following equations:

$$\tilde{c}_t = tanh(W_c * [h_{t-1}, x_t] + b_c), \tag{4}$$

$$c_t = f_t * c_{t-1} + i_t * \tilde{c}_t. \tag{5}$$

The output gate updates the hidden layer from the previous time step and is also responsible for updating the output, as given by the following:

$$o_t = \sigma(W_o * [h_{t-1}, x_t] + b_o), \tag{6}$$

$$h_t = o_t tanh(c_t). \tag{7}$$

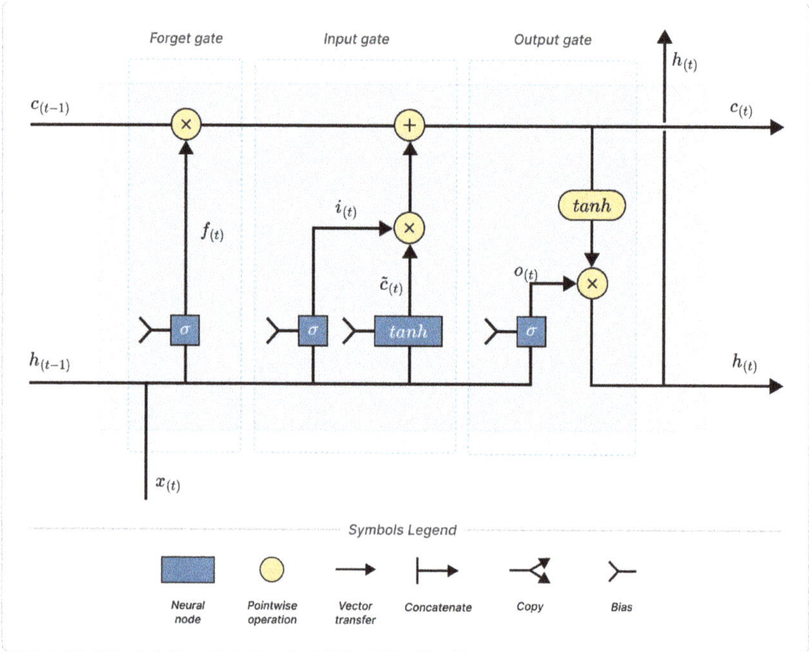

Figure 2. Schematic representation of LSTM cell (Yu et al. 2019).

2.1.3. GRU

Chung et al. (Chung et al. 2014) introduced GRU networks, which are a simplified, but equally popular, version of LSTM networks. The operation of a GRU cell is similar to that of an LSTM cell, but it uses a single hidden state that combines the forget gate and input gate into one update gate. Additionally, GRUs merge the cell state and hidden state into a single state, resulting in only two gates (update and reset gates) compared to the four gates in LSTM cells. This makes GRUs a simpler variant of LSTMs. The general architecture of a GRU cell is shown in Figure 3. The hidden state of the GRU cell is updated by the following equation (ArunKumar et al. 2021):

$$h_t = (1 - z_t) * h_{t-1} + z_t * \tilde{h}_t. \tag{8}$$

The update gate is computed using the following equation, which determines how much of the GRU unit is updated:

$$z_t = \sigma(W_z * [h_{t-1}, x_t]). \tag{9}$$

The reset gate is computed in a manner similar to the update gate, and is given by the following equation:

$$r_t = \sigma(W_r * [h_{t-1}, x_t]). \tag{10}$$

The new remember gate is generated by applying the hyperbolic tangent function to the reset gate, as described by the following equation:

$$\widetilde{h}_t = tanh(W * [r_t * h_{t-1}, x_t]). \tag{11}$$

Empirical studies have not definitively established which model is superior. However, GRUs require fewer network parameters, which makes them faster. In contrast, LSTM tends to provide a better performance when there are enough data and computational power (Alom et al. 2019).

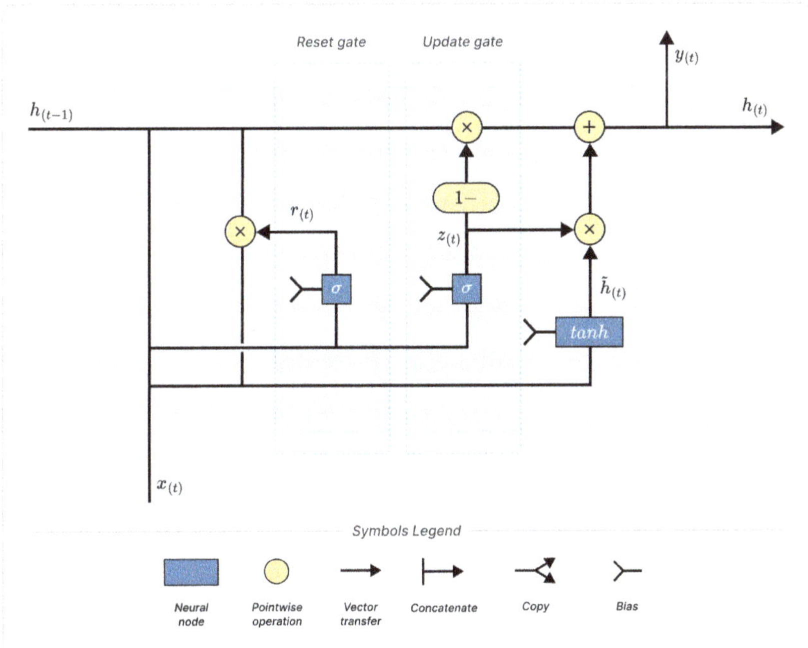

Figure 3. Schematic representation of gated recurrent unit (GRU) cell (Yu et al. 2019).

2.2. Complexity Measures

Numerous measures of complexity have been proposed in the literature. In this article, we select two widely recognized measures that have been extensively applied in financial time series analysis, as follows: the Hurst exponent and fuzzy entropy.

2.2.1. Hurst Exponent

The rescaled range analysis was developed by Hurst (1951) while investigating the statistical properties of Nile River overflows. This technique drew inspiration from Einstein's research on pure random walks, where the absolute value of particle displacement scales in proportion to the square root of time (Couillard and Davison 2005). Hurst expressed the absolute displacement in terms of rescaled cumulative deviations from the mean and defined time as the number of data points "n" used. The scaling exponent of this relationship, now referred to as the Hurst exponent (H), provides information on the presence of long-range correlations in a time series. If the dataset is purely independent, the distance traveled increases with the square root of time, and the Hurst exponent will be $1/2$. If antipersistence exists in a system, the Hurst exponent will be less than $1/2$, and if persistence occurs, the Hurst exponent will be greater than $1/2$.

By calculating the rescaled range R/S_n values for different values of n, we can estimate the Hurst exponent H. We start with a time series of length N and divide it into M contiguous subperiods, each of length n, such that $M \times n = N$. Each subperiod is labeled I_m with $m = 1, 2, \ldots, M$ and each element in I_m is labeled $N_{k.m}$ with $k = 1, 2, \ldots, n$. For each subperiod I_m, the average and standard deviation are defined as follows:

$$\mu_m = \frac{1}{n} \sum_{k=1}^{n} N_{k,m}, \tag{12}$$

$$S_m = \sqrt{\frac{1}{n} \sum_{k=1}^{n} (N_{k,m} - \mu_m)^2}. \tag{13}$$

The second step is to construct a new time series for each subperiod I_m, where each series represents the accumulated departures from the mean value. This series is defined as follows:

$$X_{k,m} = \sum_{i=1}^{k} (N_{i,m} - \mu_m), \qquad k = 1, 2, \ldots, n \tag{14}$$

Note that $X_{n,m} = 0$. We study the range of these accumulated departures from the mean, as follows:

$$R_{I_m} = \max(X_{k,m}) - \min(X_{k,m}), \quad \text{where } 1 \leq k \leq n. \tag{15}$$

Each range is rescaled by dividing it by the standard deviation of its corresponding subperiod I_m. The final rescaled range value for length n is then defined as follows:

$$R/S_n = \frac{1}{M} \sum_{m=1}^{M} R_{I_m}/S_{I_m}. \tag{16}$$

The length n is then incremented to the next higher value. We only use values of n that encompass the first and last points of the time series to ensure that the same number of points is consistently used. Using $\log(R/S_n) = \log(c) + H\log(n)$, we run a regression to find the slope.

2.2.2. Fuzzy Entropy

Expanding upon the concepts established with approximate entropy ($ApEn$) and sample entropy ($SampEn$), Chen et al. (2007, 2009) combined elements from fuzzy sets and information theory to develop a fuzzy version of $SampEn$. Fuzzy entropy ($FuzzyEn$), like its predecessors $ApEn$ and $SampEn$ (Chen et al. 2009), is a "regularity statistic" that quantifies the (un)predictability of fluctuations in a time series. For estimating $FuzzyEn$, the similarity between vectors is defined based on fuzzy membership functions and the vectors' shapes. The gradual and continuous boundaries of the fuzzy membership functions lead to several advantages, such as continuity, validity at small values, a higher accuracy, a stronger relative consistency, and less dependence on data length. $FuzzyEn$ can be considered as an upgraded alternative to $SampEn$ (and $ApEn$) for evaluating complexity, especially in short time series contaminated by noise (Balasis et al. 2013).

Similarly to *SampEn*, *FuzzyEn* excludes self-matches. However, it uses a slightly different approach for defining the initial $N - m$ vectors of a length of m, by removing a baseline, $\bar{s}_i$, as follows:

$$\bar{s}_i = m^{-1} \sum_{j=0}^{m-1} s_{i+j}, \tag{17}$$

i.e., for the *FuzzyEn* estimations, we use the first $N - m$ of the vectors, as follows:

$$\mathbf{X}_i^m = \{s_i, s_{i+1}, \ldots, s_{i+m-1}\} - \bar{s}_i, \; i = 1, 2, \ldots, N - m + 1, \tag{18}$$

Then, the similarity degree, D_{ij}^m, between each pair of vectors, $\mathbf{X}_j^m$ and $\mathbf{X}_i^m$, being within a particular distance, r, from each other is defined by a fuzzy membership function, as follows:

$$D_{ij}^m = \mu\left(d_{ij}^m, r\right), \tag{19}$$

where d_{ij}^m is, as in the case of *ApEn* and *SampEn*, the supremum norm difference between $\mathbf{X}_i^m$ and $\mathbf{X}_j^m$. For each vector, $\mathbf{X}_i^m$, we estimate the average similarity degrees with respect to all other vectors, $\mathbf{X}_j^m$, $j = 1, 2, \ldots, N - m + 1$, and $j \neq i$ (i.e., excluding itself), as follows:

$$\phi_i^m(r) = (N - m - 1)^{-1} \sum_{i=1, j \neq i}^{N-m} D_{ij}^m. \tag{20}$$

Then, we evaluate the following:

$$\varphi^m(r) = (N - m)^{-1} \sum_{i=1}^{N-m} \phi_i^m(r), \tag{21}$$

and the following:

$$\varphi^{m+1}(r) = (N - m)^{-1} \sum_{i=1}^{N-m} \phi_i^{m+1}(r). \tag{22}$$

The $FuzzyEn(m, r)$ is then defined as follows:

$$FuzzyEn(m, r) = \lim_{N \to \infty} \left[\ln \varphi^m(r) - \ln \varphi^{m+1}(r)\right], \tag{23}$$

which, for finite time series, can be calculated by the following statistic:

$$FuzzyEn(m, r, N) = \ln \varphi^m(r) - \ln \varphi^{m+1}(r). \tag{24}$$

As mentioned earlier, *FuzzyEn* estimates the complexity of a dataset. Specifically, lower *FuzzyEn* values indicate a higher likelihood that a set of data will be followed by similar data, signifying a greater regularity. Conversely, higher *FuzzyEn* values suggest a lower likelihood of similar data being repeated, indicating more irregularity. Therefore, higher *FuzzyEn* values correspond to increased randomness, disorder, and system complexity, while lower values reflect a higher degree of order/organization, as well as a lower randomness and complexity.

3. Data, Model Optimization, and Evaluation

3.1. Data Description

The forex market is a decentralized market that operates 24 h a day, except on weekends. It is the world's largest financial market, characterized by a strong liquidity and transactions amounting to trillions of US dollars daily. In our article, we focused our analysis on four highly liquid currencies (the Euro (EUR), British pound (GBP), Canadian dollar (CAD), and Swiss franc (CHF)) against the US dollar (USD). For our analyses, we used intraday data (specifically, per 4 h intervals) during the period from 28 August 2014 to 29 December 2023. All financial time series were retrieved from Dukascopy Bank, a Swiss Forex Bank and an ECN broker with its headquarters in Geneva. The data are publicly available at https://www.dukascopy.com/swiss/english/marketwatch/historical/ (last accessed 3 March 2024). In order to analyze the volatility of financial time series, we used one of the simplest and most efficient measures of volatility, known as "$Range - Based\ Volatility$", which is defined as the difference between the highest and lowest logarithmic security prices over a fixed time interval, as follows:

$$(Range - Based\ Volatility)_t = \log(High_t) - \log(Low_t). \tag{25}$$

Modifications of this volatility estimator have been used with great success in a wide range of analyses (e.g., Potirakis et al. 2013; Zitis et al. 2022), validating the views of Alizadeh et al. (2002) and Gallant et al. (1999), which support this volatility estimator as an information-rich proxy for true volatility. Furthermore, it is important to emphasize that employing Range-Based estimators for analyzing intraday data constitutes a robust methodological approach. Specifically, Andersen and Bollerslev (1998) highlighted that market microstructure issues, including non-synchronous trading effects, discrete price observations, and bid–ask spreads, can diminish the efficacy of intraday return variances or realized volatility as proxies or forecasts for volatility. In contrast, utilizing intraday high and low prices enhances the reliability and accuracy of volatility estimation (Chen et al. 2008).

3.2. Data Preprocessing

Data preprocessing is a crucial step in DL approaches and has a significant impact on the final results. One of the most commonly used data preprocessing techniques is data normalization. Nonlinear time series data, such as financial market data, often fluctuate across a large scale. Therefore, data normalization is essential for scaling the data to a smaller range, which, among other benefits, helps to accelerate the learning process of DL models. Numerous normalization techniques have been proposed in the literature. One of these techniques, which normalizes data to the range of [0, 1] using the following equation, is employed in our study:

$$x'_t = \frac{x_t - \min(x_t)}{\max(x_t) - \min(x_t)}, \tag{26}$$

where $\min(x_t)$ and $\max(x_t)$ are the minimum and maximum values of the time series, respectively. Given that the data are normalized during the model training phase, the test set output can be restored using the following formula:

$$x_t = x'_t(\max(x_t) - \min(x_t)) + \min(x_t). \tag{27}$$

3.3. Grid Search and Cross Validation Optimization

In ML models, parameters that require manual selection are known as hyperparameters. More specifically, hyperparameters are external parameters not inherent to the model itself and cannot be inferred from the dataset. Instead, they are configured by subject matter experts or through trial and error until an acceptable level of accuracy is achieved. For instance, an ANN has many such parameters, including the learning rate, the number of hidden layers, the number of nodes in each layer, and the optimizer. Hyperparameters significantly impact a model's performance; incorrect selection can lead to underfitting or overfitting. One method for optimizing hyperparameters is Grid Search Cross-Validation (GSCV). This technique systematically explores all possible combinations of candidate hyperparameters, identifying the best-performing set. GSCV enhances the accuracy of the model's generalization performance estimate. The grid search algorithm trains the model with each hyperparameter combination and selects the one with the lowest validation error. The algorithm's search process is illustrated in Figure 4 (Alhakeem et al. 2022; Hong et al. 2022).

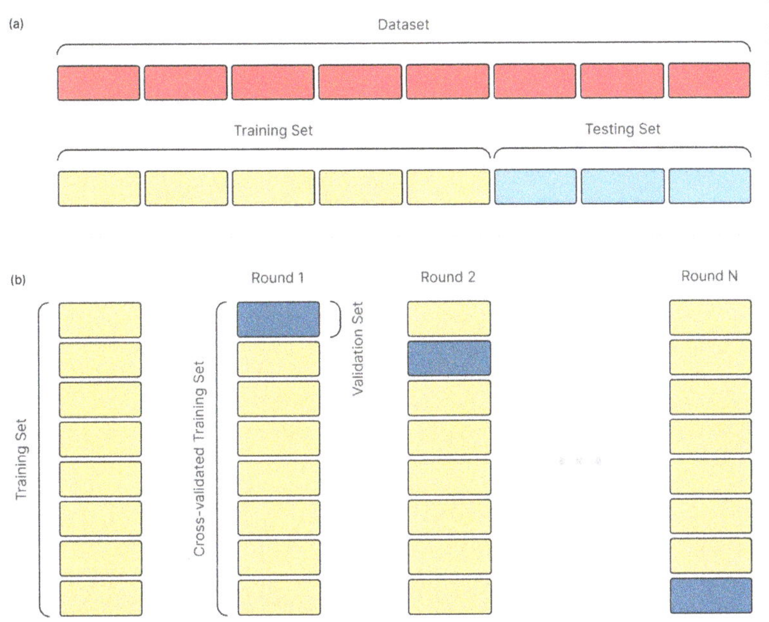

Figure 4. Partitioning of the dataset and the grid search process: (**a**) the division of the dataset into training and test sets and (**b**) a schematic representation of grid search and cross-validation.

3.4. Evaluation Measures

Evaluating the predictive performance of DL models is a crucial issue, as these measures form the basis for assessing and benchmarking the performance of each model. According to a recent review study (Kumbure et al. 2022), the majority of these measures can be classified into the following four categories: "statistical tests", "return-based", "accuracy-based", and "error-based". In our article, we utilized three of the most popular error-based metrics for measuring the forecasting performance of models (Mean Absolute Error—MAE, Root Mean Squared Error—$RMSE$, and Normalized Root Mean Squared Error—$NRMSE$) and an accuracy-based metric (Directional Symmetry—DS). The first metric that we utilized was MAE. Absolute-difference metrics like MAE limit the impact of individual outliers on model performance compared to the squared-difference metrics discussed below, making them particularly useful when dealing with data entry errors or other data quality issues (Steurer et al. 2021).

MAE measures the mean of the absolute differences between the observed values and predicted values, defined as follows:

$$MAE = \frac{1}{N}\sum_{t=1}^{N}|y_t - \hat{y}_t|, \tag{28}$$

where $\hat{y}_t$ is the forecasted value at time t, y_t is the observed value at time t, and N is the number of samples.

An alternative to mean absolute errors is mean squared errors. Squared-difference metrics are more sensitive to outliers than absolute-difference metrics, making them particularly useful in situations where minimizing large prediction errors is critical (Steurer et al. 2021). In our study, we selected $RMSE$ and $NRMSE$. The difference between $RMSE$ and $NRMSE$ is that $NRMSE$ is dimensionless, allowing for a comparison of values across different variables.

$RMSE$ measures the root mean squared difference between the predicted and actual values, defined as follows:

$$RMSE = \sqrt{\frac{\sum_{t=1}^{N}(y_t - \hat{y}_t)^2}{N}}, \tag{29}$$

where $\hat{y}_t$ is the forecasted value at time t, y_t is the observed value at time t, and N is the number of samples.

$NRMSE$ measures the normalized root mean squared difference between predicted and actual values, defined as follows:

$$NRMSE = \frac{1}{y_{max} - y_{min}}\sqrt{\frac{\sum_{t=1}^{N}(y_t - \hat{y}_t)^2}{N}}, \tag{30}$$

where $\hat{y}_t$ is the forecasted value at time t, y_t is the observed value at time t, and N is the number of samples.

The smaller the values of the three evaluation indicators, the more accurate the model's forecasting results.

On the other hand, DS measures the accuracy of a model by assessing its performance in predicting the direction of value changes, whether positive or negative. Specifically, the DS statistic represents the percentage of instances where the sign of the change in value from one time period to the next matches between the actual and predicted time series. A DS value of 100% indicates that the model perfectly predicts the direction of change in the time series from one period to the next (Sarveswararao et al. 2023).

DS is defined as follows:

$$DS = \frac{100}{N-1}\sum_{t=2}^{N} d_i, \tag{31}$$

$$d_i = \begin{cases} 1, & if\ (y_t - y_{t-1})(\hat{y}_t - \hat{y}_{t-1}) > 0 \\ 0, & otherwise \end{cases} \tag{32}$$

where $\hat{y}_t$ is the forecasted value at time t, y_t is the observed value at time t, N is the number of samples, and the direction of the value change is given by the corresponding d_i.

4. Results

As already mentioned, the forex market is a decentralized market that operates 24 h a day, except on weekends. It is the world's largest financial market, characterized by a strong liquidity and transactions amounting to trillions of US dollars daily. Its volatility significantly impacts imports and exports, capital flows, commodity prices, economic output, and employment. Therefore, the study of forex market volatility is a crucial issue. In this article, we study forex market volatility using DL models. Specifically, we investigate for the first time in the literature, to the best of our knowledge, whether incorporating complexity measures as features in DL models can improve their accuracy in predicting forex market volatility.

In our analysis, we first calculated the Range-Based Volatility estimator for four currency exchange rates, as outlined in Section 3.1. Subsequently, for the Range-Based Volatility time series corresponding to each currency rate, we estimated the Hurst exponent and $FuzzyEn$ using sliding windows of 1024 samples. The dataset was then divided into training and test subsets, with 60% of the data allocated for training the DL models and 40% reserved for evaluating their performance (Figure 5).

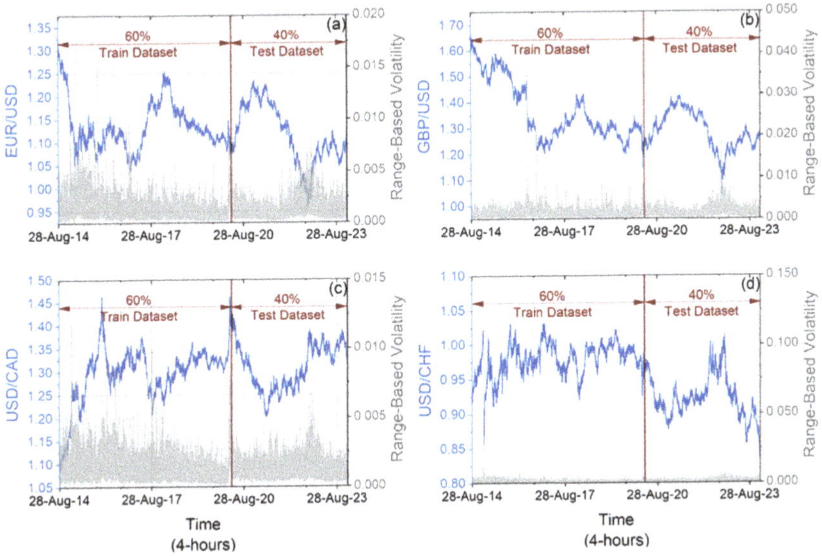

Figure 5. Evolution of four forex market currency exchange rate prices (blue curves, left vertical axis) and corresponding Range-Based volatility (grey curves, right vertical axis) over the period from 28 August 2014, to 29 December 2023: (**a**) EUR/USD, (**b**) GBP/USD, (**c**) USD/CAD, and (**d**) USD/CHF. The vertical red lines delineate the data area utilized for model training (on the left) and the data area employed for model testing (on the right).

For the training dataset, we applied normalization following the methodology described in Section 3.2. Thereafter, the DL architectures—namely RNN, LSTM, and GRU—were employed to independently forecast the Range-Based Volatility time series values for the subsequent 4 h period for each currency rate, utilizing the previous five samples of each variable as input memory. This procedure was repeated for each model using varying feature sets. Specifically, for each currency rate and model, the following feature combinations were used successively:

- Case I: Range-Based Volatility;
- Case II: Range-Based Volatility, High and Low;
- Case III: Range-Based Volatility, Hurst Exponent and $FuzzyEn$;
- Case IV: Range-Based Volatility, High, Low, Hurst Exponent, and $FuzzyEn$.

The main objective of this approach was to identify which combination of features enhanced the accuracy of the DL models. In particular, we aimed to investigate whether the inclusion of complexity measures, alongside traditional features, would provide additional insights and subsequently improve prediction accuracy. We concentrated on complexity measures, as they have been shown to offer significant insights into financial time series data (Jakimowicz 2020; Zitis et al. 2023a, 2023b; Tzouras et al. 2015). It is worth mentioning that this method of identifying optimal feature sets to improve model performance is widely recognized in the literature, e.g., (Cho and Lee 2022). It is also important to note that, for each case, we applied the GSCV methodology with three-fold cross-validation, as outlined in Section 3.3, to determine the optimal hyperparameters for each model. The list of hyperparameters and their respective search ranges were as follows: Activation: [Tanh], Batch size: [16, 32, 64], Epochs: [10, 50, 100], Optimizer: [Adam], and Neurons: [8, 16, 32, 64]. Additionally, we used a single hidden layer for each model, as adding more layers did not improve the results. The optimal hyperparameters for each model are summarized in Table 1.

Table 1. Optimal hyperparameter specifications for the RNN, LSTM, and GRU models.

Deep Learning Models	Hyperparameters	Optimal Hyperparameters															
		EUR/USD				GBP/USD				USD/CAD				USD/CHF			
		Case I	Case II	Case III	Case IV	Case I	Case II	Case III	Case IV	Case I	Case II	Case III	Case IV	Case I	Case II	Case III	Case IV
RNN	Activation	Tanh	Tanh	Tanh	Tanh	Tanh	Tanh	Tanh	Tanh	Tanh	Tanh	Tanh	Tanh	Tanh	Tanh	Tanh	Tanh
	Batch size	16	16	16	64	16	16	16	16	16	16	16	16	32	16	16	32
	Epochs	10	50	50	50	50	100	10	50	10	10	50	100	10	100	100	100
	Optimizer	Adam	Adam	Adam	Adam	Adam	Adam	Adam	Adam	Adam	Adam	Adam	Adam	Adam	Adam	Adam	Adam
	Neurons	32	16	32	16	64	32	64	64	16	16	8	32	32	32	32	64
LSTM	Activation	Tanh	Tanh	Tanh	Tanh	Tanh	Tanh	Tanh	Tanh	Tanh	Tanh	Tanh	Tanh	Tanh	Tanh	Tanh	Tanh
	Batch size	16	16	16	16	16	16	16	16	16	16	16	32	16	16	16	16
	Epochs	10	100	100	100	100	50	100	50	100	50	100	100	50	50	100	100
	Optimizer	Adam	Adam	Adam	Adam	Adam	Adam	Adam	Adam	Adam	Adam	Adam	Adam	Adam	Adam	Adam	Adam
	Neurons	32	16	16	64	16	32	64	64	16	32	32	64	16	64	32	16
GRU	Activation	Tanh	Tanh	Tanh	Tanh	Tanh	Tanh	Tanh	Tanh	Tanh	Tanh	Tanh	Tanh	Tanh	Tanh	Tanh	Tanh
	Batch size	16	16	16	32	16	16	16	16	16	16	16	16	16	32	32	16
	Epochs	10	100	50	50	10	100	100	100	50	100	50	100	100	100	100	100
	Optimizer	Adam	Adam	Adam	Adam	Adam	Adam	Adam	Adam	Adam	Adam	Adam	Adam	Adam	Adam	Adam	Adam
	Neurons	32	16	32	64	64	64	32	32	64	64	32	32	8	32	64	64

After identifying the optimal hyperparameters, the models were trained, and predictions for the Range-Based Volatility time series were generated using the test dataset (Figures 6–9).

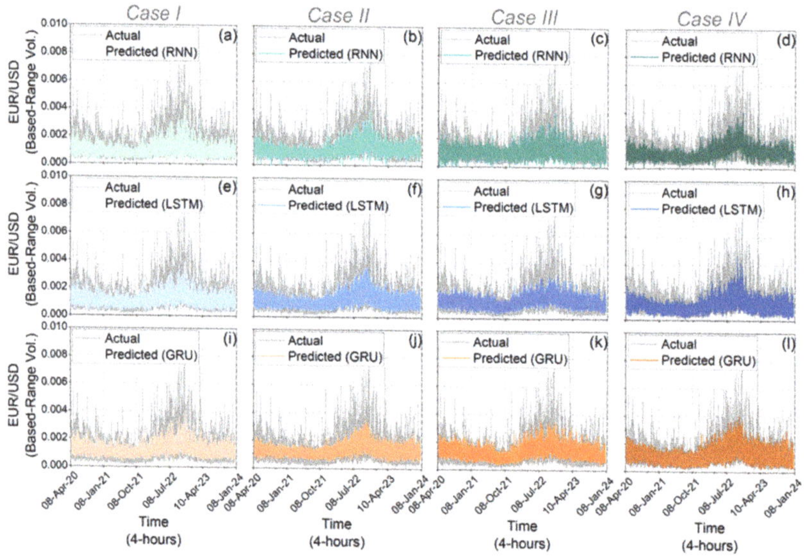

Figure 6. Actual values of the Range-Based volatility for EUR/USD (grey curves) and the model predictions (colored curves) by feature case and DL model for the test dataset (i.e., over the period 8 April 2020, to 29 December 2023). More specifically, subfigures (**a**,**e**,**i**) show the actual values of the Range-Based volatility and the predictions of the RNN, LSTM, and GRU models, respectively, for Case I (where the feature used was Range-Based Volatility). Subfigures (**b**,**f**,**j**) show the actual values of the Range-Based volatility and the predictions of the RNN, LSTM, and GRU models, respectively, for Case II (where the features used were Range-Based Volatility, High, and Low). Subfigures (**c**,**g**,**k**) show the actual values of the Range-Based volatility and the predictions of the RNN, LSTM, and GRU models, respectively, for Case III (where the features used were Range-Based Volatility, Hurst Exponent, and *FuzzyEn*). Subfigures (**d**,**h**,**l**) show the actual values of the Range-Based volatility and the predictions of the RNN, LSTM, and GRU models, respectively, for Case IV (where the features used were Range-Based Volatility, High, Low, Hurst Exponent, and *FuzzyEn*).

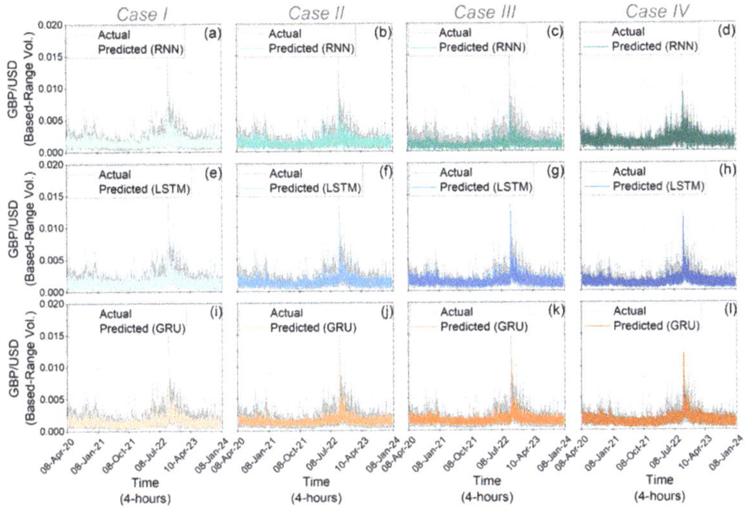

Figure 7. Actual values of the Range-Based volatility for GBP/USD (grey curves) and the model predictions (colored curves) by feature case and DL model for the test dataset (i.e., over the period 8 April 2020, to 29 December 2023). More specifically, subfigures (**a**,**e**,**i**) show the actual values of the Range-Based volatility and the predictions of the RNN, LSTM, and GRU models, respectively, for Case I (where the feature used was Range-Based Volatility). Subfigures (**b**,**f**,**j**) show the actual values of the Range-Based volatility and the predictions of the RNN, LSTM, and GRU models, respectively, for Case II (where the features used were Range-Based Volatility, High, and Low). Subfigures (**c**,**g**,**k**) show the actual values of the Range-Based volatility and the predictions of the RNN, LSTM, and GRU models, respectively, for Case III (where the features used were Range-Based Volatility, Hurst Exponent, and *FuzzyEn*). Subfigures (**d**,**h**,**l**) show the actual values of the Range-Based volatility and the predictions of the RNN, LSTM, and GRU models, respectively, for Case IV (where the features used were Range-Based Volatility, High, Low, Hurst Exponent, and *FuzzyEn*).

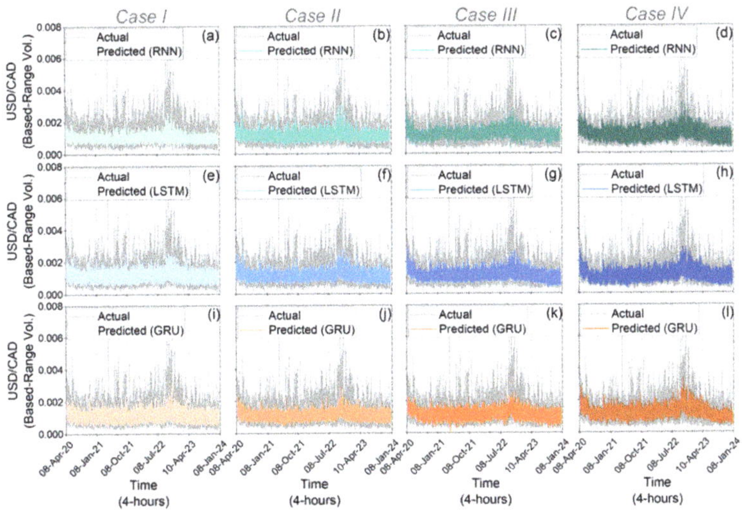

Figure 8. Actual values of the Range-Based volatility for USD/CAD (grey curves) and the model predictions (colored curves) by feature case and DL model for the test dataset (i.e., over the period 8

April 2020, to 29 December 2023). More specifically, subfigures (**a**,**e**,**i**) show the actual values of the Range-Based volatility and the predictions of the RNN, LSTM, and GRU models, respectively, for Case I (where the feature used was Range-Based Volatility). Subfigures (**b**,**f**,**j**) show the actual values of the Range-Based volatility and the predictions of the RNN, LSTM, and GRU models, respectively, for Case II (where the features used were Range-Based Volatility, High, and Low). Subfigures (**c**,**g**,**k**) show the actual values of the Range-Based volatility and the predictions of the RNN, LSTM, and GRU models, respectively, for Case III (where the features used were Range-Based Volatility, Hurst Exponent, and $FuzzyEn$). Subfigures (**d**,**h**,**l**) show the actual values of the Range-Based volatility and the predictions of the RNN, LSTM, and GRU models, respectively, for Case IV (where the features used were Range-Based Volatility, High, Low, Hurst Exponent, and $FuzzyEn$).

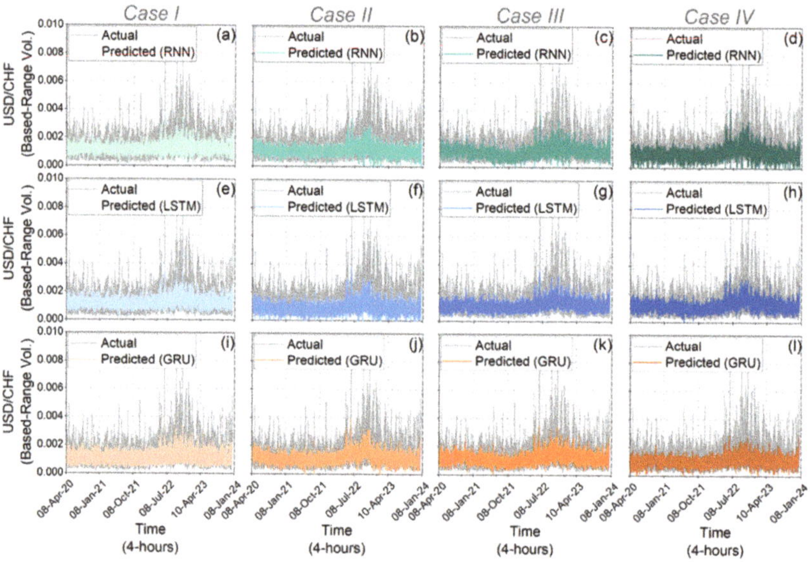

Figure 9. Actual values of the Range-Based volatility for USD/CHF (grey curves) and the model predictions (colored curves) by feature case and DL model for the test dataset (i.e., over the period 8 April 2020, to 29 December 2023). More specifically, subfigures (**a**,**e**,**i**) show the actual values of the Range-Based volatility and the predictions of the RNN, LSTM, and GRU models, respectively, for Case I (where the feature used was Range-Based Volatility). Subfigures (**b**,**f**,**j**) show the actual values of the Range-Based volatility and the predictions of the RNN, LSTM, and GRU models, respectively, for Case II (where the features used were Range-Based Volatility, High, and Low). Subfigures (**c**,**g**,**k**) show the actual values of the Range-Based volatility and the predictions of the RNN, LSTM, and GRU models, respectively, for Case III (where the features used were Range-Based Volatility, Hurst Exponent, and $FuzzyEn$). Subfigures (**d**,**h**,**l**) show the actual values of the Range-Based volatility and the predictions of the RNN, LSTM, and GRU models, respectively, for Case IV (where the features used were Range-Based Volatility, High, Low, Hurst Exponent, and $FuzzyEn$).

A subsequent evaluation of the model performance on the test dataset was conducted using four statistical metrics (i.e., MAE, $RMSE$, $NRMSE$, and DS), as detailed in Section 3.4. This evaluation was performed for each of the three models, across all currency rates, and for each of the four feature sets. The results are presented in Table 2.

Table 2. Performance measures by currency pair, DL model, and feature case.

Deep Learning Models	EUR/USD Case I	EUR/USD Case II	EUR/USD Case III	EUR/USD Case IV	GBP/USD Case I	GBP/USD Case II	GBP/USD Case III	GBP/USD Case IV	USD/CAD Case I	USD/CAD Case II	USD/CAD Case III	USD/CAD Case IV	USD/CHF Case I	USD/CHF Case II	USD/CHF Case III	USD/CHF Case IV
Mean Absolute Error																
RNN	**0.00047**	0.00048	0.00048	**0.00047**	0.00056	**0.00055**	0.00059	0.00058	0.00042	0.00043	0.00044	**0.00041**	0.00049	0.00048	**0.00047**	**0.00047**
LSTM	0.00047	0.00045	0.00047	**0.00042**	0.00052	0.00054	0.00052	**0.00051**	0.00041	0.00041	0.00040	**0.00039**	0.00049	0.00047	**0.00045**	0.00046
GRU	0.00049	0.00050	0.00049	**0.00046**	0.00055	0.00054	0.00056	**0.00052**	**0.00040**	**0.00040**	0.00041	0.00041	0.00046	0.00047	0.00046	**0.00045**
Root Mean Squared Error																
RNN	0.00074	0.00070	0.00071	**0.00069**	0.00087	**0.00086**	0.00096	**0.00086**	0.00062	0.00061	0.00060	**0.00058**	**0.00069**	**0.00069**	**0.00069**	**0.00069**
LSTM	0.00071	0.00066	0.00068	**0.00065**	0.00084	0.00082	0.00081	**0.00080**	0.00059	0.00059	**0.00058**	**0.00058**	0.00069	0.00073	0.00067	**0.00066**
GRU	0.00071	0.00068	0.00069	**0.00066**	0.00086	0.00080	0.00082	**0.00079**	0.00059	0.00058	0.00058	**0.00057**	0.00068	0.00068	**0.00067**	0.00068
Normalized Root Mean Squared Error																
RNN	1.84152	1.70613	1.75924	**1.48703**	1.65000	1.72154	2.10000	**1.32000**	2.86000	2.41000	2.22000	**1.81922**	2.20000	2.21000	1.88000	**1.61000**
LSTM	1.84268	1.51000	1.70091	**1.36055**	1.45000	1.52088	**1.32076**	1.37427	1.99000	2.20613	1.99000	**1.76000**	2.12000	1.94000	2.03000	**1.80000**
GRU	1.79000	1.63797	1.47042	**1.25040**	1.35000	1.43000	1.54000	**1.24993**	1.98000	2.16000	1.93000	**1.66000**	1.76000	**1.70000**	1.77000	2.02000
Directional Symmetry																
RNN	50.77%	52.92%	**55.24%**	54.79%	51.40%	53.13%	52.60%	**53.40%**	48.40%	49.00%	51.10%	**55.41%**	51.80%	53.50%	53.70%	**57.20%**
LSTM	51.72%	55.90%	55.02%	**58.61%**	55.10%	54.23%	**57.32%**	56.45%	55.00%	51.32%	55.20%	**55.70%**	52.10%	54.10%	54.80%	**56.20%**
GRU	51.30%	55.05%	55.08%	**57.69%**	50.80%	56.50%	57.10%	**57.96%**	55.80%	**56.80%**	54.40%	53.00%	55.60%	54.30%	55.00%	**58.00%**

Note: The feature cases with the highest performance for each model and exchange rate are highlighted using bold font.

The results indicate that, in the majority of cases, the LSTM and GRU models consistently outperform the simple RNN model. For instance, in Case IV for the EUR/USD exchange rate, a significant improvement in forecast accuracy is observed when comparing the GRU model to the RNN. Specifically, the improvements are approximately 2% for MAE, 4% for $RMSE$, 16% for $NRMSE$, and 5% for DS. Similar enhancements are noted in Case III for the GBP/USD exchange rate when comparing the LSTM model to the RNN, with improvements of approximately 12% for MAE, 16% for $RMSE$, 37% for $NRMSE$, and 9% for DS. Importantly, the enhanced predictive accuracy of the LSTM and GRU models is not limited to Cases III and IV, where complexity measures were included as features. For instance, in Case I for the USD/CAD exchange rate, the LSTM model demonstrates improvements of approximately 2% for MAE, 5% for $RMSE$, 30% for $NRMSE$, and 14% for DS when compared to the RNN. Similarly, in Case II for the USD/CHF exchange rate, the GRU model shows improvements of about 2% for MAE, 1% for $RMSE$, 23% for $NRMSE$, and 1% for DS over the RNN. This is a plausible finding, as both LSTM and GRU represent advancements over the basic RNN architecture. Furthermore, our findings align with those of previous research, which has demonstrated that the LSTM and GRU models exhibit a superior performance in forecasting the volatility of financial time series (Gunnarsson et al. 2024). Consequently, our results suggest that, for the analysis of currency rate volatility, models with more complex architectures, such as LSTM and GRU, are preferable to simpler models like the RNN.

The main finding of this study, aside from establishing that the LSTM and GRU models exhibit a higher predictive accuracy than the simpler RNN model, is that the accuracy of all models is consistently higher in Cases III and IV across various statistical metrics (Table 2). This suggests that incorporating complexity measures as features in DL models enhances their ability to predict volatility. Specifically, for the EUR/USD exchange rate, it is evident from all statistical measures that the accuracy of all three models improves when complexity measures are included as features (Table 2). For instance, a comparison of the LSTM model's performance in Case IV with Case I reveals improvements in prediction accuracy of approximately 11% for MAE, 8% for $RMSE$, 26% for $NRMSE$, and 13% for DS. The GRU model exhibits similar results; comparing Case IV with Case II, the improvements in accuracy are approximately 8% for MAE, 3% for $RMSE$, 24% for $NRMSE$, and 5% for

DS. Similarly, for the GBP/USD exchange rate, the LSTM model's performance in Case III compared to Case II shows improvements of approximately 4% for MAE, 1% for $RMSE$, 13% for $NRMSE$, and 6% for DS. Notably, even the simpler RNN model demonstrates an enhanced accuracy in predicting volatility when complexity measures are incorporated into its input. For example, in the case of the USD/CAD exchange rate, a comparison between Case IV and Case II reveals improvements in forecast accuracy of approximately 5% for MAE, 5% for $RMSE$, 25% for $NRMSE$, and 13% for DS.

In summary, the findings from our analyses suggest that the inclusion of complexity measures as features enhances the accuracy of volatility predictions. Conversely, when these measures are omitted, the models tend to perform less accurately, increasing the likelihood of underestimating or overestimating volatility. This can result in suboptimal decisions, such as inadequate risk management or inappropriate asset allocation, ultimately impacting returns and increasing exposure to unexpected losses. It is also noteworthy that, while the integration of complexity measures into DL models has not been extensively studied—and, to the best of our knowledge, no prior research has specifically applied these measures to DL models for predicting volatility in the forex market—our findings align with the broader literature. The studies we identified conclude that incorporating complexity measures as features in ML/DL models improves prediction accuracy (see Section 1: Introduction). Furthermore, our analyses reveal that, in most cases, the LSTM and GRU models outperform the RNN model in terms of volatility prediction accuracy. This result highlights the ability of LSTM and GRUs to efficiently capture long-term dependencies, unlike RNNs, where the current state is heavily influenced by the previous state.

5. Conclusions

In recent decades, predicting financial market volatility has become crucial for economic research, particularly for asset allocation and risk management. However, due to the nonlinear, chaotic nature of financial markets, traditional models often struggle to provide accurate forecasts. This challenge has spurred interest from AI and complex systems researchers, as machine learning models like ANNs can effectively capture nonlinearity without relying on prior assumptions, and complexity measures like the Hurst exponent and $FuzzyEn$ reveal long-term dependencies and randomness. Nevertheless, despite the apparent suitability of integrating ML models with complexity measures for the analysis of financial time series, this area remains relatively underexplored.

In this article, we investigated whether the incorporation of complexity measures as features within DL models can enhance their accuracy in predicting volatility in the forex market, the largest financial market globally. Specifically, we proposed the development of volatility forecasting models that integrate the Hurst exponent and $FuzzyEn$ as features into three DL architectures—RNN, LSTM, and GRU—to predict the intraday volatility of four highly liquid currency pairs (EUR/USD, GBP/USD, USD/CAD, and USD/CHF). To estimate volatility, we employed the Range-Based estimator, which is regarded as an information-rich proxy for true volatility. Our results demonstrated that the inclusion of complexity measures as features significantly enhanced the accuracy of volatility predictions. In contrast, when these measures were excluded, the models tended to perform less accurately, increasing the likelihood of underestimating or overestimating volatility, and consequently, risk. This result aligns with the literature, as the studies we identified conclude that incorporating complexity measures as features in DL models enhances prediction accuracy. Additionally, it was observed that models with more complex architectures, such as LSTM and GRUs, generally outperformed the simpler RNN model.

In summary, the contribution of our findings is threefold, as follows: (i) the primary conclusion is that incorporating complexity metrics as features in DL models can enhance model accuracy in predicting volatility. In achieving this, we illuminate a relatively underexplored area and aim to advance the discourse on the combined application of complexity metrics and DL models in finance; (ii) our results contribute to the existing literature by providing a comparative analysis of three popular DL architectures (RNN, LSTM, and GRU) in terms of their accuracy in forecasting forex market volatility; and (iii) our results have practical applications, as accurate volatility predictions can help investors to enhance returns by signaling the optimal times to enter or exit markets, enabling them to capitalize on periods of high or low uncertainty. Furthermore, precise volatility forecasts allow risk managers to design effective hedging strategies to mitigate adverse price movements. Additionally, understanding volatility trends holds significant value for market makers, high-frequency trading (HFT) participants, and options traders. Accurate volatility forecasts enable these stakeholders to evaluate the likelihood of price fluctuations and effectively manage the risks associated with automated trading strategies.

Finally, as already mentioned, this scientific field remains relatively unexplored, offering considerable scope for future research. For instance, it would be valuable to examine the predictability of these models using alternative volatility estimators. Additionally, incorporating other complexity measures beyond the Hurst exponent and fuzzy entropy could provide further insights. Future research could also explore integrating complexity measures into DL models for directly predicting price, rather than focusing on volatility prediction. Moreover, applying these models to different time periods would be an interesting avenue for investigation.

Author Contributions: Conceptualization, P.I.Z. and S.M.P.; methodology, P.I.Z., S.M.P., and A.A.; software, P.I.Z., S.M.P., and A.A.; validation, P.I.Z., S.M.P., and A.A.; formal analysis, P.I.Z.; investigation, P.I.Z. and S.M.P.; data curation, P.I.Z.; writing—original draft preparation, P.I.Z. and S.M.P.; writing—review and editing, S.M.P. and A.A.; visualization, P.I.Z. and S.M.P.; supervision, S.M.P. and A.A. All authors have read and agreed to the published version of the manuscript.

Funding: This research received no external funding.

Data Availability Statement: All financial time series used in this article are publicly available from Dukascopy Bank, a Swiss Forex Bank and an ECN broker with its headquarters in Geneva. (https://www.dukascopy.com/swiss/english/marketwatch/historical/, accessed on 20 March 2024).

Conflicts of Interest: The authors declare no conflicts of interest.

References

Ahmed, Shamima, Muneer M. Alshater, Anis El Ammari, and Helmi Hammami. 2022. Artificial Intelligence and Machine Learning in Finance: A Bibliometric Review. *Research in International Business and Finance* 61: 101646. [CrossRef]

Alhakeem, Zaineb M., Yasir Mohammed Jebur, Sadiq N. Henedy, Hamza Imran, Luís F. A. Bernardo, and Hussein M. Hussein. 2022. Prediction of Ecofriendly Concrete Compressive Strength Using Gradient Boosting Regression Tree Combined with GridSearchCV Hyperparameter-Optimization Techniques. *Materials* 15: 7432. [CrossRef] [PubMed]

Alizadeh, Sassan, Michael W. Brandt, and Francis X. Diebold. 2002. Range-Based Estimation of Stochastic Volatility Models. *The Journal of Finance* 57: 1047–91. [CrossRef]

Alom, Md Zahangir, Tarek M. Taha, Chris Yakopcic, Stefan Westberg, Paheding Sidike, Mst Shamima Nasrin, Mahmudul Hasan, Brian C. Van Essen, Abdul A. S. Awwal, and Vijayan K. Asari. 2019. A State-of-The-Art Survey on Deep Learning Theory and Architectures. *Electronics* 8: 292. [CrossRef]

Andersen, Torben G., and Tim Bollerslev. 1997. Intraday Periodicity and Volatility Persistence in Financial Markets. *Journal of Empirical Finance* 4: 115–58. [CrossRef]

Andersen, Torben G., and Tim Bollerslev. 1998. Answering the Skeptics: Yes, Standard Volatility Models Do Provide Accurate Forecasts. *International Economic Review* 39: 885. [CrossRef]

ArunKumar, K. E., Dinesh V. Kalaga, Ch. Mohan Sai Kumar, Masahiro Kawaji, and Timothy M. Brenza. 2021. Forecasting of COVID-19 Using Deep Layer Recurrent Neural Networks (RNNs) with Gated Recurrent Units (GRUs) and Long Short-Term Memory (LSTM) Cells. *Chaos, Solitons & Fractals* 146: 110861. [CrossRef]

Balasis, Georgios, Reik Donner, Stelios Potirakis, Jakob Runge, Constantinos Papadimitriou, Ioannis Daglis, Konstantinos Eftaxias, and Jürgen Kurths. 2013. Statistical Mechanics and Information-Theoretic Perspectives on Complexity in the Earth System. *Entropy* 15: 4844–88. [CrossRef]

Bengio, Yoshua, Patrice Simard, and Paolo Frasconi. 1994. Learning Long-Term Dependencies with Gradient Descent Is Difficult. *IEEE Transactions on Neural Networks* 5: 157–66. [CrossRef]

Berman, Daniel, Anna Buczak, Jeffrey Chavis, and Cherita Corbett. 2019. A Survey of Deep Learning Methods for Cyber Security. *Information* 10: 122. [CrossRef]

Chen, Cathy W. S., Richard Gerlach, and Edward M. H. Lin. 2008. Volatility Forecasting Using Threshold Heteroskedastic Models of the Intra-Day Range. *Computational Statistics & Data Analysis* 52: 2990–3010. [CrossRef]

Chen, Weiting, Jun Zhuang, Wangxin Yu, and Zhizhong Wang. 2009. Measuring Complexity Using FuzzyEn, ApEn, and SampEn. *Medical Engineering & Physics* 31: 61–68. [CrossRef]

Chen, Weiting, Zhizhong Wang, Hongbo Xie, and Wangxin Yu. 2007. Characterization of Surface EMG Signal Based on Fuzzy Entropy. *IEEE Transactions on Neural Systems and Rehabilitation Engineering* 15: 266–72. [CrossRef] [PubMed]

Cho, Poongjin, and Minhyuk Lee. 2022. Forecasting the Volatility of the Stock Index with Deep Learning Using Asymmetric Hurst Exponents. *Fractal and Fractional* 6: 394. [CrossRef]

Chung, Junyoung, Caglar Gulcehre, KyungHyun Cho, and Yoshua Bengio. 2014. Empirical Evaluation of Gated Recurrent Neural Networks on Sequence Modeling. *arXiv* arXiv:1412.3555. [CrossRef]

Couillard, Michel, and Matt Davison. 2005. A Comment on Measuring the Hurst Exponent of Financial Time Series. *Physica A: Statistical Mechanics and Its Applications* 348: 404–18. [CrossRef]

Delgado-Bonal, Alfonso. 2019. Quantifying the Randomness of the Stock Markets. *Scientific Reports* 9: 12761. [CrossRef]

Dhingra, Barkha, Shallu Batra, Vaibhav Aggarwal, Mahender Yadav, and Pankaj Kumar. 2023. Stock Market Volatility: A Systematic Review. *Journal of Modelling in Management* 19: 925–52. [CrossRef]

Fałdziński, Marcin, Piotr Fiszeder, and Peter Molnár. 2024. Improving Volatility Forecasts: Evidence from Range-Based Models. *The North American Journal of Economics and Finance* 69: 102019–19. [CrossRef]

Fama, Eugene. 1970. Efficient Capital Markets: A Review of Theory and Empirical Work. *The Journal of Finance* 25: 383–417. [CrossRef]

Feller, William. 1951. The Asymptotic Distribution of the Range of Sums of Independent Random Variables. *Annals of Mathematical Statistics* 22: 427–32. [CrossRef]

Gallant, A. Ronald, Chien-Te Hsu, and George Tauchen. 1999. Using Daily Range Data to Calibrate Volatility Diffusions and Extract the Forward Integrated Variance. *Review of Economics and Statistics* 81: 617–31. [CrossRef]

Garman, Mark B., and Michael J. Klass. 1980. On the Estimation of Security Price Volatilities from Historical Data. *The Journal of Business* 53: 67–78. [CrossRef]

Ghosh, Indranil, Manas K. Sanyal, and R. K. Jana. 2017. Fractal Inspection and Machine Learning-Based Predictive Modelling Framework for Financial Markets. *Arabian Journal for Science and Engineering* 43: 4273–87. [CrossRef]

Gong, Jue, Gang-Jin Wang, Chi Xie, and Gazi Salah Uddin. 2024. How Do Market Volatility and Risk Aversion Sentiment Inter-Influence over Time? Evidence from Chinese SSE 50 ETF Options. *International Review of Financial Analysis* 95: 103440. [CrossRef]

Gunnarsson, Elias Søvik, Håkon Ramon Isern, Aristidis Kaloudis, Morten Risstad, Benjamin Vigdel, and Sjur Westgaard. 2024. Prediction of Realized Volatility and Implied Volatility Indices Using AI and Machine Learning: A Review. *International Review of Financial Analysis* 93: 103221–21. [CrossRef]

Hochreiter, Sepp, and Jürgen Schmidhuber. 1997. Long Short-Term Memory. *Neural Computation* 9: 1735–80. [CrossRef]

Hong, Jichao, Fengwei Liang, Xun Gong, Xiaoming Xu, and Quanqing Yu. 2022. Accurate State of Charge Estimation for Real-World Battery Systems Using a Novel Grid Search and Cross Validated Optimised LSTM Neural Network. *Energies* 15: 9654. [CrossRef]

Hurst, Harold Edwin. 1951. Long-Term Storage Capacity of Reservoirs. *Transactions of the American Society of Civil Engineers* 116: 770–99. [CrossRef]

Imrana, Yakubu, Yanping Xiang, Liaqat Ali, and Zaharawu Abdul-Rauf. 2021. A Bidirectional LSTM Deep Learning Approach for Intrusion Detection. *Expert Systems with Applications* 185: 115524. [CrossRef]

Jakimowicz, Aleksander. 2020. The Role of Entropy in the Development of Economics. *Entropy* 22: 452. [CrossRef]

Karaca, Yeliz, and Dumitru Baleanu. 2020. A novel R/S fractal analysis and wavelet entropy characterization approach for robust forecasting based on self-similar time series modeling. *Fractals* 28: 2040032. [CrossRef]

Karaca, Yeliz, Yu-Dong Zhang, and Khan Muhammad. 2020. Characterizing Complexity and Self-Similarity Based on Fractal and Entropy Analyses for Stock Market Forecast Modelling. *Expert Systems with Applications* 144: 113098. [CrossRef]

Kim, Jihyun, and Howon Kim. 2015. Applying Recurrent Neural Network to Intrusion Detection with Hessian Free Optimization. In *Information Security Applications*. Edited by Ho-won Kim and Dooho Choi. Switzerland: Springer, pp. 357–69.

Kim, Sondo, Seungmo Ku, Woojin Chang, and Jae Wook Song. 2020. Predicting the Direction of US Stock Prices Using Effective Transfer Entropy and Machine Learning Techniques. *IEEE Access* 8: 111660–82. [CrossRef]

Kirisci, Melih, and Ozge Cagcag Yolcu. 2022. A New CNN-Based Model for Financial Time Series: TAIEX and FTSE Stocks Forecasting. *Neural Processing Letters* 54: 3357–74. [CrossRef]

Kumbure, Mahinda Mailagaha, Christoph Lohrmann, Pasi Luukka, and Jari Porras. 2022. Machine Learning Techniques and Data for Stock Market Forecasting: A Literature Review. *Expert Systems with Applications* 197: 116659. [CrossRef]

Kutner, Ryszard, Christophe Schinckus, and Harry Eugene Stanley. 2022. Three Risky Decades: A Time for Econophysics? *Entropy* 24: 627. [CrossRef]

Lahmiri, Salim, and Stelios Bekiros. 2021. The Effect of COVID-19 on Long Memory in Returns and Volatility of Cryptocurrency and Stock Markets. *Chaos, Solitons & Fractals* 151: 111221. [CrossRef]

Liu, Wenkai, Ping Guo, and Lian Ye. 2019. A Low-Delay Lightweight Recurrent Neural Network (LLRNN) for Rotating Machinery Fault Diagnosis. *Sensors* 19: 3109. [CrossRef]

Liu, Yifan, Zengchang Qin, Pengyu Li, and Tao Wan. 2017. Stock Volatility Prediction Using Recurrent Neural Networks with Sentiment Analysis. In *Advances in Artificial Intelligence: From Theory to Practice*. Cham: Springer, pp. 192–201. [CrossRef]

Mashrur, Akib, Wei Luo, Nayyar A. Zaidi, and Antonio Robles-Kelly. 2020. Machine Learning for Financial Risk Management: A Survey. *IEEE Access* 8: 203203–23. [CrossRef]

Minadakis, George, Stelios M. Potirakis, John Stonham, Constantinos Nomicos, and Konstantinos Eftaxias. 2012. The Role of Propagating Stress Waves on a Geophysical Scale: Evidence in Terms of Nonextensivity. *Physica A: Statistical Mechanics and Its Applications* 391: 5648–57. [CrossRef]

Neto, João Nunes De Mendonça, Luiz Paulo Lopes Fávero, and Renata Turola Takamatsu. 2018. Hurst exponent, fractals and neural networks for forecasting financial asset returns in Brazil. *International Journal of Data Science* 3: 29–49. [CrossRef]

Ni, Li-Ping, Zhi-Wei Ni, and Ya-Zhuo Gao. 2011. Stock Trend Prediction Based on Fractal Feature Selection and Support Vector Machine. *Expert Systems with Applications* 38: 5569–76. [CrossRef]

Nikolova, Venelina, Juan E. Trinidad Segovia, Manuel Fernández-Martínez, and Miguel Angel Sánchez-Granero. 2020. A Novel Methodology to Calculate the Probability of Volatility Clusters in Financial Series: An Application to Cryptocurrency Markets. *Mathematics* 8: 1216. [CrossRef]

Parkinson, Michael. 1980. The Extreme Value Method for Estimating the Variance of the Rate of Return. *The Journal of Business* 53: 61. [CrossRef]

Pearlmutter, Barak A. 1995. Gradient Calculations for Dynamic Recurrent Neural Networks: A Survey. *IEEE Transactions on Neural Networks* 6: 1212–28. [CrossRef]

Pineda, Fernando J. 1987. Generalization of Back Propagation to Recurrent and Higher Order Neural Networks. In *Neural Information Processing Systems*. Cambridge, MA: MIT Press.

Potirakis, Stelios M., Pavlos I. Zitis, and Konstantinos Eftaxias. 2013. Dynamical Analogy between Economical Crisis and Earthquake Dynamics within the Nonextensive Statistical Mechanics Framework. *Physica A: Statistical Mechanics and Its Applications* 392: 2940–54. [CrossRef]

Raubitzek, Sebastian, and Thomas Neubauer. 2021a. Combining Measures of Signal Complexity and Machine Learning for Time Series Analyis: A Review. *Entropy* 23: 1672. [CrossRef]

Raubitzek, Sebastian, and Thomas Neubauer. 2021b. Taming the Chaos in Neural Network Time Series Predictions. *Entropy* 23: 1424. [CrossRef]

Rogers, Chris, and Stephen E. Satchell. 1991. Estimating Variance from High, Low and Closing Prices. *The Annals of Applied Probability* 1: 504–12. [CrossRef]

Sarveswararao, Vangala, Vadlamani Ravi, and Yelleti Vivek. 2023. ATM Cash Demand Forecasting in an Indian Bank with Chaos and Hybrid Deep Learning Networks. *Expert Systems with Applications* 211: 118645. [CrossRef]

Selvaratnam, Somesh, and Michael Kirley. 2006. Predicting Stock Market Time Series Using Evolutionary Artificial Neural Networks with Hurst Exponent Input Windows. In *AI 2006: Advances in Artificial Intelligence*. Edited by Abdul Sattar and Byeong-Ho Kang. Switzerland: Springer, pp. 617–26.

Siegenfeld, Alexander F., and Yaneer Bar-Yam. 2020. An Introduction to Complex Systems Science and Its Applications. *Complexity* 2020: 1–16. [CrossRef]

Steurer, Miriam, Robert J. Hill, and Norbert Pfeifer. 2021. Metrics for Evaluating the Performance of Machine Learning Based Automated Valuation Models. *Journal of Property Research* 38: 99–129. [CrossRef]

Takaishi, Tetsuya. 2020. Rough Volatility of Bitcoin. *Finance Research Letters*, 101379. [CrossRef]

Todorova, Neda. 2011. Volatility Estimators Based on Daily Price Ranges versus the Realized Range. *Applied Financial Economics* 22: 215–29. [CrossRef]

Todorova, Neda, and Sven Husmann. 2011. A Comparative Study of Range-Based Stock Return Volatility Estimators for the German Market. *Journal of Futures Markets* 32: 560–86. [CrossRef]

Tzouras, Spilios, Christoforos Anagnostopoulos, and Emma McCoy. 2015. Financial Time Series Modeling Using the Hurst Exponent. *Physica A: Statistical Mechanics and Its Applications* 425: 50–68. [CrossRef]

Vortelinos, Dimitrios I. 2014. Optimally Sampled Realized Range-Based Volatility Estimators. *Research in International Business and Finance* 30: 34–50. [CrossRef]

Xu, Bing, and Jamal Ouenniche. 2012. A Data Envelopment Analysis-Based Framework for the Relative Performance Evaluation of Competing Crude Oil Prices' Volatility Forecasting Models. *Energy Economics* 34: 576–83. [CrossRef]

Yakuwa, Fuminori, Mika Yoneyama, and Yasuhiko Dote. 2004. Novel Time Series Analysis and Prediction of Stock Trading Using Fractal Theory and Time-Delayed Neural Networks. *International Journal of Hybrid Intelligent Systems* 1: 72–79. [CrossRef]

Yang, Dennis, and Qiang Zhang. 2000. Drift Independent Volatility Estimation Based on High, Low, Open, and Close Prices. *The Journal of Business* 73: 477–92. [CrossRef]

Yu, Yong, Xiaosheng Si, Changhua Hu, and Jianxun Zhang. 2019. A Review of Recurrent Neural Networks: LSTM Cells and Network Architectures. *Neural Computation* 31: 1235–70. [CrossRef]

Zhang, G. Peter, B. Eddy Patuwo, and Michael Y. Hu. 2001. A Simulation Study of Artificial Neural Networks for Nonlinear Time-Series Forecasting. *Computers & Operations Research* 28: 381–96. [CrossRef]

Zitis, Pavlos I., Shinji Kakinaka, Ken Umeno, Michael P. Hanias, Stavros G. Stavrinides, and Stelios M. Potirakis. 2023a. Investigating Dynamical Complexity and Fractal Characteristics of Bitcoin/US Dollar and Euro/US Dollar Exchange Rates around the COVID-19 Outbreak. *Entropy* 25: 214. [CrossRef] [PubMed]

Zitis, Pavlos I., Shinji Kakinaka, Ken Umeno, Stavros G. Stavrinides, Michael P. Hanias, and Stelios M. Potirakis. 2023b. The Impact of COVID-19 on Weak-Form Efficiency in Cryptocurrency and Forex Markets. *Entropy* 25: 1622. [CrossRef] [PubMed]

Zitis, Pavlos I., Stelios M. Potirakis, Georgios Balasis, and Konstantinos Eftaxias. 2021. An Exploratory Study of Geospace Perturbations Using Financial Analysis Tools in the Context of Complex Systems. *Geosciences* 11: 239. [CrossRef]
Zitis, Pavlos I., Yiannis Contoyiannis, and Stelios M. Potirakis. 2022. Critical Dynamics Related to a Recent Bitcoin Crash. *International Review of Financial Analysis* 84: 102368. [CrossRef]
Zournatzidou, Georgia, and Christos Floros. 2023. Hurst Exponent Analysis: Evidence from Volatility Indices and the Volatility of Volatility Indices. *Journal of Risk and Financial Management* 16: 272. [CrossRef]

Journal of
Risk and Financial Management

MDPI

Article

Forecasting Orange Juice Futures: LSTM, ConvLSTM, and Traditional Models Across Trading Horizons

Apostolos Ampountolas

School of Hospitality Administration, Boston University, Boston, MA 02215, USA; aampount@bu.edu

Abstract: This study evaluated the forecasting accuracy of various models over 5-day and 10-day trading horizons to predict the prices of orange juice futures (OJ = F). The analysis included traditional models like Autoregressive Integrated Moving Average (ARIMA) and advanced neural network models such as Long Short-Term Memory (LSTM), Recurrent Neural Network (RNN), Backpropagation Neural Network (BPNN), Support Vector Regression (SVR), and Convolutional Long Short-Term Memory (ConvLSTM), incorporating factors like the Commodities Index and the S&P500 Index. We employed loss function metrics and various tests to assess model performance. The results indicated that for the 5-day horizon, the LSTM and ConvLSTM consistently outperformed the other models. LSTM achieved the lowest error rates and demonstrated superior capability in capturing temporal dependencies, especially in single-factor and S&P500 Index predictions. ConvLSTM also performed strongly, effectively modeling spatial and temporal data patterns. In the 10-day horizon, similar trends were observed. LSTM and ConvLSTM models had significantly lower errors and better alignment with actual values. The BPNN model performed well when all factors were included, and the SVR model maintained consistent accuracy, particularly for single-factor predictions. The Diebold–Mariano (DM) test indicated significant differences in forecasting accuracy, favoring advanced neural network models. In addition, incorporating multiple influencing factors further improved predictive performance, enhancing investment outcomes and reducing risk.

Keywords: orange juice futures price; time series forecasting; LSTM; RNN; BPNN; SVR; ConvLSTM; machine learning; commodities

1. Introduction

The study of commodity market dynamics has been a cornerstone of financial research, offering valuable perspectives on price formation, risk management, and market efficiency. The global economy relies heavily on commodities, particularly the oil and natural gas sector, as well as other important commodities such as energy, agriculture, minerals, and metals. Among the range of commodities, orange juice futures (OJ = F) have been a particularly interesting area of study already for several decades (Roll 1984) due to their distinctive market traits and the significant impact of both natural and economic factors. In addition, evaluating orange juice prices is crucial because several interrelated factors significantly impact the global market and consumer behavior (Wang and Wei 2021; Zhang et al. 2018).

Is it possible to reliably predict commodity prices? This question has been the subject of ongoing discussion in the financial and economic literature. For example, the recent surge in orange juice prices can be attributed to extreme weather events and persistent diseases affecting major orange-producing regions, i.e., hurricanes and pest infestations (Durbin and Pollastri 2024). Weather greatly influences orange juice production, unlike other widely produced commodities. Nevertheless, commodity prices are generally considered more unpredictable than stock prices or exchange rates, posing challenges for accurate forecasting. Factors like the interaction of demand and supply, economic expansion, market predictions, government regulations, and unexpected events such as spillover effects, pandemics, war, and global debt crises all have an impact on commodity futures prices (Zhao et al. 2016). These complex factors are the primary drivers of the significant price fluctuations in the spot market prices of commodities. As a result, the expectation is that predicting commodity price trends, specifically, in this case, the orange juice futures prices, will not only help mitigate volatility and reduce risk in commodity markets but can also support governmental entities in making sound and long-term economic choices. Therefore, the motivation for this research is tied to the unique characteristics of the orange juice futures market, which is heavily influenced by various factors that create challenges for traders and investors. The study highlights the need to develop robust forecasting models to improve investment outcomes and reduce market risks, especially given the significant volatility of orange juice futures prices compared to other commodities like gold or oil.

Given the latest technological advancements, various methods are being utilized to forecast prices in the financial industry (Ampountolas 2023; Gupta and Nigam 2020). Although traditional econometric techniques, for example, the vector autoregressive model (VAR) struggle to accurately predict the non-linear aspects of commodity prices due to their robust linear assumptions (Sun et al. 2022; Wang and Fang 2022), advanced models such as machine learning techniques have gained significant attention due to their ability to observe volatility characteristics, non-linear information, and historical data effectively (Ampountolas 2024; Butler et al. 2021; Zhao et al. 2017) or combining models (Barrow and Crone 2016). Therefore, in the financial and economics literature, we have encountered many authors since the early years, for example, Kroner et al. (1995) who employed machine learning techniques, such as the Support Vector Regression (SVR), Long Short-Term Memory (LSTM), Recurrent Neural Networks (RNNs), Multi-Layer Perceptron (MLP), convolutional neural networks (CNNs), gate recurrent units (GRUs), backpropagation (BPNN) models, and many other models to validate the impact of various factors on predicting commodity futures prices.

Limited literature examines the price forecasts of orange juice futures (OJ = F) as an independent asset. Most research focuses on commodities like gold or oil, with many papers examining multiple commodities inclusively. Motivated by this and the enormous price growth during the last two years, we examine various forecasting models—ARIMA, LSTM, RNN, BPNN, SVR, NAR, and ConvLSTM—to predict commodity futures market's prices of orange juice futures prices. We also include other factors such as commodity futures (ES = F) and S&P500 Indexes. Therefore, we employ two forecasting horizons: 5 trading days and 10 trading days. Thus, this study aims to contribute to current research by analyzing and predicting the price trends of orange juice futures in the selected commodity markets. Additionally, we present a comparative analysis of the forecasting models based on loss functions and performance metrics. As such, predicting orange juice futures prices is essential because this market is highly volatile and affected by a range of unpredictable factors that have significant economic impacts. Accurate predictions can help stakeholders mitigate volatility, manage risk, and make more informed decisions in the commodity market. Moreover, given the increasing price volatility in recent years, enhanced forecasting methods can improve profitability for stakeholders involved in futures trading.

Our results revealed that for both the 5-day and 10-day horizons, advanced neural network models, particularly LSTM and ConvLSTM, consistently outperformed the other forecasting models. These models achieved the lowest error rates and demonstrated superior capability in capturing temporal dependencies, with ConvLSTM also effectively modeling spatial and temporal data patterns. The directional accuracy and Diebold and Mariano (1995) test supported the findings. In the 10-day horizon, the LSTM and ConvLSTM models again showed significantly lower errors and better alignment with actual values than ARIMA, which had the highest error rates. The BPNN model performed well when all factors were included, and the SVR model maintained consistent accuracy, especially for single-factor predictions. The DM test indicated significant differences in forecasting accuracy, favoring advanced neural network models.

Section 2 briefly overviews the current literature, and Section 3 discusses the relevant forecasting models and performance assessment metrics and details the data. Section 4 then presents an analysis of the empirical study's findings. Section 5 summarizes the study's conclusions and outlines potential directions for future research.

2. Literature Review

In one of the earliest studies, Roll (1984) confirmed that the weather condition variable impacts the market for frozen concentrated juice. Orange juice prices are impacted by high volatility as a result of concerns about extreme weather events that could affect production. However, he demonstrated that weather accounts for only a small portion of the fluctuations seen in futures prices. In another work, Kroner et al. (1995) utilized time-series approaches to generate long-term predictions of commodity price volatility by integrating investors' anticipated volatility. The authors assessed various forecasts of commodity price volatility, categorizing them into three groups: (1) forecasts based solely on expectations derived from options prices, (2) forecasts relying exclusively on time-series modeling, and (3) forecasts that combine market expectations and time-series techniques. They concluded that the forecasts proposed in category (3) outperformed the other two categories. Brooks et al. (2013) analyzed whether there is consistency in the evidence supporting two theories on commodity future pricing over time. The authors explored if the ability of commodity futures to predict prices is related to their seasonal fluctuations, and they also examined if there are changes in the pricing relationships at different times. They found more compelling evidence of seasonal patterns in the basis, which aligns with the storage theory. The findings reveal that structural changes mainly involve adjustments in the starting points rather than the trends, indicating that the predictive power of the basis remains consistent across various economic conditions. The study by Black et al. (2014) investigates how stock and commodity prices are related and whether this connection can be utilized to predict stock returns. Since both prices are associated with anticipated future economic performance, they are expected to have a lasting relationship, while shifts in sentiment toward commodity investments may impact how the response to imbalances occurs. The findings indicated that there is a long-term relationship between stock and commodity prices, and further tests identify disruptions in the predictive regression. The paper by Atsalakis et al. (2016) introduces an innovative method for predicting the price direction of 25 commodities on the global market using a neuro-fuzzy controller. The prediction system utilizes two adaptive neural fuzzy inference systems (ANFISs) to create an inverse controller for each commodity. The findings demonstrate a 68.33% hit rate with a significant improvement in return on equity compared to the buy-and-hold strategy.

In addition to traditional econometric approaches, various machine learning techniques are used to uncover the inherent complexity of commodity prices. The most common machine learning methods include neural networks (NN) and support vector machines (SVM), which are favored for their ability to model intricate characteristics like nonlinearity and volatility. Hybrid models have also demonstrated superior forecasting accuracy compared to their machine learning models. Drachal and Pawłowski (2021) briefly overviews how genetic algorithms (GA) are used to predict commodity prices. The authors concentrated on a hybrid method (i.e., combining genetic algorithms with other approaches) used in situations like determining if a complete forecasting technique can be split into two or more distinct parts, with one part being based on a GA and the other parts based on different methods. Another study by Jiang et al. (2022) utilized various machine learning techniques to confirm the influence of investor sentiment on estimating the price of crude oil futures. The authors included several forecasting models, such as the MLP, LSTM, SVR, RNN, and GRU models. The results indicated that the Long Short-Term Memory model yielded the best results when combined with the composite sentiment index. This was attributed to a reduced rate of accuracy errors and improved directional accuracy when forecasting next-day-ahead prices for time-series analysis. In a similar study, Guo et al. (2023) utilized machine learning to analyze historical data, volatility, and non-linear characteristics. They assessed the predictive capabilities of neural network models such as the GRU, MLP, LSTM, RNN, CNN, SVR, and BPNN models on crude oil futures. The set of assessment tests illustrated that the GRU model surpassed other models in terms of accuracy and performance when forecasting crude oil futures prices. Moreover, the incorporation of relevant factors resulted in enhanced forecast accuracy for the proposed models. A recent study by Zheng et al. (2024) reported the effectiveness of hybrid models in enhancing the accuracy of crude oil price forecasts when compared to single models. Their research introduces an innovative interval-based approach. Initially, they apply variational mode decomposition (VMD) to split the original training series into low- and high-frequency components. The low-frequency component is considered an inseparable random set. It is forecasted using a newly developed autoregressive conditional interval (ACI) model, while the high-frequency component is predicted using interval Long Short-Term Memory (iLSTM) networks. The final interval-valued prediction is obtained by combining the forecasts of both components. Additionally, the study designs and implements a daily trading strategy based on interval-valued data.

Ren et al. (2024) introduced an innovative imaging technique to predict the daily price data of crude oil futures. Utilizing convolutional neural networks (CNNs), they achieved higher accuracy in predicting future price trends than other standard forecasting methods. The findings indicate that images can capture more nonlinear information, which is advantageous for energy price prediction, particularly during significant fluctuations in crude oil prices. In a different study, Ampountolas (2024) studied GARCH models and the Support Vector Regression (SVR) model to understand better how volatility changes in commodity returns, like gold and cocoa, as well as the financial market index S&P500. The evaluation showed that Support Vector Regression (SVR) performs better than traditional GARCH models for short-term forecasting, suggesting it could be a valuable alternative for predicting financial market trends. These results highlight the importance of choosing the right modeling techniques for specific types of assets and forecasting time frames.

In conclusion, an extensive body of literature discusses predicting volatility in commodity futures markets, mainly for energy, crude oil, or metals. Throughout the years, forecasting techniques have progressed from traditional econometric approaches to innovative machine learning methods. Consequently, the accuracy of forecast models is gradually increasing, and at the same time, it has been demonstrated that the variables influencing the prediction of commodity futures prices are varied.

3. Data and Methodology

3.1. Data

This study's data set contained daily historical time series data for three financial assets: orange juice futures (OJ = F), S&P500 futures (ES = F), and the S&P500 Index (GSPC). The dependent variable for this study is the price of orange juice futures. We aim to accurately forecast the price of orange juice futures in the USA market. The dataset covers the period from July 2022 to June 2024 and has 504 observations. The data were obtained from Yahoo Finance. In addition, we utilized the S&P500 futures index and the stock market, i.e., the S&P500 Index, as impact factors in the orange juice futures price estimation model.

3.2. Descriptive Statistics

3.2.1. Dataset Trend

Figure 1 illustrates a noticeable upward trend in the price of orange juice futures (OJ = F) over the two years, characterized by substantial volatility and periodic corrections. Similarly, the trend index confirms the bullish trajectory, with the futures price increasing by 145.17% from the beginning date for the dataset. In this context, the analysis highlights the potential for significant returns while emphasizing the volatility of commodity futures markets. Such insights are vital for investors and market analysts to make informed trading and investment decisions.

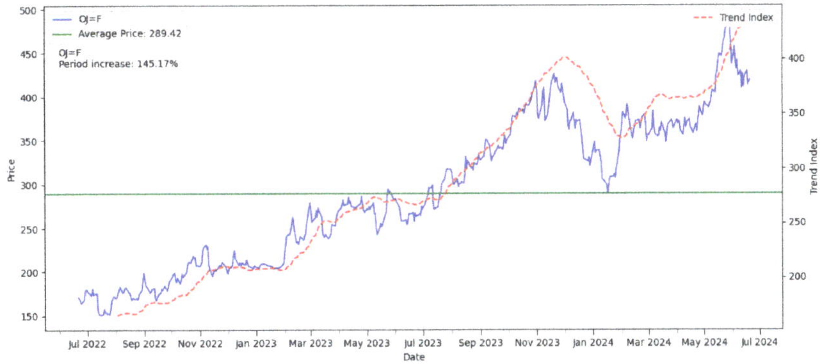

Figure 1. Orange juice futures price and trend.

3.2.2. Summary Statistics

Moreover, Table 1 reports a comprehensive overview of the study's summary statistics of the three financial assets: OJ = F, ES = F, and GSPC. OJ = F has a standard deviation of 82.74, which, relative to its mean, suggests significant variability in prices. This is also supported by the OJ = F price range, which shows a broad price range that aligns with its high standard deviation. In contrast, ES = F and GSPC have higher absolute standard deviations of 483.97 and 478.46, respectively, but these are small relative to their higher mean values and thus have relatively low volatility compared to OJ = F. Finally, OJ = F has a kurtosis of −1.1256, suggesting less frequent extreme deviations from the mean. ES = F and GSPC have kurtosis values of −0.7725 and −0.7436, respectively, indicating a similar but slightly less pronounced platykurtic distribution. At the same time, OJ = F shows a slight positive skewness of 0.1262, suggesting a marginally longer right tail. The financial indices, ES = F and GSPC, have higher positive skewness values of 0.5726 and 0.5850, respectively, indicating a more noticeable asymmetry with a longer right tail.

Table 1. Dataset summary statistics.

Asset	Obs	Mean	Std. Dev	Min	Max	Kurtosis	Skewness
OJ = F	504	289.4238	82.7351	150.6500	487.2000	−1.1256	0.1262
Financial Indices							
ES = F	504	4394.4995	483.9666	3588.5000	5491.0000	−0.7725	0.5726
GSPC	503	4376.1165	478.4562	3577.0300	5487.0298	−0.7436	0.5850

3.3. *Forecasting Models*

3.3.1. Autoregressive Integrated Moving Average (ARIMA)

The Autoregressive Integrated Moving Average (ARIMA) model is a prominent statistical forecasting technique within the ARMA linear model class. According to Hyndman and Athanasopoulos (2018), the development of exponential smoothing models hinges on identifying trends and seasonality in the data. In contrast, ARIMA models are adept at handling stationary, non-stationary, and seasonal processes of order (p, d, q). The general form of the ARIMA model is represented as

$$(1-\phi_1 B)\,(1-\Phi_1 B^4)(1-B)(1-B^4)y_t = (1+\theta_1 B)\,(1+\Theta_1 B^4)\varepsilon_t \tag{1}$$

In this equation, y_t denotes the observed value at time t, and ε_t represents the error term, assumed to be white noise with a Gaussian distribution, having a mean of zero and a constant variance σ^2. The ARIMA model is denoted by ARIMA(p, d, q), where selecting the appropriate order (p, d, q) is a critical aspect of the ARIMA modeling procedure.

ARIMA models can be applied to both seasonal and non-seasonal data. Seasonal ARIMA requires a more intricate specification of the model components. Prior to estimating the time series models, it is essential to perform the augmented Dickey–Fuller (ADF) test Dickey and Fuller (1979) to determine the stationarity of the dataset. If the series is found to be non-stationary, data transformation is necessary. The ADF test is defined as follows:

$$\Delta x_t = \alpha_0 + b_0 x_{t-1} + \sum_{i=1}^{k} c_0 \Delta x_{t-1} + w_t \tag{2}$$

Here, Δ denotes the difference operator; α_0, b_0, and c_0 are coefficients to be estimated; x is the variable under examination; and w is the white noise error term. The null hypothesis ($b_0 = 0$) indicates that the series is non-stationary, while the alternative hypothesis ($b_0 < 0$) suggests that the series is stationary.

3.3.2. Recurrent Neural Network (RNN)

The RNN is structured with input, hidden, and output layers, allowing it to handle and retain new data simultaneously, thus enabling information transfer to subsequent periods (Henrique et al. 2018). Due to its feedback mechanism, the RNN incorporates historical data in its predictions. However, it struggles with retaining long-term data and may suffer from gradient explosion issues (Jiang et al. 2022). The RNN calculations are as follows:

$$h_t = f_h(u_t x_t + W_{t-1} h_{t-1}) \tag{3}$$

$$y_{t+T} = f_y(v_t h_t + b_y) \tag{4}$$

where h_t represents the hidden layer vector, x_t is the input layer vector, y_{t+T} is the output layer, u_t is the input-to-hidden weight at time t, v_t is the hidden-to-output weight at time t, and W_{t-1} is the weight from the output state at time $t-1$ to the hidden state at time t.

3.3.3. Long Short-Term Memory (LSTM)

LSTM is an advanced version of RNN featuring forget, input, and output gates. It leverages RNN's strengths while mitigating its weaknesses, making it suitable for time series prediction. Based on Jiang et al. (2022), the transfer process is detailed as follows:

$$F_t = \rho(W_{fx} x_t + W_{fh} h_{t-1} + b_f) \tag{5}$$

$$I_t = \rho(W_{ix} x_t + W_{ih} h_{t-1} + b_i) \tag{6}$$

$$O_t = \rho(W_{ox} x_t + W_{oh} h_{t-1} + b_o) \tag{7}$$

$$C_t = f_t \circ c_{t-1} + i_t \circ \tanh(W_{cx} x_t + W_{ch} h_{t-1} + b_c) \tag{8}$$

$$h_t = o_t \circ \tanh(c_t) \tag{9}$$

where F_t is the forget gate at time t, W is the weight matrix, x_t is the input vector at time t, b the bias parameter, h_t is the hidden state vector at time t, I_t is the input gate at time t, O_t is the output gate at time t, ρ and tanh are the activation functions, and C_t is the candidate set.

3.3.4. Convolutional Long Short-Term Memory (ConvLSTM)

The Convolutional Long Short-Term Memory (ConvLSTM) model represents an advanced neural network architecture specifically designed to handle spatiotemporal data by integrating convolutional operations within the LSTM framework. The traditional fully connected LSTM (FC-LSTM) is powerful for sequence modeling but lacks the capability to effectively capture spatial correlations, as it uses fully connected layers that disregard spatial information. ConvLSTM addresses this limitation by incorporating convolutional structures in both the input-to-state and state-to-state transitions, allowing it to capture local spatial dependencies better.

The fundamental equations governing ConvLSTM are as follows:

$$i_t = \sigma(W_{xi} * X_t + W_{hi} * H_{t-1} + W_{ci} \circ C_{t-1} + b_i) \tag{10}$$

$$f_t = \sigma(W_{xf} * X_t + W_{hf} * H_{t-1} + W_{cf} \circ C_{t-1} + b_f) \tag{11}$$

$$C_t = f_t \circ C_{t-1} + i_t \circ \tanh(W_{xc} * X_t + W_{hc} * H_{t-1} + b_c) \tag{12}$$

$$o_t = \sigma(W_{xo} * X_t + W_{ho} * H_{t-1} + W_{co} \circ C_t + b_o) \tag{13}$$

$$H_t = o_t \circ \tanh(C_t) \tag{14}$$

Here, i_t, f_t, and o_t represent the input, forget, and output gates, respectively. The symbols X_t and H_t denote the input and hidden state at time t, while C_t is the cell state. The convolution operator is represented by *, and the Hadamard product is represented by $\circ$.

The ConvLSTM model thus maintains the advantages of traditional LSTM in handling long-term dependencies while enhancing its ability to process data with spatial structures. This makes ConvLSTM particularly suitable for applications like precipitation nowcasting, where capturing both spatial and temporal patterns is crucial. By stacking multiple ConvLSTM layers and forming an encoding–forecasting structure, the model achieves robust performance predicting future states from historical data, significantly outperforming traditional FC-LSTM models in spatiotemporal sequence forecasting tasks.

3.3.5. Backpropagation Neural Network (BPNN)

The Backpropagation Neural Network (BPNN) is among the most popular and extensively used models in artificial neural networks, renowned for its robustness and simplicity. BPNN employs a Multi-Layer Perceptron structure, typically consisting of an input layer, one or more hidden layers, and an output layer. The core principle of BPNN is the backpropagation algorithm, which adjusts the network weights to minimize the error between the predicted outputs and the actual targets. This is achieved through an iterative process of forward and backward passes.

During the forward pass, input data are propagated through the network, generating an output. The error is then calculated using a loss function, such as the mean squared error (MSE):

$$E = \frac{1}{2}\sum_{i=1}^{n}(y_i - \hat{y}_i)^2 \tag{15}$$

where y_i is the actual target value and $\hat{y}_i$ is the value predicted by the network.

This error is propagated backward through the network to update the weights in the backward pass. The learning algorithm performs a gradient descent optimization on the weights linking the nodes in each layer. The weight update rule is derived from the gradient descent method, where the weights are adjusted in the direction that reduces the error. The update for a weight w_{ij} from neuron i to neuron j is given by

$$\Delta w_{ij} = -\eta \frac{\partial E}{\partial w_{ij}} \tag{16}$$

where η is the learning rate, controlling the step size of the weight update. The partial derivative $\frac{\partial E}{\partial w_{ij}}$ is computed using the chain rule, which involves calculating the gradient of the error concerning the weights.

Despite its advantages, BPNN has shortcomings, such as long training times and potential overtraining. However, its robustness and generally good performance across a wide range of applications make it a valuable tool in neural network modeling. Due to its effectiveness and ease of use, BPNN is often considered a benchmark for comparing the performance of other neural network models. This iterative weight adjustment process continues until the network converges to a state where the error is minimized, thereby improving the model's accuracy. BPNN's ability to fine-tune weights through gradient descent is highly effective for various applications, including pattern recognition, time series forecasting, and complex function approximation.

3.3.6. Support Vector Regression (SVR)

Support Vector Regression (SVR) is a non-linear regression technique based on Support Vector Machine (SVM) principles. SVR excels in approximating functions and works by identifying a regression hyperplane in a high-dimensional feature space with minimal risk. According to Kazem et al. (2013), the formulation of SVR can be expressed as follows:

$$f(x) = w^T\phi(x) + b \tag{17}$$

Minimize

$$\frac{1}{2}||w||^2 + C\sum_{i=1}^{n}(\xi_i + \xi_i^*) \tag{18}$$

Subject to

$$y_i - (w \cdot \phi(x_i) + b) \leq \epsilon + \xi_i \tag{19}$$

$$(w \cdot \phi(x_i) + b) - y_i \leq \epsilon + \xi_i^* \tag{20}$$

$$\xi_i, \xi_i^* \geq 0 \tag{21}$$

In this formulation, $x_i \in \mathbb{R}^k$ for $i = 1, 2, ..., n$ and $y_i \in \mathbb{R}$. Here, y_i represents the target value of x_i, w is the weight vector, $\phi(x)$ denotes a non-linear mapping function and b is a bias term. The variables ξ_i and ξ_i^* are slack variables that account for deviations from the margin of tolerance ϵ.

SVR aims to determine the optimal hyperplane that approximates the data with a minimal margin of error and maintains the model's generalization ability by managing the trade-off between the hyperplane's flatness and the error tolerance.

3.3.7. Non-Linear Autoregressive (NAR) Neural Network

A neural network is a computational model designed for data processing that can capture relationships within data. One of the significant advantages of artificial neural networks (ANNs) over other forecasting and modeling approaches is their ability to approximate complex functions with high precision and identify nonlinear patterns in input data without preset assumptions. Dynamic neural networks, particularly the NAR model, are extensively utilized for modeling and forecasting time series data, such as financial time series.

The NAR model addresses nonlinear time series problems by utilizing a single time series and predicting its future values based solely on its past values. Mathematically, the future value of a time series Y_t is forecasted using its previous values $Y_{t-1}, Y_{t-2}, \ldots, Y_{t-d}$, where f represents the mapping function performed by the neural network:

$$Y_t = f(Y_{t-1}, \ldots, Y_{t-d}) \tag{22}$$

This model aims to learn the optimal weights for the neurons to minimize the error between the network's output and the actual values. A crucial aspect of neural-network-based forecasting is the network's architecture, which defines the number of neurons in each layer and the connections between them. A feed-forward network with a hidden layer is commonly employed for time series modeling and forecasting. The NAR neural network typically features a feed-forward structure with a tansigmoid transfer function in the hidden layer and a linear transfer function in the output layer.

Determining the number of hidden neurons and the number of delays in observations (denoted by d) is essential because these parameters significantly influence the autocorrelation structure of the time series. Researchers often rely on trial-and-error experiments to choose these parameters due to the lack of a theoretical method for their determination. In one-step-ahead forecasting tasks, the number of neurons in the output layer is usually set to one.

3.4. Assessment Indicators

3.4.1. Loss Functions

The study presents a comprehensive analysis of the forecasting accuracy of various loss functions, including the commonly used Mean Absolute Percentage Error (MAPE), as well as the Mean Absolute Error (MAE) and Root Mean Square Error (RMSE).

$$\text{Mean Absolute Error: MAE} = \frac{1}{h}\sum_{j=1}^{h}\left|y_{t+j} - \hat{y}_{t+j}\right|, \tag{23}$$

$$\text{Root Mean Square Error: RMSE} = \sqrt{\frac{1}{h}\sum_{j=1}^{h}\left(y_{t+j} - \hat{y}_{t+j}\right)^2}, \tag{24}$$

$$\text{Mean Absolute Percentage Error: MAPE} = \frac{1}{h}\sum_{j=1}^{h}\frac{y_{t+j} - \hat{y}_{t+j}}{y_{t+j}}, \tag{25}$$

where $\hat{y}_{t+j}$ indicates the model's forecast at time t. y_{t+j} refers to the dataset's actual values, h refers to the forecasting horizon, and finally, j indicates the number of historical observations. A lower value obtained from these evaluation indicators signifies a smaller error, indicating that the predictive model effectively converges toward accurate results.

3.4.2. Forecasting Performance Metrics

In addition, we utilize the directional accuracy (DA) and accuracy improvement (AI) metrics and the Diebold and Mariano (DM) test to evaluate the performance of forecasting models.

The directional accuracy (DA) is a metric used to assess forecasting models by measuring their ability to predict the direction of changes in observed values. This is especially valuable in financial forecasting, where accurately predicting whether prices will increase or decrease is often more important than predicting the exact value. A higher DA indicates better forecasting model performance in predicting the direction of changes.

$$DA = \frac{100}{T}\sum_{t=1}^{T} d_t \tag{26}$$

where d_t is defined as

$$d_t = \begin{cases} 1 & \text{if } (Y(t) - Y(t-1))(\hat{Y}(t) - \hat{Y}(t-1)) \geq 0 \\ 0 & \text{otherwise} \end{cases} \tag{27}$$

where $Y(t)$ and $\hat{Y}(t)$ are the actual and predicted values at time t, respectively, and T is the sample size. The indicator function d_t checks whether the predicted change in the value (from $t-1$ to t) matches the actual change in the value. If both the actual and predicted changes are in the same direction (both up or both down), d_t equals 1, indicating a correct prediction. If the directions do not match, d_t equals 0, indicating an incorrect prediction.

We have also employed the accuracy improvement (AI) and the Diebold and Mariano (DM) tests to compare the forecasting models more accurately.

The accuracy improvement (AI) is designed to compare two forecasting models. The accuracy improvement is defined as

$$\text{AI} = \frac{S - S_p}{S} \times 100\% \tag{28}$$

where the sum of the absolute errors for a specified model is denoted as S, and the sum of the absolute errors for the proposed model is denoted as S_p. If $AI > 0$, it indicates that the proposed forecasting model performs better, whereas if $AI < 0$, it implies that the proposed model has not overcome the specified model's drawback. The index AI provides a more intuitive way to compare precision.

Finally, we used the predictive accuracy test suggested by Diebold and Mariano (1995) to assess the statistical significance of enhancements in forecast accuracy. This test is commonly utilized to compare the predictive capabilities of various models and ascertain if the differences in accuracy are statistically meaningful.

$$DM = \frac{\bar{d}}{\sqrt{\hat{\sigma}_d^2 / T}} \quad (29)$$

where $\bar{d}$ refers to the mean of the loss differential series d_t and d_t represents the difference between the loss from the first model and the loss from the second model. T represents the number of observations and $\hat{\sigma}_d^2$ indicates an estimate of the variance of d_t.

4. Estimation Results

This study's estimation results present forecasts with a horizon of 5 trading days and 10 trading days. According to the whole evaluation forecasting model, we initially conducted a forecast without influencing factors (single factor—OJ = F). Then, considering the influencing variables, we added the ES = F factor along with the OJ = F. Afterward, we introduced the OJ = F and the S&P500 Index factor, conducting a new estimation, and finally, we performed estimations including all factors in the forecasting process.

4.1. Forecast Results in the 5-Trading Day Horizon

Table 2 presents the forecast accuracy results for the study's various models and the evaluation indicators across different financial indices (Single-factor (OJ = F), Commodities Index, S&P500 Index, and a combined category of all factors) in a 5-trading-day horizon (steps). Compared to advanced models, the traditional ARIMA model shows the highest error rates across all metrics, indicating its limited capacity to handle complex time series data. LSTM stands out with the lowest error rates, particularly excelling in single-factor and S&P500 Index predictions, showcasing its strength in modeling temporal dependencies with high accuracy (e.g., MAE of 12.4155 and 9.4766 and MAPE of 3.1107% and 2.4010%, respectively). RNN and BPNN also perform well, though RNN shows higher errors in the Commodities Index, indicating variability in performance across different data types. SVR exhibits consistent but moderate accuracy, with relatively low errors but less effectiveness than neural networks. BPNN shows low errors, specifically when introducing the Commodities Index and when we combine all factors to forecast the daily price of orange juice futures. While improving over ARIMA, NAR still presents higher errors, especially in the combined category of all factors. ConvLSTM demonstrates robust performance with low errors across most categories, second only to LSTM, highlighting its efficacy in capturing spatial and temporal data patterns. Overall, the results emphasize the superiority of advanced neural network models, particularly BPNN, LSTM, and ConvLSTM, in achieving accurate forecasts in financial time series data.

Table 3 compares the performance of various models in terms of directional accuracy and average improvement over a 5-day prediction period. The ARIMA model, serving as a baseline, shows a directional accuracy of 50.53%. The ConvLSTM model outperforms all others, with the highest directional accuracy of 62.11% and an average improvement of 65.33%. SVR also demonstrates strong performance with a 58.95% directional accuracy and 56.13% average improvement. The LSTM and BPNN models provide moderate enhancements, with directional accuracies of 55.79% and 51.58%, respectively, and average improvements of 39.11% and 51.82%. Interestingly, despite its poor directional accuracy of 46.32%, the NAR model shows the highest average improvement at 66.86%, suggesting it may excel in other prediction aspects. RNN, with a directional accuracy of 47.37%, shows a significant average improvement of 53.59%. Overall, ConvLSTM is the most reliable model for directional predictions, followed by SVR, while NAR and RNN might enhance different prediction metrics beyond directional accuracy.

Table 2. Accuracy of models' forecasting results in 5-trading-day steps.

Models	Metrics	Single Factor	Commodities Index	S&P500 Index	All
ARIMA	MAE	75.3148	77.0628	52.4859	52.3981
	MSE	6904.3332	7212.5565	3565.8827	3546.0604
	RMSE	83.0923	84.9268	59.7150	59.5488
	MAPE	18.8555	19.2984	13.0741	13.0551
LSTM	MAE	12.4155	19.1915	9.4766	14.4386
	MSE	254.8753	522.2959	158.0147	341.6509
	RMSE	15.9648	22.8538	12.5704	18.4838
	MAPE	3.1107	4.8310	2.4010	3.5943
RNN	MAE	13.7396	26.1952	14.7374	14.3007
	MSE	316.8579	970.6563	401.1044	329.8499
	RMSE	17.8005	31.1554	20.0276	18.1618
	MAPE	3.4733	6.6225	3.6936	3.6512
BPNN	MAE	8.4186	42.2337	10.2134	9.9090
	MSE	137.5138	1943.8305	155.2525	159.2351
	RMSE	11.7266	44.0889	12.4600	12.6188
	MAPE	2.1074	10.9688	2.6142	2.5316
SVR	MAE	8.6390	10.7829	10.8827	10.1447
	MSE	142.4235	165.7649	166.9276	156.7200
	RMSE	11.9341	12.8750	12.9200	12.5188
	MAPE	2.1728	2.8067	2.8366	2.6253
NAR	MAE	14.1338	13.7667	13.6553	19.1757
	MSE	289.0329	288.4339	288.7256	501.5138
	RMSE	17.0010	16.9833	16.9919	22.3945
	MAPE	3.6222	3.5077	3.4741	4.9971
ConvLSTM	MAE	11.4094	11.4070	10.4159	14.5008
	MSE	185.1033	182.2130	162.6494	272.5280
	RMSE	13.6053	13.4986	12.7534	16.5084
	MAPE	2.9474	2.9387	2.6706	3.7759

Table 3. Directional accuracy and accuracy improvement—5-day steps (all factors).

	Models	Directional Accuracy (%)	Average Improvement (%)
5-day steps	ARIMA	50.53	–
	LSTM	55.79	39.11
	RNN	47.37	53.59
	BPNN	51.58	51.82
	SVR	58.95	56.13
	NAR	46.32	66.86
	ConvLSTM	62.11	65.33

Next, in Figure 2, we compare each prediction model's estimated results and actual values in the 5-trading day horizon. We observe that the ARIMA model shows poor performance, as its forecasted values are flat and do not capture the trend and volatility of the actual data. LSTM and ConvLSTM models, on the other hand, performed well, closely aligning with the actual data and accurately capturing both the upward trend and fluctuations. The RNN model shows moderate accuracy, better than ARIMA, but still missed some key variations in the data. The BPNN also performs reasonably well, capturing the overall trend with some deviations. However, the SVR displayed substantial divergence from the actual data, indicating its inadequacy in this forecasting context. The NAR model improves upon ARIMA and SVR, capturing the general trend but still missing several peaks and troughs. We conclude that advanced neural network models, particularly LSTM and ConvLSTM, demonstrate superior forecasting capabilities and effectively handle the complexities and nonlinearities present in the time series data.

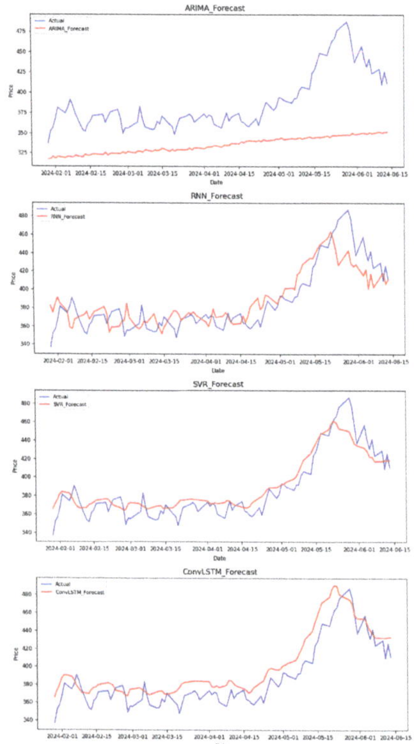

Figure 2. Comparison of forecasting models' actual and predicted values—5-day steps.

Finally, in Table 4, we present the results of the Diebold–Mariano test. The findings reveal significant differences in forecasting accuracy among various models, with ARIMA showing highly significant differences ($p < 0.01$) compared to all other models, suggesting its distinct performance characteristics. Notably, LSTM consistently outperforms other models, as indicated by significant positive DM statistics across all comparisons ($p < 0.01$). In contrast, RNN exhibits a notable negative DM value when compared with the BPNN, indicating inferior performance while showing better performance against SVR, NAR, and ConvLSTM. The BPNN model shows significant differences with SVR, NAR, and ConvLSTM, highlighting its unique predictive capabilities. The SVR and NAR comparisons also indicate significant differences, suggesting varied forecasting strengths. Furthermore, the comparison between ConvLSTM and NAR shows no significant difference, implying similar performance. As such, we observe that the DM test results underscore the variability in forecasting accuracy among the models.

Table 4. Diebold–Mariano (DM) test results among forecasting models in 5-day steps.

Models	Benchmark					
	LSTM	**RNN**	**BPNN**	**SVR**	**NAR**	**ConvLSTM**
ARIMA	17.8053 ***	24.3258 ***	20.7271 ***	25.5028 ***	24.4659 ***	22.6057 ***
LSTM		16.8237 ***	26.5703 ***	50.8174 ***	26.8106 ***	30.5143 ***
RNN			−1.9965 **	3.0291 *	18.2003 ***	9.1926 ***
BPNN				9.5119 ***	18.0418 ***	19.7829 ***
SVR					11.7014 ***	12.5263 ***
NAR						−1.6399

Note: * Significance at 10% level, ** at the 5% level, *** at the 1% level.

4.2. Forecast Results in 10-Trading Day Horizon

Table 5 presents the accuracy of the forecasting models evaluated over 10-day (horizon—trading day) steps across different datasets, similar to 5-day steps. The ARIMA model consistently shows the highest error rates across all metrics and datasets, with an MAE ranging from 51.4101 to 75.0684 and a MAPE from 12.8525% to 18.8773%, indicating its limited efficacy in forecasting complex time series data. In contrast, the LSTM model demonstrates significantly lower errors, with an MAE between 17.7515 and 19.3754 and a MAPE around 4.4288% to 4.7611%, highlighting its superior ability to capture temporal dependencies. The RNN model also performs well, particularly for the Commodities Index, but shows higher variability with an MAE from 18.9532 to 40.0245 and a MAPE from 4.6796% to 10.0940%. The BPNN model exhibits robust performance with the lowest errors among the neural networks in the category of all factors, achieving an MAE of 11.7737 and a MAPE of 2.9399%. The SVR outperforms the other models and maintains consistent, higher accuracy across datasets with an MAE from 12.4496 to 13.9587 and a MAPE of around 3.0931% to 3.4438%. It is noticeable that the SVR is the most accurate model for a single factor, including the Commodities Index and the S&P500 Index. While improving over ARIMA, the NAR model still shows higher errors than LSTM and BPNN, with an MAE between 18.7106 and 19.4742 and a MAPE from 4.7287% to 4.8448%. Lastly, ConvLSTM displays strong forecasting capability, excelling in the Commodities Index with the lowest MSE of 407.6756 and an RMSE of 20.1910 and maintaining a competitive performance across other datasets. These empirical results indicate that the SVR model and, in one case, the BPNN model are the most accurate models for the forecasting of orange juice futures prices, even if additional influencing factors are included in the prediction process. These findings are, to an extent, similar to the estimation results in the 5-trading day horizon, although in the 5-day step forecasts, the LSTM and the ConvLSTM demonstrated superior forecasting accuracy in some cases. Additionally, concurrently incorporating extra relevant factors can enhance all predictive models' performance. Thus, it has been shown once more that integrating influencing factors can decrease the forecasting model's prediction error and boost the accuracy of forecasting orange juice (OJ = F) futures prices.

Table 6 presents the results of the directional accuracy (DA) and accuracy improvement (AI) criterion for various forecasting models over 10-day steps. Directional accuracy measures the percentage of the correctly predicted direction of changes, while AI reflects the percentage improvement over a baseline model, in this study the ARIMA model. ARIMA shows a directional accuracy of 48.89%, serving as the AI baseline. Among the models, BPNN achieves the highest directional accuracy at 54.44%, indicating superior predictive capability in capturing the direction of changes. ConvLSTM, despite having a directional accuracy of 50.00%, shows the most substantial average improvement (63.75%) over ARIMA, highlighting its efficacy in enhancing forecasting accuracy. NAR and LSTM exhibit notable average improvements despite lower directional accuracies (45.56% and 44.44%). RNN and SVR demonstrate moderate directional accuracies (51.11% and 52.22%) but differ in accuracy improvement, with RNN showing a significant improvement (33.30%)

compared to SVR (8.20%). Therefore, the results suggest that while directional accuracy varies across models, advanced neural networks like ConvLSTM and NAR substantially improve forecasting accuracy.

Table 5. Models forecast results accuracy in 10-trading day horizon.

Models	Metrics	Single Factor	Commodities Index	S&P500 Index	All
ARIMA	MAE	67.8574	75.0684	51.4101	51.4660
	MSE	5836.0380	6898.8519	3465.5084	3473.0407
	RMSE	76.3940	83.0593	58.8686	58.9325
	MAPE	17.0000	18.8773	12.8525	12.8667
LSTM	MAE	18.8399	19.2947	17.7515	19.3754
	MSE	640.2273	668.2661	586.0565	707.8805
	RMSE	25.3027	25.8508	24.2086	26.6060
	MAPE	4.6487	4.7541	4.4288	4.7611
RNN	MAE	40.0245	20.8836	18.9532	21.0377
	MSE	2206.0296	812.4532	647.3866	900.3059
	RMSE	46.9684	28.5036	25.4438	30.0051
	MAPE	10.0940	5.1418	4.6796	5.1378
BPNN	MAE	14.5993	17.1953	14.3158	11.7737
	MSE	377.5428	426.3074	344.9291	256.9264
	RMSE	19.4305	20.6472	18.5723	16.0289
	MAPE	3.6595	4.4805	3.5939	2.9399
SVR	MAE	12.9888	12.4810	12.4496	13.9587
	MSE	345.7689	285.5075	284.0731	374.0397
	RMSE	18.5949	16.8970	16.8545	19.3401
	MAPE	3.1915	3.1000	3.0931	3.4438
NAR	MAE	18.7106	18.9656	18.9775	19.4742
	MSE	622.8136	621.6618	633.2322	649.2775
	RMSE	24.9562	24.9331	25.1641	25.4809
	MAPE	4.7287	4.7720	4.7523	4.8448
ConvLSTM	MAE	19.2422	15.5235	15.8455	17.5845
	MSE	621.6677	407.6756	408.7932	495.4774
	RMSE	24.9333	20.1910	20.2186	22.2593
	MAPE	4.9771	3.9664	4.0803	4.5623

Table 6. Directional accuracy and accuracy improvement—10-day steps (all factors).

	Models	Directional Accuracy (%)	Average Improvement (%)
10-day steps	ARIMA	48.89	–
	LSTM	44.44	40.33
	RNN	51.11	33.30
	BPNN	54.44	42.88
	SVR	52.22	8.20
	NAR	45.56	47.96
	ConvLSTM	50.00	63.75

Then, we evaluated the forecasted values from the estimation models, which take into account all the relevant factors with the actual value, as shown in Figure 3. We can observe that the ARIMA model significantly underperforms, failing to capture the upward trend and volatility, indicating its limitations in forecasting complex, nonlinear patterns. On the other hand, the LSTM and ConvLSTM models demonstrate a closer alignment with actual values, particularly in capturing the general upward trend and peak levels, highlighting their superior ability to handle time series data with temporal dependencies. The RNN and BPNN models exhibit moderate performance, capturing some trends but with notable deviations and missed volatility. The SVR model shows substantial divergence from actual values, at least in this context, reflecting its inadequacy. Finally, while better than ARIMA, the NAR model still shows significant discrepancies, particularly in capturing peak values. Therefore, by comparing the predicted and actual values, we find that the LSTM and ConvLSTM models stand out for their enhanced forecasting capabilities, which effectively model the underlying patterns and trends in the data.

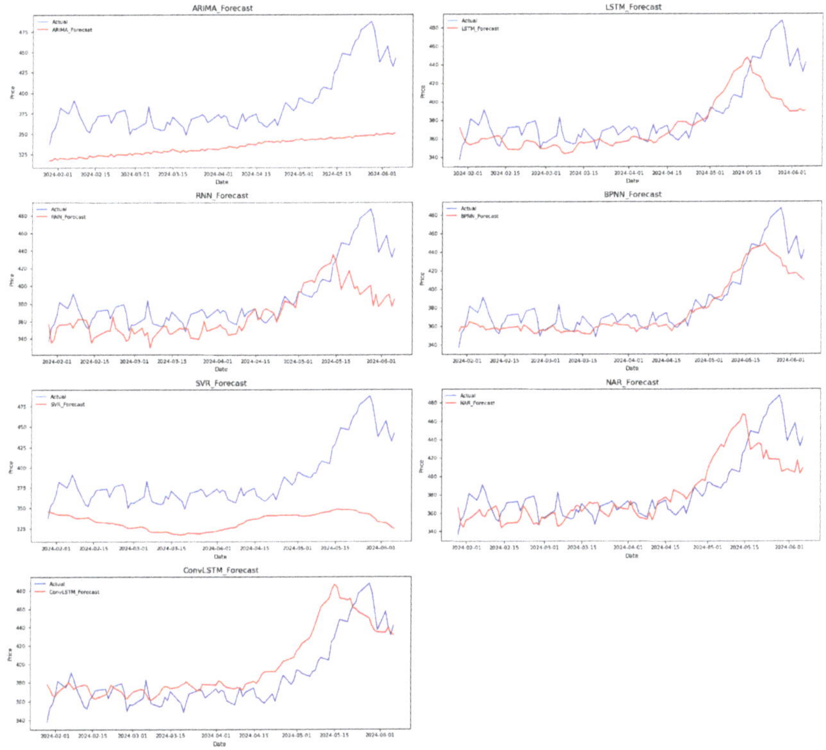

Figure 3. Forecasts model comparison of actual and predicted values—10-day steps.

Finally, we employed the Diebold–Mariano (DM) test to examine the forecasting accuracy of the various models over 10-day steps. Table 7 presents the test results. More specifically, the ARIMA model shows highly significant differences ($p < 0.01$) with all models except SVR, where it slightly underperforms (−0.6466 ***), suggesting ARIMA's generally distinct predictive behavior. LSTM exhibits significantly better performance compared to RNN (−8.3953 ***) and SVR (−17.9334 ***) but slightly outperforms BPNN (1.8406 ***) and demonstrates superior accuracy against NAR and ConvLSTM. RNN's performance is significantly worse than SVR (−16.0307 ***) but better than BPNN (5.8633 ***) and significantly improved over NAR and ConvLSTM. BPNN shows similar trends, underperforming against SVR (−16.2270 ***) but outperforming NAR and ConvLSTM. SVR demonstrates significant superiority over NAR (16.5782 ***) and ConvLSTM (19.7874 ***). Lastly, NAR's performance is significantly outperformed by ConvLSTM (15.6224 ***). In these findings, we observe that the variable forecasting capabilities across models with advanced neural networks like LSTM and ConvLSTM often exhibit superior performance compared to traditional models such as ARIMA, particularly in handling complex time series data.

Table 7. Diebold–Mariano (DM) test results among forecasting models in 10-day steps.

Models	Benchmark					
	LSTM	**RNN**	**BPNN**	**SVR**	**NAR**	**ConvLSTM**
ARIMA	18.5606 ***	17.0005 ***	17.7258 ***	−0.6466 ***	18.1408 ***	21.2885 ***
LSTM		−8.3953 ***	1.8406 ***	−17.9334 ***	8.5297 ***	19.5791 ***
RNN			5.8633 ***	−16.0307 ***	14.6996 ***	19.0879 ***
BPNN				−16.2270 ***	3.1734 ***	19.2480 ***
SVR					16.5782 ***	19.7874 ***
NAR						15.6224 ***

Note: *** Significance at the 1% level.

5. Conclusions

This study evaluated the forecasting accuracy of various models with different configurations over 5-day and 10-day trading horizons to forecast orange juice futures (OJ = F) prices. We have employed a dataset from July 2022 to June 2024. Our analysis included traditional models like ARIMA and advanced neural network models such as LSTM, RNN, BPNN, SVR, and ConvLSTM, with varying influencing factors like the Commodities Index and the S&P500 Index. In addition, we have adopted a set of loss function metrics to evaluate the accuracy of each model and various tests to assess the performance of each forecasting model.

For the 5-trading day forecasting horizon, the advanced neural network models, particularly LSTM and ConvLSTM, consistently outperformed traditional models like ARIMA. LSTM achieved the lowest error rates and demonstrated superior capability in capturing temporal dependencies, especially in single-factor and S&P500 Index predictions. ConvLSTM also exhibited strong performance, highlighting its effectiveness in modeling spatial and temporal data patterns. The directional accuracy and Diebold–Mariano test further supported the superiority of LSTM and ConvLSTM over other models.

In the 10-trading day forecasting period, we observed similar trends. While ARIMA displayed the highest error rates, the LSTM and ConvLSTM models showed significantly lower errors and better alignment with actual values. The BPNN model also performed well, mainly when we incorporated all factors. The SVR model maintained consistent accuracy across datasets, especially for single-factor predictions. The Diebold–Mariano test results indicated significant differences in forecasting accuracy, with advanced neural network models generally outperforming traditional models.

The findings of this study demonstrate that advanced models such as LSTM and ConvLSTM outperform traditional methods like ARIMA in forecasting orange juice futures prices. Specifically, LSTM achieved the lowest error rates across various factors, including the Commodities Index and S&P500 Index. This differs from previous research on commodities such as crude oil and gold, which favored machine learning techniques (e.g., LSTM, GRU) while emphasizing different influencing factors such as investor sentiment and macroeconomic indicators. For example, research by Guo et al. (2023) highlighted the superior performance of GRU in crude oil forecasting, particularly when considering relevant factors like volatility and historical data. Furthermore, while previous studies applied hybrid models to energy commodities, this study demonstrates the advantage of neural network models for commodity markets, emphasizing the need to customize forecasting tools to the distinctive characteristics of each market.

Our empirical results also have practical implications. Therefore, investors and analysts can promptly analyze market trends and identify potential risks based on the forecasting model results. As we have observed, the findings emphasize the superiority of advanced neural network models, particularly LSTM and ConvLSTM, in forecasting complex time series data. These models effectively capture underlying patterns and trends, offering enhanced forecasting capabilities compared to traditional models like ARIMA. Incorporating influencing factors further improves the predictive performance of these models, underscoring the importance of considering multiple variables in the forecasting of financial assets. This optimization enhances investors' investment performance and reduces risk. Therefore, the DM test in both periods supports the above findings by indicating that models like LSTM and ConvLSTM not only provide statistically better predictions but also can offer traders and investors more reliable forecasts for decision-making. This could lead to improved returns and reduced risks, especially in volatile markets such as orange juice futures.

Limitations and Further Research

Despite the promising results, this study, like any other, has limitations that warrant further research. First, the dataset was limited to specific financial indices and assets. As such, future research could explore a broader range of variables and datasets to enhance the generalizability of the findings. In addition, we observed only two forecasting horizons (5-trading day and 10-trading day steps). Examining shorter- or longer-term forecasting estimations could provide more insights into the robustness and reliability of these models.

Second, while advanced neural network models showed superior performance, model optimization is also very important. Future studies should explore different optimization methods to enhance forecasting accuracy or incorporate additional forecasting models, such as hybrid models and parameters. At the same time, although neural networks like LSTM and ConvLSTM can effectively model nonlinear relationships, they require extensive data for training to avoid overfitting, especially in highly volatile markets like orange juice futures. Additionally, neural networks are computationally intensive, requiring significant time and resources for both training and fine-tuning, particularly as the complexity of the network increases. Finally, another practical consideration is the interpretability of these models. Neural networks are often seen as black boxes, making it difficult for users to understand how predictions are derived.

Finally, the study primarily focused on point forecasts. Introducing probabilistic forecasting methods could offer a more comprehensive evaluation of model performance by considering uncertainty and confidence intervals in predictions. Furthermore, the economic implications of these forecasts were not analyzed. Future research should assess the practical applications and financial benefits of employing advanced neural network models for trading and investment strategies.

Nevertheless, the study demonstrated the potential of the models utilized in financial forecasting, and further research could lead to even more robust and practical forecasting solutions.

Funding: This research received no external funding.

Data Availability Statement: Data are publicly available.

Conflicts of Interest: The authors declare no conflict of interest.

References

Ampountolas, Apostolos. 2023. Comparative analysis of machine learning, hybrid, and deep learning forecasting models: Evidence from european financial markets and bitcoins. *Forecasting* 5: 472–486. [CrossRef]

Ampountolas, Apostolos. 2024. Enhancing forecasting accuracy in commodity and financial markets: Insights from garch and svr models. *International Journal of Financial Studies* 12: 59. [CrossRef]

Atsalakis, George, Dimitrios Frantzis, and Constantin Zopounidis. 2016. Commodities' price trend forecasting by a neuro-fuzzy controller. *Energy Systems* 7: 73–102. [CrossRef]

Barrow, Devon K., and Sven F. Crone. 2016. Cross-validation aggregation for combining autoregressive neural network forecasts. *International Journal of Forecasting* 32: 1120–1137. [CrossRef]

Black, Angela J., Olga Klinkowska, David G. McMillan, and Fiona J. McMillan. 2014. Forecasting stock returns: Do commodity prices help? *Journal of Forecasting* 33: 627–639. [CrossRef]

Brooks, Chris, Marcel Prokopczuk, and Yingying Wu. 2013. Commodity futures prices: More evidence on forecast power, risk premia and the theory of storage. *The Quarterly Review of Economics and Finance* 53: 73–85. [CrossRef]

Butler, Sunil, Piotr Kokoszka, Hong Miao, and Han Lin Shang. 2021. Neural network prediction of crude oil futures using b-splines. *Energy Economics* 94: 105080. [CrossRef]

Dickey, David A., and Wayne A. Fuller. 1979. Distribution of the estimators for autoregressive time series with a unit root. *Journal of the American Statistical Association* 74: 427–431.

Diebold, X. Francis, and S. Roberto Mariano. 1995. Comparing predictive accuracy. *Journal of Business & Economic Statistics* 13: 134–144.

Drachal, Krzysztof, and Michał Pawłowski. 2021. A review of the applications of genetic algorithms to forecasting prices of commodities. *Economies* 9: 6. [CrossRef]

Durbin, Dee-Ann, and Tatianna Pollastri. 2024. High Orange Juice Prices May Be on the Table for a While Due to Disease and Extreme Weather—finance.yahoo.com. Available online: https://finance.yahoo.com/news/high-orange-juice-prices-may-151316322.html (accessed on 18 July 2024).

Guo, Lili, Xinya Huang, Yanjiao Li, and Houjian Li. 2023. Forecasting crude oil futures price using machine learning methods: Evidence from china. *Energy Economics* 127: 107089. [CrossRef]

Gupta, Nalini, and Shobhit Nigam. 2020. Crude oil price prediction using artificial neural network. *Procedia Computer Science* 170: 642–647. [CrossRef]

Henrique, Bruno Miranda, Vinicius Amorim Sobreiro, and Herbert Kimura. 2018. Stock price prediction using Support Vector Regression on daily and up to the minute prices. *The Journal of Finance and Data Science* 4: 183–201. [CrossRef]

Hyndman, Rob J., and George Athanasopoulos. 2018. *Forecasting: Principles and Practice*. Melbourne: OTexts. Available online: http://OTexts.com/fpp2/ (accessed on 10 July 2024).

Jiang, Zhe, Lin Zhang, Lingling Zhang, and Bo Wen. 2022. Investor sentiment and machine learning: Predicting the price of china's crude oil futures market. *Energy* 247: 123471. [CrossRef]

Kazem, Ahmad, Ebrahim Sharifi, Farookh Khadeer Hussain, Morteza Saberi, and Omar Khadeer Hussain. 2013. Support Vector Regression with chaos-based firefly algorithm for stock market price forecasting. *Applied Soft Computing* 13: 947–958. [CrossRef]

Kroner, Kenneth F., Kevin P. Kneafsey, and Stijn Claessens. 1995. Forecasting volatility in commodity markets. *Journal of Forecasting* 14: 77–95. [CrossRef]

Ren, Xiaohang, Wenting Jiang, Qiang Ji, and Pengxiang Zhai. 2024. Seeing is believing: Forecasting crude oil price trend from the perspective of images. *Journal of Forecasting* 43: 2809–2821. [CrossRef]

Roll, Richard. 1984. Orange juice and weather. *The American Economic Review* 74: 861–880.

Sun, Yongxuan, Bowen Zhang, Zhizhong Ding, Momiao Zhou, Mingxi Geng, Xi Wu, Jie Li, and Wei Sun. 2022. Environment-aware vehicle lane change prediction using a cumulative probability mapping model. *International Journal of Sensor Networks* 40: 1–9. [CrossRef]

Wang, Donghua, and Tianhui Fang. 2022. Forecasting crude oil prices with a wt-fnn model. *Energies* 15: 1955. [CrossRef]

Wang, Wenting, and Longbao Wei. 2021. Impacts of agricultural price support policy on price variability and welfare: Evidence from china's soybean market. *Agricultural Economics* 52: 3–17. [CrossRef]

Zhang, Dongqing, Guangming Zang, Jing Li, Kaiping Ma, and Huan Liu. 2018. Prediction of soybean price in china using qr-rbf neural network model. *Computers and Electronics in Agriculture* 154: 10–17. [CrossRef]

Zhao, Lin, Xun Zhang, Shouyang Wang, and Shanying Xu. 2016. The effects of oil price shocks on output and inflation in china. *Energy Economics* 53: 101–110. [CrossRef]

Zhao, Yang, Jianping Li, and Lean Yu. 2017. A deep learning ensemble approach for crude oil price forecasting. *Energy Economics* 66: 9–16. [CrossRef]

Zheng, Li, Yuying Sun, and Shouyang Wang. 2024. A novel interval-based hybrid framework for crude oil price forecasting and trading. *Energy Economics* 130: 107266. [CrossRef]

Journal of
Risk and Financial Management

MDPI

Article

Financial Distress Prediction in the Nordics: Early Warnings from Machine Learning Models

Nils-Gunnar Birkeland Abrahamsen [1], Emil Nylén-Forthun [1], Mats Møller [1], Petter Eilif de Lange [2] and Morten Risstad [1,*]

[1] Department of Industrial Economics and Technology Management, Norwegian University of Science and Technology, 7491 Trondheim, Norway

[2] Department of International Business, Norwegian University of Science and Technology, 6001 Ålesund, Norway; petter.e.delange@ntnu.no

* Correspondence: morten.risstad@ntnu.no; Tel.: +47-97166263

Abstract: This paper proposes an explicable early warning machine learning model for predicting financial distress, which generalizes across listed Nordic corporations. We develop a novel dataset, covering the period from Q1 2001 to Q2 2022, in which we combine idiosyncratic quarterly financial statement data, information from financial markets, and indicators of macroeconomic trends. The preferred LightGBM model, whose features are selected by applying explainable artificial intelligence, outperforms the benchmark models by a notable margin across evaluation metrics. We find that features related to liquidity, solvency, and size are highly important indicators of financial health and thus crucial variables for forecasting financial distress. Furthermore, we show that explicitly accounting for seasonality, in combination with entity, market, and macro information, improves model performance.

Keywords: financial distress prediction; credit risk; machine learning; explainable AI; Nordics

1. Introduction

For decades financial distress prediction has been on the agenda of both practitioners and researchers. On the backdrop of globalization and increased economic complexity, researchers have developed quantitative models which can infer the true state of companies beyond what can be captured by simple and rigid methodologies, with machine learning (ML) methods now representing the state of the art.

Regardless of its definition, financial distress prediction relies on data reflecting the company's true situation. Data derived from financial statements play a critical role in this regard. However, as pointed out by Jan (2021), relying solely on information from financial statements for distress prediction is risky due to information asymmetry. Businesses may use different accounting practices, implying that the probability of financial distress can differ for companies with otherwise similar financial statements. This encourages expanding the feature space of prediction models to include macro variables and forward-looking market variables that are helpful in identifying the true state of a company beyond what is available from periodically disclosed financial statements. Furthermore, financial distress prediction is often analyzed on a micro- or lower macroeconomic scale, evaluating either a set of companies within a single country or a specific industry. Arguably, this may be too narrow a scope given the increasingly globalized economy and the scarcity of distressed companies.

This paper makes three distinct contributions to the body of literature. To our knowledge, we are the first to study financial distress among Nordic listed companies over this sample period, the latter covering important economic events such as the financial crisis, the Euro area sovereign and banking crises, and the COVID-19 pandemic. This is of interest for different reasons. Even though the Nordic sovereigns in general are financially sound, the level of political and monetary integration with Europe varies strongly. Thus, it is likely that business risk in the Nordics is different from central Europe. Hence, the empirical results of this paper are of particular relevance for banks and providers of credit who need to monitor the loss potential in their loan portfolios. Moreover, we combine idiosyncratic quarterly financial statement data with information from financial markets and macroeconomic indicators. Through employing this comprehensive feature set within supervised machine learning classification frameworks, and explicitly accounting for seasonality, we show improved model performance compared to traditional methods. We also propose an end-to-end framework for default prediction, which should be useful for both practitioners and scholars.

Our empirical analysis shows that the LightGBM model yields the most accurate results, surpassing the remaining models by a notable margin. Interpreting our results using explainable AI methods, we generally find that the most important predictors align well with the existing literature. Hence, it is reasonable to attribute the superior performance of the LightGBM model to its capability to exploit the complex dynamics of a high-dimensional feature space. Our results are robust to different choices of evaluation metrics.

The rest of this paper is organized as follows: In Section 2 we provide a literature overview. Section 3 introduces data and variables, including our definition of financial distress. Section 4 discusses the models and methodologies employed in our study. Sections 5 and 6 present and discuss the results, respectively, and finally, Section 7 concludes the paper.[1]

2. Literature Review

Since the seminal contributions of Beaver (1966) and Altman (1968), financial ratios have been key ingredients in credit risk analysis. Ohlson (1980) questioned the practical applications of these models and claimed that the output from their discriminant analysis approach could not be intuitively interpreted. Proposed approaches to alleviate these concerns include binary response models (Kim et al. 2020) and conditional probability models (Balcaen and Ooghe 2006). The latter include Linear Probability Modeling (LPM), Logistic Regression (LR), and Probit Analysis (PA). LR is by far the most prevalent approach among the three conditional probability models discussed above and has become a prominent and highly trusted prediction tool in studies on financial distress (Balcaen and Ooghe 2006). Traditional LR is still utilized as a benchmark approach in comparative studies such as Moscatelli et al. (2020).

Luoma and Laitinen (1991) show that observable change in company-specific financial ratios over time exhibits predictive power for default risk. However, there is also a stochastic element in a company's performance caused by exogenous factors, such as industry and market volatility. Recognizing the potentially high number of relevant predictors and their complex dynamics, Jensen (1992); Tam (1991); Yang et al. (1999) and Frydman et al. (1985); Messie and Hansen (1988) introduced machine learning techniques, more specifically artificial neural networks (ANNs) and decision trees (DTs). The ability of ANNs to model highly complex and large quantities of data, dealing with non-linear relationships between input and output variables, has led to the application of ANNs for distress prediction (Iturriaga and Sanz 2015) and credit ratings (Abiyev 2014; Falavigna 2012). Using a broad set of machine learning models, Jiang (2023) found that a firm's idiosyncratic risk and cross-ownership relation with the rating agency were important attributes for predicting ratings. Furthermore, ensemble methods that combine the predictive power of several DTs in their decision process have become a highly effective alternative. Two ensemble methods that have become increasingly popular in recent years are Light Gradient Boosting Machine (LightGBM) and Extreme Gradient Boosting (XGBoost), both of which utilize boosting. Boosting is a sequential ensembling technique, which combines classifiers by putting more weight on misclassified observations in previous steps and generally outperforms non-boosting ensemble methods such as Random Forest (RF) (Bentejac et al. 2021). Ensemble methods which utilize boosting represent the state of the art within corporate financial distress prediction and have shown to be accurate (Qian et al. 2022; Son et al. 2019). XGBoost models, proposed by Chen and Guestrin (2016), entail relatively low computational complexity, are easily adjustable in terms of hyperparameters, and are highly accurate, which makes these models suitable for prediction problems (Du et al. 2020). To further improve computational efficiency, LightGBM was developed by Ke et al. (2017). In a study targeting financial distress prediction for Chinese companies, Qian et al. (2022) used a wrapper-based feature selection process and showed that XGBoost and LightGBM both generally outperformed other classification methods such as LR, ANN, Support Vector Machine (SVM), and RF. A comparison of the results obtained with and without feature selection imposed on the data testified to the selection's positive effect on model performance.

Explainable artificial intelligence (XAI) helps overcome the black-box nature of many machine learning models. The Shapley Additive Explanations (SHAP) framework, and variations thereof, originally proposed by Lundberg and Lee (2017), is the predominant approach to feature importance analysis. Bussmann et al. (2021) applied TreeSHAP for explaining an XGBoost model predicting default risk in Southern European SMEs. The results showed that the most important features for non-defaulting companies were profits before taxes plus interests paid and EBITDA (profitability), and the most important feature for defaulting companies was total assets (size). Recent applications of XAI in the context of credit assessment include De Lange et al. (2022); Melsom et al. (2022) and Hjelkrem and de Lange (2023).

3. Data and Variables

3.1. Definition of Financial Distress

As a continuation of Malakauskas and Lakštutienė (2021) and similar studies' descriptions of financial distress, we employed a proxy-based definition which allowed for an early warning model to recognize companies in early stages of distress. As proxies of default, we used target values of the ICR (Interest Coverage Ratio) in combination with the CR (Current Ratio). The ICR is a solvency measure that describes a company's ability to generate sufficient earnings to cover its interest payments, while the CR is a liquidity measure describing the ability to service its short-term debt or, correspondingly, to withstand short-term fluctuations in earnings. These metrics are commonly used in the credit rating industry as proxies for financial distress; see, for instance, NCR's Corporate Rating Methodology (https://nordiccreditrating.com/uploads/2023-05/Nordic%20Credit%20Rating%20-%20Corporate%20Rating%20Methodology.pdf, accessed on 1 June 2022). Further, ICR and CR are often included in debt covenants, dictating a minimum level of liquidity.[2] Mohammed and Kim-Soon (2012) and Awais et al. (2015) used Altman's Z-score in parallel with a CR value of 1.1 to predict company failure. Both studies found that CR was useful for predicting default. Kozlovskyi et al. (2019) showed that there was a general agreement among experts that a CR lower than one typically indicated a high risk of bankruptcy for a company.

We propose the following thresholds for distress to be used during class labeling of the data: A company that does not generate sufficient earnings to meet bond covenants (ICR less than 1.5, i.e., interest paid exceeding two-thirds of EBIT), and simultaneously suffers from a low degree of liquidity (CR less than one, i.e., current liabilities exceeding current assets), is deemed to be in a financially distressed situation. In total, our distress proxy with the assigned numerical thresholds finds support in both industry practices and the financial literature.[3]

3.2. Dataset

The dataset collected for this project was comprised of quarterly reported financial key figures from Nordic listed companies (excl. Iceland) for the time interval from Q1 2001 to Q2 2022, complemented by macro and financial market data. The data were retrieved from Bloomberg.

We collected data for companies with non-missing values of the Current Ratio (CR) and Interest Coverage Ratio (ICR) during at least 5% of the sample period, since these variables constituted our default proxy definition. Table 1 shows the distribution of companies and classification samples with respect to country of listing.

Table 1. Number of companies per country before and after data cleaning.

Country	Number of Listed Companies	Number of Companies after Data Cleaning	Number of Samples	Number of Distress Samples
Sweden	1092	379 (34.7%)	5383	598 (11.1%)
Norway	589	130 (22.1%)	2745	364 (13.3%)
Denmark	357	67 (18.8%)	1572	131 (8.3%)
Finland	279	63 (22.6%)	1344	112 (8.3%)
Total	**2317**	**639 (27.6%)**	**11,044**	**1205 (10.9%)**

We generated a set of features from the raw data. Table 2 shows the list of initial features and their corresponding category and formula or explanation, if applicable. Some features were unavailable or not in the required format and were thus computed as part of the data pre-processing. We used stock data in conjunction with Global Industry Classification Standard (GICS) codes and corresponding Morgan Stanley Capital International (MSCI) Europe to calculate stock quarterly log returns, industry quarterly log returns, and industry-stock beta for each company. GICS codes are hierarchically structured, and we used the 11 industry sectors at the top level to categorize the different companies. There is little discrepancy in the literature regarding the omission of financial institutions from corporate distress prediction due to their inherently unique structure. Thus, *Financials* (GICS prefix 40), i.e., banks and insurance companies, were excluded from the dataset. Table 3 shows the top-level GICS codes used and their corresponding MSCI index and sector name. In line with common practice, linear interpolation was used to fill gaps in stock data, but extrapolation was avoided to minimize the risk of creating overly synthetic samples. Industry beta values were estimated in a historical trailing-twelve-month manner using Equation (1) (with sample variance and covariance) on log returns from common trading days of MSCI indices and stocks, labeled R_i and R_s, respectively. Conventional market beta values indicating movement of a company's stock price relative to its respective stock exchange index were created similarly. Market betas were assessed relative to the OMXS30 Index, the OSEBX Index, the OMXC20 Index, and the OMXH25 Index for Swedish, Norwegian, Danish, and Finnish companies, respectively. These were market value-weighted indices representing the main stock exchanges of Stockholm, Oslo, Copenhagen, and Helsinki, respectively.

$$\beta_i^s = \frac{Cov(R_s, R_i)}{Var(R_i)} \tag{1}$$

The final type of variables in Table 2 is comprised of the categorical variables GICS Code, Quarter, and Country. Categorical variables are not intended to be interpreted directly as numeric values but rather as discrete nominal groupings. By effect of its tree-based structure, the LightGBM is inherently able to handle categorical values. The ANN and LR, on the other hand, require the categorical variables to be transformed into numerical values in order to interpret them. For this task, we used one-hot encoding[4]. In order to avoid the dummy variable trap[5] associated with the one-hot encoded variables, a single binary entry was dropped per categorical variable.

As evident from Table 1, the minority class constituted a mere 10.9% of samples in the final dataset. To exploit the entire dataset, over-sampling was chosen to combat class imbalance since this achieves class balance by increasing the size of the minority class instead of decreasing the size of the majority class.

Table 2. Feature engineering space. * Firms with dilutive securities issued include the effects of these securities in the calculation of EPS.

Variable Name	Category	Formula/Explanation
Current Ratio	Liquidity Ratio	Current Assets/Current Liabilities
WCTA	Liquidity Ratio	Working Capital/Total Assets
Asset Turnover Ratio	Efficiency ratio	Operating Revenue/Total Assets
Fixed Asset Turnover	Efficiency ratio	Operating Revenue/Fixed Assets
Fixed BEP Ratio	Efficiency ratio	EBIT/Fixed Assets
BEP Ratio	Profitability ratio	EBIT/Total Assets
Profit Margin	Profitability ratio	EBIT/Operating Revenue
ROA	Profitability ratio	Net Income/Total Assets
ROE	Profitability ratio	Net Income/Shareholder Funds
Debt Asset Ratio	Solvency ratio	Total Debt/Total Assets
Debt to Capital Ratio	Solvency ratio	Current Liabilities/Capital
Interest Coverage Ratio	Solvency ratio	EBIT/Interest Paid
Working Capital	Raw value	N/A
EBIT	Raw value	N/A
Total Sales	Raw value	N/A
Total Assets	Raw value	N/A
Capital Expenditure	Raw value	N/A
Fixed Assets	Raw value	N/A
Current Assets	Raw value	N/A
Current Liabilities	Raw value	N/A
Government Bond Spread	Macro variable	10Y Bond Yield—6M Bond Yield
GDP Growth	Macro variable	Quarterly GDP Growth
Industry Beta	Macro variable	See Equation (1)
Industry Index Return	Macro variable	Quarterly Log Return on MSCI-Index
Stock Volatility	Market variable	Annualized Quarterly Stock Volatility
P/B	Market variable	Price per Share/Book Value per Share
P/E	Market variable	Price per Share/Earnings per Share
P/S	Market variable	Price per Share/Sales per Share
Market Capitalization	Market variable	Share Price · Shares Outstanding
Market Index Return	Market variable	Log Return on Stock Exchange Index
Market Beta	Market variable	See Equation (1)
Stock Return	Market variable	Log Return of Stock
EPS	Market variable	Income Available to Common Stockholders/Weighted Average Number of Common Shares Outstanding *
GICS Code	Categorical variable	Affiliated Industry
Quarter	Categorical variable	Seasonal Indicator
Country	Categorical variable	Affiliated Country

Table 3. GICS industry sectors and their corresponding MSCI Europe indices. Number of companies and classification samples are numbers after data cleaning, i.e., from the final dataset.

GICS Prefix	Sector Name	MSCI Index	No. Companies	No. Samples
10	Energy	MXEUEN	46	1202
15	Industrials	MXEUMT	38	739
20	Materials	MXEUIN	153	2755
25	Consumer Discretionary	MXEUCD	57	1130
30	Consumer Staples	MXEUCS	29	651
35	Health Care	MXEUHC	112	1534
40	Financials	MXEUFN	N/A	N/A
45	Information Technology	MXEUIT	100	1467
50	Communication Services	MXEUTC	39	541
55	Utilities	MXEUUT	7	174
60	Real Estate	MXEURE	58	851

3.3. Features

Financial variables: In a comprehensive survey on business failure, Dimitras et al. (1996) reviewed a broad scope of scientific journals from the period 1932–1994 and found from 47 papers that the most important financial ratios could be categorized as solvency and profitability ratios. Working Capital to Total Assets (WCTA) was found to be the single most applied ratio, followed by Total Debt to Total Assets, both solvency ratios. Liang et al. (2016) supported these findings and argued that solvency and profitability ratios held the most important information in predicting bankruptcy when applying several ML models. Other studies such as Lin and Piesse (2004) and Xu and Wang (2009) shed light on operation efficiency, or correspondingly, management inefficiency, pointing to how well the firm and its assets were managed. Financial ratios in this category include Retained Earnings to Total Assets and Total Assets Turnover. Appendix B.1 contains an overview of financial ratios applied most commonly in the financial distress literature between 1930 and 2007, provided that they have been applied in five studies or more. The list, retrieved from Bellovary et al. (2007), shows that the most common ratios include Net Income to Total Assets (NITA), Current Assets to Current Liabilities (Current Ratio), WCTA, EBIT to Total Assets (EBITA), and Sales to Total Assets. We note that the leading ratios are mostly related to profitability, liquidity, and efficiency.

Accordingly, we grouped 12 financial ratios into four categories: liquidity, solvency, profitability, and operation efficiency. The intention behind this classification was to represent a broad spectrum of company characteristics while avoiding outliers.

Market and macro variables: Bonfim (2009) combines firm-level information and macro variables and reports substantial model improvement from including the latter. Charalambakis and Garrett (2018) and Jiang and Jones (2018) report similar results. Campbell et al. (2008) combine equity market data and financial statements data as explanatory variables in their study on corporate distress risk. Chava and Jarrow (2004) obtain superior results from including market variables related to publicly traded equity, compared to accounting-based bankruptcy prediction models. Similar effects are reported by Jiang and Jones (2018) and Jones et al. (2017), from including valuation multiples and market capitalization, respectively. Campbell et al. (2008) report highly variable returns and high CAPM betas for distressed companies, reflecting exposure to overall market conditions. The relevance of industry specific factors has been less frequently explored, one notable exception being Agrawal and Maheshwari (2019) who find that high industry betas are associated with increased probabilities of default. As the targeted companies in this report were listed at various Nordic stock exchanges, we examined betas linked to both industry and stock exchange returns.

Feature selection: Minimizing noise is paramount in applications of ML models. A primary source of noise is found in non-informative features, which complicate the model training and prediction. We used a supervised elimination approach for feature selection. By examining SHAP values of features that were classified by a default-tuned computationally efficient LightGBM using the TreeSHAP algorithm, we conducted a one-step backward elimination to select our final set of features. A subtle but important detail to address is the issue of data leakage since the feature selection process has the potential to extract information from parts of the future test set and apply it before testing. To avoid this, only 50% of the data were used for feature selection and subsequently excluded from the test set.

Figure 1 shows the relative importance of the top 34 features obtained from the feature selection dataset, in terms of the predictions made on a validation set. Features at the top indicate high explanatory power, while those at the bottom are considered less informative. Table 4 shows the final set of features used in this study.

Figure 2 displays the process for generating classification samples from the dataset. A rolling window methodology was used, which entailed a window that moved across the time dimension generating feature–target pairs.

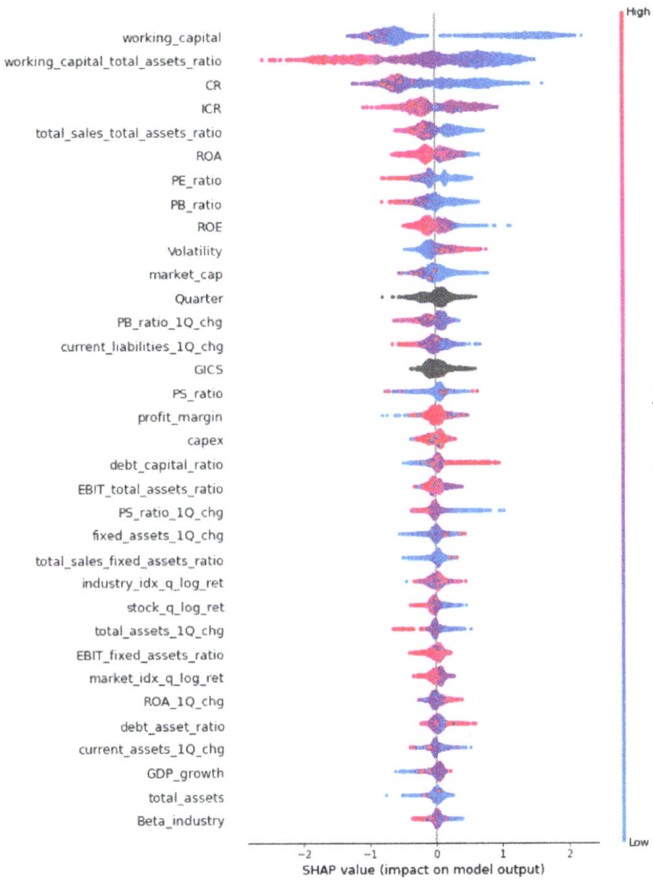

Figure 1. SHAP beeswarm plot showing the 34 most important features. Clusters of SHAP values, represented as dots, left of zero, indicate a feature associated with non-distress. Similarly, clusters right of zero indicate feature association with distress.

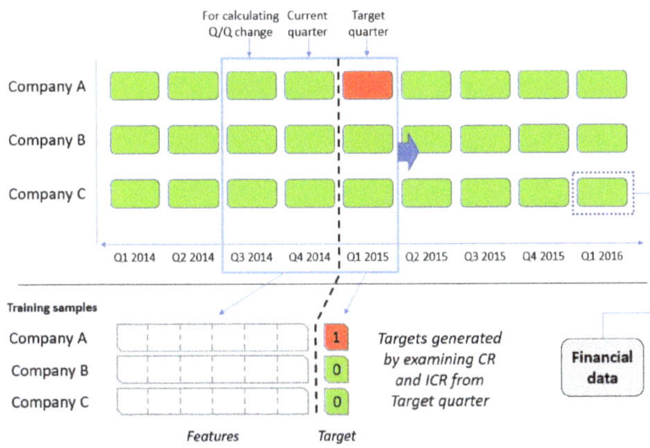

Figure 2. Process for generating training samples: a rolling window using two consecutive quarters of financial data from a company to generate both static and inter-quarter change features.

Table 4. Descriptive statistics for the 32 numerical features included in the final dataset. Ratio and inter-quarter change features are grouped at the top, while inflation-adjusted reported numbers are shown at the bottom.

Feature	Mean	Std	Min	25%	50%	75%	Max
Beta_industry	0.53	0.41	−2.88	0.26	0.5	0.77	2.57
CR	2.14	5.63	0.01	0.98	1.4	2.11	461.95
EBIT_fixed_assets_ratio	−2.18	76.73	−4781.08	−0.02	0.04	0.17	3169.67
EBIT_total_assets_ratio	−0.02	1.95	−203.72	−0.01	0.01	0.03	21.98
GDP_growth	0.89	2.49	−9.3	0.1	0.8	1.9	8.9
ICR	−275.27	13405.7	−1,261,175.0	−1.46	3.34	11.68	88,912.0
PB_ratio	11.2	221.95	0.0	1.11	2.6	6.31	15,659.98
PB_ratio_1Q_chg	0.41	16.77	−1.0	−0.05	−0.01	0.05	1348.27
PE_ratio	52.73	583.28	0.0	0.0	13.37	36.8	41,883.26
PS_ratio	249.3	4982.21	0.02	0.88	2.31	7.83	199,054.15
PS_ratio_1Q_chg	0.04	2.1	−1.0	−0.05	−0.01	0.01	177.71
ROA	−2.64	23.18	−271.88	−4.24	3.12	7.26	221.92
ROA_1Q_chg	0.26	22.35	−477.2	−0.16	0.0	0.18	1661.41
ROE	−4.69	59.95	−1653.96	−10.3	7.57	17.88	1059.74
Volatility	0.38	0.26	0.05	0.22	0.3	0.45	4.67
current_assets_1Q_chg	0.2	10.6	−1.0	−0.09	−0.0	0.09	1107.62
current_liabilities_1Q_chg	0.21	9.7	−1.0	−0.08	0.01	0.13	1013.68
debt_asset_ratio	25.99	19.25	0.0	10.08	24.04	38.76	116.23
debt_capital_ratio	34.96	23.43	0.0	15.74	35.59	51.53	214.29
fixed_assets_1Q_chg	0.67	25.53	−1.0	−0.04	−0.0	0.04	1908.94
industry_idx_q_log_ret	0.02	0.1	−0.61	−0.01	0.04	0.08	0.29
market_idx_q_log_ret	0.03	0.09	−0.38	−0.01	0.03	0.08	0.25
profit_margin	−1747.83	36,474.2	−2,076,500.0	−7.72	3.41	10.53	650,400.0
stock_q_log_ret	0.01	0.26	−2.66	−0.1	0.02	0.14	1.93
total_assets_1Q_chg	0.15	10.11	−1.0	−0.03	0.0	0.04	1061.27
total_sales_fixed_assets_ratio	20.31	407.45	−0.07	0.24	1.09	3.57	23,625.0
total_sales_total_assets_ratio	0.24	3.0	−0.0	0.07	0.19	0.29	304.08
WCTA	0.13	0.23	−0.96	−0.01	0.1	0.24	0.98
capex	−1,695,777	7,675,879	−445,616,793	−555,831	−68,453	−2892	0
market_cap	172,517,645	615,970,230	25,086	2,885,847	16,626,234	76,901,804	10,033,746,355
total_assets	124,749,445	406,931,326	14,030	2,050,788	14,036,938	65,435,701	5,149,789,660
working_capital	11,213,372	72,113,719	−320,357,815	−16,567	508,127	3,947,463	1,117,249,711

Table 5 shows the final dataset after conducting an 80/20 stratified training/test split.

Table 5. Distribution of minority and majority classes in final training and test set.

	Non-Distressed (Label 0)	Distressed (Label 1)	Total
Training	7871	964	**8835**
Test	1968	241	2209
Total	9839	1205	11,044

4. Models

From the literature review in Section 2, we inferred that ML approaches tended to outperform classical models in financial classification tasks. Among supervised learning models Athey and Imbens (2019), we distinguish between linear models, tree-based models, and neural networks. For the purpose of this paper, we did not consider linear models, for instance LASSO, to be appropriate since an a priori specification of feature interactions would be required. Tree-based models and neural networks, however, are well suited to learning such complex and non-linear dependencies from data. Hence, we restricted the empirical analysis to ANN and LightGBM. Furthermore, we employed the LR model as a benchmark due to its frequent appearance and proven track record both in the literature and in the financial industry.

Unlike ANN and LightGBM, the LR model has very few tuneable hyperparameters. Testing revealed no significant improvement from hyperparameter tuning. Our ANN and LightGBM applications, including hyperparameter tuning, are described in Sections 4.1 and 4.2.

4.1. Artificial Neural Network

An artificial neural network (ANN) is a method well suited to solving optimization problems with non-linear relationships. An ANN consists of connected nodes labeled artificial neurons, which resemble neurons in the human brain. The neurons can transmit signals to one another. The neurons are organized in layers, an input layer, intermediate hidden layers, and an output layer. A multi-layer network with more than two hidden layers is called a deep neural network. See Murphy (2012) for a textbook treatment of ANNs.

ANNs are known to be data-hungry and prone to overfitting. Our hyperparameter tuning, including steps taken to address data augmentation (i.e., oversampling) and regularization, is summarized in Table 6 and outlined in the following.

Table 6. Hyperparameters and the corresponding values that were tested during ANN tuning. Lists define discrete values, while U denotes the range of parameter values from a uniform distribution.

Hyperparameter	Values
Number of hidden layers	(2, 3)
Perceptrons in layer 1	$U_{64,512}$
Perceptrons in layer 2	$U_{32,256}$
Perceptrons in layer 3	(0, 16, 32)
Activation function	(ReLU, ELU)
Optimizer	(Adam, SGD w./momentum)
Dropout rate	$U_{0.4,0.8}$
Learning rate Adam	$U_{0.001,0.1}$
Learning rate SGD	Cyclical (0.001, 0.1)
Momentum	SGD (0.9, 0.98)

Number of hidden layers: A model with no hidden layers, i.e., just an input and output layer, is only capable of linear separation. Since our data were linearly inseparable, two and three hidden layers were tested.

Number of perceptrons in each hidden layer: The optimal number of perceptrons in each layer is determined by a trade-off between capturing complex connections and overfitting to the training data. Despite the existence of rules of thumb and research aimed at determining the optimal number of perceptrons, the most common approach is still trial and error Xu and Chen (2008). The number of perceptrons in each hidden layer was chosen randomly from a uniform distribution ranging from 64 to 512 for the first layer and 32 to 256 for the second layer. If present, the third layer was made up of either 32 or 16 perceptrons to limit the search space.

Activation function: The activation function of a perceptron determines how the weighted sum of the inputs is transformed into an output of that perceptron. Since this study deals with binary classification, the Sigmoid function was applied for the output layer. The Sigmoid function transforms any input to a value between 0 and 1, which can thus be interpreted as a probability when there is only one perceptron in the output layer. For the hidden layers, we investigated the Rectified Linear Unit (ReLU) Parhi and Nowak (2020) and the Exponential Linear Unit (ELU) Clevert et al. (2015) functions, primarily motivated by their ability to promote sparsity by reducing the number of active neurons.

Optimizer: Adaptive Moment Estimation (Adam) has recently been proposed as the preferred optimizer for ANNs Desai (2020). However, Desai (2020) demonstrated that Stochastic Gradient Descent (SGD) with momentum outperformed Adam and generalized better under certain conditions. Consequently, we tested both Adam and SGD with momentum, where two common values for momentum were tested, namely 0.9 and 0.98.

Learning rate: The learning rate is arguably the most critical hyperparameter when training a neural network. Setting the learning rate too low causes slower training and raises the probability of convergence to a local optimum, whereas setting the learning rate too high may lead the network to diverge. We evaluate cyclical learning rates with momentum for SGD, as suggested by Smith (2017) as well as non-cyclical learning rates with Adam.

Regularization: Dropout layers combat overfitting by randomly removing perceptrons, along with their associated weight and bias, during training Srivastava et al. (2014). The dropout rate for hyperparameter tuning was selected from a uniform distribution between 0.4 and 0.8.

Figure 3 shows the importance and correlation of hyperparameters with respect to the validation ROC-AUC score achieved by the different ANN configurations. Importance represents each hyperparameter's contribution to the metric, while correlation relates their values. The statistics are based on the top 1000 different model configurations. Since the search through the hyperparameter space was carried out using a Bayesian approach, parameter values that yielded higher ROC-AUC scores were favored by receiving a higher likelihood of showing up in the following configurations. The exact parameter values were chosen based on the analysis below and an assessment of the five top-performing models to avoid choosing unstable model configurations that performed well on the validation data by pure chance.

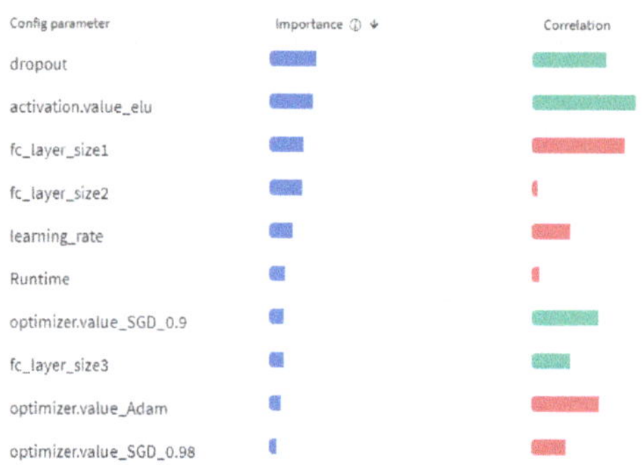

Figure 3. ANN hyperparameter importance with respect to ROC-AUC score on the validation set from WandB. Importance represents the contribution of each hyperparameter to the metric, while correlation relates their values. Green color indicates positive correlation to the ROC-AUC score, while red color indicates negative correlation.

As depicted in Figure 3, the dropout hyperparameter had the highest importance, and the positive correlation coefficient (indicated with green color) suggested that choosing a value in the upper range would be beneficial. We further discovered that three fully connected hidden layers were the best choice for our task and that the number of neurons in each layer should equal 92, 125, and 32, respectively. The optimizer that performed best was clearly SGD with a momentum equal to 0.9. This optimizer was implemented with a cyclical learning rate and was kept for final testing. Finally, ELU was chosen as the internal activation function.

Table 7 shows the hyperparameter configuration chosen for the ANN to be evaluated on the final test set. The batch size of 100 was maintained for final training, but the number of epochs was increased from 100 to 200 to ensure that the final model could find an optimal point of lowest validation loss during training.

Table 7. Final hyperparameter values for ANN.

Hyperparameter	Values
Number of hidden layers	3
Number of perceptrons in each hidden layer	(92, 125, 32)
Activation function	ELU
Optimizer	SGD
Dropout rate	0.7
Learning rate SGD	Cyclical (0.001, 0.1)
Momentum	SGD 0.9

4.2. Light Gradient Boosting Machine

LightGBM is a gradient boosting framework for machine learning based on decision tree algorithms. It grows trees leafwise. We employed the LightGBM framework due to its ability to handle unbalanced data and categorical features, its performance in terms of training speed and accuracy, and its popularity in the literature. Due to its tree-based structure, there is no need to scale or transform input data, and the LightGBM does not rely on assumptions about the input distribution to function optimally. Since they do not employ distance metrics, decision trees, in general, are insensitive to high variance and outliers in the form of extensively large or small values. The fact that several features in our dataset exhibited extreme minimum and maximum values justified the choice of this model. What distinguishes, and makes LightGBM exceptionally fast, compared to similar gradient boosting algorithms, can be explained through three properties: Gradient-Based One-Sided Sampling (GOSS), Exclusive Feature Bundling (EBF), and histogram-based splitting (binning). Table 8 displays the LightGBM hyperparameter training space.

Table 8. Hyperparameter values tested during LightGBM tuning.

Hyperparameter	Values
Gradient boosting method	GBDT, DART, GOSS
L2 regularization	(0, 0.1, 0.3)
Early-stopping rounds	(25, 50)
Number of iterations	(50, 100, 200)
Number of leaves	(8, 16, 31, 50)
Maximum depth	(−1, 25, 50, 75)
Learning rate	(0.01, 0.1, 0.05, 0.2)

The hyperparameter importance and correlation shown in Figure 4 are based on the top 1000 LightGBM configurations from WandB. Contrary to the ANN, the search through this hyperparameter space was performed in a gridlike manner, which ensured that all 3456 configurations[6] of hyperparameter values were trained and tested on the validation set. The most important hyperparameter for the LightGBM in terms of ROC-AUC score was the number of leaves, as is evident from Figure 4. The number of leaves' correlation coefficient was positive, leading us to select the highest value among the top five models, which was the default value of 31. The learning rate and max depth were chosen as the median values of the top-performing models due to their insignificant importance and correlations. The boosting type GOSS was employed with a lower L2 rate of 0.1 despite a negative correlation, due to the fact that all of the top-performing models utilized GOSS and regularization. Finally, choosing too high a value for early stopping seemed to be ineffective, so a value of 25 was selected for the final model. Table 9 displays the final hyperparameter configuration for the LightGBM.

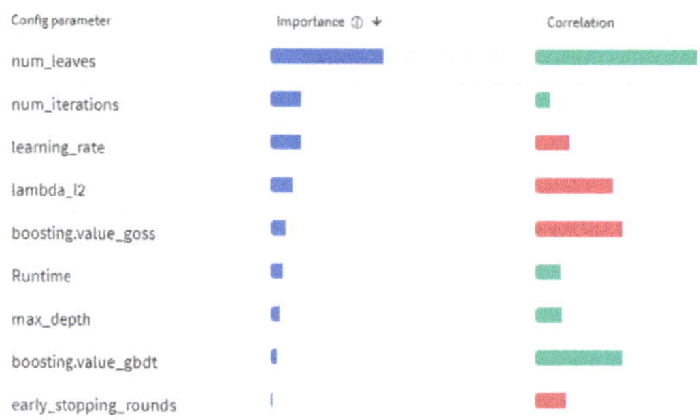

Figure 4. LightGBM hyperparameter importance with respect to ROC-AUC score on the validation set from WandB. Importance represents the contribution of each hyperparameter to the metric, while correlation relates their values. Green color indicates positive correlation to the ROC-AUC score, while red color indicates negative correlation.

Table 9. Final hyperparameter values for LightGBM.

Hyperparameter	Values
Gradient boosting method	GOSS
L2 regularization	0.1
Early-stopping rounds	25
Number of iterations	200
Number of leaves	31
Maximum depth	50
Learning rate	0.05

5. Results

Table 10 shows the precision, recall, F1, and ROC-AUC scores obtained by the final tuned models described above.[7] The results show that the ML methods LightGBM and ANN were superior to the benchmark LR model in terms of F1 score, which was in line with findings in related research highlighted in Section 2. The LightGBM outperformed the ANN on both F1 and ROC-AUC scores. Their similar and superior performance compared to the benchmark model indicated that they were both capable of capturing complex relationships that the benchmark model could not recognize, supporting our belief that there were, in fact, significant non-linear interactions at play between variables in the data.

Table 10. Precision, recall, F1, and ROC-AUC scores for all three models on the test set. LightGBM is the superior model in terms of F1 and ROC-AUC score.

Model	Precision	Recall	F1	ROC-AUC
LightGBM	0.52	0.78	0.63	0.93
ANN	0.46	0.82	0.59	0.92
LR	0.74	0.46	0.57	0.92

Figure 5 displays the ROC and precision–recall curves for the three models. It is evident from the precision–recall plot that a stable, high precision value cannot be obtained by any of the models at a level above 0.8. Nevertheless, considering the severity of type II errors, our focus should be on the middle-right part of the curves, where recall is high and type II errors are minimized. Consistent with results from Table 10, the ANN proved to be prioritizing recall, clearly underperforming the others in the range where precision and recall were balanced but performing well in the area where recall was about 0.8 and precision was between 0.4 and 0.5. The LR model exhibited the opposite behavior, favoring precision over recall. It performed roughly equal to the LightGBM in the middle-left range but was outperformed for recall scores larger than 0.5. LightGBM exhibited a behavior compatible with our analysis of error types by favoring recall while still maintaining the highest level of precision among models in that range.

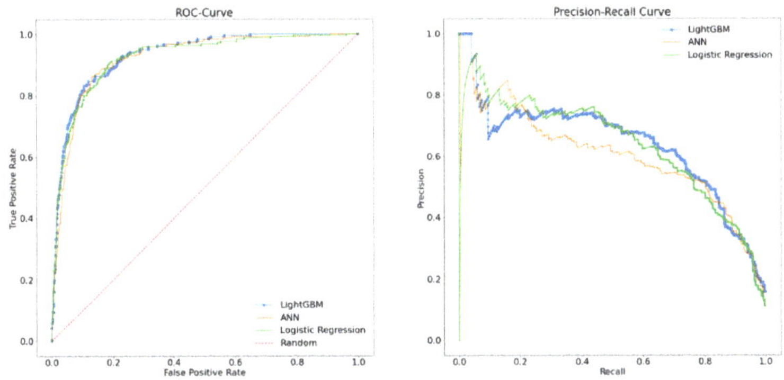

Figure 5. ROC and precision–recall curves for all three models on the test set. The red dashed line in the ROC plot represents a random classifier.

Figure 5 shows that the models performed more or less equally well in terms of ROC but varied in terms of precision–recall curve. A precision score above 0.8 could not be achieved with stability by any of the models. ANN performed poorly in the balanced precision–recall range but surpassed the LR model by a slight margin for recall values around 0.8. LightGBM showed clear superiority in the top right part of the graph, where recall was high (type II errors were minimized), and precision was maintained. Based on the above results, we argue that the LightGBM is the superior model.

6. Discussion

6.1. The Trade-Off between Type I and Type II Errors

As outlined in Appendix A, precision and recall, the components of the F1 score, are closely related to type I and type II errors, respectively. To reiterate, in the context of this task, a type I error represented the event that an otherwise healthy company was classified as distressed, while a type II error represented the event where a distressed firm was classified as healthy. From a creditor's perspective, one can argue that a type II error is more severe than a type I error since the loss associated with a distressed firm significantly outweighs the potential income from successful interest payments. Therefore, we argue that when evaluating a default model, one should put more emphasis on recall than precision. It is clear that the LR favored precision over recall, in contrast to the other two models. The LightGBM balanced precision and recall better than the ANN, which yielded a higher F1 score. However, in light of the severity of type II errors described above, one could argue that the ANN was superior due to a higher recall, indicating fewer "missed" distress cases. Nevertheless, a precision score below 0.5 meant that more than half of the positively predicted test samples were erroneous, which could be considered unacceptable in practical applications.

The ROC curves in Figure 5 display each model's inclination to trade off true positives (defaulting firms) against false positives (non-defaulting firms classified as defaulters). All three models performed well, and we only see slight variations in the top left range. We observe that the most considerable difference in behavior, although small, was between the LR and the ANN, where the ANN had a somewhat greater tendency to generate false positives when the true positive rate was low. In contrast, the LR generated more false positives when the true positive rate was high. This observation added some nuance to the otherwise equal performance in terms of ROC-AUC score.

6.2. Interpreting Predictors with SHAP

Many ML models are not inherently interpretable and need to be accompanied by an explanation model, which is an interpretable approximation to the model itself. The XAI framework of Lundberg and Lee (2017), SHAP, which builds on Shapley values, uses a linear function of binary variables as an explanation model. This makes SHAP an additive feature attribution method, which can be represented by Equation (2) below:

$$g(z') = \phi_0 + \sum_{i=1}^{M} \phi_i z'_i \tag{2}$$

Here, g represents the explanation model, $z' \in \{0,1\}$ is the vector of simplified input features, M is the number of simplified input features, and $\phi_i \in \mathbb{R}$ is the attribution effect of some feature i. A Shapley value can be interpreted as the marginal contribution of each feature averaged over the set of all feature combinations. It can thus be used to explain the contribution of individual features for a specific instance. SHAP can be used for both local and global interpretations. It helps us to gain insight into to how feature values from the entire dataset contribute to individual predictions and understanding how the contribution of the features on a single prediction score may be measured.

SHAP is based on an assumption of independence between features. Several alternative applications have been suggested, depending on the specific models applied, in order to improve and adjust the computation of SHAP. The TreeSHAP application of Lundberg et al. (2018) can be used to explain the results of LightGBM models. An advantage with TreeSHAP is that it assumes less feature independence than similar methods, meaning that it accounts for some but not all dependence (Aas et al. 2021).

TreeSHAP assumes less feature independence than other XAI approaches. Hence, this section applied TreeSHAP to the LightGBM model to interpret the behavior that led to the results presented in the previous section.

6.2.1. Global Explanations

As is evident from Figure 6, the most important features were closely related to liquidity, solvency, and company size. It is not surprising that working capital, CR, and ICR ranked high on feature importance. This is because current information about the two ratios, whose future values will determine the target, must be of high relevance. Intuitively, when attempting to say something about a state that involves a future value of a variable, one must examine the current value of that variable.

However, the mixed coloring of these variables' rows in the beeswarm plot clearly suggested that these features were not able to separate the data independently. This was further illustrated by the dependence plots shown in Figure 7. WCTA, ROA, and volatility, on the other hand, displayed more apparent signs of independent separation (blue and red dots are mostly on different sides of the middle line) albeit with a lower impact in terms of SHAP values. Still significant additional information was captured by the interaction effects of these latter variables as well, illustrated by, for instance, the ROA–WCTA dependence plot in the bottom right corner of Figure 7.

Several features in Figure 6 exhibit behaviors that coincide with our intuition. For example, red dots (high values) in the volatility plot generally lead to a higher model output, which indicates distress. Furthermore, blue dots (low values) in the working capital, WCTA, CR, and ICR plots should lead to a higher predicted probability of distress, which the plots confirms. We further note that accounting for seasonality and industry sector was appropriate, since both Quarter and GICS appeared in the mid to upper range of the beeswarm plot. Dependence plots included in Appendix B.2 further demonstrate the benefit of adding seasonality and macro and market information. These traits are captured by Quarter, GICS, GDP growth, and quarterly log returns of the stock and industry index, some of which provide clear advantageous interaction effects with more important variables.

The working capital plot in the upper left corner of Figure 7 shows that companies with low ROA (blue dots) were given higher output than those with high ROA (red dots) conditional upon the working capital being lower than 100,000 (left part of the graph area). The CR plot shows a similar tendency, i.e., high volatility was more heavily punished (higher SHAP contribution toward distress) when CR was below 0.9. A clear switch was observable in the ICR and ROA plots, where the impact of a low versus a high WCTA was the opposite depending on whether or not ICR/ROA was above or below zero. If a company had a low WCTA (blue dot), it received a higher SHAP value than if it had a high WCTA (red dot), conditional upon ICR/ROA being negative (left part of the graph area). On the other hand, when the condition was changed to ICR/ROA being positive (right part of the graph area), we observed that a low WCTA was actually less punished than a high WCTA in terms of SHAP value contribution.

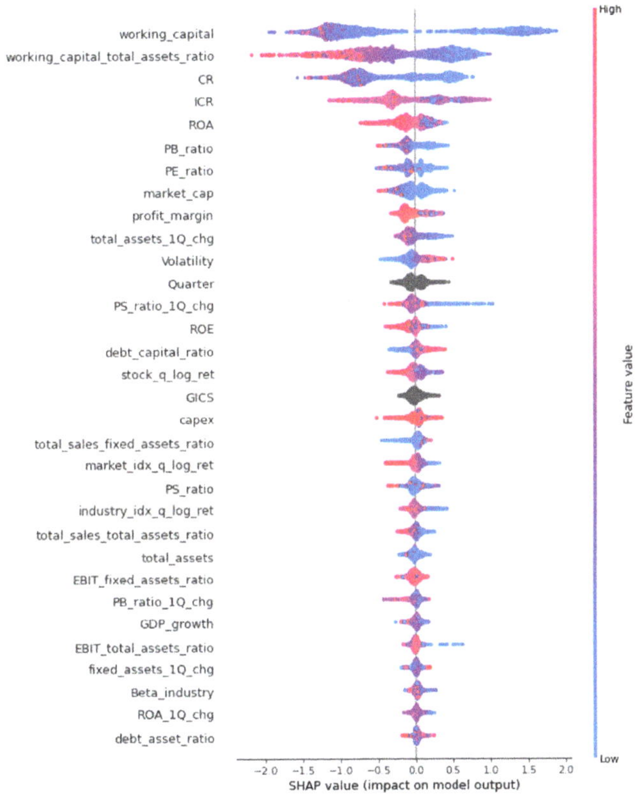

Figure 6. SHAP beeswarm plot of model predictions on the test set. Vertical ordering signifies the predictive power of features, each dot represents a single observed instance, and the color of each dot indicates the feature value for that instance. Clear color separation means that the feature independently separates the data—the degree to which it separates is indicated by the horizontal spread. Mixed coloring indicates significant feature interaction, i.e., that the SHAP value produced by a single value of that feature varies significantly depending on other feature values.

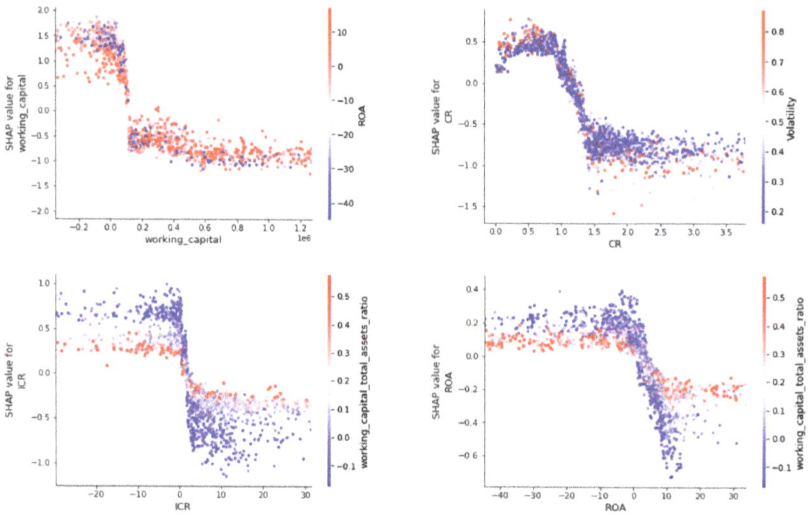

Figure 7. Dependence plots for working capital, CR, ICR, and ROA. The interaction feature on the right-hand side of each plot is selected by the highest degree of interaction and is automatically chosen by TreeSHAP.

6.2.2. Local Explanations

Local explanations, meaning interpretability of predictions for individual instances, can be displayed by waterfall plots. Similar to beeswarm plots, feature importance and SHAP values (positive or negative) are indicated by top-to-bottom rank and bar color, respectively. Starting from the expected model output which is learned during training, $E[f(x)]$ (denoted ϕ_0 in Equation (2)), the waterfall plot illustrates how the most important features each contribute to the model's final predicted value, $f(x)$ (denoted $g(z')$ in Equation (2)), for an individual sample. By default, the units on the x-axis of the waterfall plot, $E[f(x)]$ and $f(x)$, are given in log odds, and the relation between predicted value, expected value, and SHAP values can be expressed as:

$$f(x) = E[f(x)] + \sum_{i=1}^{M} \phi_i x_i \tag{3}$$

Probability, which has a more intuitive interpretation than log odds, is given by:

$$Probability = \frac{e^{ln(odds)}}{1 + e^{ln(odds)}} \tag{4}$$

Note that Equation (3) expresses the same relation as Equation (2). In order to explain model behavior, we examined examples of predictions that were labeled true positives and true negatives, i.e., correctly classified as distressed and non-distressed, respectively.

Figure 8 shows a waterfall plot of a true positive example from the test set. Using Equation (4), the sample was predicted to be in a state of distress in the ensuing quarter with a probability of 57%. It is evident that CR and ICR offset one another for this specific instance, providing little combined explanation for the prediction. A P/B ratio of less than one indicated that the company's assets may have been underpriced in the market or that the company was struggling with its ROA. The plot displays a negative ROA and negative change in total assets supporting the low P/B ratio and the impact on the prediction towards a state of distress. By examining the ROA dependence plot from Figure 7, we observe that a negative ROA combined with a low value for WCTA will have a high, positive SHAP contribution to the model output. This explains how the model determines that a company which is currently not in distress could be expected to be in distress in the next quarter.

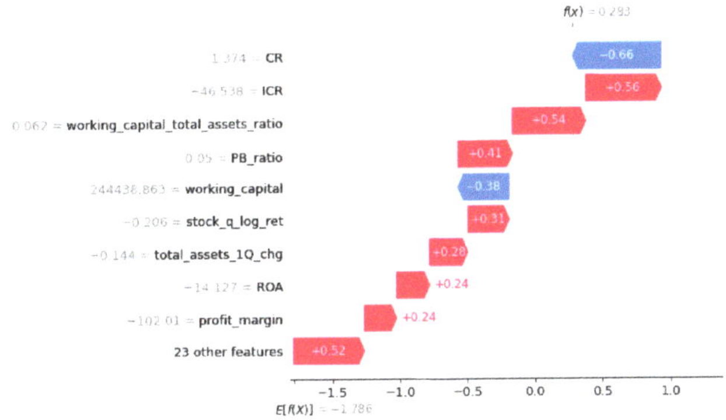

Figure 8. Waterfall plot for a true positive example. The sample was predicted to be in a state of distress in the ensuing quarter with a probability of 57%. Red arrows indicate a contribution toward a positive prediction, while blue arrows draw the prediction in the opposite direction. The length of the arrows represents the magnitude of the SHAP values, i.e., each feature's contribution to the output (financial distress) for this sample. Despite a positive CR and a relatively high working capital, the company was correctly classified as distressed.

Figure 9 shows a waterfall plot of a true negative from the test set. Using Equation (4), the sample was predicted to be in a state of distress in the ensuing quarter with a probability of only 2.1%. In addition to having a negative working capital and a large negative value of WCTA, the company displayed signs of low liquidity, indicated by a low CR. Red arrows signify that these factors contributed toward a positive prediction (distress), but the impact was mitigated by a high degree of liquidity in terms of earnings. A is evident from Figure 6, a low feature value of WCTA usually contributed towards a positive prediction, but combined with a high ICR, which was an attribute of this particular company, the SHAP value became much smaller. This is in line with the trend we observed in the ICR dependence plot in Figure 7, illustrating how a high ICR (right part of the graph area) reduces the SHAP contribution for negative WCTA values (blue dots). This example illustrates how the model extracts and weights relevant information to determine if a company that was not in a state of financial distress could be expected to stay in that state in the next quarter.

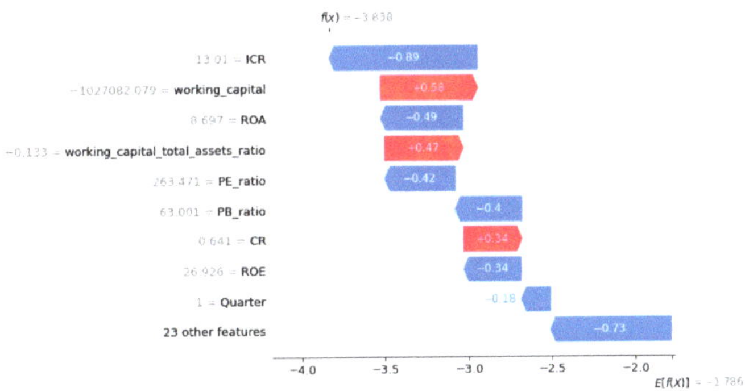

Figure 9. Waterfall plot for a true negative example. The sample was predicted to be in a state of distress in the ensuing quarter with a probability of 2.1%. Red arrows indicate a contribution toward a positive prediction, while blue arrows draw the prediction in the opposite direction. The length of the arrows represents the magnitude of the SHAP values, i.e., each feature's contribution to the output (financial non-distress) for this sample. Despite evidence indicating a low degree of solvency and liquidity, signified by red working capital, WCTA and CR, the company was correctly classified as healthy since it performed well in terms of earnings.

7. Conclusions

This paper proposed an interpretable early warning model for financial distress among listed Nordic corporations. Predictions were based on company-specific financial statement data and information about financial markets and macroeconomic trends. Using a proxy-based definition of financial distress rather than relying on juridically recorded credit events, our model proved effective as an early warning tool. Our proxy employed bond and loan covenants, i.e., measures of solvency and liquidity, and was in line with financial intuition and industry practices. All three models achieve ROC-AUC scores between 0.92 and 0.93, and the highest F1 score of 0.63 was obtained by the LightGBM, surpassing the remaining models by a notable margin.

Our results suggest that it is possible to generalize firm characteristics and behavior across Nordic countries. This view finds support in the feature selection step, as the categorical feature intended to capture geographical effects received very low feature importance. The other categorical features, capturing industry sector and seasonality, proved far more important. Findings from the data cleaning process also implied cross-border generality, with relatively similar class distributions in the four targeted countries. Similarities in political governing, legal systems, and audit standards are likely explanations in this respect.

Although LightGBM is not inherently interpretable, we provided insight into how the different input features affected both the model's overall output and predictions for individual instances by applying TreeSHAP. Our findings showed that features related to liquidity, solvency, and size were highly important to the model output. Furthermore, including macro, market, and seasonality information provided clear advantageous interaction effects with other variables. Machine learning models in general are well suited to capture such complex dynamics, and LightGBM performed particularly well in this study.

As closing remarks, we put forward certain limiting factors and areas for future improvement. Three particular areas of particular interest include (i) a further investigation of the characteristics of companies moving between states of distress and non-distress in subsequent time intervals, (ii) measures to improve data quality, and (iii) examining time-dependent effects such as structural breaks. First, to properly observe the characteristics of companies transitioning between states in subsequent time intervals, a richer dataset would be preferable. Possible solutions to mitigate this issue could be the merger of financial databases, data-filling techniques, and more analytical approaches to the trade-off between dropping rows and dropping features. Efforts to improve the dataset are recommended as a first step to further research, as we believe that any additional advancement of the model essentially hinges upon the size and quality of the dataset. Finally, even though our model accounts for time-dependent effects to some extent, structural breaks are not explicitly accounted for. A deeper look into, for instance, structural break indicator variables or in-quarter transformations to handle time-dependent effects is therefore a suggested area for further research. Lastly, given that the Nordic countries in our study are economically integrated with the European Union to varying degrees, evaluating our proposed model on non-Nordic data would be interesting.

Author Contributions: Conceptualization, N.-G.B.A., E.N.-F., M.M., M.R., and P.E.d.L.; methodology, N.-G.B.A., E.N.-F., and M.M.; software, N.-G.B.A., E.N.-F., and M.M.; formal analysis, N.-G.B.A., E.N.-F., and M.M.; validation, P.E.d.L. and M.R.; writing—original draft preparation, N.-G.B.A., E.N.-F., and M.M.; writing—review and editing, P.E.d.L. and M.R.; supervision, P.E.d.L. and M.R. All authors have read and agreed to the published version of the manuscript.

Funding: This research was partially funded by The Research Council of Norway throughout the project COMPAMA (https://www.ntnu.edu/compama/, accessed on 1 June 2022), with grant number 314609.

Data Availability Statement: The data are publicly available. Due to constrains from some of the data providers, the authors are not in a position to distribute the data.

Conflicts of Interest: The authors declare no conflicts of interest.

Appendix A. Measuring Model Performance

To compare the performance of different models, it is necessary to apply metrics that evaluate the different techniques on the same premise. After classification, predictions will belong to one of four categories, illustrated by the confusion matrix in Figure A1.

		Predicted: **Positive**	Predicted: **Negative**	
Actual	**Positive**	True Positive (TP)	False Negative (FN) **Type II Error**	Recall $\frac{TP}{TP+FN}$
Actual	**Negative**	False positive (FP) **Type I Error**	True negative (TN)	Specificity $\frac{TN}{TN+FP}$
		Precision $\frac{TP}{TP+FP}$	Negative Predictive Value $\frac{TN}{TN+FN}$	Accuracy $\frac{TP+TN}{TP+TN+FP+FN}$

Figure A1. Confusion matrix showing the four different categories for a prediction. Metrics are described along the bottom and right-hand edge. Illustration adapted from https://www.debadityachakravorty.com/ai-ml/cmatrix/ (accessed on 1 June 2022).

As is evident from the confusion matrix, there are two types of errors, type I and type II. In our case, type I errors referred to non-distressed companies classified as distressed, and type II errors were distressed companies classified as non-distressed. The existence of two types of errors naturally poses a trade-off between precision and recall. For example, a model with high recall typically lacks precision and will correctly classify a large share of the actual positives at the cost of including many actual negatives among its positive classifications. The trade-off is best visualized using a precision–recall curve. The curve is created by varying the classification threshold between zero to one while plotting the precision and recall achieved at each threshold. Even though such a curve is highly informative, it complicates the process of comparing models since it lacks a straightforward numerical metric. To circumvent this issue, the curve can be reduced to the F1 score, given by Equation (A1), which is the harmonic mean of precision and recall. Since models are implicitly trained with a default threshold of 0.5, the F1 score essentially represents a single, realistic point on the precision–recall curve.

$$F1 = \frac{2 \cdot \text{Precision} \cdot \text{Recall}}{\text{Precision} + \text{Recall}} \tag{A1}$$

Another popular way of assessing a classifier's performance is the Receiver Operating Characteristic (ROC) curve. The curve is constructed by varying the classification threshold and plotting the true positive rate (recall) against the false positive rate ($= 1 - Specificity$). Put simply, it shows a classifier's ability to sort the data based on their resemblance to the positive class. Optimally, the curve should "hug" the top left corner, indicating that the classifier found all positive examples without erroneously including a negative. Following the equivalent argumentation as given above, the ROC-Area Under the Curve (ROC-AUC) score was used to reduce the curve down to a numerical metric for automated comparison during hyperparameter tuning. The ROC-AUC score essentially calculates how close the model's performance is to the optimal curve. As a point of reference, a completely random classifier will receive a score close to 0.5, and a perfect classifier will obtain a score of 1. Even though the ROC-AUC score works best for balanced datasets, it serves as a comparable summary of a model's performance when evaluated in conjunction with the F1 score.

Appendix B. Supplementary Figures

Appendix B.1. Ratio Frequencies

Factor/Consideration	Number of Studies that Include
Net income / Total assets	54
Current ratio	51
Working capital / Total assets	45
Retained earnings / Total assets	42
Earnings before interest and taxes / Total assets	35
Sales / Total assets	32
Quick ratio	30
Total debt / Total assets	27
Current assets / Total assets	26
Net income / Net worth	23
Total liabilities / Total assets	19
Cash / Total assets	18
Market value of equity / Book value of total debt	16
Cash flow from operations / Total assets	15
Cash flow from operations / Total liabilities	14
Current liabilities / Total assets	13
Cash flow from operations / Total debt	12
Quick assets / Total assets	11
Current assets / Sales	10
Earnings before interest and taxes / Interest	10
Inventory / Sales	10
Operating income / Total assets	10
Cash flow from operations / Sales	9
Net income / Sales	9
Long-term debt / Total assets	8
Net worth / Total assets	8
Total debt / Net worth	8
Total liabilities / Net worth	8
Cash / Current liabilities	7
Cash flow from operations / Current liabilities	7
Working capital / Sales	7
Capital / Assets	6
Net sales / Total assets	6
Net worth / Total liabilities	6
No-credit interval	6
Total assets (log)	6
Cash flow (using net income) / Debt	5
Cash flow from operations	5
Operating expenses / Operating income	5
Quick assets / Sales	5
Sales / Inventory	5
Working capital / Net worth	5

Figure A2. Frequency of financial ratios applied in literature between 1930 and 2007, given their appearance in five or more studies. Retrieved from (Bellovary et al. 2007, p.42).

Appendix B.2. Dependence Plots

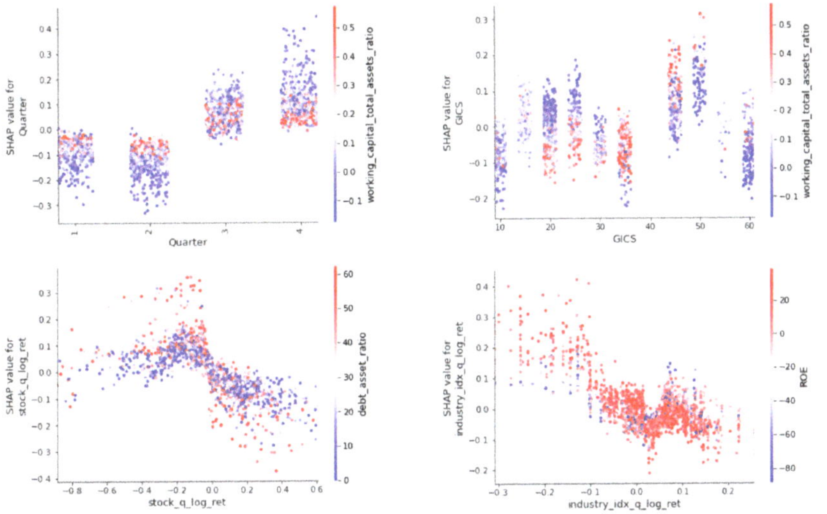

Figure A3. Dependence plot for categorical, macro, and market variables. Quarter shows clear interactive effects with WCTA, displaying that WCTA values have opposite impacts on the model output depending on whether the observation is from the first half or second half of the year. Similar effects observable for Stock Log Returns, where high values of Debt Asset Ratio have opposite impacts depending on whether the quarterly log returns are positive or negative.

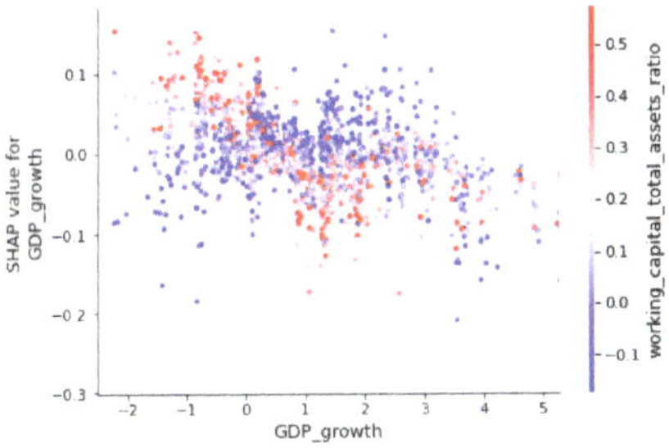

Figure A4. Dependence plot for GDP Growth. Clear interaction effect showing that WCTA yields opposite SHAP impact dependent on whether the economy is experiencing a recession or a boom.

Notes

1 This paper is based on the M.Sc thesis by Birkeland Abrahamsen et al. (2022).

2 Credit rating agencies report that an ICR value below 1.5 often coincides with non-investment grade entities, see, for instance, Standard & Poor's (https://www.spratings.com/scenario-builder-portlet/pdfs/CorporateMethodology.pdf, accessed on 1 June 2022), Moody's (https://www.moodys.com/researchandratings/methodology/003006001/rating-methodologies/methodology/003006001/003006001/-/0/0/-/0/-/-/en/global/rr, accessed on 1 June 2022), Fitch (https://www.fitchratings.com/research/corporate-finance/corporate-rating-criteria-15-10-2021, accessed on 1 June 2022), Morningstar (https://www.dbrsmorningstar.com/research/394214/general-corporate-methodology, accessed on 1 June 2022), and Nordic Credit Rating (https://nordiccreditrating.com, accessed on 1 June 2022).

3 Balcaen and Ooghe (2006) bring forth several other reasons why judicial credit events serve as a poor foundation for dichotomous classification. Among these are the fact that it may take several years before failure is formally recorded, making the actual point of distress challenging to determine, and the possibility of other juridical exits such as merger, absorption, dissolution, and liquidation, which act to conceal distress.

4 The conversion of categorical variables into binary indicators.

5 Introducing perfect multicollinearity by redundantly specifying a dummy variable for each category.

6 $3 \cdot 3 \cdot 2 \cdot 3 \cdot 4 \cdot 4 \cdot 4 \cdot 4 = 3456$ different hyperparameter configurations.

7 See Appendix A for definitions and a discussion of these model performance metrics.

References

Aas, Kjersti, Martin Jullum, and Anders Løland. 2021. Explaining individual predictions when features are dependent: More accurate approximations to Shapley values. *Artificial Intelligence* 298: 103502. [CrossRef]

Abiyev, Rahib H. 2014. Credit rating using type-2 fuzzy neural networks. *Mathematical Problems in Engineering* 2014: 460916. [CrossRef]

Agrawal, Khushbu, and Yogesh Maheshwari. 2019. Efficacy of industry factors for corporate default prediction. *IIMB Management Review* 31: 71–77. [CrossRef]

Altman, Edward. 1968. Financial ratios, discriminant analysis and the prediction of corporate bankruptcy. *The Journal of Finance* 23: 589–609. [CrossRef]

Athey, Susan, and Guido W. Imbens. 2019. Machine learning methods that economists should know about. *Annual Review of Economics* 11: 685–725. [CrossRef]

Awais, Mustabsar, Faisal Hayat, Noreen Mehar, and W. Ul-Hassan. 2015. Do z-score and current ratio have ability to predict bankruptcy. *Developing Country Studies* 5: 30–36.

Balcaen, Sofie, and Hubert Ooghe. 2006. 35 years of studies on business failure: An overview of the classic statistical methodologies and their related problems. *The British Accounting Review* 38: 63–93. [CrossRef]

Beaver, William H. 1966. Financial ratios as predictors of failure. *Journal of Accounting Research* 4: 71–111. [CrossRef]

Bellovary, Jodi L., Don E. Giacomino, and Michael D. Akers. 2007. A review of bankruptcy prediction studies: 1930 to present. *Journal of Financial Education* 33: 1–42.

Bentejac, Candice, Anna Csorgo, and Gonzalo Martinez-Munoz. 2021. A comparative analysis of gradient boosting algorithms. *Artificial Intelligence Review* 54: 1937–67. [CrossRef]

Birkeland Abrahamsen, Nils-Gunnar, Emil Nylén-Forthun, and Mats Møller. 2022. Financial Distress Prediction Using Machine Learning and Xai: Developing an Early Warning Model for Listed Nordic Corporations. Master's thesis, Norwegian University of Science and Technology, Trondheim, Norway.

Bonfim, Diana. 2009. Credit risk drivers: Evaluating the contribution of firm level information and of macroeconomic dynamics. *Journal of Banking & Finance* 33: 281–99.

Bussmann, Niklas, Paolo Giudici, Dimitri Marinelli, and Jochen Papenbrock. 2021. Explainable machine learning in credit risk management. *Computational Economics* 57: 203–16. [CrossRef]

Campbell, John Y., Jens Hilscher, and Jan Szilagyi. 2008. In search of distress risk. *The Journal of Finance* 63: 2899–939. [CrossRef]

Charalambakis, Evangelos C., and Ian Garrett. 2018. On corporate financial distress prediction: What can we learn from private firms in a developing economy? evidence from greece. *Review of Quantitative Finance and Accounting* 52: 467–91. [CrossRef]

Chava, Sudheer, and Robert A. Jarrow. 2004. Bankruptcy prediction with industry effects. *Review of Finance* 8: 537–69. [CrossRef]

Chen, Tianqi, and Carlos Guestrin. 2016. Xgboost: A scalable tree boosting system. Paper presented at the 22nd ACM SIGKK International Conference on Knowledge Discovery and Data Mining, San Francisco, CA, USA, August 13–17. pp. 785–94.

Clevert, Djork-Arné, Thomas Unterthiner, and Sepp Hochreiter. 2015. Fast and accurate deep network learning by exponential linear units (elus). *arXiv* arXiv:1511.07289.

De Lange, Petter Eilif, Borger Melsom, Christian Bakke Vennerød, and Sjur Westgaard. 2022. Explainable ai for credit assessment in banks. *Journal of Risk and Financial Management* 15: 556. [CrossRef]

Desai, Chitra. 2020. Comparative analysis of optimizers in deep neural networks. *International Journal of Innovative Science and Research Technology* 5: 959–62.

Dimitras, Augustinos I., Stelios H. Zanakis, and Constantin Zopounidis. 1996. A survey of business failures with an emphasis on prediction methods and industrial applications. *European Journal of Operational Research* 90: 487–513. [CrossRef]

Du, Xudong, Wei Li, Sumei Ruan, and Li Li. 2020. Cus-heterogeneous ensemble-based financial distress prediction for imbalanced dataset with ensemble feature selection. *Applied Soft Computing* 97: 106758. [CrossRef]

Falavigna, Greta. 2012. Financial ratings with scarce information: A neural network approach. *Expert Systems with Applications* 39: 1784–92. [CrossRef]

Frydman, Halina, Edward Altman, and Duen-Li Kao. 1985. Introducing recursive partitioning for financial classification: The case of financial distress. *The Journal of Finance* 40: 269–91. [CrossRef]

Hjelkrem, Lars Ole, and Petter Eilif de Lange. 2023. Explaining deep learning models for credit scoring with shap: A case study using open banking data. *Journal of Risk and Financial Management* 16: 221. [CrossRef]

Iturriaga, Félix J López, and Iván Pastor Sanz. 2015. Bankruptcy visualization and prediction using neural networks: A study of us commercial banks. *Expert Systems with Applications* 42: 2857–69. [CrossRef]

Jan, Chyan-Long. 2021. Financial information asymmetry: Using deep learning algorithms to predict financial distress. *Symmetry* 13: 443. [CrossRef]

Jensen, Herbert L. 1992. Using neural networks for credit scoring. *Managerial Finance* 18: 15–26. [CrossRef]

Jiang, Yi, and Stewart Jones. 2018. Corporate distress prediction in china: A machine learning approach. *Accounting & Finance* 58: 1063–109.

Jiang, Yixiao. 2023. A primer on machine learning methods for credit rating modeling. In *Econometrics—Recent Advances and Applications*. London: IntechOpen.

Jones, Stewart, David Johnstone, and Roy Wilson. 2017. Predicting corporate bankruptcy: An evaluation of alternative statistical frameworks. *Journal of Business Finance & Accounting* 44: 3–34.

Ke, Guolin, Qi Meng, Thomas Finley, Taifeng Wang, Wei Chen, Weidong Ma, Qiwei Ye, and Tie-Yan Liu. 2017. Lightgbm: A highly efficient gradient boosting decision tree. *Advances in Neural Information Processing Systems* 30: 3146–54.

Kim, Hyeongjun, Hoon Cho, and Doojin Ryu. 2020. Corporate default predictions using machine learning: Literature review. *Sustainability* 12: 6325. [CrossRef]

Kozlovskyi, Serhii, Boris Poliakov, Ruslan Lavrov, and Natalya Ivanyuta. 2019. Management and comprehensive assessment of the probability of bankruptcy of ukrainian enterprises based on the methods of fuzzy sets theory. *Problems and Perspectives in Management* 17: 370–81. [CrossRef]

Liang, Deron, Chia-Chi Lu, Chih-Fong Tsai, and Guan-An Shih. 2016. Financial ratios and corporate governance indicators in bankruptcy prediction: A comprehensive study. *European Journal of Operational Research* 252: 561–72. [CrossRef]

Lin, Lin, and Jenifer Piesse. 2004. Identification of corporate distress in uk industrials: A conditional probability analysis approach. *Applied Financial Economics* 14: 73–82. [CrossRef]

Lundberg, Scott, Gabriel Erion, and Su-In Lee. 2018. Consistent individualized feature attribution for tree ensembles. *arXiv* arXiv:1802.03888.

Lundberg, Scott M., and Su-In Lee. 2017. A unified approach to interpreting model predictions. *Advances in Neural Information Processing Systems* 30: 4765–74.

Luoma, Martti, and Erkki K. Laitinen. 1991. Survival analysis as a tool for company failure prediction. *Omega* 19: 673–78. [CrossRef]

Malakauskas, Aidas, and Aušrinė Lakštutienė. 2021. Financial distress prediction for small and medium enterprises using machine learning techniques. *Inžinerinė ekonomika* 32: 4–14. [CrossRef]

Melsom, Borger, Christian B. Vennerød, Petter de Lange, Lars Ole Hjelkrem, and Sjur Westgaard. 2022. Explainable artificial intelligence for credit scoring in banking. *Journal of Risk* 25. [CrossRef]

Messier, William F., Jr., and James V. Hansen. 1988. Inducing rules for expert system development: An example using default and bankruptcy data. *Management Science* 34: 1403–15. [CrossRef]

Mohammed, Ali Abusalah Elmabrok, and Ng Kim-Soon. 2012. Using Altman's model and current ratio to assess the financial status of companies quoted in the Malaysian stock exchange. *International Journal of Scientific and Research Publications* 2: 1–11.

Moscatelli, Mirko, Fabio Parlapiano, Simone Narizzano, and Gianluca Viggiano. 2020. Corporate default forecasting with machine learning. *Expert Systems with Applications* 161: 113567. [CrossRef]

Murphy, Kevin P. 2012. *Machine Learning: A Probabilistic Perspective*. Cambridge, MA: MIT Press.

Ohlson, James A. 1980. Financial ratios and the probabilistic prediction of bankruptcy. *Journal of Accounting Research* 18: 109–31. [CrossRef]

Parhi, Rahul, and Robert D. Nowak. 2020. The role of neural network activation functions. *IEEE Signal Processing Letters* 27: 1779–83. [CrossRef]

Qian, Hongyi, Baohui Wang, Minghe Yuan, Songfeng Gao, and You Song. 2022. Financial distress prediction using a corrected feature selection measure and gradient boosted decision tree. *Expert Systems with Applications* 190: 116202. [CrossRef]

Smith, Leslie N. 2017. Cyclical learning rates for training neural networks. Paper presented at 2017 IEEE Winter Conference on Applications of Computer Vision (WACV), Santa Rosa, CA, USA, March 24–31. pp. 464–72.

Son, Hwijae, C. Hyun, Du Phan, and Hyung Ju Hwang. 2019. Data analytic approach for bankruptcy prediction. *Expert Systems with Applications* 138: 112816. [CrossRef]

Srivastava, Nitish, Geoffrey E. Hinton, Alex Krizhevsky, Ilya Sutskever, and Ruslan Salakhutdinov. 2014. Dropout: A simple way to prevent neural networks from overfitting. *The Journal of Machine Learning Research* 15: 1929–58.

Tam, Kar Yan. 1991. Neural network models and the prediction of bank bankruptcy. *Omega* 19: 429–45. [CrossRef]

Xu, Shuxiang, and Ling Chen. 2008. A novel approach for determining the optimal number of hidden layer neurons for fnn's and its application in data mining. Paper presented at 5th International Conference on Information Technology and Applications (ICITA 2008), Cairns, Australia, June 23–26. pp. 683–86.

Xu, Xiaoyan, and Yu Wang. 2009. Financial failure prediction using efficiency as a predictor. *Expert Systems with Applications* 36: 366–73. [CrossRef]

Yang, Z. R., Marjorie B. Platt, and Harlan D. Platt. 1999. Probabilistic neural networks in bankruptcy prediction. *Journal of Business Research* 44: 67–74. [CrossRef]

Journal of
Risk and Financial Management

MDPI

Systematic Review

Bibliometric Analysis of the Machine Learning Applications in Fraud Detection on Crowdfunding Platforms

Luis F. Cardona, Jaime A. Guzmán-Luna * and Jaime A. Restrepo-Carmona

Facultad de Minas, Universidad Nacional de Colombia Sede Medellín, Medellín 050001, Colombia;
luisfernandocardona7@gmail.com (L.F.C.); jarestrepoca@unal.edu.co (J.A.R.-C.)
* Correspondence: jaguzman@unal.edu.co

Abstract: Crowdfunding platforms are important for startups, since they offer diverse financing options, market validation, and promotional opportunities through an investor community. These platforms provide detailed company information, aiding informed investment decisions within a regulated and secure environment. Machine learning (ML) techniques are important in analyzing large data sets, detecting anomalies and fraud, and enhancing decision-making and business strategies. A systematic review employed PRISMA guidelines, which studied how ML improves fraud detection on digital crowdfunding platforms. The analysis includes English-language studies from peer-reviewed journals published between 2018 and 2023 to analyze the pre- and post-COVID-19 pandemic. The findings indicate that ML techniques such as Random Forest, Support Vector Machine, and Artificial Neural Networks significantly enhance the predictive accuracy and utility of tax planning for startups considering equity crowdfunding. The United States, Germany, Canada, Italy, and Turkey do not present statistically significant differences at the 95% confidence level, standing out for their notable academic visibility. Florida Atlantic and Cornell Universities, Springer and John Wiley & Sons Ltd. publishing houses, and the *Journal of Business Ethics and Management Science* magazines present the highest citations without statistical differences at the 95% confidence level.

Keywords: crowdfunding; fraud; machine learning; PRISMA; statistical analysis

1. Introduction

Crowdfunding platforms are fundraising methods in which people contribute different amounts of money through online platforms, facilitating access to capital for projects and businesses (Brown et al. 2017). These platforms positively impact the economy, benefiting small and medium-sized businesses by reducing transaction costs, improving investment efficiency, attracting non-professional investors, promoting financial accessibility, fostering innovation and entrepreneurship, and validating market concepts (Ellman and Hurkens 2019a, 2019b). Within this order of ideas, crowdfunding promotes job creation, increases tax revenue, and supports innovative high-tech companies. Through these mechanisms, crowdfunding drives economic growth and strengthens the financial ecosystem (Cicchiello et al. 2019). According to Freedman and Jin (2011), the crowdfunding market in North America generates more than USD 17 billion annually and is projected to grow to USD 300 billion by 2030. There are different types of crowdfunding platforms, including those based on rewards, actions, donations, and loans (Markas and Wang 2019; Petrov and Emelyanova 2021). The elements of crowdfunding campaigns include the creator, project, funding goal, investors, incentives, and sponsors. The platform selection should reflect user trust through ethical practices and security measures to prevent fraud (Markas and Wang 2019). Additionally, companies can gain a competitive advantage by identifying and prioritizing key innovation opportunities (Markas and Wang 2019).

Crowdfunding platforms are a powerful tool for financing projects, businesses, and personal causes. However, the risk of fraud can appear as fake projects or misappropriation of funds (Ellman and Hurkens 2019b; Bafna et al. 2023). These anomalous behaviors affect investor confidence and reduce public–private funding. Additionally, fraud can attract negative media and public attention, affecting the flexibility and accessibility of crowdfunding (Bafna et al. 2023; Xu et al. 2023). Platforms should invest in security and control systems and algorithms to prevent and detect fraud. The operations can be conducted for identity verification, monitoring suspicious transactions, and providing channels to report fraud. Traditional fraud detection methods in crowdfunding include rule-based systems, fundamental statistical analysis, and manual review to report suspicious or unusual transactions (Cumming et al. 2021). However, these methods are vulnerable to tax evasion by fraudsters and can be slow and error-prone (Petrov and Emelyanova 2021; Winoto and Wulandari 2023).

Behl et al. (2022) evaluated the uses of Artificial intelligence (AI) tools in donation-based crowdfunding platforms. The employing of AI technology can improve operational performance in disaster relief operations. However, the community perceives indicators of risk, privacy, transaction security, and fraud, negatively. Burtch et al. (2016) studied digital platforms and found they must balance information control to avoid harming campaigns' visibility and success. It is important to note that crowdfunding platforms must be visible and clearly show all the investors their finances. For these reasons, Machine Learning (ML) significantly enhances fraud detection. These techniques can identify complex patterns in transactions and fraudulent behaviors. Elitzur (2024) invites businesses and industries to leverage ML to improve real-time fraud alert systems, optimize resources, and minimize losses, making it a powerful tool in the fight against fraud. ML provides advanced data visualization tools essential for identifying complex and non-linear patterns that can influence the success of campaigns. Different authors in their publications motivate the studies of fraud and anomalous-behavior detection in financial processes in other areas, such as business (Goodell et al. 2021) and healthcare (Bassani et al. 2019).

A subset of Artificial Intelligence (AI) is ML, which uses several algorithms to improve predictions using historical data without explicit programming. ML is divided into different approaches, as supervised and unsupervised algorithms. Supervised methods are algorithms trained on labeled data, while unsupervised methods identify patterns in unlabeled data (Butt et al. 2020; Sharifani and Amini 2023). These algorithms are used in fraud detection, recommendation systems, image recognition, natural language processing, and medical diagnosis (Sharifani and Amini 2023; Yadav et al. 2023). Traditional fraud detection methods are less precise and require manual review, while ML-based methods are faster and more accurate, analyze large volumes of data in real time, and adapt to new frauds (Yadav et al. 2023). However, ML algorithms require significant computational resources and high-quality data to avoid false positives (Sharifani and Amini 2023; Yadav et al. 2023). Artificial Neural Networks (ANNs), k-Nearest Neighbors (K-NN), Support Vector Machines (SVMs), Naive Bayes (NB), K-Means, and Singular Value Decomposition (SVD) are examples of ML methods employed in fraud detection (Sharifani and Amini 2023; Yadav et al. 2023; Cardona et al. 2024). Artificial Neural Networks (ANNs) detect fraud anomalies in real time by recognizing patterns in network traffic. K-Nearest Neighbors (K-NN) classifies data to implement suitable security measures. Support Vector Machines (SVMs) and Naive Bayes (NB) identify threats by differentiating data classes using probabilistic models. Unsupervised learning methods such as K-Means and Singular Value Decomposition (SVD) are effective for anomaly detection and data dimensionality reduction (Butt et al. 2020).

This study employs bibliometric analysis to report whose ML methods are used for identifying and preventing fraudulent activities. It is important to clarify that this manuscript is based on the strategies used in the literature to detect fraud in crowdfunding platforms and does not study the prediction of crowdfunding campaigns' success. Creating a fraud detection system with machine learning presents significant challenges in enhancing political e-government systems and industry 4.0. These include needing high-quality data, explaining decisions from complex models, compliance with regulations such as the

General Data Protection Regulation, and ethical considerations. Despite these challenges, the global fraud detection and prevention market is expected to grow significantly, driven by the increasing use of digital technologies and the adoption of risk-based authentication and fraud analysis solutions. Digital crowdfunding platforms are increasingly used in different contexts, showing exponential growth (Freedman and Jin 2011). However, these platforms are susceptible to different types of fraud, leading to distrust and discouraging user investment. For these reasons, it is necessary to integrate AI, especially ML techniques, to improve the early detection of fraud and anomalous behavior on these platforms. Digital platforms have increased after the COVID-19 pandemic (Zribi 2022), so this study evaluates those works published from 2018 to April 2024. This research undertakes a comprehensive and systematic analysis to identify the countries, universities, and industries investing in the study of fraud on crowdfunding platforms using machine learning techniques. The analysis, conducted through a statistical approach, reveals the most significant associations based on bibliometric variables such as the year of publication, total citations, number of institutions and authors, and the journal's quartile. This approach will also unveil the most frequently used machine learning techniques and their effectiveness in fraud identification and control on digital crowdfunding platforms. In conclusion, this work aims to compile and analyze the primary studies on the subject. The PRISMA methodology (Page et al. 2021) is employed for this purpose. The study is guided by the following research questions, which will be thoroughly explored and answered in this work. This analysis will provide a comprehensive understanding of the use of machine learning techniques in detecting fraud on digital crowdfunding platforms.

- RQ1: What are the most promising machine learning techniques in detecting fraud on digital crowdfunding platforms?
- RQ2: Which types of fraud are commonly found in studies?
- RQ3: What representative works were developed to detect fraud in digital crowdfunding platforms?
- RQ4: Which countries or groups of countries have the highest academic output in fraud detection on digital crowdfunding platforms? Are there any significant differences in their contributions compared to the total citations?
- RQ5: What are the clusters and statistical comparison analyses between the universities, publishers, and journals, compared to the total citations? Are there any statistical differences between those variables compared to the total citations?
- RQ6: What future trends and developments are expected in this area of research?

2. Materials and Methods

2.1. Bibliometric Analysis

To address these questions, the PRISMA methodology (Preferred Reporting Items for Systematic Reviews and Meta-Analyses) is employed. This method improves the transparency and quality of systematic reviews and meta-analyses. It is based on a set of guidelines and a checklist that ensures that studies are identified, selected, and reported clearly and systematically. PRISMA helps researchers conduct and present systematic reviews rigorously and transparently. In addition, it allows us to identify the most relevant works, countries, and research centers that are most notable in academic production, whether articles, conferences, or books (Page et al. 2021; Pranckutė 2021). The PRISMA methodology characteristics employed in this work are detailed below.

- Research must be related to fraud detection and types of fraud on digital crowdfunding platforms. For this reason, research topics related to cryptocurrencies, marketing, blockchain, e-commerce, and cryptocurrency are excluded.
- For this study, two of the most remarkable and widely used databases in the academic and scientific world, Scopus and Web of Science (WoS), were selected. These two databases have been used in various review works, providing robust conceptual tools for the state of a particular investigation (Pranckutė 2021).

- The years of the search were chosen to span from 2018 to April 2024, covering the pre- and post-COVID-19 pandemic periods. This choice corresponds to the period of growth in digital platforms, underscoring the pertinence and timeliness of our research. The AND connector used and separated combinations of the following keys: equity, crowdfunding, fraud, detection, machine learning, tax planning, and security.
- Journals, working papers, and conference documents must be peer-reviewed and belong to institutional universities or research centers. It is important to clarify that conference papers were selected because they typically provide information on the latest innovations and trends before they appear in journal publications.
- All PRISMA steps were carried out manually and humanly without requiring artificial intelligence. The authors reviewed the title, abstract, and conclusions and then conducted a subsequent reading of the document.

Figure 1 shows the number of documents extracted using the PRISMA methodology. Of the 925 records taken until April 2024 in the two databases (Scopus and WoS), a first data cleansing was carried out based on the year and the English language, resulting in the exclusion of 167 records (13 documents after 2018 and 154 duplicate records). Of the remaining 758 records, keyword-based filters were applied, excluding terms such as cryptocurrency, blockchain, commerce, and marketing. In total, 623 records were excluded using the above keywords. After this filter, 135 records remained, reduced to 39 after a manual reading of the title, summary, and conclusions. A total of 96 reports are assessed for eligibility. Finally, each article was carefully read, focusing on those that met the study's purpose of detecting fraud through machine learning. This process resulted in 26 records that will be analyzed in depth. It is essential to highlight that a bibliometric extraction from these 26 records will be carried out to make relevant inferences.

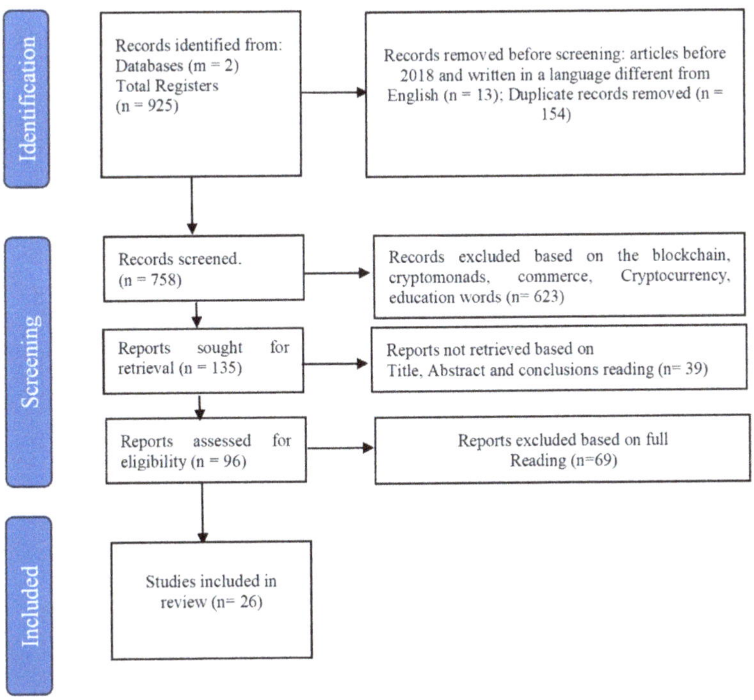

Figure 1. PRISMA flow diagram for crowdfunding-platform fraud detection.

2.2. Statistical Analysis

Statistical analyses with the list of the most representative works are carried out. A table that presents key variables is constructed, enabling us to address the guiding research questions. The variables considered, such as the journal's title and its quartile, the year of publication, the type of fraud studied, the number of citations and self-citations, the number of institutions involved in the studies, the publisher, the country, and the number of countries that have participated in the study, are crucial in our understanding of fraud studies. Subsequently, the information is tabulated, and a series of descriptive graphs are crafted, effectively enhancing the visualization of the data.

The Principal Component Analysis (PCA) is used to optimize manufacturing and control processes, analyze failures, and optimize product design (Minh et al. 2023). Additionally, PCA concentrates the most relevant information in the first principal components, making it easier to visualize the data and identify patterns, similarities, and clustering (Granato et al. 2018). The biplot and dendrogram graphs were used to analyze the relationships between the variables under study. In this work, the PCA analysis is employed to identify variable aggregation.

On the other hand, an ANOVA analysis is used to compare countries, universities, journals, and publisher, regarding the number of citations at the 95% confidence level. The results of this analysis identify which factors have significant statistical differences at the 95% confidence level. It is important to note that total citation is a key factor employed in the comparison, since it provides valuable information to understand the impact and relevance of academic publications in different contexts (Aksnes et al. 2019). The statistical analysis shows that if a pair of means overlaps, there are no statistically significant differences between both means. On the other hand, if a pair of means does not overlap, this implies a statistically significant difference at a 5% significance level (Montgomery and Runger 2020). Statistical analyses are performed using Statgraphics Centurion XVI software. It is important to note that the normality test results determine the type of group comparison test, whether parametric or non-parametric. Parametric tests, including ANOVA and Fisher's LSD intervals, are used when the data follow a normal distribution. The Kruskal–Wallis test uses the non-parametric approach. The Kruskal–Wallis test compares three or more independent groups, and determines whether they come from the same distribution (Montgomery and Runger 2020).

3. Results

3.1. Overview of Main Works

Table 1 summarizes the most important characteristics of the collected works. Table 1, detailed below, provides the following observations.

- 1.4% of the works were published before 2018, so 98.6% of the documents were published in recent years. The above reaffirms that the post-pandemic period has represented the development of digital crowdfunding platforms and the need to analyze and detect fraud using machine learning techniques.
- The machine learning algorithm most employed by the different studies is Random Forest (with 9% of the total methods used in the studies), followed by Latent Dirichlet Allocation and Support Vector Machine (both methods with 7% of the total studies), and finally the methods of Decision Trees, Logistic Regression, Long Short-Term Memory and Neural Networks (RQ1 is Answered).
- 42% of the studies were published in high-impact journals in Q1, followed by Q2 with 8% and Q3 and Q4 with 12% and 8%, respectively. It is important to highlight that Q1 articles concentrate the highest number of citations around 91%, followed by Q2 journals with 6%, and finally, 3% of citations with unclassified journals.
- Cumming et al. (2021) is the article with the highest number of citations of 185 and self-citations of 20. On the other hand, Belavina et al. (2020) have 136 citations and ten self-citations. The two studies described above use Propensity Score Matching (PSM) and sequential testing to model the early detection of fraud on digital crowdfunding

platforms. Although some recent studies have few or no citations, common in recent publications, the diversity of methods used, and international collaboration underlines the importance and growing interest in fraud detection using advanced techniques.

- The most frequent publishers include Elsevier, Springer, and MDPI, indicating their relevance in this field of research. Institutional collaboration is mostly between one or two institutions.
- The main types of fraud on crowdfunding platforms include personal fraud, such as plagiarism of content and collusion with auditors, and the creation of fraudulent projects, which may be feasible but undeliverable, impractical, or technically unfeasible. There are also frauds related to hacking attacks on microgrid investment platforms and fraud in rewards-based campaigns. Other types of fraud include misinformation about technologies such as 5G, diversion of funds and misuse of money, and fraud in donation-based crowdfunding campaigns. Also included are prevented fraud, where campaigns were stopped before transferring funds and attempted fraud, where the fraud was discovered after funds were received (RQ2 is Answered).
- Digital platforms used in the studies include GoFundMe, Kickstarter, Indiegogo (Belavina et al. 2020; Perez et al. 2022), LendingClub, and Seedrs (Huo et al. 2024).
- Research in fraud detection and risk management on crowdfunding platforms has explored different methodologies. Xu et al. (2023) and Bafna et al. (2023) propose decentralized systems based on blockchain and Ethereum smart contracts to ensure proper utilization of funds, avoiding external influences and fraud. On the other hand, Hou and Qu (2023) and Li and Qu (2022) use machine learning models such as BERT, BNB, MT5, and hybrid classifiers to detect logical contradictions and misleading narratives in crowdfunding projects. Prateek et al. (2021) and Shafqat et al. (2020) demonstrate the effectiveness of combining machine learning classifiers with rule-based models to identify fraud. Wu et al. (2022) highlight the importance of evaluating crowdfunding platforms for investments in microgrids, while Cumming et al. (2021) and Lee et al. (2022) highlight the precision of logistic regression to detect fraud. Furthermore, studies such as that of Winoto and Wulandari (2023) and Meoli et al. (2022) analyze the impact of regulation and financial literacy on the crowdfunding ecosystem to mitigate risks such as adverse selection and moral hazard. Finally, Elmer and Ward-Kimola (2023) and Han and Dang (2020) investigate how crowdfunding platforms can spread disinformation. Also, these authors concluded the importance of ML algorithms for early warning systems in proactive fraud prevention. Table 1 displays the most representative works. (RQ3 is Answered). The above authors report high accuracy values, around 98%, in fraud detection (Shafqat et al. 2020; Choi et al. 2022). It is important to note that machine learning techniques have been successfully used in other contexts and applications. For example, in predicting the success of crowdfunding campaigns, Logistic Regression, with or without PCA, showed an appropriate performance, reaching an accuracy of 84%. Random Forest with PCA obtained an accuracy of 82%, while XGBoost with PCA achieved an accuracy of 83% (Raflesia et al. 2023). Other applications detect fake news information, where the Bi-LSTM algorithm showed an accuracy of 96.77% (Hamed et al. 2023). These applications show an excellent opportunity for machine learning algorithms to be used in fake news and fraud prediction.

Figure 2 shows the countries with the most citations. The United States has the highest number of citations, indicating its research's academic and scientific impact. Western Europe, with countries such as Germany, and Asia, China, and Japan, also have representative citations, reflecting their strong presence in this field of research. Africa, Latin America, and some Asian countries have significantly fewer citations, which indicates less contribution or recognition in the international academic literature.

Table 1. Overview of PRISMA selected studies that employed machine learning on fraud detection in crowdfunding digital platforms.

Study	First Author (Reference)	Journal Title	Type of Document	Publication Year	Fraud Type Evaluated	Fraud Detection in Crowdfunding Platforms	Number of Citations (Auto Citations)	Number of Institutions Involved	Publisher	Number of Countries	Journal Quartile
1	Mohammadi et al. (2025)	*International Journal of Finance & Managerial Accounting*	Journal Article	2025	Fraudsters may use asymmetric information and regulatory loopholes to deceive investors.	NN	0 (0)	1	Inderscience	1	Q3
2	Huo et al. (2024)	*Information Processing & Management*	Journal Article	2024	Risks and challenges associated with information disclosure on crowdfunding platforms and how they affect resource acquisition for digital ventures.	STM	1 (0)	5	Elsevier	3	Q1
3	Bafna et al. (2023)	*Journal of Information and Computational Science*	Journal Article	2023	Embezzlement of funds, lack of value returned to contributors, misuse of money.	Not Applied	0 (0)	1	Binary Information Press	1	Q4
4	Bianda et al. (2023)	*Journal of World Science*	Journal Article	2023	Types of frauds related to crowdfunding services based on Sharia principles (Riba, Gharar, Maysir, Tadlis, Dharar, Al-Ta'addi, Al-Taqshir, Mukhalafah al-shurut, Zhulm).	Not Applied	3 (0)	1	Riviera Publishing	1	NC
5	Elmer and Ward-Kimola (2023)	*Media, Culture & Society*	Journal Article	2023	Electoral fraud, disinformation about 5G.	Not Applied	6 (2)	2	SAGE Publications Ltd.	1	Q1
6	Hou and Qu (2023)	*Current applied science and technology*	Journal Article	2023	Feasible but fraudulent projects, impractical fraudulent projects.	BERT, MT5, SP, AFT	0 (0)	1	King Mongkut's Institute of Technology Ladkrabang	2	Q4
7	Lathifah et al. (2022)	*2022 10th International Conference on Cyber and IT Service Management (CITSM)*	conference	2022	Unauthorized access control in administrative areas, advanced SQL injection vulnerabilities, insecure design, misconfiguration of security, vulnerable and outdated components, software and data integrity failures.	Not Applied	2 (0)	1	IEEE Xplore	1	NC
8	Winoto and Wulandari (2023)	*Management Studies and Entrepreneurship Journal*	Journal Article	2023	Fraud in data verification, explorative analysis, fraud in project presentation, fraud in project execution, asymmetric information risk.	Not Applied	0 (0)	1	YRPI	1	NC
9	Xu et al. (2023)	*Information Sciences*	Journal Article	2023	Personal fraud, content plagiarism, collusion with auditors.	Not Applied	5 (0)	2	Elsevier	1	Q1

Table 1. *Cont.*

Study	First Author (Reference)	Journal Title	Type of Document	Publication Year	Fraud Type Evaluated	Fraud Detection in Crowdfunding Platforms	Number of Citations (Auto Citations)	Number of Institutions Involved	Publisher	Number of Countries	Journal Quartile
10	Zkik et al. (2023)	*Electronic Commerce Research*	Journal Article	2024	Re-entry attacks, infinite loop attacks, block timestamp attacks, Advanced Persistent Threats (APTs), malware, Distributed Denial-of-Service (DDoS) attacks.	AdaBoost, XGBoost, RF	4 (0)	3	Springer	3	Q1
11	Choi et al. (2022)	*KSII Transactions on Internet and Information Systems*	Journal Article	2022	Detect fraudulent activities within health-related crowdfunding campaigns on platforms like GoFundMe.	LDA, CF	0 (0)	3	Korea Society of Internet Information	1	Q3
12	Lee et al. (2022)	*Sensors*	Journal Article	2022	Fraud in reward-based crowdfunding campaigns.	LR, FSLR	2 (0)	2	MDPI	2	Q1
13	Li and Qu (2022)	*Songklanakarin Journal of Science & Technology*	Journal Article	2022	Projects with logically feasible and practical concepts and technically infeasible projects.	BNB, NO, BK	0 (0)	1	Songklanakarin Journal of Science & Technology	2	Q3
14	Meoli et al. (2022)	*Corporate Governance: An International Review*	Journal Article	2022	Fraud related to equity-based crowdfunding, especially concerning investor financial literacy.	Not Applied	50 (7)	2	Emerald Group Publishing Ltd.	1	Q1
15	Perez et al. (2022)	*Proceedings of the 14th ACM Web Science Conference 2022*	conference	2020	Embezzlement fraud, opportunistic fraud, total fraud.	RF, AdaBoost, DT, k-NN, NB, SVM, EC, MLP	12 (1)	3	arXiv	2	NC
16	Riadi et al. (2022)	*Engineering Science Letter*	Journal Article	2022	Fraud related to the security of crowdfunding services in charitable organizations.	Not Applied	0 (0)	1	The Indonesian Institute of Science and Technology	1	NC
17	Wu et al. (2022)	*Financial Innovation*	Journal Article	2022	Fraud and hacking attacks on crowdfunding platforms for investments in microgrid projects.	q-ROFSs, M-SWARA, DEMATEL, TOPSIS, IFS and PFS	40 (17)	2	Springer	2	Q1
18	Cumming et al. (2021)	*Journal of Business Ethics*	Journal Article	2021	Prevented fraud, attempted fraud, fraud in campaigns with delays of more than a year, no communication for six months, and no rewards.	PSM	185 (20)	5	Springer	3	Q1
19	Prateek et al. (2021)	*WISP 2021 Proceedings. 2.*	conference	2021	Fraudulent campaigns on donation-based crowdfunding platforms.	RF, SVM	0 (0)	1	AIS Electronic Library	1	NC

Table 1. *Cont.*

Study	First Author (Reference)	Journal Title	Type of Document	Publication Year	Fraud Type Evaluated	Fraud Detection in Crowdfunding Platforms	Number of Citations (Auto Citations)	Number of Institutions Involved	Publisher	Number of Countries	Journal Quartile
20	Belavina et al. (2020)	*Management Science*	Journal Article	2020	Embezzlement of funds, and performance opacity.	ST	136 (10)	2	INFORMS	1	Q1
21	Han and Dang (2020)	*Proceedings of the 7th International Conference on Management of e-Commerce and e-Government*	conference	2020	Failure to pay promised returns, delayed return payments, breach of established agreements, and lack of post-sale services.	RF, SVM	0 (0)	1	ACM DL	1	NC
22	Petrov and Emelyanova (2021)	*CEUR Workshop Proceedings*	conference	2021	Bankruptcy risks, fraud or unfair practices, risks associated with public offerings and unlicensed activities, information disclosure risks, and illegal platform use risks.	SA, LR, NN, DT, NBC	2 (0)	2	CEUR Workshop Proceedings	1	NC
23	Shafqat et al. (2020)	*Applied Sciences*	Journal Article	2020	Successfully funded but not delivered projects, canceled projects, and projects suspended for fraud.	LDA, LSTM.	4 (0)	2	MDPI	1	Q2
24	Ellman and Hurkens (2019a)	*Economics Letters*	Journal Article	2019	Fraud in the context of reward-based crowdfunding.	Not Applied	27 (3)	1	Elsevier	1	Q2
25	Shafqat and Byun (2019)	*Applied Sciences*	Journal Article	2019	Misrepresentation of ideas, advance fee fraud, investment fraud, non-payment or non-delivery, personal data breach.	LSTM-LDA	18 (4)	1	MDPI	1	Q1
26	Zenone and Snyder (2019)	*Policy & Internet*	Journal Article	2019	Faking or exaggerating one's own illness, faking or exaggerating someone else's illness, identity theft, and misuse of funds.	Not Applied	51 (3)	1	John Wiley and Sons Ltd.	1	Q1

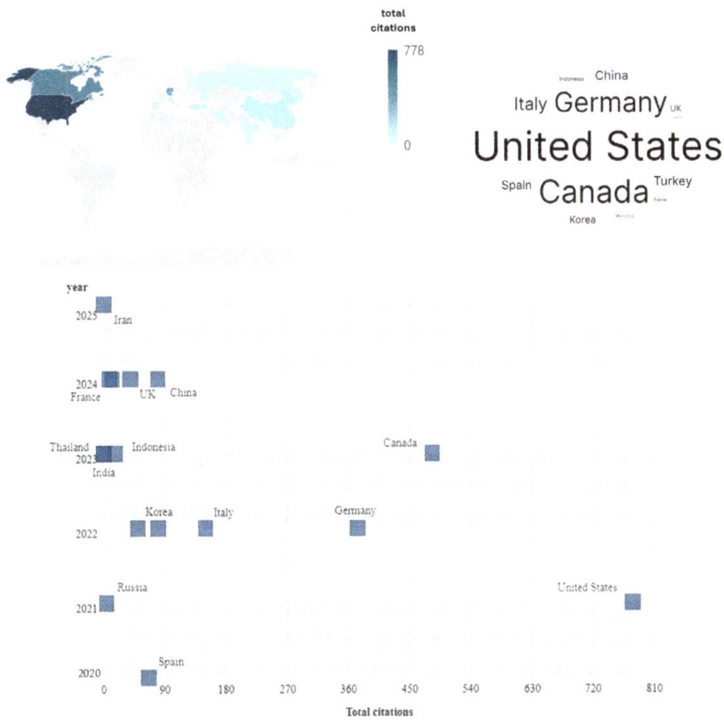

Figure 2. Country distribution of the total citations of the main works gathered.

Figure 3 shows the universities' distribution of the total citations. Concordia University leads with 376 citations, followed by the University of Pennsylvania with 272. Florida Atlantic University, Poschingerstraße, the University of Birmingham, and the University of Bremen are tied, with 185 citations each. The University of Bergamo has 150 citations, Cornell University 136, Simon Fraser University-Health Sciences 102, and İstanbul Medipol University 80. Concordia University and the University of Pennsylvania stand out, suggesting the need to analyze their publication and collaboration strategies.

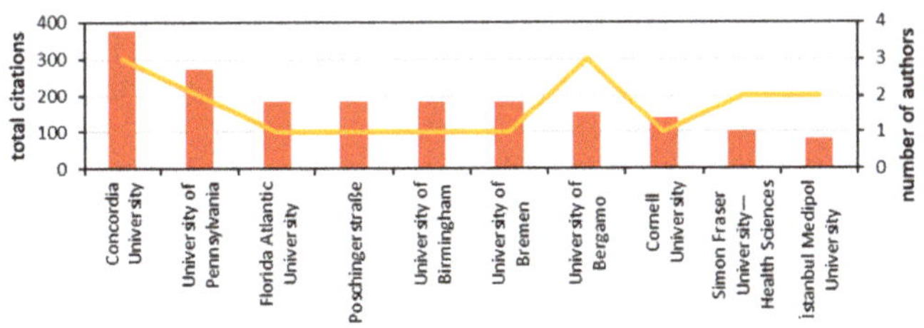

Figure 3. Universities' research distribution of the total citations, and the number of authors of the main works gathered.

Figure 4 shows the authors' most remarkable citations and publications in the field of research. Cumming, D. stands out with 360 citations in three publications, reflecting strong influence, while the results for Belavina, E., with 130 citations in one publication, suggest great relevance and innovation. Cumming's citation efficiency is 120 citations per publication, and Belavina's is 130. In contrast, Sharfqat, W. and Shang, W. L., with three publications each, do not exceed 120 citations, indicating lower comparative efficiency.

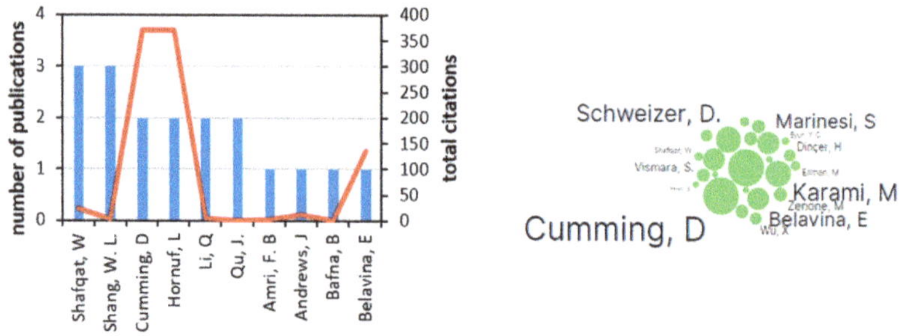

Figure 4. Author distribution between the total citations and the number of publications carried out in the field of research.

3.2. *Principal Component Analysis (PCA) Results*

In a PCA analysis, the components 1 and 2 are represented on the X and Y axes. These components are linear combinations of the original variables and manage to capture most of the variability present in the data. Figure 5a shows the country's biplot distribution. The biplot axes represent the first two principal components (Component 1 and Component 2). The variables used to carry out the analysis in Figure 5 are the countries, the total number of publications, the number of authors, the year, the number of institutions, and the number of articles published in Q1 or Q2. The first principal component (Component 1) is influenced by the "number of authors", "number of institutions", and "Q1", since these vectors are mainly aligned with the axis of the first component. The second principal component (Component 2) is influenced by "year", since this vector is mainly aligned with the axis of the second component. Figure 5b shows the university's biplot distribution. The "total citations" arrow indicates a strong association with the second principal component (Component 2). The variables "year" and "Journal Article" have similar directions, suggesting a possible correlation between them. The variable "conference" is in the opposite direction to "Journal Article", suggesting contrasting characteristics between these types of publications. The variables "Q1" and "Q2" can be related to the journal's quartile, showing different patterns of association. Finally, the "number of authors" is oriented horizontally, indicating its more significant relationship with the first principal component (Component 1).

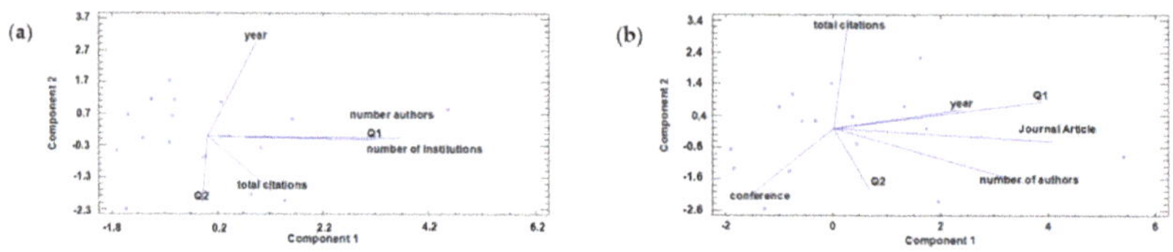

Figure 5. Biplot analysis of the country (**a**) and the university's (**b**) component distribution.

Figure 6 shows the dendrogram diagram of the country analysis. The dendrogram provided is made using the nearest neighbor method and the squared Euclidean distance. The analysis of this dendrogram allows us to understand the similarity between different countries based on several variables: total citations, number of authors per year, number of institutions, articles in Q1, and articles in Q2. The distance in the dendrogram shows the dissimilarity among the countries; the greater the distance, the greater the difference in the values of the variables studied. In the multi-country clustering analysis, several groups are identified based on similarity in variables such as citations, number of authors, institutions, and articles in Q1 and Q2. Canada, France, Morocco, Thailand, India, the United Kingdom, and Italy form a close group, indicating similar values in the mentioned variables. Germany and Iran, although grouped together, show moderate differences from the other groups. The United States and Japan are further apart, indicating more significant differences, while Spain and Indonesia are also together but at some distance. The United States and Spain are also similar, but present notable differences from the previous group. Finally, China and Korea are in the most distant group, suggesting significantly different values in the analyzed variables (RQ4 is Answered).

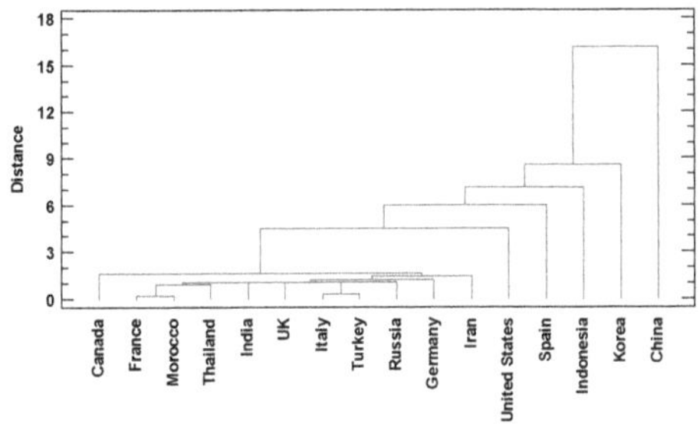

Figure 6. Dendrogram analysis of the country aggrupation.

Figure 7 shows the university's dendrogram using the nearest neighbor method with the squared Euclidean approach. The closest universities in the dendrogram have similar characteristics in the variables considered. The top 14 universities employed in the analysis are described as follows: Concordia University (U1), University of Pennsylvania (U2), Florida Atlantic University (U3), Poschingerstraße (U4), University of Birmingham (U5), University of Bremen (U6), University of Bergamo (U7), Cornell University (U8), Simon Fraser University-Health Sciences (U9), İstanbul Medipol University (U10), Campus UAB (U11), Jeju National University (U12), Normal University (U13) and Hunan University (U14). Institutions that cluster at greater distances (such as U12 and U14) have unique profiles compared to the others. The primary groups identified present different levels of similarity among the institutions. Group 1 is composed of U1, U2, U3, U4, U5, U6, U7, U8, U9, and U10, and shows a very high level of similarity, with distances less than 8, which indicates that these institutions have quite similar profiles in the mentioned variables. Group 2 is composed of U11, U12, U13, and U14, and also presents relatively low distances, although not as low as the first group, suggesting a moderate similarity between them. Finally, Group 3 is composed of U15, U16, U17, U18, U19, and U20, constituting a different group with moderate similarity. Within Group 1, a subgroup from U1 to U6 has a very low distance, approximately 2, and another subgroup from U7 to U10 has a slightly larger distance, approximately 4 to 6. On the other hand, U21 is an isolated institution that is not grouped with any other, up to a distance greater than 16, which indicates a very different profile in the variables analyzed (RQ5 is Answered).

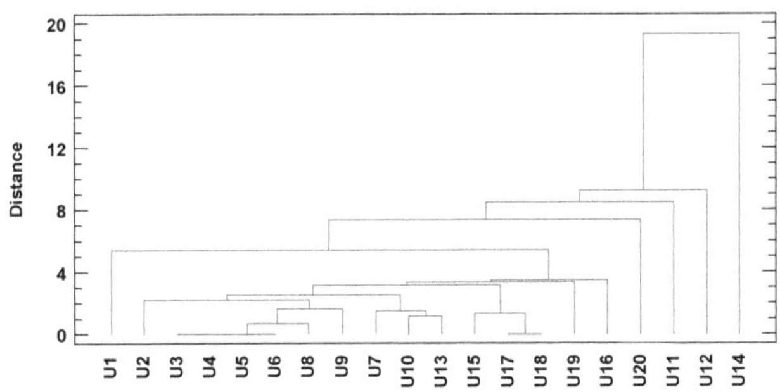

Figure 7. Dendrogram analysis of the university's aggrupation using nearest neighbor method coupled with squared Euclidean.

3.3. Statistical Comparison Analysis

The normal probability plot using the residuals showed that the standard skewness and the kurtosis statistics values were outside the range of −2 to +2, which indicates significant normality departure. For these reasons, the authors employed a Kruskal–Wallis nonparametric test for statistical comparison. Figure 8 shows the statistical comparison of total citations between countries, universities, publishers, and journals. In this figure, the error bars correspond to the Kruskal–Wallis intervals at a 95% confidence level, and the point between the lines corresponds to the mean of the total citations. The *p*-values of the Kruskal–Wallis test for different groups are as follows: in countries, it is 6.61×10^{-5}; in universities, it is 1.26×10^{-4}; in publishing houses, it is 1.89×10^{-8}; and in academic journals, it is 5.67×10^{-9}. As can be seen, the *p*-value is less than 0,05, which implies a statistically significant difference amongst the medians at the 95% confidence level. Below are the observations derived from the results in Figure 8.

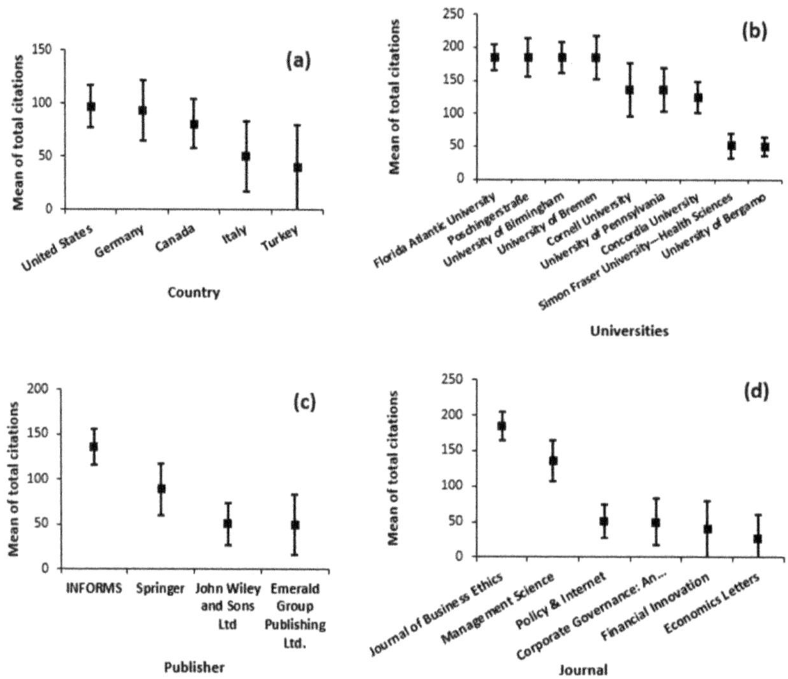

Figure 8. Comparison of the statistical analysis of the (**a**) country, (**b**) universities, (**c**) publisher, and (**d**) journal with the total citations, at a 95% confidence level.

- The comparison of the five countries with the highest citations shows no statistically significant differences at the 95% confidence level. The above implies that the United States, Germany, Canada, Italy, and Turkey are the most representative countries in terms of total citations, and are the countries whose works have had remarkable visualization in the academic community (RQ4 is Answered).
- The comparison of the universities reveals two groups. The first group comprises Florida Atlantic University, Poschingerstraße, University of Birmingham, University of Bremen, Cornell University, University of Pennsylvania, and Concordia University. The second group includes Simon Fraser University-Health Sciences and the University of Bergamo. For the universities in the first group, no statistically significant differences are observed at the 95% confidence level, which indicates that their academic production is being recognized and that they are the most proficient

universities for producing some research work. However, with fewer citations, the second group presents significant differences from the first group (RQ5 is Answered).

- The comparison of the publishers shows three groups. The first group, with the highest citations, consists of Springer and John Wiley and Sons Ltd. The second group includes Emerald Group Publishing Ltd. and *Proceedings of the 14th ACM Web Science*. The last group consists of the *Proceedings of the 14th ACM Web Science*. The first group's editorials present more citations and significant differences from the other two groups. It is essential to highlight that these publishers' focus on publishing works related to fraud, identification, and control, using machine learning techniques (RQ5 is Answered).
- The comparison of journals shows two groups. The first group includes *the Journal of Business Ethics and Management Science*, while the second group includes *Policy & Internet, Corporate Governance: An International Review, Financial Innovation*, and *Economics Letters*. All these journals and their editors are interested in improving their research on fraud identification using machine learning methods on crowdfunding platforms (RQ5 is Answered).

Finally, the effect sizes of the non-parametric test are estimated. The effect size is a research tool that complements tests of statistical significance, providing information about the magnitude of the observed effect (Aarts et al. 2014). This approach not only helps validate the results, but also provides a more complete and accurate view of the academic landscape, facilitating the identification of the most influential and prominent entities in the field of study (Aarts et al. 2014). The effects observed in different groups show that 48% are registered in countries, 91% in universities, 56% in publishing houses, and 100% in academic journals. Universities and journals have the most significant effect sizes, implying that they are important in publishing. Publishers and countries follow them. The authors highlight the importance of conducting a bibliometric analysis using different statistical methods to identify the most prolific countries and universities in a research topic.

4. Challenges and Further Studies on Fraud Detection in Crowdfunding Platforms

4.1. Data Challenges and ML Algorithms

High-quality, well-structured, labeled data are fundamental for building precise and efficient machine learning models to learn relevant patterns and make accurate predictions (Mvula et al. 2023). Machine learning provides continuous feedback, allowing models to adapt, improve, and address new fraud tactics. Through data analysis, user and transaction segmentation can be performed, enhancing fraud detection strategies by targeting specific segments prone to fraudulent activities. Advanced data visualization tools are crucial in understanding complex, non-linear patterns, helping analysts quickly identify problematic areas and make informed decisions (Elitzur 2024). Additionally, companies must identify and access valuable internal and external data sources, ensuring availability through crawling algorithms or database access. Innovative and research projects utilizing machine learning can uncover new insights, while a data-driven approach helps identify innovative product development opportunities (Bafna et al. 2023; Xu et al. 2023).

Further work can be carried out with advanced linguistic techniques to improve the detection of fraudulent reviews (Lee and Sohn 2019; Raflesia et al. 2023). Evaluating new ensemble and deep-learning algorithms, such as neural networks and SVM, could increase accuracy (Lee and Sohn 2019; Raflesia et al. 2023). Creating adaptive methods that respond to changes in reviewer behavior will improve the robustness of the model (Raflesia et al. 2023). Optimizing hyperparameters with techniques such as GridSearchCV maximizes performance on ML algorithms (Butt et al. 2020; Raflesia et al. 2023). Furthermore, policies and regulations tailored to specific contexts must be developed to protect crowdfunding stakeholders (Wonglimpiyarat 2018). Figure 9 presents recent ML approaches for cybersecurity intrusion detection in different applications. Louati et al. (2024) employ unsupervised learning with a MARL model based on the NSL-KDD dataset, achieving high accuracy and low false-positive and negative incidence. Kalinin and Krundyshev (2023) and Talukder et al. (2024) use supervised learning, achieving accuracies of up to 99.95%, using neural networks and oversampling techniques. Jemili et al. (2023) and Roshan and Zafar (2024) studied online supervised and adaptive learning models, combining algorithms such as Random Forest, XGBoost, and K-Nearest Neighbors. These authors found that the evaluated ML algorithms present more accuracies than 98% using different cybersecurity data sets (RQ6 is Answered).

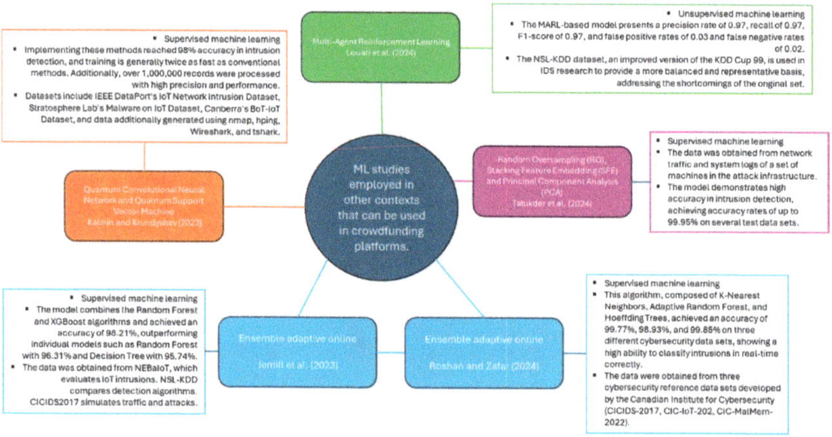

Figure 9. Advanced machine learning approaches for cybersecurity intrusion detection (Kalinin and Krundyshev 2023; Louati et al. 2024; Talukder et al. 2024; Jemili et al. 2023; Roshan and Zafar 2024).

4.2. Improvements in Crowdfunding Platforms: Design, Policies and Inter-Operability

Figure 10 shows the main topics for further research for detecting fraud and anomalous behaviors on digital crowdfunding platforms. Future research on crowdfunding platforms can focus on the following aspects (RQ6 is Answered).

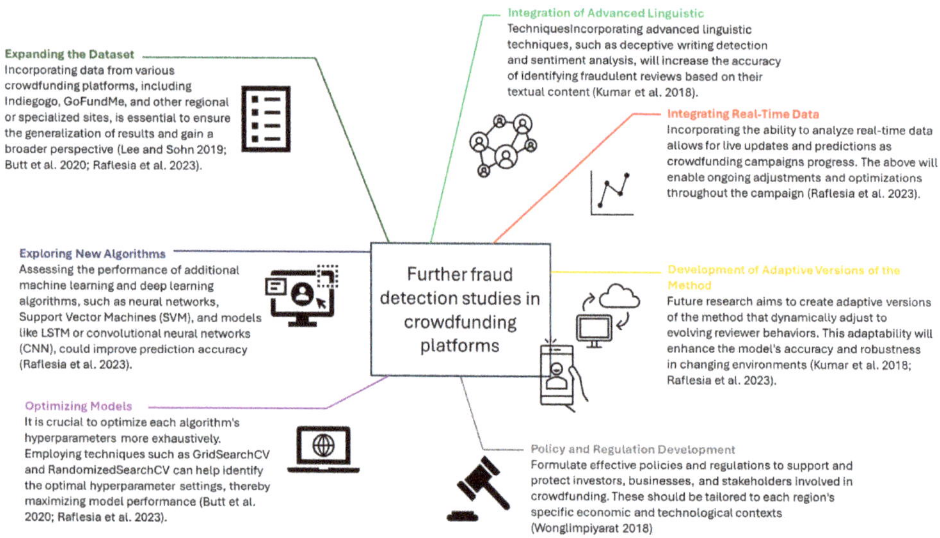

Figure 10. Challenges of Machine Learning in Fraud Detection on Crowdfunding Platforms (Lee and Sohn 2019; Butt et al. 2020; Raflesia et al. 2023; Kumar et al. 2018; Wonglimpiyarat 2018).

- Analyze how new technologies such as blockchain, big data, augmented reality, and virtual reality can increase transparency and trust in these platforms. These technologies can improve project presentation and sponsor engagement (Zhou et al. 2023; Ratten 2023; Yang et al. 2023). In addition, it is important to explore innovative business models that integrate analytical and digital marketing services. The above could strengthen the long-term financial sustainability of crowdfunding platforms and make them more resilient (Zhou et al. 2023; Ratten 2023; Yang et al. 2023).
- The competition between platforms and how this influences their strategies can help them effectively differentiate themselves in the market (Zhou et al. 2023). Further work in AI can be carried out to personalize and adapt the user experience to their interests and behaviors (Yang et al. 2023; Gawer 2021; Chen et al. 2022).
- Ensuring transparency and ethical practices to safeguard user data privacy and foster trust (Yang et al. 2023; Chen et al. 2022; Vicari and Kirby 2023). Implementing incentive and control mechanisms can enhance relationship management with project creators and contributors (Chen et al. 2022).
- The role of crowdfunding platforms in supporting entrepreneurship, particularly in times of global crises, is not just a theoretical concept but a practical solution for entrepreneurs and small businesses (Ratten 2023). This aspect warrants further investigation.
- Facilitating networking and inter-operability among entrepreneurs, investors, and consumers, and examining effective digital marketing strategies can attract more participants to these platforms (Ratten 2023; Yang et al. 2023).
- The regulatory environment can be studied to maintain competitiveness and innovation while mitigating risks such as fraud and privacy issues (Gawer 2021, 2022). Future studies should consider how platform- and policy-design changes can improve well-being and market efficiency, testing different design elements and policy interventions to observe their impact on contributor behavior and campaign success.
- Deeper research is needed to understand endogenous anonymity election and its broader implications, exploring the various factors that lead contributors to choose anonymity and how these choices affect the overall crowdfunding ecosystem (Burtch et al. 2016; Wonglimpiyarat 2018).
- It is important to incorporate crowdfunding campaigns with traditional marketing channels such as social media, email marketing, and public relations to maximize their reach. Furthermore, these campaigns contribute to brand building and long-term customer loyalty and have great potential in B2B markets, facilitating the launch of industrial products and technologies. It is important to explore the impact of equity crowdfunding on investor relations and corporate governance and its ability to foster innovation and support new technologies and business models. Considering the regulatory environment and legal implications ensures compliance and effectiveness of campaigns (Brown et al. 2017). Addressing ethical considerations and social impact ensures responsible practices and a positive societal effect.
- Finally, comparative studies between different countries can provide valuable insights into how cultural, economic, and regulatory environments influence the success of crowdfunding platforms, helping to identify best practices and areas for improvement (Bassani et al. 2019).

4.3. Strategies and Challenges in Cybersecurity and Fraud Education: Methods, Academic Programs and Gamification Learning Platforms

Figure 11 shows different studies of educational and social communications. Cybersecurity and fraud education for children and younger people and equipment management processes in an industry are most effective when self-directed instruction, collaboration, and traditional teaching methods are used, significantly improving assessment results. Best practices for topic selection include using age-appropriate materials published by government agencies, which educators should actively seek out. Nationwide implementation faces challenges such as lack of standardized curriculum, shortage of trained professionals, and resource limitations, especially in low-income and rural schools, highlighting the need for better funding and increased fraud awareness. Educational programs have proven effective, significantly increasing student interest and knowledge, with a 15% increase after workshops (Solis-Diaz 2023). Furthermore, game-based learning platforms, especially those using mobile applications, are highly engaging for primary school students, and improve learning outcomes through personalized content.

Figure 11. Aspects of social education and knowledge appropriation of fraud (Solis-Diaz 2023; Ahmad et al. 2021).

4.4. Implementing Machine Learning for Fraud Detection in Crowdfunding Platforms

To carry out a machine learning (ML) project to identify fraud on a crowdfunding platform, it is essential first to pinpoint the issue and the specific sector that requires improvement. Then, high-quality data must be collected and prepared, which includes tasks such as data cleaning, identifying outliers, handling missing values, and normalization. Once the data are prepared, the most appropriate ML algorithm, such as Random Forest, SVM, ANNs, KNN, or Naive Bayes, is selected, depending on the characteristics of the data and the problem to be solved. It is essential to divide the data into training and test sets, to evaluate the model's performance. Evaluation metrics such as Recall, F1-score, and ROC-AUC serve to evaluate and validate the model, continuously monitoring it to make necessary adjustments when new data appear or conditions change. Throughout this process, it is essential to consider ethical and security aspects to ensure compliance with current legal and privacy regulations. Figure 12 shows this fact. It is important to note that to develop a machine learning system, tools such as the Scikit-Learn, TensorFlow, or PyTorch libraries are used to build models. These models are often deployed on cloud platforms such as AWS, Google Cloud, or Microsoft Azure. In addition, a data team composed of data scientists, data engineers, and domain-specific experts is essential for managing and optimizing the process.

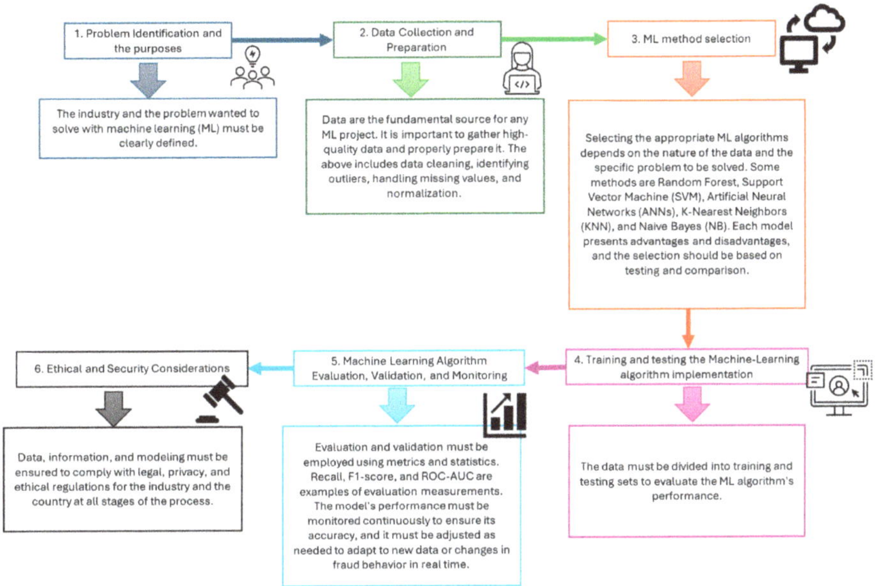

Figure 12. Machine Learning implementation process for fraud detection on crowdfunding platforms.

5. Limitations of the Study

This study has several significant limitations. First, the amount of data available fluctuates, due to continuous updates in the WoS and Scopus databases, which may affect the consistency of the results. Secondly, the study topics were selected during the data recovery phase, which could introduce bias in the results obtained. Third, the search terms used were derived from the existing scientific literature, which could have excluded some relevant keywords. Further research could help identify new search keywords. Fourth, bibliometric analyses were limited to articles written in English, which could have introduced sampling bias and consequently influenced the study results. Furthermore, future research should consider including articles in other languages to provide a more complete view and reduce potential bias.

6. Conclusions

- In this work, a bibliometric analysis is carried out to identify the most relevant studies on fraud detection in digital crowdfunding platforms using machine learning techniques. The analyses were carried out during the COVID-19 pandemic and post-pandemic period, from 2018 to 2024. Using the PRISMA methodology, 26 works were retrieved from the two databases, Scopus and Web of Science. The common fraud methods in this digital platform are fraud in crowdfunding campaigns based on rewards, fraudulent campaigns based on donations, embezzlement and misuse of funds, fraud due to embezzlement, use of information asymmetric, and regulatory loopholes to deceive investors. Furthermore, machine learning techniques used at industrial and academic levels include Random Forest (RF), Support Vector Machine (SVM), Logistic Regression (LR), Neural Networks (NN), Naive Bayes (NB), Decision Trees (DT), Latent Dirichlet Allocation (LDA), and Long Short-Term Memory (LSTM), among others.
- The results of the analysis reveal that Cumming, D., followed by Belavina, E., are the authors with the highest publications and citations. At the same time, Sharfqat, W. and Shang, W. L. have the lowest citations. It is important to note that the universities with the highest number of publications and citations are Concordia University, with

more than 350 citations; the University of Pennsylvania, with around 250 citations; and Florida Atlantic University and Poschingerstraße, with about 150 citations each. Other institutions in the topmost prolific universities, although with fewer than 150 citations, include Birmingham, Bremen, Bergamo, and Cornell Universities.

- The analysis of the principal components shows that two principal components influence the countries where the authors are affiliated. The first component is influenced by "number of authors", "number of institutions", and "Q1", while Component 2 is influenced by "year." Regarding institutions, the first component is related to "year" and "Journal Article", while "conference" is in the opposite direction to "Journal Article", showing contrasting characteristics. The authors prefer to publish in scientific journals rather than conferences, and the journal quartile (Q1 and Q2) reflects different patterns of association. The "number of authors" relates primarily to Component 1. The analysis also shows that Canada, France, Morocco, Thailand, India, the United Kingdom, and Italy form a close group, indicating similar values in publications, citations, and several institutions participating in the research. Germany and Iran present moderate differences. The United States and Japan are further apart, pointing to significant differences. Spain and Indonesia are together, but at some distance, while the United States and Spain are similar to each other but different from the previous group. China and Korea form the most distant group, suggesting very different values.
- Further studies that will impact this research topic are highlighted by the need to expand the data set and integrate advanced linguistic analyses, allowing for a more complete analysis. Incorporating real-time data and developing adaptive versions of the method will improve responsiveness. Exploring new algorithms and optimizing models are important to increase accuracy. Developing appropriate policies and regulations aims to ensure a practical operational framework. These joint approaches will strengthen early anomaly detection and improve efficiency in industrial contract management.
- This work provides tools for understanding recent studies of fraud detection on crowdfunding platforms using machine learning techniques. The above enables accurate and faster identification of fraudulent activities, thereby protecting investors and reducing associated financial risks. Furthermore, collaboration between academic institutions and industries facilitates the development of new technologies and methodologies to address practical problems and strengthens the regulatory framework and trust in these platforms. So, this work identifies global trends, future research directions, and opportunities for continued innovations in the security and efficiency of crowdfunding platforms.

Author Contributions: The three authors participated in all steps of the manuscript preparation: methodology, investigation, formal analysis, writing—original draft, writing—review and editing. All authors have read and agreed to the published version of the manuscript.

Funding: This research was funded by Universidad Nacional de Colombia and the Contraloría General de la República (CGR) de Colombia with the inter-administrative contract No. 1550 of 2023.

Data Availability Statement: No new data were created or generated in the article.

Acknowledgments: The authors are grateful for the support of the Universidad Nacional de Colombia and the Contraloría General de la República (CGR) de Colombia with the inter-administrative contract No. 1550 of 2023. The contract aims to provide scientific and technological services to the Dirección de Información, Análisis y Reacción Inmediata through applied research activities, technological development, innovation, and knowledge transfer to promote the deployment of methodologies, techniques, and technological solutions for developing the Digital Government Policy in the Contraloría General de la República de Colombia to strengthen surveillance and fiscal control.

Conflicts of Interest: The authors declare that they have no known competing financial interests or personal relationships that could have appeared to influence the work reported in this paper.

List of Abbreviations

AFT	Adaptive Fuzzy Training
AI	Artificial Intelligence
ANAC	Italy's National Anti-Corruption Authority
ANN	Artificial Neural Network
AR	Augmented Reality.
BBN	Bayesian Belief Network
BERT	Bidirectional Encoder Representations from Transformers
BK	Balanced K-means
BNB	Binomial Naive Bayes
CART	Classification and Regression Trees
CBS	Cost Breakdown Structure
CF	Collaborative Filtering
DEMATEL	Decision-Making Trial and Evaluation Laboratory
DNN	Deep Neural Network
DT	Decision Trees
EmPULIA	Digital platform for public tenders in Apulia
EU	European Union
FSLR	Forward Stepwise Logistic Regression
GBM	Gradient Boosting Machine
IEEE	Institute of Electrical and Electronics Engineers
IF	Isolation Forest
IFS	Intuitionistic Fuzzy Sets
INCM	Portuguese Mint and Official Printing Office
IoT	Internet of Things
KNN	K-Nearest Neighbors
k-NN	k-Nearest Neighbors
LaBSE	Language-agnostic BERT Sentence Embedding
LASER	Language-Agnostic SEntence Representations
LDA	Latent Dirichlet Allocation
LR	Logistic Regression
LSTM	Long Short-Term Memory
LSTM-LDA	Long Short-Term Memory—Latent Dirichlet Allocation
MBERT	Bidirectional Encoder Representations from Transformers Multilingüe
MDL	Minimum Description Length
ML	Machine Learning
MLP	Multilayer Neural Network
MLP	Multilayer Perceptron
M-SWARA	Modified Step-wise Weight Assessment Ratio Analysis
MT5	Multilingual Text-to-Text Transfer Transformer
NB	Naive-Bayes
Neural	Network
NLP	Natural Language Processing
PCA	Principal Component Analysis
PFS	Pythagorean Fuzzy Sets
PRISMA	Preferred Reporting Items for Systematic Reviews and Meta-Analyses
PSA	Production Sharing Agreements
PSM	Propensity Score Matching
Q	Quartile
q-ROFSs	q-Rung Orthopair Fuzzy Sets
RBFN	Radial Basis Function Network
RF	Random Forest
RQ	Research Question
SciML	Scientific Machine Learning
SCSC	Supply Chain Smart Contract
SD	Standard Deviation
SMS	Safety Management Systems

SP	Stochastic Programming
ST	Sequential Testing
STM	Structural Topic Modelling
SVM	Support Vector Machine
TOPSIS	Technique for Order of Preference by Similarity to Ideal Solution
UAV	Unmanned Aerial Vehicles
WBS	Work Breakdown Structure
XGBoost	Extreme Gradient Boosting
XLMR	Cross-lingual Language Model Pretraining

References

Aarts, Sil, Marjan Van Den Akker, and Bjorn Winkens. 2014. The Importance of Effect Sizes. *The European Journal of General Practice* 20: 61–64. [CrossRef] [PubMed]

Ahmad, Norita, Phillip A. Laplante, Joanna F. DeFranco, and Mohamad Kassab. 2021. A Cybersecurity Educated Community. *IEEE Transactions on Emerging Topics in Computing* 10: 1456–63. [CrossRef]

Aksnes, Dag W., Liv Langfeldt, and Paul Wouters. 2019. Citations, Citation Indicators, and Research Quality: An Overview of Basic Concepts and Theories. *Sage Open* 9: 2158244019829575. [CrossRef]

Bafna, Bhavana, Vedant Daigavane, Shlok Shaha, Gaurav Shinde, and Sachin Shelke. 2023. Decentralized Transaction System for Detection and Prevention of Fraud in Crowdfunding Platforms. *Journal of Information and Computational Science* 13: 133–38.

Bassani, Gaia, Nicoletta Marinelli, and Silvio Vismara. 2019. Crowdfunding in Healthcare. *The Journal of Technology Transfer* 44: 1290–310. [CrossRef]

Behl, Abhishek, Pankaj Dutta, Zongwei Luo, and Pratima Sheorey. 2022. Enabling Artificial Intelligence on a Donation-Based Crowdfunding Platform: A Theoretical Approach. *Annals of Operations Research* 319: 761–89. [CrossRef]

Belavina, Elena, Simone Marinesi, and Gerry Tsoukalas. 2020. Rethinking Crowdfunding Platform Design: Mechanisms to Deter Misconduct and Improve Efficiency. *Management Science* 66: 4980–97. [CrossRef]

Bianda, Ryan, Aang Gunaepi, and Muhammad Misbakul Munir. 2023. Offering Sharia Securities Through Technology-Based Crowdfunding Services Based on Sharia Principles According to MUI Fatwa. *Journal of World Science* 2: 332–40. [CrossRef]

Brown, Terrence E., Edward Boon, and Leyland F. Pitt. 2017. Seeking Funding in Order to Sell: Crowdfunding as a Marketing Tool. *Business Horizons* 60: 189–95. [CrossRef]

Burtch, Gordon, Anindya Ghose, and Sunil Wattal. 2016. Secret Admirers: An Empirical Examination of Information Hiding and Contribution Dynamics in Online Crowdfunding. *Information Systems Research* 27: 478–96. [CrossRef]

Butt, Umer Ahmed, Muhammad Mehmood, Syed Bilal Hussain Shah, Rashid Amin, M. Waqas Shaukat, Syed Mohsan Raza, Doug Young Suh, and Md. Jalil Piran. 2020. A Review of Machine Learning Algorithms for Cloud Computing Security. *Electronics* 9: 1379. [CrossRef]

Cardona, Luis F., Jaime A. Guzmán-Luna, and Jaime A. Restrepo-Carmona. 2024. Bibliometric Analysis of Intelligent Systems for Early Anomaly Detection in Oil and Gas Contracts: Exploring Recent Progress and Challenges. *Sustainability* 16: 4669. [CrossRef]

Chen, Liang, Tong W. Tong, Shaoqin Tang, and Nianchen Han. 2022. Governance and Design of Digital Platforms: A Review and Future Research Directions on a Meta-Organization. *Journal of Management* 48: 147–84. [CrossRef]

Choi, Jaewon, Jaehyoun Kim, and Ho Lee. 2022. Hybrid Fraud Detection Model: Detecting Fraudulent Information in the Healthcare Crowdfunding. *KSII Transactions on Internet and Information Systems (TIIS)* 16: 1006–27.

Cicchiello, Antonella Francesca, Francesca Battaglia, and Stefano Monferrà. 2019. Crowdfunding Tax Incentives in Europe: A Comparative Analysis. *The European Journal of Finance* 25: 1856–82. [CrossRef]

Cumming, Douglas, Lars Hornuf, Moein Karami, and Denis Schweizer. 2021. Disentangling Crowdfunding from Fraudfunding. *Journal of Business Ethics* 1: 26.

Elitzur, Ramy. 2024. Machine Learning and Non-Investment Crowdfunding Research: A Tutorial. *Journal of Alternative Finance* 1: 109–27. [CrossRef]

Ellman, Matthew, and Sjaak Hurkens. 2019a. Fraud Tolerance in Optimal Crowdfunding. *Economics Letters* 181: 11–16. [CrossRef]

Ellman, Matthew, and Sjaak Hurkens. 2019b. Optimal Crowdfunding Design. *Journal of Economic Theory* 184: 104939. [CrossRef]

Elmer, Greg, and Sabrina Ward-Kimola. 2023. Crowdfunding (as) Disinformation: 'Pitching' 5G and Election Fraud Campaigns on GoFundMe. *Media, Culture and Society* 45: 578–94. [CrossRef]

Freedman, Seth, and Ginger Zhe Jin. 2011. *Learning by Doing with Asymmetric Information: Evidence from Prosper.com*. Working Paper. New York: National Bureau of Economic Research, Inc.

Gawer, Annabelle. 2021. Digital Platforms' Boundaries: The Interplay of Firm Scope, Platform Sides, and Digital Interfaces. *Long Range Planning* 54: 102045. [CrossRef]

Gawer, Annabelle. 2022. Digital Platforms and Ecosystems: Remarks on the Dominant Organizational Forms of the Digital Age. *Innovation* 24: 110–24. [CrossRef]

Goodell, John W., Satish Kumar, Weng Marc Lim, and Debidutta Pattnaik. 2021. Artificial Intelligence and Machine Learning in Finance: Identifying Foundations, Themes, and Research Clusters from Bibliometric Analysis. *Journal of Behavioral and Experimental Finance* 32: 100577. [CrossRef]

Granato, Daniel, Jânio S. Santos, Graziela B. Escher, Bruno L. Ferreira, and Rubén M. Maggio. 2018. Use of Principal Component Analysis (PCA) and Hierarchical Cluster Analysis (HCA) for Multivariate Association Between Bioactive Compounds and Functional Properties in Foods: A Critical Perspective. *Trends in Food Science & Technology* 72: 83–90.

Hamed, Suhaib Kh, Ab Aziz, Mohd Juzaiddin, and Mohd Ridzwan Yaakub. 2023. Fake news detection model on social media by leveraging sentiment analysis of news content and emotion analysis of users' comments. *Sensors* 23: 1748. [CrossRef]

Han, Wenying, and Hao Dang. 2020. Product Crowdfunding Default Risk Warning Based on Random Forest Model. Paper present at the 7th International Conference on Management of e-Commerce and e-Government, Jeju Island, Republic of Korea, July 1–3; pp. 99–105.

Hou, Wenting, and Jian Qu. 2023. BM5-SP-SC: A Dual Model Architecture for Contradiction Detection on Crowdfunding Projects. *Current Applied Science and Technology* 10: 55003. [CrossRef]

Huo, Hong, Chen Wang, Chunjia Han, Mu Yang, and Wen-Long Shang. 2024. Risk Disclosure and Entrepreneurial Resource Acquisition in Crowdfunding Digital Platforms: Evidence from Digital Technology Ventures. *Information Processing and Management* 61: 103655. [CrossRef]

Jemili, Farah, Rahma Meddeb, and Ouajdi Korbaa. 2023. Intrusion detection based on ensemble learning for big data classification. *Cluster Computing* 27: 3771–98. [CrossRef]

Kalinin, Maxim, and Vasiliy Krundyshev. 2023. Security Intrusion Detection Using Quantum Machine Learning Techniques. *Journal of Computer Virology and Hacking Techniques* 19: 125–36. [CrossRef]

Kumar, Naveen, Deepak Venugopal, Liangfei Qiu, and Subodha Kumar. 2018. Detecting Review Manipulation on Online Platforms with Hierarchical Supervised Learning. *Journal of Management Information Systems* 35: 350–80. [CrossRef]

Lathifah, Ari, Faaza Bil Amri, and Ani Rosidah. 2022. Security Vulnerability Analysis of the Sharia Crowdfunding Website Using OWASP-ZAP. Paper present at the 2022 10th International Conference on Cyber and IT Service Management (CITSM), Yogyakarta, Indonesia, September 20–21; New York: IEEE, pp. 1–5.

Lee, SeungHun, Wafa Shafqat, and Hyun-Chul Kim. 2022. Backers Beware: Characteristics and Detection of Fraudulent Crowdfunding Campaigns. *Sensors* 22: 7677. [CrossRef]

Lee, Won Sang, and So Young Sohn. 2019. Discovering Emerging Business Ideas Based on Crowdfunded Software Projects. *Decision Support Systems* 116: 102–13. [CrossRef]

Li, Qi, and Jian Qu. 2022. A Novel BNB-NO-BK Method for Detecting Fraudulent Crowdfunding Projects. *Songklanakarin Journal of Science and Technology* 44: 1209–19.

Louati, Faten, Farah Barika Ktata, and Ikram Amous. 2024. Big-IDS: A Decentralized Multi Agent Reinforcement Learning Approach for Distributed Intrusion Detection in Big Data Networks. *Cluster Computing* 27: 6823–6841. [CrossRef]

Markas, Ruhaab, and Yisha Wang. 2019. Dare to Venture: Data Science Perspective on Crowdfunding. *SMU Data Science Review* 2: 19.

Meoli, Michele, Alice Rossi, and Silvio Vismara. 2022. Financial Literacy and Security-Based Crowdfunding. *Corporate Governance: An International Review* 30: 27–54. [CrossRef]

Minh, Pham Son, Hung-Son Dang, and Nguyen Canh Ha. 2023. Optimization of 3D Cooling Channels in Plastic Injection Molds by Taguchi-Integrated Principal Component Analysis (PCA). *Polymers* 15: 1080. [CrossRef] [PubMed]

Mohammadi, Ali, Fraydoon Rahnamay Roodposhti, Hoda Hemmati, and Narges Yazdanian. 2025. Identification and Modeling of Crowdfunding Risk Indicators in FinTech-Based Businesses Based on the Combined Approach of Thematic Analysis and Partial Least Squares in SEM. *International Journal of Finance and Managerial Accounting* 10: 13–24.

Montgomery, Douglas C., and George Runger. 2020. *Applied Statistics and Probability for Engineers*. New York: John Wiley & Sons Ltd.

Mvula, Paul K., Paula Branco, Guy-Vincent Jourdan, and Herna L. Viktor. 2023. A Systematic Literature Review of Cyber-Security Data Repositories and Performance Assessment Metrics for Semi-Supervised Learning. *Discover Data* 1: 4. [CrossRef]

Page, Matthew J., Joanne E. McKenzie, Patrick M. Bossuyt, Isabelle Boutron, Tammy C. Hoffmann, Cynthia D. Mulrow, Larissa Shamseer, Jennifer M. Tetzlaff, Elie A. Akl, Sue E. Brennan, and et al. 2021. The PRISMA 2020 Statement: An Updated Guideline for Reporting Systematic Reviews. *BMJ* 372: n71. [CrossRef]

Perez, Beatrice, Sara Machado, Jerone Andrews, and Nicolas Kourtellis. 2022. I Call BS: Fraud Detection in Crowdfunding Campaigns. Paper present at the 14th ACM Web Science Conference, Barcelona, Spain, June 26–29; pp. 1–11.

Petrov, Lev F., and Ellina S. Emelyanova. 2021. The Crowdfunding: Financial Flows and Risks. *CEUR Workshop Proceedings* 2830: 41–51.

Pranckutė, Raminta. 2021. Web of Science (WoS) and Scopus: The Titans of Bibliographic Information in Today's Academic World. *Publications* 9: 12. [CrossRef]

Prateek, Pranay, Dan J. Kim, and Ling Ge. 2021. Detection of Fraudulent Campaigns on Donation-Based Crowdfunding Platforms Using a Combination of Machine. Paper present at the 16th Pre-ICIS Workshop on Information Security and Privacy, Austin, TX, USA, December 12; pp. 1–9.

Raflesia, Sarifah Putri, Dinda Lestarini, Rizka Dhini Kurnia, and Dinna Yunika Hardiyanti. 2023. Using Machine Learning Approach Towards Successful Crowdfunding Prediction. *Bulletin of Electrical Engineering and Informatics* 12: 2438–45. [CrossRef]

Ratten, Vanessa. 2023. Digital Platforms and Transformational Entrepreneurship During the COVID-19 Crisis. *International Journal of Information Management* 72: 102534. [CrossRef] [PubMed]

Riadi, Imam, Ariqah Adliana Siregar, and Adiniah Gustika Pratiwi. 2022. Security on Charity Crowdfunding Services Using KAMI Index 4.1. *Engineering Science Letter* 1: 15–19.
Roshan, Khushnaseeb, and Aasim Zafar. 2024. Ensemble Adaptive Online Machine Learning in Data Stream: A Case Study in Cyber Intrusion Detection System. *International Journal of Information Technology*. [CrossRef]
Shafqat, Wafa, and Yung-Cheol Byun. 2019. Topic Predictions and Optimized Recommendation Mechanism Based on Integrated Topic Modeling and Deep Neural Networks in Crowdfunding Platforms. *Applied Sciences* 9: 5496. [CrossRef]
Shafqat, Wafa, Yung-Cheol Byun, and Namje Park. 2020. Effectiveness of Machine Learning Approaches Towards Credibility Assessment of Crowdfunding Projects for Reliable Recommendations. *Applied Sciences* 10: 9062. [CrossRef]
Sharifani, Koosha, and Mahyar Amini. 2023. Machine Learning and Deep Learning: A Review of Methods and Applications. *World Information Technology and Engineering Journal* 10: 3897–904.
Solis-Diaz, Christian Javier. 2023. *Education as a Solution to Combat Rising Cybercrime Rates against Children and Teenagers*. Electronic Theses, Projects, and Dissertations. Available online: https://scholarworks.lib.csusb.edu/etd/1811 (accessed on 12 July 2024).
Talukder, Alamin, Manowarul Islam, Ashraf Uddin, Khondokar Fida Hasan, Selina Sharmin, Salem A. Alyami, and Mohammad Ali Moni. 2024. Machine Learning-Based Network Intrusion Detection for Big and Imbalanced Data Using Oversampling, Stacking Feature Embedding and Feature Extraction. *Journal of Big Data* 11: 33. [CrossRef]
Vicari, Stefania, and Daniel Kirby. 2023. Digital Platforms as Socio-Cultural Artifacts: Developing Digital Methods for Cultural Research. *Information, Communication & Society* 26: 1733–55.
Winoto, Wahyu, and Permata Wulandari. 2023. Explorative Analysis of Securities Crowdfunding: Pillars, Business Flow and Risk Mitigation in MSME Funding in Indonesia. *Management Studies and Entrepreneurship Journal (MSEJ)* 4: 3206–21.
Wonglimpiyarat, Jarunee. 2018. Challenges and Dynamics of FinTech Crowdfunding: An Innovation System Approach. *The Journal of High Technology Management Research* 29: 98–108. [CrossRef]
Wu, Xiaohang, Hasan Dinçer, and Serhat Yüksel. 2022. Analysis of Crowdfunding Platforms for Microgrid Project Investors via a Q-Rung Orthopair Fuzzy Hybrid Decision-Making Approach. *Financial Innovation* 8: 52. [CrossRef]
Xu, Yang, Quanlin Li, Cheng Zhang, Yunlin Tan, Ping Zhang, Gguojun Wang, and Yaoxue Zhang. 2023. A Decentralized Trust Management Mechanism for Crowdfunding. *Information Sciences* 638: 118969. [CrossRef]
Yadav, Pavinder, Nidhi Gupta, and Pawan Kumar Sharma. 2023. A Comprehensive Study Towards High-Level Approaches for Weapon Detection Using Classical Machine Learning and Deep Learning Methods. *Expert Systems with Applications* 212: 118698. [CrossRef]
Yang, Yunpeng, Nan Chen, and Hongmin Chen. 2023. The Digital Platform, Enterprise Digital Transformation, and Enterprise Performance of Cross-Border E-Commerce-From the Perspective of Digital Transformation and Data Elements. *Journal of Theoretical and Applied Electronic Commerce Research* 18: 777–94. [CrossRef]
Zenone, Marco, and Jeremy Snyder. 2019. Fraud in Medical Crowdfunding: A Typology of Publicized Cases and Policy Recommendations. *Policy and Internet* 11: 215–34. [CrossRef]
Zhou, Xiaoyang, He Liu, Jialu Li, Kai Zhang, and Benjamin Lev. 2023. Channel Strategies When Digital Platforms Emerge: A Systematic Literature Review. *Omega* 120: 102919. [CrossRef]
Zkik, Karim, Anass Sebbar, Oumaima Fadi, Sachin Kamble, and Amine Belhadi. 2023. Securing Blockchain-Based Crowdfunding Platforms: An Integrated Graph Neural Networks and Machine Learning Approach. *Electronic Commerce Research* 1: 37. [CrossRef]
Zribi, Sirine. 2022. Effects of Social Influence on Crowdfunding Performance: Implications of the COVID-19 Pandemic. *Humanities and Social Sciences Communications* 9: 192. [CrossRef]

Journal of
Risk and Financial Management

MDPI

Article

Exploring Calendar Anomalies and Volatility Dynamics in Cryptocurrencies: A Comparative Analysis of Day-of-the-Week Effects before and during the COVID-19 Pandemic

Sonal Sahu [1], Alejandro Fonseca Ramírez [2] and Jong-Min Kim [3,*]

[1] Escuela de Negocios, Tecnologico de Monterrey, Monterrey 64700, Mexico; sonalsahu@tec.mx
[2] EGADE Business School, Tecnologico de Monterrey, Monterrey 66269, Mexico; afonseca@tec.mx
[3] Division of Science and Mathematics, University of Minnesota Morris, Moris, MN 56267, USA
* Correspondence: jongmink@morris.umn.edu

Abstract: This study investigates calendar anomalies and their impact on returns and volatility patterns in the cryptocurrency market, focusing on day-of-the-week effects before and during the COVID-19 pandemic. Using advanced statistical models from the GARCH family, we analyze the returns of Binance USD, Bitcoin, Binance Coin, Cardano, Dogecoin, Ethereum, Solana, Tether, USD Coin, and Ripple. Our findings reveal significant shifts in volatility dynamics and day-of-the-week effects on returns, challenging the notion of market efficiency. Notably, Bitcoin and Solana began exhibiting day-of-the-week effects during the pandemic, whereas Cardano and Dogecoin did not. During the pandemic, Binance USD, Ethereum, Tether, USD Coin, and Ripple showed multiple days with significant day-of-the-week effects. Notably, positive returns were generally observed on Sundays, whereas a shift to negative returns on Mondays was evident during the COVID-19 period. These patterns suggest that exploitable anomalies persist despite the market's continuous operation and increasing maturity. The presence of a long-term memory in volatility highlights the need for robust trading strategies. Our research provides valuable insights for investors, traders, regulators, and policymakers, aiding in the development of effective trading strategies, risk management practices, and regulatory policies in the evolving cryptocurrency market.

Keywords: calendar anomalies; volatility; cryptocurrencies; day-of-the-week effect; GARCH model; dummy variables; ANOVA; COVID-19; EGARCH; GJR-GARCH; FIGARCH; Lo's modified R/S test

JEL Classification: C58; G10; G12; G14; G15

1. Introduction

The study of anomalies in financial time-series datasets that occur on specific dates dates back more than a century. Seasonal and psychological factors affect these anomalies, also referred to as calendar anomalies, which represent patterns or effects that conventional asset pricing models cannot explain (Chatzitzisi et al. 2021). These anomalies challenge the Efficient Market Hypothesis (EMH) by suggesting that predictable trends in asset prices can be exploited for abnormal returns, facilitating the development of effective trading techniques (Kumar 2023).

Cryptocurrencies present new challenges for the study of calendar anomalies. With over 22,235 cryptocurrencies listed on CoinMarketCap, the emergence of digital assets has introduced significant changes to traditional monetary systems, prompting a reevaluation of established standards (Weber 2016; Baek and Elbeck 2014). As cryptocurrencies gain popularity, retail investors are increasingly including them in their portfolios (Zhao and Zhang 2021). This evolving trend involves extending the research on calendar anomalies to encompass the rapidly growing cryptocurrency industry.

The Adaptive Market Hypothesis (AMH) contradicts established financial theories by arguing that market efficiency and inefficiency can coexist, allowing investors and participants to adjust to changing market conditions (Enow 2022). This hypothesis suggests that market participants modify their strategies based on their changing knowledge and market dynamics, resulting in more accurate pricing models and trading strategies (Naz et al. 2023). Miralles-Quirós and Miralles-Quirós (2022) found evidence of calendar anomalies in cryptocurrencies, including the day-of-the-week effect, which showed predictable patterns in returns based on specific days. AMH's emphasis on market adaptability is consistent with the reported anomalies in cryptocurrency markets, where investors may modify trading methods based on calendar impacts (Khuntia and Pattanayak 2021). Understanding these anomalies is crucial for developing effective investment strategies and regulatory frameworks.

To improve risk management, regulatory implications, and forecasting accuracy, it is critical to model volatility and day-of-the-week effects in cryptocurrencies using advanced statistical models. Symmetric and asymmetric generalized autoregressive conditional heteroscedasticity (GARCH) models are suitable for this purpose. They help regulators analyze crypto risk and volatility (Ngunyi et al. 2019), facilitate market monitoring (Omari and Ngunyi 2021), provide insights into market risks (Aggarwal and Jha 2023), and influence crypto regulatory policies (Ampountolas 2022).

This study investigates whether the cryptocurrency market exhibits calendar effects given its unique 24/7 operations, including holidays and weekends. Unlike traditional financial markets with set trading hours, cryptocurrency markets immediately reflect any published information in prices. This continuous operation suggests that returns should be uniform across days and times. However, the potential for varying returns throughout the year and week makes studying calendar effects in cryptocurrencies difficult. We specifically explore the day-of-the-week effects by analyzing the returns of the top ten cryptocurrencies by market capitalization, extending the focus beyond Bitcoin and Ethereum. Using statistical models such as GARCH, EGARCH, GJR-GARCH, and FIGARCH, we provide a comprehensive analysis of these effects.

Additionally, this study addresses a notable gap in the literature regarding a comparative analysis of the day-of-the-week effects in the cryptocurrency market before and during the COVID-19 pandemic. The pandemic's seismic shifts in global financial markets prompted us to investigate how cryptocurrency efficiency and volatility evolved during this period and how temporal patterns and anomalies shifted. By analyzing the top ten cryptocurrencies, this study offers valuable insights for investors, traders, regulators, and policymakers. The use of asymmetric GARCH models enhances our understanding of how different types of news impact the day-of-the-week effects. Testing for long-term memory using the FIGARCH model reveals the persistence of volatility over time, which is crucial for the development of robust trading strategies. The continuous and global trading nature of cryptocurrencies highlights the importance of non-stop market operations in analyzing these effects.

The remainder of this paper is structured as follows: Section 2 reviews the pertinent literature; Section 3 expounds on our data and methodology; Section 4 presents the empirical data analysis and discussion; and Section 5 concludes our study.

2. Literature Review

Studying anomalies and volatility is crucial for developing smart investment strategies, effective risk management, and market stability (Tadepalli and Jain 2018). Anomalies challenge the efficient market hypothesis, which suggests that regular asset price patterns can be exploited for abnormal returns (Dong et al. 2021). These anomalies may vary over time owing to changing market conditions, necessitating a detailed analysis of their dynamics. Researchers have noted calendar anomalies in various markets, including the Russian bond and stock markets (Compton et al. 2013), Turkish markets (Aydoğan and Booth 2003), US markets (Plastun et al. 2019), Asia-Pacific stock markets (Aziz and Ansari

2017), Thai stock markets (Wuthisatian 2021), Gulf Cooperation Council stock exchanges (Siriopoulos and Youssef 2019), Nigerian stock markets (Adaramola and Adekanmbi 2020), and Swedish stock markets (Eidinejad and Dahlem 2021).

Empirical studies primarily focus on the effects of the day of the week and month of the year, categorizing them into religious and non-religious anomalies (Sejati et al. 2022). Religious anomalies include festive religious days, such as the Yom Kippur, Diwali, and Ramadan effects (Kliger and Qadan 2019), whereas non-religious anomalies encompass the day of the week, month of the year, Halloween, turn-of-the-month, and turn-of-the-year effects (Mehta and Chander 2009). While calendar impacts on stock markets are well documented, our understanding of calendar effects on cryptocurrency markets remains limited, especially among cryptocurrencies other than Bitcoin (Robiyanto et al. 2019).

Various authors have suggested factors that explain calendar anomalies in cryptocurrency markets, attributing them to market sentiment, liquidity, and other external factors (Naz et al. 2023; Caporale and Plastun 2019). The sentiment analysis of social media data and liquidity dynamics plays a crucial role in cryptocurrency markets and can influence the occurrence of calendar anomalies (Valencia et al. 2019; Wan et al. 2023). Understanding these dynamics is essential for comprehending the underlying factors driving calendar anomalies in cryptocurrency markets.

The COVID-19 pandemic has profoundly affected global financial markets, including cryptocurrencies (Lahmiri and Bekiros 2020). Several studies have investigated these effects across different markets, highlighting their significant impact on both the equity and cryptocurrency markets (Sahoo 2021). The pandemic has transformed the global role of cryptocurrencies and has adversely affected various economies (Lee et al. 2022). Despite the initial shocks, cryptocurrencies such as Bitcoin, Ethereum, and Litecoin demonstrated resilience but suffered significant negative return shocks during the initial wave of the pandemic (Marobhe 2022).

Researchers have widely adopted GARCH models, including asymmetric GARCH models, to study calendar anomalies and volatility in the cryptocurrency markets (Kim et al. 2021; Ampountolas 2022). These models are crucial for capturing the time-varying nature of volatility, a prominent characteristic of cryptocurrency markets. Asymmetric GARCH models, such as the Exponential GARCH (EGARCH) and Glosten-Jagannathan-Runkle GARCH (GJR-GARCH), are particularly well suited for modeling volatility and cryptocurrency anomalies because they can capture asymmetric volatility patterns (Naimy et al. 2021). This asymmetry is significant, as it reflects the different reactions of market volatility to positive and negative shocks, often observed in highly speculative and sentiment-driven cryptocurrency markets.

These models offer valuable insights into cryptocurrency market dynamics, such as the impact of macroeconomic announcements, market sentiment, and regulatory news on volatility. By accurately modeling these dynamics, asymmetric GARCH models enhance risk management and forecasting capabilities, providing investors and policymakers with tools to better understand and mitigate the risks associated with cryptocurrency investments. Predicting volatility patterns helps develop robust trading strategies, optimize portfolio allocations, and improve overall market efficiency.

Furthermore, the Fractionally Integrated Generalized Autoregressive Conditional Heteroskedasticity (FIGARCH) model is particularly advantageous for analyzing the day-of-the-week effect in the cryptocurrency market for several reasons (Ampountolas 2024). FIGARCH models capture long-term memory in volatility, which is crucial given that past volatility in cryptocurrencies can have a prolonged impact on future volatility. This model's flexibility allows for a more accurate representation of volatility dynamics, which is essential for detecting patterns over different days of the week. Additionally, FIGARCH models account for autocorrelation in returns, a significant factor influencing day-of-the-week effects.

FIGARCH models are robust to non-stationarity, accommodating the changing statistical properties often observed in cryptocurrency markets. They effectively utilize daily data, making them suitable for detecting periodic volatility patterns that may occur weekly. This comprehensive framework ensures a sophisticated understanding of how day-of-the-week effects manifest in volatile and often unpredictable cryptocurrency markets.

Kinateder and Papavassiliou (2021) investigated seasonality and calendar effects in cryptocurrencies, specifically focusing on how the day of the week influences returns and volatility. Their study utilized daily data from major cryptocurrencies to identify patterns and anomalies that could impact trading strategies. Aharon and Qadan (2019) provide empirical evidence of the day-of-the-week effect, highlighting distinct patterns in price movements and volatility on certain days. They analyze the daily returns of Bitcoin and Ethereum, showing that Mondays and Fridays exhibit higher volatility than other days. Dangi (2020) explored the implications of these calendar effects and offered insights into the unique behaviors of cryptocurrency markets. This study examines a broad range of cryptocurrencies and finds that certain weekdays consistently show abnormal returns, suggesting potential opportunities for traders. İmre and Ölçen (2022) further analyze these effects, demonstrating how understanding day-of-the-week patterns can inform investment strategies and risk management. They use a comprehensive dataset spanning several years and multiple cryptocurrencies, revealing that day-of-the-week effects are significant and can be exploited for better portfolio management.

Analyzing cryptocurrency data from pre-COVID-19 (1 January 2017 to 19 March 2020) and during COVID-19 (20 March 2020 to 5 May 2023) provides a comprehensive perspective on market dynamics and anomalies. This period encompasses significant events and developments within the cryptocurrency market, offering rich insights into market behavior and efficiency. Dividing the data into pre-COVID-19 and during the COVID-19 periods is a strategic approach to analyzing the cryptocurrency market, given the profound impact of the pandemic on financial markets.

The pre-COVID-19 period includes the 2017 cryptocurrency boom, the 2018 market correction, and a gradual recovery up to early 2020. This period reflects a market driven primarily by retail investors, speculative trading, and initial regulatory development. In contrast, the COVID-19 period captures the market crash and rapid recovery in March 2020, significant bull runs, increased institutional adoption, and the rise of Decentralized Finance (DeFi). This period also includes the third Bitcoin halving in May 2020, which is historically correlated with price increases. Additionally, economic stimulus measures, low interest rates, and inflation concerns during the pandemic have influenced market dynamics. This division allows for a comprehensive examination of how the COVID-19 pandemic has affected the cryptocurrency market. This extended period encompasses significant events and developments within the cryptocurrency market, offering rich insights into market behavior and efficiency. This understanding enables informed decision-making and the development of strategies to effectively navigate the market.

The literature review highlights critical aspects of cryptocurrency anomalies and volatility, emphasizing the importance of calendar effects in these markets. It is evident that traditional and cryptocurrency markets exhibit calendar anomalies, which challenge the EMH and support the AMH. The use of advanced statistical models, particularly GARCH and its variants, is crucial for capturing the time-varying nature of volatility and for providing valuable insights into market dynamics.

This study aims to fill the gap in the literature by focusing on the day-of-the-week effects in the cryptocurrency market, particularly before and during the COVID-19 pandemic. By analyzing the top ten cryptocurrencies by market capitalization, we aim to provide a general understanding of how the market operates. Employing advanced models such as GARCH, EGARCH, GJR-GARCH, and FIGARCH, this study provides a comprehensive analysis of these effects, offering valuable insights for investors, traders, regulators, and policymakers. Understanding these anomalies and volatility patterns is essential for developing effective trading strategies, risk management practices, and regulatory frameworks, particularly in the rapidly evolving cryptocurrency market.

3. Data and Methodology

3.1. Data Description

In our empirical investigation, we analyzed a dataset of daily closing prices in US dollars obtained from CoinMarketCap (https://coinmarketcap.com/coins/ accessed on 16 February 2024). We focused on the following top cryptocurrencies in terms of diffusion and market capitalization: Binance USD, Bitcoin, Binance Coin, Cardano, Dogecoin, Ethereum, Solana, Tether, USD Coin, and Ripple.

Cryptocurrency exchanges operate continuously without formal closing times. Thus, data providers typically determine the "closing price" based on a specific point in time each day, usually at the end of the UTC day. Each exchange might calculate the closing price differently; some use the last trade price before midnight UTC, while others use an average price over the last few minutes of the day. Higher liquidity exchanges tend to have more stable prices, whereas lower liquidity exchanges may experience greater volatility and price discrepancies.

The "closing auction process" in cryptocurrency trading establishes the closing price of digital assets at the end of the trading session. During this process, buy and sell orders are matched to determine the equilibrium price, which serves as the official closing price for the asset. CoinMarketCap aggregates prices from multiple exchanges to determine the daily closing price, averaging prices across different exchanges weighted by trading volume. This methodology provides a representative closing price. Differences in the methodologies used by data providers can lead to slight variations in the reported closing prices.

3.2. Data Preparation

Our investigation began by checking the database for normality using the Jacque–Bera (JB) and Anderson–Darling (AD) tests. We then calculate the returns, defined as the natural logarithm of the ratio between two consecutive prices, using the following formula:

$$\mathrm{Rn} = In(CP\mathrm{n}) - In(CP_{\mathrm{n}-1}) \times 100 \quad (1)$$

where R_n denotes returns on an nth day in percentage; CP_{n} denotes closing price on an nth day; $CP^{(\mathrm{n}^{-1})}$ denotes the closing price on the previous trading day; and In is a natural log.

We used log returns in the subsequent models because they allow for continuous compounding and tend to exhibit stationarity, making them more suitable for statistical analysis. We assessed the return series for all ten coins using both the Augmented Dickey–Fuller (ADF) and Phillips–Perron tests, confirming their stationarity.

3.3. Parametric and Non-Parametric Tests

We applied a diverse set of quantitative approaches encompassing both parametric and non-parametric tests. Specifically, we use the conventional regression model with dummy variables and Analysis of Variance (ANOVA) as parametric tests (Basdas 2011). To address potential biases arising from dummy variables, especially in the presence of abrupt fluctuations, we incorporated non-parametric testing techniques such as the mood Median Test (Mood's Median Test), following the recommendations of Chien et al. (2002).

3.4. Regression Analysis

We apply GARCH models to check for volatility. Initially, we employed a dummy regression model that assumed a constant return variance for cryptocurrencies. The ordinary least squares (OLS) regression equation was as follows:

$$\begin{aligned}\mathrm{Return}_t = {} & \beta_1\mathrm{MONDAY}_t + \beta_2\mathrm{TUESDAY}_t + \beta_3\mathrm{WEDNESDAY}_t + \beta_4\mathrm{THURSDAY}_t + \beta_5\mathrm{FRIDAY}_t + \\ & \beta_6\mathrm{SATURDAY}_t + \beta_7\mathrm{SUNDAY}_t + \varepsilon_t\end{aligned} \quad (2)$$

where MONDAY, TUESDAY, WEDNESDAY, THURSDAY, FRIDAY, SATURDAY, and SUNDAY are dummy variables for each day of the week returns (e.g., if the day is Monday, then the dummy variable Monday will be 1 and 0 otherwise); β_1, β_2, β_3, β_4, β_5, β_6, and β_7 are coefficients; and ε_t is error term. The coefficients of these seven dummy variables represent the returns for each day of the week. To prevent perfect multicollinearity, we excluded the intercept term and included dummy variables for all seven days of the week.

3.5. Volatility Modelling

We checked the residuals from the least-squares regression equation for autoregressive conditional heteroscedasticity using the ARCH test. If the ARCH effect becomes apparent in the residuals, we apply the GARCH family model.

To capture the leptokurtic distributions, volatility clustering, leverage effects, and long-term memory properties of cryptocurrencies, we applied symmetric, asymmetric, and fractionally integrated volatility models. We use the widely employed GARCH (*p*, *q*) model to model symmetric volatility. The conditional variance equation of the GARCH (*p*, *q*) model is as follows:

$$\sigma_t^2 = +\sum_{i=1}^{p} \alpha_i \varepsilon_{t-i}^2 + \sum_{j=1}^{q} \beta j \sigma_{t-j}^2 \quad (3)$$

where, α_i, and βj are coefficients, $\varepsilon^2{}_{t-i}$ is the previous-period ARCH term, and $s^2{}_{t-j}$ is the previous-period GARCH term.

To capture the asymmetric effect, also known as the leverage effect, we apply the EGARCH and GJR-GARCH models. The conditional variance equation of the EGARCH (p, q) model is as follows:

$$log\left(\sigma_t^2\right) = \omega + \sum_{i=1}^{p} \left[\alpha_i \left(\frac{|\varepsilon_{t-i}|}{\sigma_{t-i}} - \sqrt{\frac{2}{\pi}}\right) + \gamma_i \left(\frac{\varepsilon_{t-i}}{\sigma_{t-i}}\right)\right] + \sum_{j=i}^{q} \beta_j log\left(\sigma_{t-j}^2\right) \quad (4)$$

α_i measures the magnitude of the shock, β_j measures the persistence of the conditional volatility of the shocks to the market; and γ_ι is the asymmetric pattern that measures the leverage effect.

The conditional variance equation of the GJR-GARCH (*p*, *q*) model is as follows:

$$\sigma_t^2 = \omega + \sum_{i=1}^{p} (\alpha_i + \gamma_i I_{t-i}) \varepsilon_{t-i}^2 + \sum_{j=1}^{q} \beta_j \sigma_{t-j}^2 \quad (5)$$

where, $\omega \geq 0$, $\alpha_i \geq 0$, $\beta_j \geq 0$, $\alpha_i + \gamma_\iota \geq 0$.

To account for the long-term memory properties in volatility, we apply the FIGARCH model. The conditional variance equation of the FIGARCH (*p*, *d*, *q*) model is as follows:

$$(1 - \beta(L))(1 - L)^d \sigma_t^2 = \omega + \alpha(L) \varepsilon_t^2 \quad (6)$$

where σ_t^2 is the conditional variance at time *t*, *L* is the lag operator, *β(L)* is a polynomial in the lag operator *L* with parameters β_i, representing the autoregressive component of the conditional variance, $(1 - L)^d$ is the fractional differencing operator with parameter and (where $0 \leq d \leq 10$), capturing long memory in the volatility process.

The FIGARCH (1, *d*, 1) model captures the long-term memory and persistence of volatility observed in cryptocurrency returns. By accommodating long-range dependence, the FIGARCH model *addresses* the limitations of traditional GARCH models and provides a more accurate representation of volatility dynamics. The fractional differencing parameter d in the FIGARCH model quantifies the degree of long-term memory, offering deeper insights into the volatility behavior of cryptocurrencies before and during the COVID-19 pandemic.

To assess the presence of long-term memory in the residuals of the FIGARCH (1, *d*, 1) model, we applied Lo's modified R/S test. We first calculated the modified R/S statistic for the residuals using a specified number of lags based on an autocorrelation function (ACF) plot. To determine the critical values, we conducted a Monte Carlo simulation, generating 10,000 white noise time series of the same length as the actual data. For each simulated series, we computed the modified R/S statistic, which allowed us to build a distribution of the statistic under the null hypothesis of no long-term memory. We then extracted the critical values corresponding to 1%, 5%, and 10% significance levels from this distribution. Finally, we compared the calculated modified R/S statistic for the residuals with these critical values. If the calculated statistic exceeds the critical value at the 5% significance level, we reject the null hypothesis and conclude that long-term memory is present in the time series. Conversely, if the calculated statistic is below the critical value, we do not find any evidence of long-term memory.

3.6. Model Adequacy and Selection

To ensure the adequacy of the GARCH models, we applied the Ljung–Box and Lagrange multiplier (LM) tests (Engle 2001) to check for autocorrelation or volatility clustering in the residuals. We then used the Akaike Information Criterion (AIC) to select the best GARCH models. The AIC is designed to minimize the expected estimated Kullback–Leibler (K-L) information loss and balance the model fit and complexity (Burnham and Anderson 2004). This criterion is particularly useful for our large sample size and complex model structures, ensuring that we select models that provide a good fit to the data without being overly complex.

4. Empirical Data Analysis and Discussion

We begin our analysis with fundamental statistics and parametric/non-parametric tests. We conducted a descriptive analysis of the ten selected cryptocurrencies, as outlined in Tables 1 and 2. Before the COVID-19 pandemic, Binance Coin exhibited the highest average return, followed by Ripple. During the COVID-19 period, Binance Coin clearly led in average returns, followed by Cardano, which showed significant growth in popularity and value. Among the ten cryptocurrencies, USD Coin had the least fluctuation during both the pre-COVID-19 and COVID-19 periods. The distribution of returns during the pre-COVID-19 period skewed leftward favorably for Binance USD, Ethereum, and Tether and positively for the remaining coins. During the COVID-19 period, most cryptocurrencies, including Binance USD, Bitcoin, Binance Coin, Cardano, Solana, Ethereum, and Ripple, exhibited a leftward skew.

To ensure robustness, we followed Caporale and Plastun's (2019) recommendation by employing both parametric and non-parametric models. To investigate variations across days of the week, we conducted one-way ANOVA and Mood Median tests. We applied the Jarque–Bera and Anderson–Darling tests for normality to all ten cryptocurrencies. The results indicate that in both the pre- and during the COVID-19 periods, the null hypothesis of normality in returns should be rejected at the 5% significance level, consistent with Szczygielski et al. (2019) and Agyei et al. (2022) (see Table A1 in Appendix A).

Table 1. Daily descriptive statistics of ten cryptocurrencies in the pre-COVID-19 period.

Descriptive Statistics	Bitcoin	Binance Coin	Cardano	Dogecoin	Ethereum	Tether	USD Coin	Ripple
Mean	12.015%	58.287%	2.719%	20.358%	−12.189%	−0.017%	−0.110%	31.179%
Maximum	2870.990%	32,699.360%	8721.609%	4553.488%	2625.760%	1265.370%	253.691%	8812.683%
Minimum	−2251.580%	−10,024.390%	−2698.714%	−4781.982%	−2185.820%	−2833.380%	−209.640%	−4962.824%
Standard Deviation	4.393	15.609	7.708	6.921	5.152	1.486	0.475	7.703
Coefficient of Variation	36.563	26.780	283.529	33.996	−42.271	−9004.824	−431.951	24.706
Skewness	0.076	10.643	2.920	0.829	−0.201	−5.635	0.186	2.437
Kurtosis	7.796	237.267	31.126	12.965	5.857	148.928	9.022	27.515

Source: Elaborated by the author.

Table 2. Daily descriptive statistics of ten cryptocurrencies during the COVID-19 periods.

Descriptive Statistics	Binance USD	Bitcoin	Binance Coin	Cardano	Dogecoin	Solana	Ethereum	Tether	USD Coin	Ripple
Mean	−0.025%	9.981%	29.489%	24.346%	−11.627%	37.451%	23.580%	0.005%	−0.033%	8.463%
Maximum	650.371%	1760.260%	5526.562%	2691.957%	7324.953%	3844.862%	2194.057%	250.046%	192.579%	4233.534%
Minimum	−649.448%	−4337.140%	−5590.344%	−5244.024%	−4667.967%	−4521.549%	−5630.799%	−197.281%	−158.485%	−5495.483%
Standard Deviation	0.428	3.874	5.700	5.859	7.457	7.792	5.209	0.292	0.282	6.276
Coefficient of Variation	−1697.480	38.813	19.330	24.065	−64.137	20.806	22.092	5760.118	−854.539	74.162
Skewness	−0.107	−1.429	−0.185	−0.442	1.464	−0.058	−1.464	0.159	0.045	−0.205
Kurtosis	106.763	19.683	24.491	11.051	24.921	6.640	18.420	15.488	9.884	17.856

Source: Elaborated by the author.

Upon scrutinizing the one-way ANOVA results at a 95% confidence level, we observed no significant differences in mean returns among days of the week for all coins during both the pre- and during COVID-19 periods. We employ Mood's median test, a robust non-parametric test, to examine the median equality for log returns across the seven days. In the pre-COVID-19 period, Ethereum and Tether exhibited p-values < 0.05, suggesting a day-of-week effect. However, during the COVID-19 period, no coins yielded significant p-values, indicating no observed day-of-week effects, consistent with Kaiser's (2019) findings.

Furthermore, we tested for equal variances between days of the week to assess the variability and potential day-of-week effects. For the pre-COVID-19 period, Bitcoin, Cardano, Ethereum, and Ripple rejected the null hypothesis at the 95% confidence level. During the COVID-19 period, Bitcoin, Binance Coin, Cardano, Dogecoin, Solana, Ethereum, and Ripple rejected the null hypothesis at 95% confidence, indicating significant differences in variances among days.

While parametric and non-parametric tests confirm the presence of day-of-the-week effects, we further validate these findings by incorporating dummy variables into GARCH models. This approach allows for the modeling of time-varying volatility patterns, leading to more accurate forecasts and a better understanding of how specific days of the week impact financial returns and volatility. This transition to GARCH models enhances our ability to capture the dynamic nature of cryptocurrency markets and provides deeper insights into day-of-the-week effects.

To ensure the robustness of our GARCH model, it is essential to confirm the stationarity of the data. We rigorously examined stationarity through unit root tests employing both the Augmented Dickey–Fuller (ADF) and Phillips–Perron (PP) tests, which are standard tools in time-series analyses. The results, displayed in Tables A2 and A3, consistently revealed p-values below 0.05 for all ten cryptocurrencies studied. This compelling evidence led to the rejection of the null hypothesis at the 95% confidence level, confirming the stationarity of our time-series data.

After confirming stationarity, we used dummy variables in an ordinary least squares (OLS) regression and conducted Engle's ARCH test. This test reveals the presence of volatility clustering both before and after the COVID-19 pandemic (see Table A4 in Appendix A). The presence of ARCH effects was confirmed as all p-values were less than 0.05. These results support the use of GARCH frameworks for modeling volatility.

To incorporate the leptokurtic nature of cryptocurrencies, we implement a Normal Inverse Gaussian (NIG) distribution for the error element in the GARCH model. This distribution can capture the additional skewness and kurtosis in the residual return series (Osterrieder et al. 2017). We first identify the best GARCH (p, q) model to accurately model the volatility of ten cryptocurrencies. To ensure the reliability of our chosen GARCH (p, q) models, all the coefficients (ω, αi, *and* βj) in the GARCH (p, q) model must be non-negative and satisfy the condition $\alpha i + \beta j < 1$. Higher αi values suggest greater volatility responses to market shocks, whereas larger βj coefficients indicate the occurrence of market shocks.

As indicated in Tables 3 and 4 (period preceding COVID-19 and period during COVID-19), the fact that the coefficients $\beta_1 + \beta_2 > \alpha_1$ indicates that when attempting to forecast present volatility, attention is directed towards the enduring consequences of past shocks rather than recent occurrences. Furthermore, we evaluate the volatility persistence by summing the values of α_1, β_1, and β_2. The sum of these parameters, which is a critical indicator of the model stability, must not exceed one. The high value of coefficient β_1 suggests the presence of volatility clustering.

Table 3. Summary of GARCH (p,q) model parameters and diagnostics (pre-COVID-19 period).

	Bitcoin	Binance Coin	Cardano	Dogecoin	Ethereum	Tether	USD Coin	Ripple
Best GARCH (p,q) Model	**GARCH (1,2)**	**GARCH (1,1)**	**GARCH (1,1)**	**GARCH (1,1)**	**GARCH (1,1)**	**GARCH (1,1)**	**GARCH (1,1)**	**GARCH (1,2)**
ω	1.539	6.653	0.558	0.658	9.588	0.003	0.090	2.550
ω (p-value)	0.000	0.018	0.049	0.004	0.018	0.003	0.010	0.000
α_1	0.139	0.348	0.055	0.376	0.455	0.305	0.090	0.392
α_1 (p-value)	0.000	0.006	0.002	0.000	0.031	0.000	0.001	0.000
β_1	0.055	0.623	0.936	0.555	0.524	0.667	0.900	0.200
β_1 (p-value)	0.032	0.000	0.000	0.000	0.000	0.000	0.000	0.040
β_2	0.757							0.419
β_2 (p-value)	0.032							0.000
Volatility persistence	0.951	0.971	0.992	0.931	0.979	0.972	0.990	1.011
AIC Value	5.405	6.541	6.304	5.964	5.999	0.805	0.433	5.980
Ljung box test p-value	0.146	0.742	0.232	0.149	0.538	0.606	0.344	0.089
ARCH LM-Test p-value	0.673	0.671	0.640	0.977	0.713	0.800	0.298	0.760

Source: Elaborated by the author.

Table 4. Summary of GARCH (p,q) model parameters and diagnostics (during the COVID-19 period).

	Binance USD	Bitcoin	Binance Coin	Cardano	Dogecoin	Solana	Ethereum	Tether	USD Coin	Ripple
Best GARCH (p,q) Model	GARCH(1,2)	GARCH(1,1)	GARCH(1,1)	GARCH(1,1)	GARCH(1,1)	GARCH(1,1)	GARCH(1,1)	GARCH(1,2)	GARCH(1,1)	GARCH(1,1)
ω	0.000	0.321	0.974	2.383	8.317	2.557	1.076	0.000	0.000	1.676
ω (p-value)	0.021	0.041	0.001	0.001	0.016	0.003	0.005	0.132	0.176	0.002
α_1	1.282	0.096	0.181	0.211	0.833	0.146	0.117	0.615	0.377	0.237
α_1 (p-value)	0.049	0.001	0.000	0.000	0.016	0.000	0.000	0.003	0.000	0.000
β_1	0.307	0.900	0.806	0.747	0.537	0.820	0.849	0.258	0.608	0.719
β_1 (p-value)	0.014	0.000	0.000	0.000	0.000	0.000	0.000	0.036	0.000	0.000
β_2	0.315							0.466		
β_2 (p-value)	0.003							0.000		
Volatility persistence	1.904	0.997	0.988	0.958	1.370	0.966	0.966	1.339	0.985	0.955
AIC Value	−0.600	5.155	5.580	5.983	5.931	6.617	5.741	−0.796	−0.615	5.745
Ljung box test p-value	0.486	0.425	0.637	0.830	0.500	0.786	0.995	0.689	0.208	0.963
ARCH LM-Test p-value	0.669	0.978	0.465	0.622	0.787	0.105	0.788	0.839	0.000	0.682

Source: Elaborated by the author.

Ripple shows a heightened susceptibility to negative leaps and eruptive behavior, as indicated by the equation $\alpha_1 + \beta_1 + \beta_2 > 1$, during both periods. This pattern suggests a decline in volatility, which aligns with the findings of Idrees and Akhtar (2023). Consistent with the findings of Queiroz and David (2023), the GARCH (1,1) model performs well in predicting volatility across most cryptocurrencies during both the pre-COVID-19 and during the COVID-19 periods, leaving only Bitcoin and Ripple during the pre-COVID-19 period and Binance USD and Tether during the COVID-19 period, for which GARCH (1,2) provides a better fit.

We also examine the EGARCH and GJR-GARCH asymmetric GARCH models for ten distinct cryptocurrencies before and during the COVID-19 pandemic. To account for heavy tails and high kurtosis, these models capture inherent volatility asymmetry, specifically, as they relate to positive and negative returns in an effective manner. The optimal p-q model with the lowest AIC score was then selected. Tables 5 and 6 (pre-COVID-19 and during COVID-19) illustrate the optimal selection of the asymmetric models.

Our findings indicate a significant shift in the leverage effect dynamics before and during the COVID-19 period. In the pre-COVID period, Binance Coin, Cardano, Dogecoin, and Ripple exhibited leverage effects, meaning that negative returns led to greater increases in volatility than positive returns of the same magnitude. However, during the COVID-19 pandemic, this dynamic changed substantially. Only Bitcoin, Ethereum, and Tether continued to show leverage effects, whereas the previously mentioned cryptocurrencies did not exhibit the same behavior.

This shift can be attributed to the changing market conditions and investor behavior during the pandemic, where Bitcoin, Ethereum, and Tether became more prominent as stable and reliable assets, leading to different volatility dynamics compared to other cryptocurrencies. This analysis highlights the importance of considering the market context and the evolving nature of leverage effects in financial markets.

Table 5. Summary of asymmetric GARCH (p,q) model parameters and diagnostics (pre-COVID-19 period).

	Bitcoin	Binance Coin	Cardano	Dogecoin	Ethereum	Tether	USD Coin	Ripple
Best GARCH (p,q) Model	No asymmetric model is a good fit	**EGARCH (1,1)**	**EGARCH (1,1)**	**EGARCH (2,1)**	No asymmetric model is a good fit	No asymmetric model is a good fit	No asymmetric model is a good fit	**EGARCH (2,1)**
ω ω (p-value)		−0.036 0.033	−0.053 0.039	−0.109 0.000				−0.072 0.006
α_1 α_1 (p-value)		0.294 0.000	0.163 0.000	0.500 0.000				0.679 0.000
α_2				−0.260				−0.498
α_2 (p-value)				0.002				0.000
γi		−0.032	−0.008	0.049				0.056
γi (p-value)		0.028	0.007	0.046				0.028
β_1 β_1 (p-value)		0.971 0.000	0.985 0.000	0.982 0.000				0.985 0.000
AIC Value		6.539	6.314	6.005				5.987
Ljung box test p-value		0.762	0.140	0.167				0.320
ARCH LM-Test p-value		0.951	0.435	0.813				0.416

Source: Elaborated by the author.

Table 6. Summary of asymmetric GARCH (p,q) model parameters and diagnostics (during the COVID-19 period).

	Binance USD	Bitcoin	Binance Coin	Cardano	Dogecoin	Solana	Ethereum	Tether	USD Coin	Ripple
Best GARCH (p,q) Model	No asymmetric model is a good fit	**EGARCH (1,2)**	No asymmetric model is a good fit	No asymmetric model is a good fit	No asymmetric model is a good fit	No asymmetric model is a good fit	**GJR-GARCH (1,1)**	**EGARCH (1,2)**	No asymmetric model is a good fit	No asymmetric model is a good fit
ω		0.040					0.778	−0.381		
ω (p-value)		0.004					0.000	0.000		
α_1		0.087					0.108	0.511		
α_1 (p-value)		0.000					0.000	0.000		
α_2		−0.039						0.117		
α_2 (p-value)		0.000						0.021		
γi		1.469					0.046	0.617		
γi (p-value)		0.000					0.009	0.000		
β_1		−0.507					0.848	0.358		
β_1 (p-value)		0.000					0.000	0.020		
AIC Value		5.489					5.880	−0.818		
Ljung box test p-value		0.844					0.829	2.254		
ARCH LM-Test p-value		0.450					0.633	0.156		

Source: Elaborated by the author.

We conducted a FIGARCH (1, d, 1) model to capture the long-term memory and persistence in volatility observed in cryptocurrency returns, as shown in Tables 7 and 8 (pre-COVID period and during the COVID-19 period). The results show that in the pre-COVID period, only Bitcoin and USD Coin do not have significant p-values for the fractional differencing parameter d at the 95% confidence level. During the COVID period, Tether, USD Coin, and Ripple also did not show significant d p-values at the 95% confidence level.

Table 7. Summary of FIGARCH (1,d,1) model parameters and diagnostics (pre-COVID-19 period).

	Bitcoin	Binance Coin	Cardano	Dogecoin	Ethereum	Tether	USD Coin	Ripple
ω	0.385	11.313	0.284	0.582	23.714	0.003	−0.003	0.271
ω (p-value)	0.064	0.009	0.395	0.014	0.000	0.000	0.755	0.114
α	0.277	−0.166	0.752	0.314	0.860	0.156	−0.057	0.792
α (p-value)	0.053	0.368	0.000	0.002	0.000	0.031	0.714	0.000
β	0.791	0.224	0.897	0.728	0.595	0.773	0.071	0.891
β (p-value)	0.000	0.292	0.000	0.000	0.000	0.000	0.665	0.000
d	0.726	0.699	0.397	0.760	0.618	1.001	0.385	0.549
d (p-value)	0.004	0.000	0.002	0.000	0.000	0.000	0.003	0.000
AIC Value	5.406	6.531	6.287	5.963	6.077	0.817	0.553	5.959
Ljung box test p-value	0.132	0.098	0.286	0.208	0.591	0.524	0.590	0.155
ARCH LM-Test p-value	0.890	0.321	0.953	0.787	0.254	0.852	0.308	0.630

Source: Elaborated by the author.

Table 8. Summary of FIGARCH (1,d,1) model parameters and diagnostics (during the COVID-19 period).

	Binance USD	Bitcoin	Binance Coin	Cardano	Dogecoin	Solana	Ethereum	Tether	USD Coin	Ripple
ω	0.000	0.800	0.960	2.387	1.519	0.820	4.316	−0.001	0.000	1.717
ω (*p*-value)	0.461	0.168	0.308	0.111	0.076	0.064	0.001	0.090	0.904	0.155
α	0.206	0.120	−0.105	0.195	0.671	0.472	−0.190	0.156	0.234	−0.090
α (*p*-value)	0.001	0.044	0.046	0.037	0.000	0.351	0.017	0.376	0.015	0.797
β	0.807	0.781	0.161	0.427	0.505	0.011	0.078	0.391	0.611	0.027
β (*p*-value)	0.000	0.000	0.020	0.010	0.004	0.008	0.041	0.514	0.000	0.942
d	0.943	0.718	0.394	0.457	0.249	0.231	0.360	0.478	0.658	0.399
d (*p*-value)	0.000	0.016	0.000	0.002	0.035	0.004	0.000	0.074	0.163	0.060
AIC Value	−0.533	5.156	5.569	5.981	5.914	6.659	5.746	0.074	−0.598	5.758
Ljung box test *p*-value	0.324	0.433	0.481	0.820	0.550	0.965	0.857	0.611	0.059	0.854
ARCH LM-Test *p*-value	0.739	0.815	0.035	0.609	0.818	0.128	0.991	0.633	0.130	0.977

Source: Elaborated by the author.

To further confirm the presence of long-range dependence, we applied Lo's modified R/S test at the 95% confidence level. We compared the resulting test statistic Q_n with the critical values at the 1%, 5%, and 10% significance levels, as shown in Table 9 for the pre-COVID period and Table 10 for the COVID period. The consistency of Lo's test results with our FIGARCH findings reaffirms the presence of long-range dependence in the dataset, thus validating the robustness of our initial FIGARCH results. These results are consistent with those of previous studies on Bitcoin and Ethereum by Soylu et al. (2020) and Sheraz et al. (2022), which also showed long-term memory in these cryptocurrencies. However, our results differ from those of Sheraz et al. (2022) regarding Ripple, which did not exhibit long-term memory during the COVID-19 period.

Table 9. Summary Lo's modified R/S test results (pre-COVID-19 period).

	Calculated Lo's Modified R/S Statistic Q_n	Critical Value (1%)	Critical Value (5%)	Critical Value (10%)	Interpretation
Bitcoin	57.105	64.894	57.348	53.288	No long-term memory detected
Binance Coin	73.294	68.748	56.386	54.987	Long-term memory detected
Cardano	59.978	57.803	51.957	48.356	Long-term memory detected
Dogecoin	59.445	54.675	50.857	47.348	Long-term memory detected
Ethereum	68.429	64.944	57.242	53.268	Long-term memory detected
Tether	64.657	62.559	55.463	51.572	Long-term memory detected
USD Coin	37.329	41.739	37.458	34.949	No long-term memory detected
Ripple	59.384	58.886	51.952	48.556	Long-term memory detected

Source: Elaborated by the author.

Table 10. Summary Lo's modified R/S test results (during the COVID-19 period).

Currency	Calculated Lo's Modified R/S Statistic	Critical Value (1%)	Critical Value (5%)	Critical Value (10%)	Interpretation
Binance USD	59.106	54.984	51.987	49.681	Long-term memory detected
Bitcoin	65.194	65.652	58.275	54.301	Long-term memory detected
Binance Coin	69.924	66.133	58.243	54.170	Long-term memory detected
Cardano	66.927	65.652	58.275	54.301	Long-term memory detected
Dogecoin	64.839	64.937	57.293	54.628	Long-term memory detected
Solana	68.746	65.258	57.543	53.251	Long-term memory detected
Ethereum	69.201	65.912	54.836	53.228	Long-term memory detected
Tether	57.188	65.893	58.396	54.532	No long-term memory detected
USD Coin	51.208	66.097	58.345	54.284	No long-term memory detected
Ripple	57.299	65.893	58.396	54.532	No long-term memory detected

Source: Elaborated by the author.

After conducting all the tests, we first selected the best GARCH (p, q) model for each cryptocurrency. Next, we identify the best asymmetric model by choosing between EGARCH (p, q) and GJR-GARCH (p, q). Finally, we determined the best FIGARCH (1,d,1) model. Among these, we selected the optimal model based on the lowest Akaike Information Criterion (AIC).

We performed Q-Q plot tests on the residuals from the best-fitted GARCH models, including GARCH, EGARCH, GJR-GARCH, and FIGARCH, as shown in Figure 1 (pre-COVID) and Figure 2 (during COVID-19). By comparing the Q-Q plots of the residuals against the theoretical NIG distribution, we evaluated which model residuals most closely followed this expected pattern. Figures 1 and 2 also indicate which GARCH model provides the best fit for each cryptocurrency. We then used this best-fit model to model the volatility of the top ten cryptocurrencies, incorporating dummy variables to determine whether a day-of-the-week effect exists.

From the best-fitted GARCH model, we scrutinized the significant anomalies and observed a notable trend on Sundays, where the majority of cryptocurrencies exhibited positive returns during both the pre-COVID-19 and COVID-19 periods. All coefficients of cryptocurrencies are positive, indicating higher average returns on that day. A day with a positive coefficient may be seen as a good day to hold or sell if you look to capitalize on higher returns. Traders might prefer to sell on these days to maximize profits. This finding deviates from the previously reported negative Sunday effect by Dorfleitner and Lung (2018) but corroborates the findings of Naz et al. (2023).

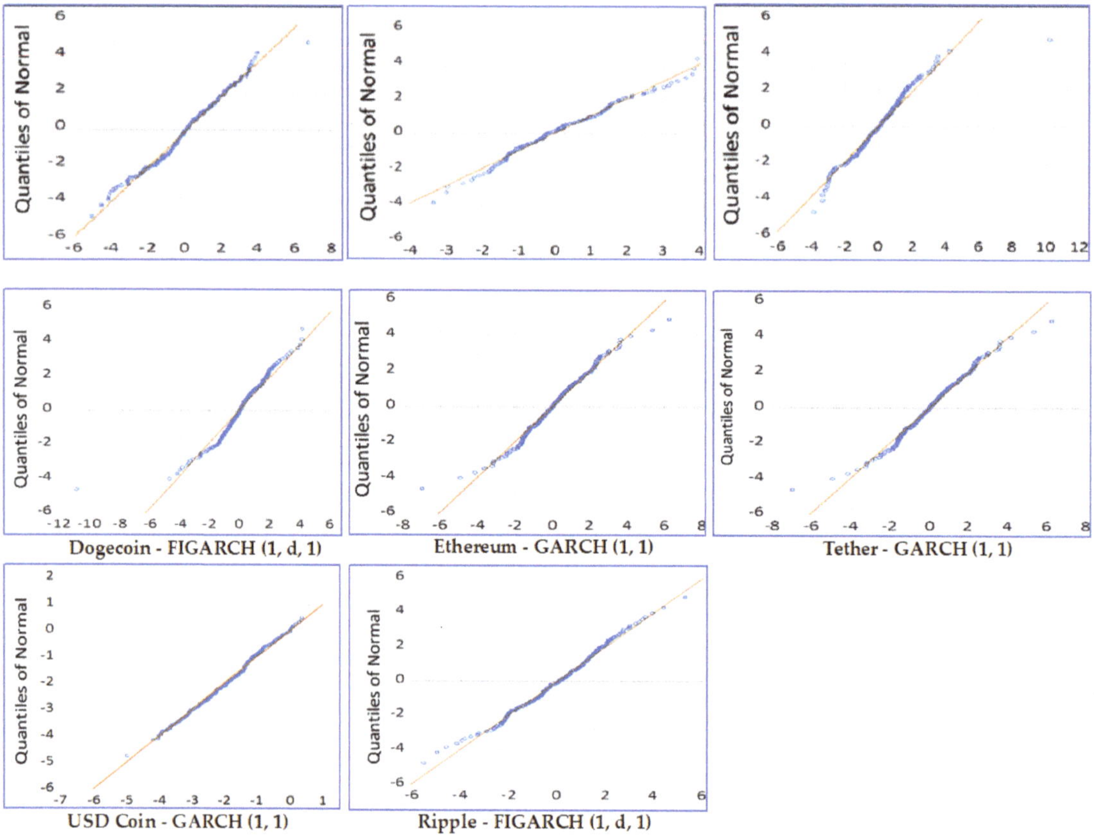

Figure 1. Q-Q plot of residuals in the pre-COVID-19 period.

In addition, a noticeable shift occurred in Monday returns. During the pre-COVID-19 period, cryptocurrencies displayed positive returns, consistent with the findings of Ma and Tanizaki (2019), Hamurcu (2022), López-Martín (2023), and Naz et al. (2023). However, during the COVID-19 period, this trend reversed, and all the coins had negative coefficients, indicating lower average returns on that day. This aligns with the findings of Baur et al. (2019) and Hinny and Szabó (2022). Days with negative coefficients may be seen as better days to buy, as prices tend to be lower. This provides a buying opportunity for traders looking to purchase at lower prices and sell at higher prices on subsequent days with positive coefficients like Thursday, Friday, and Sunday. This alignment supports the adaptive market hypothesis. Tables 11 and 12 present the coefficients and *p*-values for the day-of-the-week effects, further detailing the observed trends.

Binance Coin, Ethereum, Tether, USD Coin, and Ripple continued to exhibit anomalies throughout the observed period. During the COVID-19 period, Bitcoin, Ethereum, and Ripple experienced a shift in anomalies to Tuesdays, with positive coefficients indicating higher returns for investors. Ripple consistently maintained its anomalies on Tuesdays and Fridays, with positive returns on these days during the COVID-19 period. Bitcoin showed a day-of-the-week effect with positive returns on Tuesday, in line with the study by Aharon and Qadan (2019), which contradicts their finding of a Monday effect on Bitcoin. Binance Coin's effect was observed on Sundays. Solana exhibited a day-of-the-week effect with negative returns on Wednesdays, which is consistent with the findings of López-

Martín (2023). Notably, Cardano and Dogecoin did not show any anomalies during the COVID-19 period.

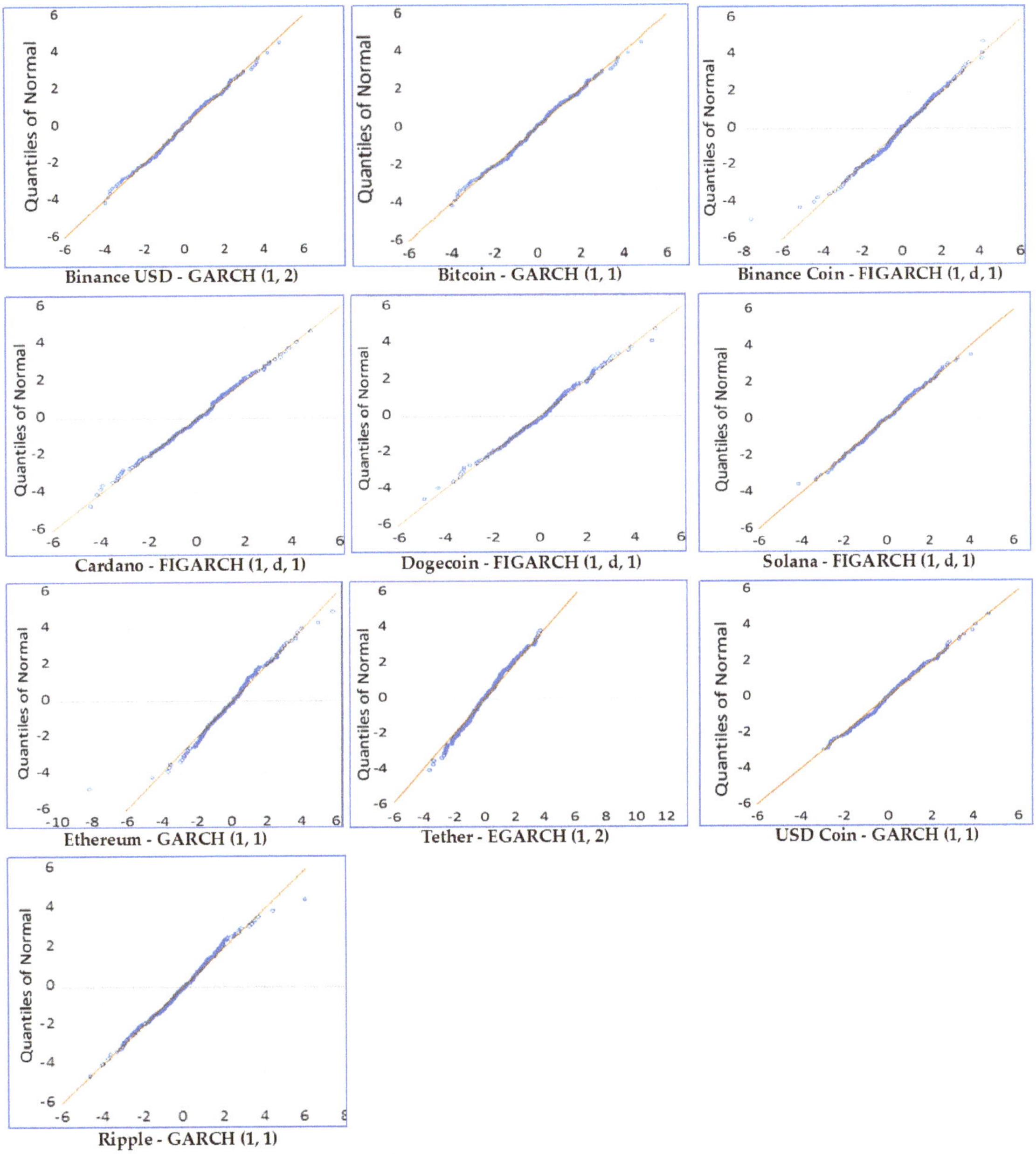

Figure 2. Q-Q plot of residuals during the COVID-19 Period.

Table 11. Coefficients and p-values (pre-COVID-19 period) for day-of-week effects from the best-fit GARCH model.

		Monday	Tuesday	Wednesday	Thursday	Friday	Saturday	Sunday
Bitcoin	Coefficient	0.306	0.037	0.129	0.320	−0.130	0.419	0.184
	p-value	0.183	0.838	0.521	0.130	0.529	0.055	0.448
Binance Coin	Coefficient	0.110	−0.188	−0.276	−0.476	−0.081	0.801	0.023
	p-value	0.772	0.580	0.434	0.193	0.815	**0.029**	0.955
Cardano	Coefficient	0.347	−0.640	−0.444	−0.454	−1.307	0.596	0.380
	p-value	0.374	0.082	0.250	0.250	**0.002**	0.143	0.423
Dogecoin	Coefficient	0.055	−0.432	−0.357	−0.006	−0.717	0.237	−0.069
	p-value	0.823	**0.037**	0.121	0.978	**0.004**	0.354	0.795
Ethereum	Coefficient	0.365	−0.228	−0.163	−0.277	−0.395	0.751	0.169
	p-value	0.214	0.384	0.563	0.359	0.182	**0.014**	0.579
Tether	Coefficient	0.005	−0.031	−0.003	0.002	0.020	−0.007	0.018
	p-value	0.687	**0.012**	0.833	0.892	0.163	0.586	0.230
USD Coin	Coefficient	0.027	0.001	0.014	0.023	0.023	−0.018	0.000
	p-value	0.206	0.953	0.586	0.316	0.355	0.433	0.996
Ripple	Coefficient	0.075	−0.593	−0.090	−0.227	−1.073	0.220	0.223
	p-value	0.642	**0.001**	0.497	0.100	**0.000**	0.213	0.192

Source: Elaborated by the author. Note: The p-values in bold indicate statistically significant day-of-the-week effects at the 95% significance level for specific days.

Table 12. Coefficients and p-values (during the COVID-19 period) for day-of-week effects from the best-fit GARCH model.

		Monday	Tuesday	Wednesday	Thursday	Friday	Saturday	Sunday
Binance USD	Coefficient	−0.017	−0.009	−0.003	−0.001	0.016	0.011	−0.008
	p-value	**0.001**	0.116	0.587	0.833	**0.006**	**0.032**	0.201
Bitcoin	Coefficient	−0.132	0.666	−0.059	0.224	0.071	−0.038	0.214
	p-value	0.511	**0.000**	0.741	0.222	0.714	0.860	0.323
Binance Coin	Coefficient	−0.446	0.445	−0.142	0.185	0.188	0.124	0.622
	p-value	0.052	0.051	0.517	0.393	0.404	0.631	**0.008**
Cardano	Coefficient	−0.554	0.274	−0.267	0.001	0.158	−0.379	0.521
	p-value	0.077	0.336	0.339	0.997	0.594	0.241	0.119
Dogecoin	Coefficient	−0.372	−0.057	−0.408	−0.060	−0.088	−0.067	0.359
	p-value	0.138	0.809	0.099	0.800	0.719	0.777	0.180
Solana	Coefficient	−0.538	0.568	−0.967	−0.029	0.285	−0.478	0.831
	p-value	0.222	0.154	**0.017**	0.944	0.492	0.278	0.083
Ethereum	Coefficient	−0.128	0.790	−0.139	0.605	0.281	−0.105	0.530
	p-value	0.666	**0.002**	0.593	**0.021**	0.283	0.718	0.091
Tether	Coefficient	−0.012	−0.010	−0.002	−0.014	0.015	0.024	0.001
	p-value	**0.044**	0.149	0.712	**0.030**	**0.035**	**0.000**	0.915
USD Coin	Coefficient	−0.021	−0.012	−0.004	0.000	0.026	0.021	0.013
	p-value	**0.000**	0.102	0.465	0.941	**0.000**	**0.000**	**0.001**
Ripple	Coefficient	−0.238	0.932	−0.089	0.297	0.769	−0.245	0.225
	p-value	0.328	**0.005**	0.787	0.367	**0.024**	0.488	0.529

Source: Elaborated by the author. Note: The p-values in bold indicate statistically significant day-of-the-week effects at the 95% significance level for specific days.

Binance Coin, Ethereum, Tether, and USD Coin displayed anomalies on multiple days. Binance Coin showed anomalies on Mondays, Fridays, and Saturdays, with Mondays having a negative coefficient and Fridays and Saturdays having positive coefficients. This pattern suggests that investors in Binance Coin could benefit from buying on Mondays and selling on Fridays or Saturdays. Ethereum exhibits a day-of-the-week effect with positive coefficients on Tuesday and Friday, indicating that these days are optimal for selling to gain higher returns. Tether had a day-of-the-week effect, with negative coefficients on Monday and Thursday making these days better for buying, while positive coefficients on Friday and Saturday indicated better days for selling. Similarly, USD Coin's pattern suggests that investors should consider buying on Monday and selling on Fridays, Saturdays, and Sundays.

The effect of market sentiment is implicitly observed in our analysis of day-of-the-week anomalies and shifts in return patterns during the COVID-19 period. Market sentiment significantly influences cryptocurrency prices, often leading to herding behavior, where investors follow the actions of others rather than their own independent analysis. This behavior amplifies price movements and contributes to the observed day-of-the-week effects. The shifts in returns and anomalies during the COVID-19 period likely reflect changes in market sentiment as investors react to the rapidly evolving economic and social conditions.

While this study offers significant insights, its limitations include the following: future research could benefit from incorporating intraday data to provide more detailed insights. While market sentiment significantly influences cryptocurrency prices, we did not include specific variables to quantify sentiment. Future research should consider incorporating sentiment analysis from social media trends, news sentiments, and investor surveys to provide a more detailed understanding of market dynamics. Furthermore, our model is backward-looking, meaning that the day-of-the-week effects detected in historical data may not persist under current market conditions. Market dynamics evolve, and past patterns may not necessarily hold true today. A post-pandemic analysis can reveal if trends have changed since COVID-19.

5. Conclusions

This study delves into calendar anomalies and volatility patterns within the cryptocurrency market, focusing on day-of-the-week effects before and during the COVID-19 pandemic. We leverage advanced statistical models, including GARCH, EGARCH, GJR-GARCH, and FIGARCH, to analyze the top ten cryptocurrencies by market capitalization. The continuous 24/7 operation of cryptocurrency markets, which includes holidays and weekends, offers a unique context for this investigation that is distinct from traditional financial markets.

Our findings reveal notable shifts in volatility dynamics and day-of-the-week effects due to the pandemic. The pre-COVID period shows pronounced leverage effects in Binance Coin, Cardano, Dogecoin, and Ripple, with negative returns leading to greater increases in volatility. However, during the COVID-19 period, this behavior was observed only in Bitcoin, Ethereum, and Tether, indicating significant changes in market dynamics and investor behavior. These shifts underscore the importance of considering the evolving market context when analyzing financial anomalies.

We find compelling evidence of day-of-the-week anomalies, particularly in the returns of all studied coins, except for Cardano and Dogecoin, during the COVID-19 period. Bitcoin, which did not show any day-of-the-week effect pre-COVID-19, began to exhibit such effects during the pandemic. This finding challenges the notion of market efficiency in the cryptocurrency space, suggesting that exploitable anomalies persist despite a market's continuous operation and increasing maturity.

The use of FIGARCH models provides deeper insights into long-term memory and the persistence of volatility in cryptocurrency returns. The presence of long-term memory in most cryptocurrencies before and during the COVID-19 period highlights the need for robust trading strategies that account for prolonged volatility effects. Our application of

Lo's modified R/S test further validates these findings, confirming long-range dependence in the dataset.

Our analysis also demonstrated day-of-the-week effects on cryptocurrency returns, with different patterns emerging before and during the pandemic. Positive returns are generally observed on Sundays, whereas a shift to negative returns on Mondays is evident during the COVID-19 period. These patterns suggest strategic opportunities for investors, such as buying on days with negative coefficients and selling on days with positive coefficients, to maximize returns.

Several macroprudential strategies can enhance investor confidence and mitigate fear and uncertainty, especially in the face of anomalies and exogenous shocks, such as crises and pandemics. Enhanced transparency and reporting, including real-time reporting of trading volumes and significant trades, helps investors make informed decisions and reduce uncertainty. Establishing market stabilization funds to intervene during periods of extreme volatility can help stabilize prices and prevent panic selling. Investor education programs on market anomalies and risk management techniques empower better investment decisions, reduce fear, and promote confidence. Regular stress testing and scenario analysis of major exchanges ensure preparedness for potential shocks and inform market-stability strategies. Developing comprehensive regulatory frameworks that address the unique aspects of cryptocurrency markets provides a stable environment for investors.

In conclusion, our study provides valuable insights for investors, traders, regulators, and policymakers to navigate the complexities of the cryptocurrency market. The identified volatility patterns and day-of-the-week effects inform the development of effective trading strategies, risk-management practices, and regulatory frameworks. As the cryptocurrency market continues to evolve, analysis and adaptation are essential to capitalize on emerging opportunities and mitigate associated risks.

Author Contributions: Conceptualization, S.S. and J.-M.K.; methodology, S.S. and J.-M.K.; software: S.S.; validation, S.S., A.F.R. and J.-M.K.; formal analysis, S.S.; investigation, S.S.; resources, S.S.; data curation: S.S.; writing—original draft preparation, S.S.; writing—review and editing: S.S., A.F.R.; visualization, S.S.; supervision: J.-M.K.; project administration, S.S.; funding acquisition: J.-M.K. All authors have read and agreed to the published version of the manuscript.

Funding: This research received no external funding.

Data Availability Statement: The data used were downloaded from publicly available sources: https://coinmarketcap.com/coins/ (accessed on 16 February 2024).

Conflicts of Interest: The authors declare no conflicts of interest.

Appendix A

Table A1. Results of the parametric and non-parametric tests on cryptocurrencies in pre- and during the COVID-19 periods.

	Normality Test		Central Tendency Test				Variance Test			
	Anderson Darling Test *p*-Values		Mood Median Test *p*-Values		One-Way ANOVA *p*-Values		Levene's Test *p*-Values		Bartlett's Test *p*-Values	
	Pre	During	Pre	During	Pre	During	Pre	During	Pre	During
Binance USD	-	<0.05	-	0.402	-	0.885	-	0.588	-	0.61
Bitcoin	<0.05	<0.05	0.249	0.733	0.645	0.676	0.026	0.000	0.101	0.000
Binance Coin	<0.05	<0.05	0.346	0.992	0.673	0.955	0.243	0.000	0.62	0.001
Cardano	<0.05	<0.05	0.058	0.762	0.137	0.331	0.048	0.001	0.148	0.003
Dogecoin	<0.05	<0.05	0.482	0.368	0.481	0.728	0.559	0.009	0.953	0.036
Solana	-	<0.05	-	0.941	-	0.741	-	0.011	-	0.033
Ethereum	<0.05	<0.05	0.042	0.674	0.302	0.675	0.049	0.000	0.044	0.001
Tether	<0.05	<0.05	0.024	0.444	0.156	0.449	0.959	0.592	0.947	0.545
USD Coin	<0.05	<0.05	0.960	0.147	0.983	0.462	0.943	0.456	0.950	0.604
Ripple	<0.05	<0.05	0.129	0.857	0.826	0.888	0.004	0.001	0.033	0.002

Source: Elaborated by the author.

Table A2. Augmented Dickey–Fuller test results before and during the COVID-19 pandemic.

Augmented Dickey–Fuller Test Statistics										
Pre-COVID-19 Period										
	Binance USD	Bitcoin	Binance Coin	Cardano	Dogecoin	Solana	Ethereum	Tether	USD Coin	Ripple
t-Statistic	−12.454	−33.183	−31.552	−16.336	−20.820	N/A	−28.069	−25.340	−14.962	−20.492
p-value	0.000	0.000	0.000	0.000	0.000		0.000	0.000	0.000	0.000
During the COVID-19 Period										
t-Statistic	−26.466	−33.829	−21.147	−33.867	−25.908	−32.832	−34.677	−24.210	−23.482	−32.970
p-value	0.000	0.000	0.000	0.000	0.000	0.000	0.000	0.000	0.000	0.000

Source: Elaborated by the author.

Table A3. Phillips–Perron test results before and during the COVID-19 period.

Phillips–Perron Test Statistic										
Pre-COVID-19 Period										
	Binance USD	Bitcoin	Binance Coin	Cardano	Dogecoin	Solana	Ethereum	Tether	USD Coin	Ripple
t-Statistic	−16.307	−33.201	−31.727	−27.945	−31.612	N/A	−28.245	−68.989	−33.266	−33.572
p-value	0.000	0.000	0.000	0.000	0.000		0.000	0.000	0.000	0.000
During the COVID-19 Period										
t-Statistic	−30.657	−33.784	−43.953	−34.209	−32.753	−33.492	−29.931	−74.346	−41.548	−35.457
p-value	0.000	0.000	0.000	0.000	0.000	0.000	0.000	0.000	0.000	0.000

Source: Elaborated by the author.

Table A4. Test results for Engle's Arch test.

1	Binance USD	During COVID-19	F-statistic	236.151	Prob. F	0.000
			Obs*R-squared	324.169	Prob. Chi-Square	0.000
2	Bitcoin	Pre-COVID-19	F-statistic	19.672	Prob. F	0.000
			Obs*R-squared	38.077	Prob. Chi-Square	0.000
		During COVID-19	F-statistic	0.142	Prob. F	0.049
			Obs*R-squared	0.284	Prob. Chi-Square	0.049
3	Binance Coin	Pre-COVID-19	F-statistic	0.038	Prob. F	0.963
			Obs*R-squared	0.076	Prob. Chi-Square	0.963
		During COVID-19	F-statistic	23.340	Prob. F	0.000
			Obs*R-squared	44.775	Prob. Chi-Square	0.000
4	Cardano	Pre-COVID-19	F-statistic	26.171	Prob. F	0.000
			Obs*R-squared	49.309	Prob. Chi-Square	0.000
		During COVID-19	F-statistic	8.806	Prob. F	0.000
			Obs*R-squared	17.365	Prob. Chi-Square	0.000
5	Dogecoin	Pre-COVID-19	F-statistic	16.792	Prob. F	0.000
			Obs*R-squared	32.669	Prob. Chi-Square	0.000
		During COVID-19	F-statistic	24.146	Prob. F	0.000
			Obs*R-squared	44.661	Prob. Chi-Square	0.000

Table A4. *Cont.*

6	Solana	During COVID-19	F-statistic	18.776	Prob. F	0.000
			Obs*R-squared	36.201	Prob. Chi-Square	0.000
7	Ethereum	Pre-COVID-19	F-statistic	6.232	Prob. F	0.002
			Obs*R-squared	12.313	Prob. Chi-Square	0.002
		During COVID-19	F-statistic	3.724	Prob. F	0.025
			Obs*R-squared	7.416	Prob. Chi-Square	0.025
8	Tether	Pre-COVID-19	F-statistic	7.657	Prob. F	0.001
			Obs*R-squared	15.133	Prob. Chi-Square	0.001
		During COVID-19	F-statistic	234.791	Prob. F	0.000
			Obs*R-squared	322.888	Prob. Chi-Square	0.000
9	USD Coin	Pre-COVID-19	F-statistic	37.645	Prob. F	0.000
			Obs*R-squared	64.870	Prob. Chi-Square	0.000
		During COVID-19	F-statistic	122.120	Prob. F	0.000
			Obs*R-squared	197.782	Prob. Chi-Square	0.000
10	Ripple	Pre-COVID-19	F-statistic	52.853	Prob. F	0.000
			Obs*R-squared	96.619	Prob. Chi-Square	0.000
		During COVID-19	F-statistic	23.880	Prob. F	0.000
			Obs*R-squared	45.766	Prob. Chi-Square	0.000

Source: Elaborated by the author.

References

Adaramola, Anthony Olugbenga, and Kehinde Oladeji Adekanmbi. 2020. Day-of-the-week effect in Nigerian stock exchange: Adaptive market hypothesis approach. *Investment Management and Financial Innovations* 17: 97–108. [CrossRef]

Aggarwal, Khushboo, and Mithilesh Kumar Jha. 2023. Day-of-the-week effect and volatility in stock returns: Evidence from the Indian stock market. *Managerial Finance* 49: 1438–52. [CrossRef]

Agyei, Samuel Kwaku, Anokye Mohammed Adam, Ahmed Bossman, Oliver Asiamah, Peterson Owusu Junior, Roberta Asafo-Adjei, and Emmanuel Asafo-Adjei. 2022. Does volatility in cryptocurrencies drive the interconnectedness between the cryptocurrencies market? Insights from wavelets. *Cogent Economics & Finance* 10: 1–34.

Aharon, David Y., and Mahmoud Qadan. 2019. Bitcoin and the day-of-the-week effect. *Finance Research Letters*. 31. Available online: https://www.sciencedirect.com/science/article/abs/pii/S1544612317307894 (accessed on 26 June 2024).

Ampountolas, Apostolos. 2022. Cryptocurrencies Intraday High-Frequency Volatility Spillover Effects Using Univariate and Multivariate GARCH Models. *International Journal of Financial Studies* 10: 51. [CrossRef]

Ampountolas, Apostolos. 2024. Enhancing Forecasting Accuracy in Commodity and Financial Markets: Insights from GARCH and SVR Models. *International Journal of Financial Studies* 12: 59. [CrossRef]

Aydoğan, Kürsat, and G. Geoffrey Booth. 2003. Calendar anomalies in the Turkish foreign exchange markets. *Applied Financial Economics* 13: 353–60. [CrossRef]

Aziz, Tariq, and Valeed Ahmad Ansari. 2017. The Turn of the Month Effect in Asia-Pacific Markets: New Evidence. *Global Business Review* 19: 214–26. [CrossRef]

Baek, Chung, and Matt Elbeck. 2014. Bitcoins as an investment or speculative vehicle? A first look. *Applied Economics Letters* 22: 30–34. [CrossRef]

Basdas, Ülkem. 2011. The day-of-the-week effect for Istanbul stock exchange: A stochastic dominance approach. *Journal of Applied Finance and Banking* 1: 223.

Baur, Dirk G., Daniel Cahill, Keith Godfrey, and Zhangxin (Frank) Liu. 2019. Bitcoin time-of-day, day-of-week and month-of-year effects in returns and trading volume. *Finance Research Letters* 31: 78–92. [CrossRef]

Burnham, Kenneth P., and David R. Anderson. 2004. Multimodel Inference. *Sociological Methods & Research* 33: 261–304.

Caporale, Guglielmo Maria, and Alex Plastun. 2019. The day of the week effect in the cryptocurrency market. *Finance Research Letters* 31: 258–69. [CrossRef]

Chatzitzisi, Evanthia, Stilianos Fountas, and Theodore Panagiotidis. 2021. Another look at calendar anomalies. *The Quarterly Review of Economics and Finance* 80: 823–40. [CrossRef]

Chien, Chin-Chen, Cheng-Few Lee, and Andrew M. L. Wang. 2002. A note on stock market seasonality: The impact of stock price volatility on the application of dummy variable regression model. *The Quarterly Review of Economics and Finance* 42: 155–62. [CrossRef]

Compton, William, Robert A. Kunkel, and Gregory Kuhlemeyer. 2013. Calendar anomalies in Russian stocks and bonds. *Managerial Finance* 39: 1138–54. [CrossRef]

Dangi, Vandana. 2020. Day of the Week Effect in Cryptocurrencies' Returns and Volatility. *Ramanujan International Journal of Business and Research/Ramanujan International Journal of Business and Research* 5: 139–67. [CrossRef]

Dong, Xi, Yan Li, David E. Rapach, and Guofu Zhou. 2021. Anomalies and the Expected Market Return. *The Journal of Finance/The Journal of Finance* 77: 639–81. [CrossRef]

Dorfleitner, Gregor, and Carina Lung. 2018. Cryptocurrencies from the perspective of euro investors: A re-examination of diversification benefits and a new day-of-the-week effect. *Journal of Asset Management* 19: 472–94. [CrossRef]

Eidinejad, Shahin, and Elena Dahlem. 2021. The existence and historical development of the holiday effect on the Swedish stock market. *Applied Economics Letters* 29: 1855–58. [CrossRef]

Engle, Robert. 2001. GARCH 101: The Use of ARCH/GARCH Models in Applied Econometrics. *Journal of Economic Perspectives/The Journal of Economic Perspectives* 15: 157–68. [CrossRef]

Enow, Samuel Tabot. 2022. Evidence of Adaptive Market Hypothesis in International Financial Markets. *Journal of Academic Finance* 13: 48–55. [CrossRef]

Hamurcu, Cagri. 2022. Bitcoin'de Haftanın Günü Ve Yılın Ayı Anomalilerinin Varlığının İncelenmesi. *Kırklareli Üniversitesi İktisadi ve İdari Bilimler Fakültesi Dergisi* 11: 162–83. [CrossRef]

Hinny, Robin, and Dorottya Kata Szabó. 2022. Cryptocurrency Market Anomalies: The Day-of-the-Week Effect: A Study on the Existence of the Day-of-the-Week Effect in Cryptocurrencies and Crypto Portfolios. Bachelor's thesis, Jönköping University, Jönköping, Sweden. Available online: https://urn.kb.se/resolve?urn=urn:nbn:se:hj:diva-57129 (accessed on 26 June 2024).

Idrees, Muhammad Abdullah, and Saima Akhtar. 2023. An Investigative Analysis of Volatility in the Cryptocurrency Market. *International Journal of Trends and Innovations in Business & Social Sciences* 1: 80–86.

İmre, Süreyya, and Olcay Ölçen. 2022. The Day of the Week Effect in Euro and Bitcoin: Evidence from Volatility Models. *International Journal of Entrepreneurship and Management Inquiries* 6: 1–17.

Kaiser, Lars. 2019. Seasonality in cryptocurrencies. *Finance Research Letters* 31: 232–38. [CrossRef]

Khuntia, Sashikanta, and J. K. Pattanayak. 2021. Adaptive calendar effects and volume of extra returns in the cryptocurrency market. *International Journal of Emerging Markets* 17: 2137–65. [CrossRef]

Kim, Jong-Min, Dong H. Kim, and Hojin Jung. 2021. Estimating yield spreads volatility using GARCH-type models. *The North American Journal of Economics and Finance* 57: 101396. [CrossRef]

Kinateder, Harald, and Vassilios G. Papavassiliou. 2021. Calendar effects in Bitcoin returns and volatility. *Finance Research Letters* 38: 101420. [CrossRef]

Kliger, Doron, and Mahmoud Qadan. 2019. The High Holidays: Psychological mechanisms of honesty in real-life financial decisions. *Journal of Behavioral and Experimental Economics* 78: 121–37. [CrossRef]

Kumar, Vinod. 2023. Is the Beta Anomaly Real? A Correction in Existing Theories of Cost of Capital and Asset Pricing. *Journal of Emerging Market Finance* 22: 135–63. [CrossRef]

Lahmiri, Salim, and Stelios Bekiros. 2020. The impact of COVID-19 pandemic upon stability and sequential irregularity of equity and cryptocurrency markets. *Chaos, Solitons, and Fractals* 138: 109936. [CrossRef] [PubMed]

Lee, Yen-Sheng, Ace Vo, and Thomas A. Chapman. 2022. Examining the Maturity of Bitcoin Price through a Catastrophic Event: The Case of Structural Break Analysis During the COVID-19 Pandemic. *Finance Research Letters* 49: 103165. [CrossRef]

López-Martín, Carmen. 2023. Dynamic analysis of calendar anomalies in cryptocurrency markets: Evidences of adaptive market hypothesis. *Spanish Journal of Finance and Accounting/Revista Española de Financiación Y Contabilidad* 52: 559–92. [CrossRef]

Ma, Donglian, and Hisashi Tanizaki. 2019. The day-of-the-week effect on Bitcoin return and volatility. *Research in International Business and Finance* 49: 127–36. [CrossRef]

Marobhe, Mutaju Isaack. 2022. Cryptocurrency as a safe haven for investment portfolios amid COVID-19 panic cases of Bitcoin, Ethereum and Litecoin. *China Finance Review International* 12: 51–68. [CrossRef]

Mehta, Kiran, and Ramesh Chander. 2009. Seasonality in Indian Stock Market: A re-examination of January Effect. *Asia Pacific Business Review* 5: 28–42. [CrossRef]

Miralles-Quirós, José Luis, and María Mar Miralles-Quirós. 2022. A new perspective of the day-of-the-week effect on Bitcoin returns: Evidence from an event study hourly approach. *Oeconomia Copernicana* 13: 745–82. [CrossRef]

Naimy, Viviane, Omar Haddad, Gema Fernández-Avilés, and Rim El Khoury. 2021. The predictive capacity of GARCH-type models in measuring the volatility of crypto and world currencies. *PLoS ONE* 16: e0245904. [CrossRef] [PubMed]

Naz, Farah, Madeeha Sayyed, Ramiz-Ur Rehman, Muhammad Akram Naseem, Shamsul Nahar Abdullah, and Muhammad Ishfaq Ahmad. 2023. Calendar anomalies and market volatility in selected cryptocurrencies. *Cogent Business & Management* 10: 2171992.

Ngunyi, Anthony, Simon Mundia, and Cyprian Omari. 2019. modelling volatility dynamics of cryptocurrencies using garch models. *Journal of Mathematical Finance* 09: 591–615. [CrossRef]

Omari, Cyprian, and Anthony Ngunyi. 2021. The predictive performance of extreme value analysis based-models in forecasting the volatility of cryptocurrencies. *Journal of Mathematical Finance* 11: 438–65. [CrossRef]

Osterrieder, Joerg, Martin Strika, and Julian Lorenz. 2017. Bitcoin and Cryptocurrencies—Not for the Faint-Hearted. *International Finance and Banking* 4: 56. [CrossRef]
Plastun, Alex, Xolani Sibande, Rangan Gupta, and Mark E. Wohar. 2019. Rise and Fall of Calendar Anomalies over a Century. Social Science Research Network. *The North American Journal of Economics and Finance* 49: 181–205. [CrossRef]
Queiroz, Rhenan Gomes dos Santos, and Sergio David. 2023. Performance of the Realized-GARCH Model against Other GARCH Types in Predicting Cryptocurrency Volatility. *Risks* 11: 211. [CrossRef]
Robiyanto, Robiyanto, Yosua Arif Susanto, and Rihfenti Ernayani. 2019. Examining the day-of-the-week-effect and the-month-of-the-year-effect in cryptocurrency market. *Jurnal Keuangan dan Perbankan* 23: 361–375. [CrossRef]
Sahoo, Pradipta Kumar. 2021. COVID-19 pandemic and cryptocurrency markets: An empirical analysis from a linear and nonlinear causal relationship. *Studies in Economics and Finance* 38: 454–68. [CrossRef]
Sejati, Hiro, Irham Lihan, and Ernie Hendrawaty. 2022. Analysis of Ramadan Effect on Indonesian Islamic Stock Market: Jakarta Islamic Index (JII) (2016–2020). *Asian Journal of Economics, Business and Accounting* 22: 470–80. [CrossRef]
Sheraz, Muhammad, Silvia Dedu, and Vasile Preda. 2022. Volatility dynamics of non-linear volatile time series and analysis of information flow: Evidence from cryptocurrency data. *Entropy* 24: 1410. [CrossRef] [PubMed]
Siriopoulos, Costas, and Layal Youssef. 2019. The January barometer in emerging markets: New evidence from the Gulf Cooperation Council stock exchanges. *Investment Management and Financial Innovations/Investment Management & Financial Innovations* 16: 61–71.
Soylu, Pınar Kaya, Mustafa Okur, Özgür Çatıkkaş, and Z. Ayca Altintig. 2020. Long memory in the volatility of selected cryptocurrencies: Bitcoin, ethereum and ripple. *Journal of Risk and Financial Management* 13: 107. [CrossRef]
Szczygielski, Jan Jakub, Andreas Karathanasopoulos, and Adam Zaremba. 2019. One shape fits all? A comprehensive examination of cryptocurrency return distributions. *Applied Economics Letters* 27: 1567–73. [CrossRef]
Tadepalli, Meher Shiva, and Ravi Kumar Jain. 2018. Persistence of calendar anomalies: Insights and perspectives from literature. *American Journal of Business* 33: 18–60. [CrossRef]
Valencia, Franco, Alfonso Gómez-Espinosa, and Benjamín Valdés-Aguirre. 2019. Price movement prediction of cryptocurrencies using sentiment analysis and machine learning. *Entropy* 21: 589. [CrossRef] [PubMed]
Wan, Yang, Yuncheng Song, Xinqian Zhang, and Zhichao Yin. 2023. Asymmetric volatility connectedness between cryptocurrencies and energy: Dynamics and determinants. *Frontiers in Environmental Science* 11. [CrossRef]
Weber, Beat. 2016. Bitcoin and the legitimacy crisis of money. *Cambridge Journal of Economics* 40: 17–41. [CrossRef]
Wuthisatian, Rattaphon. 2021. An examination of calendar anomalies: Evidence from the Thai stock market. *Journal of Economic Studies* 49: 422–34. [CrossRef]
Zhao, Haidong, and Lini Zhang. 2021. Financial literacy or investment experience: Which is more influential in cryptocurrency investment? *The International Journal of Bank Marketing* 39: 1208–26. [CrossRef]

Journal of
Risk and Financial Management

MDPI

Article

Prediction of Currency Exchange Rate Based on Transformers

Lu Zhao and Wei Qi Yan *

School of Engineering, Computer and Mathematical Sciences, Auckland University of Technology, Auckland 1010, New Zealand
* Correspondence: weiqi.yan@aut.ac.nz

Abstract: The currency exchange rate is a crucial link between all countries related to economic and trade activities. With increasing volatility, exchange rate fluctuations have become frequent under the combined effects of global economic uncertainty and political risks. Consequently, accurate exchange rate prediction is significant in managing financial risks and economic instability. In recent years, the Transformer models have attracted attention in the field of time series analysis. Transformer models, such as Informer and TFT (Temporal Fusion Transformer), have also been extensively studied. In this paper, we evaluate the performance of the Transformer, Informer, and TFT models based on four exchange rate datasets: NZD/USD, NZD/CNY, NZD/GBP, and NZD/AUD. The results indicate that the TFT model has achieved the highest accuracy in exchange rate prediction, with an R^2 value of up to 0.94 and the lowest RMSE and MAE errors. However, the Informer model offers faster training and convergence speeds than the TFT and Transformer, making it more efficient. Furthermore, our experiments on the TFT model demonstrate that integrating the VIX index can enhance the accuracy of exchange rate predictions.

Keywords: Transformer; Informer; TFT; currency exchange rate

1. Introduction

The exchange rate is a fundamental economic factor, significantly impacting domestic and international economic relations. The exchange rate acts as a bridge for financial communication between various countries (Pradeepkumar and Ravi 2018). Its instabilities not only affect the country's international trade and capital flows but also directly impact the international investment of enterprises, foreign trade and individual investment. Forecasting exchange rate trends is an essential basis for judging the timing of exchange rate transactions.

The exchange rate market is a nonlinear dynamic market characterized by complexity, diversity and uncertainty (Niu and Zhang 2017). This makes exchange rate forecasting more challenging. With the advent of artificial intelligence, the existing research work on financial time series forecasting has also obtained more and more attention. In contrast to traditional time series methods, it can manage the nonlinear, chaotic, noisy and complex data of exchange rate markets, allowing for more effective forecasts (Rout et al. 2017). The dataset is crucial in exchange rate forecasting, mainly including exchange rate prices, volatility, etc. However, if the selected time series is long and has high dimensions, it is tough to achieve the expected results by using the existing models for exchange rate prediction (Lai et al. 2018). Afterward, with the rapid growth in artificial intelligence (AI), the usage of deep learning models to process time-series-related tasks has recently become mainstream, and a series of neural network models for time series tasks has appeared. Early proposed models such as Recurrent Neural Networks (RNN), Long Short-Term Memory (LSTM) and Gated Recurrent Unit (GRU) are considered suitable for processing time series tasks (Pirani et al. 2022).

As the most popular mainstream architecture of deep learning in recent years, the Transformer models are widely adopted in typical tasks such as text classification, sentiment analysis, target detection, speech recognition, etc. However, there are few related works in the field of time series analysis, and multiple financial time series analysis research works still use traditional sequence prediction methods. Therefore, this paper proposes the research questions as follows:

- Question 1: How does the Transformer model perform in predicting the exchange rate?
- Question 2: By comparing the Transformer, Informer and Temporal Fusion Transformer, which algorithm performs best in predicting the exchange rate?

This paper aims to achieve exchange rate predictions based on NZD and discover the most advanced algorithms fitting for exchange rate predictions through deep learning. Based on transformers, we have studied two recent algorithms, Informer and TFT. During our experiments on Google Colab, we trained the model, adjusted parameters, and obtained results established on four processed datasets. Subsequently, the performance of the three algorithms was compared and analyzed to determine the optimal forecast exchange rate model. Eventually, this paper explored the pros and cons of the model, summarized the experimental results, and provided references for other related research work.

The structure of this paper is outlined as follows: Section 2 presents the related works and elaborates on the methodologies of the three models. Section 3 displays the results through experiments on the three models. Section 4 contains the conclusion by comparing the performance of the three models and analyzing them in conjunction with their own characteristics.

2. Materials and Methods

This section consists of related work based on traditional time series models and proposed models: Transformer, Informer, and TFT. In addition, it also illustrates the corresponding methodologies. Subsequently, the experimental processes are presented, and the measures for model evaluation are clarified.

2.1. Related Work Based on Traditional Time Series Models

Since the exchange rate is non-stationary in mean and variance, its relationship with other data series changes dynamically due to nonlinear and dynamic changes in the exchange rate over time (Xu et al. 2019). As international trade continues to grow at an increasing rate, it is becoming more and more common, and the factors affecting exchange rates gradually increase.

2.1.1. ARIMA

ARIMA is one of the most universal linear methods for forecasting time series, and its research has achieved great success in academic and industrial applications (Khashei and Bijari 2011). In the study of the USD/TRY exchange rate forecast, Yıldıran and Fettahoğlu (2017) generated long-term and short-term models based on the ARIMA framework. Through comparison, it was found that ARIMA is more fitting for short-term forecasts. Similarly, Yamak et al. (2019) used a dataset of Bitcoin prices and applied the ARIMA, LSTM and GRU models for prediction analysis. The results showed that ARIMA delivered the best results among these models, with a MAPE and RMSE of 2.76% and 302.53, respectively.

2.1.2. RNN

RNN is one of the neural networks specifically designed to handle time series problems (Hu et al. 2021). It can extract information from a time series, allow the information to persist, and use previous knowledge to infer subsequent patterns. Traditional neural networks such as the Backpropagation Neural Network (BPNN) are also used for time series modeling, while the time series information of such models is usually less than RNN.

2.1.3. LSTM

Although RNN has outstanding advantages in dealing with time series problems, as the training time rises and the number of network layers increases after the nodes of the neural network have been calculated in many stages, the features of the previous relatively long time slice have been covered, so problems such as vanishing gradient or exploding gradient are prone to occur, which leads to the incapability to learn the relationship between information, thereby losing the ability to process long-term series data (Li et al. 2018).

2.2. Related Work Based on Transformer, Informer, and TFT

2.2.1. Transformer

Transformer was initially explored by Vaswani et al. (2017), and it no longer stuck to the framework of RNN and CNN, and attention was applied to the seq-to-seq structure to form the Transformer model and to process natural language tasks. Since then, the Transformer model has generated outstanding results in fields such as computer vision (Han et al. 2022). Moreover, the research work on Transformer in time series has also aroused great interest (Wen et al. 2023). Through experimental research on 12 public datasets with time series, it was found that Transformer can capture long-term dependencies and obtain the most accurate prediction results in five of the dataset trainings (Lara-Benítez et al. 2021). However, its calculation is more complex than CNN, so the training process is relatively slow.

Despite in-depth research outcomes on the Transformer, it is evident from the literature that most studies primarily focus on reducing the computational requirements of the Transformer model (Tay et al. 2022). However, they overlook the importance of capturing the dependencies among neighboring elements, addressing the heterogeneity between the values of time series data, the temporal information corresponding to the time series, and the positional information of each dimension within the time series.

2.2.2. Informer

To solve the heterogeneity of time information, position information and numbers, a model based on Transformer architecture and attention mechanism was offered (Zhou et al. 2021). For the first time, time coding, position coding and scalar were introduced in the embedding layer to crack the long sequence input problem. ProbSparse self-attention captures long-distance dependencies and lessens the time complexity in the computation process. Using the distillation mechanism can effectively decrease the time dimension of the feature map and lower memory consumption. Although Informer outperforms LSTM in time series forecasting tasks, its inability to capture dependencies among neighboring elements with a multihead attention mechanism leads to insufficient capture of the time series local information. This results in lower prediction accuracy and higher memory consumption, which could be more conducive to large-scale deployment. A relative coding algorithm (Gong et al. 2022) was based on the Informer framework to predict the heating load. The experimental results indicate that the improved Informer model is more robust. Moreover, based on Informer and the proposed Autoformer (Wu et al. 2021), a new decomposition architecture was designed with an autocorrelation mechanism. The model breaks the preprocessing convention of sequence decomposition and updates it into the fundamental internal blocks of the deep model. This design enables Autoformer to progressively decompose complex time series. Moreover, inspired by the random process theory, Autoformer designed an autocorrelation mechanism based on sequence periodicity, replacing the Self-Attention module in Transformer with autocorrelation mode. In long-term forecasting, Autoformer achieves outstanding accuracy.

2.2.3. TFT

Transformer model has demonstrated its outstanding performance in both natural language processing and computer vision (Bi et al. 2021). Applying this model to capture long-term dependencies and data interaction in time series has become the focus. The general method for processing time series data is to treat data in all dimensions with equal weight. This may cause the model to ignore critical input information or be interfered with by noise, which is also a shortcoming of traditional processing methods. Temporal Fusion Transformer (TFT) is a Transformer model for multistep prediction tasks, which is developed to effectively process different types of input information (i.e., static, known or observed inputs) and construct feature representations to achieve high predictive performance (Lim et al. 2021). The TFT model (Zhang et al. 2022) was proposed to predict short-term highway speed by collecting Minnesota traffic data and applying them to the training and testing of the model. Compared with traditional models, the TFT model performs best when the prediction range exceeds 30 min.

2.3. Methods Based on Transformer, Informer and TFT

2.3.1. Transformer

In Transformers, the self-attention mechanism has received a higher recognition rate compared to other neural network models that utilize the attention mechanism. The attention mechanism in Transformers excels at capturing the internal correlation within data and features, and more effectively solves the problem of long-distance dependence (Wang et al. 2022).

Contrary to other models that only make use of a single attention module, the Transformer employs multihead attention modules to operate in parallel (Sridhar and Sanagavarapu 2021). In this step, the original queries, keys and values of dimension D_m are each mapped into spaces of dimensions D_k , D_m and D_v using H different learned vectors. The model computes each of these mapped queries, keys and values according to Equation (1), outputting attention weights for each. Then, it concatenates all these outputs and converts them back into an D_m dimensional representation.

$$\begin{aligned} MultiHeadAttn(Q,K,V) &= Concat(head_1,\cdots,head_H)W^O, \\ where \quad head_i &= Attention\left(QW_i^Q, KW_i^K, VW_i^V\right) \end{aligned} \tag{1}$$

where $head_i$ is computed by applying the attention function to the transformed inputs. W^O represents the weight matrix applied after concatenating the outputs of all attention heads.

2.3.2. Informer

Informer model has been proposed to address the long-sequence forecasting issues in the Transformer. This model provides an improved self-attention module to reduce time complexity (Sun et al. 2022).

In the Informer network, probabilistic sparse self-attention replaces traditional self-attention. Each input vector is utilized to calculate query, key and value vectors in the self-attention mechanism. Then, attention weights are calculated by computing the dot product of query vectors and key vectors. The attention weights represent the similarity between each and all input vectors. In the probabilistic sparse self-attention mechanism, query vectors compute the similarity with each key vector, generating an attention distribution. The probabilistic sparse self-attention calculation is shown in Equation (2).

$$ProbAttn\left(\hat{Q}^l, K^i, V^i\right) = softmax\left(\frac{\hat{Q}^l K^{i^T}}{\sqrt{d}}\right)V^i \tag{2}$$

where $\hat{Q}^l$ represents the distance calculated using KL divergence among the attention distribution and the uniform distribution to determine the value of each query point, thus specifying which queries should be allocated computational resources, it then selects the active query with the most significant distance.

In general, in probabilistic sparse self-attention calculation, attention is only given to the far-active queries. In contrast, the dot products for other queries are substituted with the mean of the value vectors, thus reducing the computational task.

2.3.3. TFT

Temporal Fusion Transformer (TFT) is a time series prediction model based on the Transformer architecture, aiming to solve the limitations of traditional time series prediction models (Lim et al. 2021). TFT introduces a novel method to capture features and nonlinear relationships across multiple time scales (Fayer et al. 2023). TFT employs recurrent layers for localized processing and interpretable attention layers to manage long-term dependencies. The algorithm also leverages specialized components for feature selection and a sequence of gating layers to filter out unnecessary elements, thereby maintaining the optimal performance of this model across various scenarios. The main components of this TFT model are the Gating mechanism and variable selection network, Static covariate encoder, and Temporal fusion decoder.

2.4. Data Collection and Preprocessing

Due to the changes in the exchange rate being impacted by multiple aspects, they display diverse characteristics of change. We selected four representative currencies, USD, GBP, CNY, and AUD, as training and test samples because of their significant impact on the global economy, widespread usage in international trade, and substantial influence on foreign exchange markets. These currencies are representative of major economic regions, providing a comprehensive and diverse dataset for robust predictive modeling. The datasets of NZD against these four currencies are all from Yahoo! Finance (https://nz.finance.yahoo.com) and Investing website (www.investing.com). To enhance the learning ability of our proposed model for unexpected fluctuations, each sample includes daily data from 3 January 2005 to 2 February 2024, totaling 4980 entries. The primary variables of the dataset include closing, opening, highest, lowest and floating prices of the day. We select the closing price as the experimental objective as shown in Figure 1.

Figure 1. The trend of NZD against the four selected currencies.

We adopt Equation (4) for imputing missing values.

$$X_i = \frac{X_{i-1} + X_{i+1}}{2} \quad (3)$$

where X_i defines the data to be imputed, X_{i-1} represents the data from the day before the missing data, and X_{i+1} illustrates the data from the day after the missing data.

The most common method, min–max standardization, is also utilized in data preprocessing. The calculation process is

$$X^* = \frac{X - X_{min}}{X_{max} - X_{min}}. \quad (4)$$

where X^* represents the dimensionless data after normalization, X means the observation value, X_{min} denotes the minimum value, and X_{max} tells the maximum value. Denormalization is restoring normalized data to facilitate subsequent data analysis and other operations.

2.5. Data Description

After preprocessing the four datasets, the total number of samples for each is 4980. To better understand the data's characteristics and distribution features and utilize the relevant data for modeling, it is essential to conduct a descriptive statistical analysis before modeling. Table 1 provides the descriptive statistics for the four datasets.

Table 1. The descriptive statistics of NZD against four currency exchange rates.

Currency	Mean	Min	Max	Median	Standard Deviation	Kurtosis	Skewness
USD	0.709	0.494	0.882	0.703	0.073	−0.369	0.118
CNY	4.827	3.371	6.163	4.79	0.484	−0.148	0.258
GBP	0.473	0.328	0.597	0.497	0.063	−0.726	−0.693
AUD	0.884	0.728	0.997	0.91	0.064	−0.886	−0.686

Table 1 shows that the standard deviation for NZD/USD is 0.073, indicating that the exchange rate fluctuates within a narrow range. A kurtosis value of −0.369 and a skewness value of 0.118 suggest that the distribution of NZD/USD deviates slightly from a normal distribution, showing slight flatness and right skewness. Still, overall, it is close to symmetry. Compared to NZD/CNY, there is a significant difference between its minimum and maximum values, which are 3.371 and 6.163, respectively. The median of 4.79 is slightly lower than the average, implying a skewed distribution to the right. The standard deviation is 0.484, indicating the volatility is higher than the other three currency pairs. The kurtosis and skewness are −0.148 and 0.258, respectively, indicating a relatively flat and slightly right-skewed distribution. The statistical results for NZD/GBP show that the average exchange rate for NZD/GBP is 0.473, with a minimum of 0.328 and a maximum of 0.597, revealing a smaller fluctuation range and, hence, a relatively stable exchange rate. The median of 0.497 is very close to the mean, reflecting the central tendency of the data. Its standard deviation of 0.063 is the smallest among the four currency pairs, showing the lowest volatility. The average exchange rate for NZD/AUD is 0.884, with a fluctuation range from 0.728 to 0.997, which is relatively moderate. The median of 0.91 is higher than the average, exhibiting more data points in the higher value range. A standard deviation of 0.064 indicates lower volatility. The kurtosis of −0.886 and skewness of −0.686 present a skewed and peaked distribution, suggesting a frequent occurrence of lower values.

Throughout this detailed analysis, we summarize that these four datasets demonstrate diverse levels of volatility and distribution characteristics. NZD/GBP and NZD/AUD show relatively lower volatility, while NZD/USD and NZD/CNY exhibit higher volatility. In the experiment, we divided the dataset into two parts for the training process of the three models: 80% for training and 20% for testing.

2.6. Experiment Implementation

2.6.1. The Experimental Implementation of Transformer

In the training process of the Transformer model, it is vital to set essential parameters, which are continuously adjusted and optimized. Due to the complexity of the Transformer, we employ a lower learning rate parameter of 0.0005. Although this means that the model learns more slowly, it can help the model adapt more finely to the training data, leading to better stable and accurate predictions. The value of input_window is set to 7, which allows for more suitable capturing of weekly patterns or trends in the data for time series data like exchange rates, a typical setting in financial sequences. We experimented with the multiple training epochs, setting them at 50, 100, 150 and 200, and finally found that 150 is the best, avoiding the risk of overfitting.

2.6.2. The Experimental Implementation of Informer

Unlike the parameter settings of the Transformer, through multiple attempts, we have set the number of epochs to 60. Since the Informer optimizes computational complexity, reducing unnecessary computations and parameter usage, it achieves better results in a shorter training time. The table below details the model parameters of the Informer.

2.6.3. The Experimental Implementation of TFT

The model training of TFT is conducted within a PyTorch-lightning framework. In this environment, it is possible to adjust the model's hyperparameters promptly during the data training process. This setup integrates with the Early-Stopping mechanism to obtain an outstanding combination of parameters. For the TFT model, a learning rate of 0.001 is a moderate value that supports balanced training speed and convergence quality. Setting the hidden layer's size to 32 means the TFT model is relatively simple and computationally efficient. Since no overly complex recognition tasks exist, we set the number of attention heads to 1.

2.7. Evaluation Methods

In our experiment of exchange rate prediction, to reflect the reliability of the predictive performance accurately and objectively, we utilize four evaluation metrics, including root mean square error (RMSE), mean absolute error (MAE), coefficient of determination (R^2), mean absolute percentage error (MAPE). The smaller the RMSE and MAE, the closer the predictions are to the actual values. A larger R^2 indicates a better fit of the model. MAPE provides a comprehensive indication of the model's overall predictive effectiveness.

3. Results

3.1. Experimental Results of Transformer

In this experiment, the initial model we trained on Google Colab for the four exchange rate datasets was the Transformer model. By considering both the training on the training set and the predictions on the test set, the Transformer has achieved satisfactory results. Figure 2 displays the actual and predictive results of the test set.

From the prediction results related to the four test sets, the trend of NZD/USD is very close to the actual result, reaching highs and lows at almost the same time, and the high degree of overlap between the two lines indicates that the Transformer can effectively capture the trends and seasonal changes in the exchange rate. However, from the NZD/CNY prediction graph, we discover the deviations during periods of high volatility, and the Transformer model has yet to capture the peaks and troughs of the exchange rate perfectly. Despite this, the overall prediction trend still tracks the real exchange rate well. Similar to NZD/AUD, though the figure shows a strong correlation between prediction and reality, the Transformer still underestimates or overestimates the peaks in some intervals. Regarding the NZD/GBP trend, the prediction accuracy is high for most of the timeline, showing that the Transformer is robust. Table 1 shows more details of the experimental evaluation results of the Transformer.

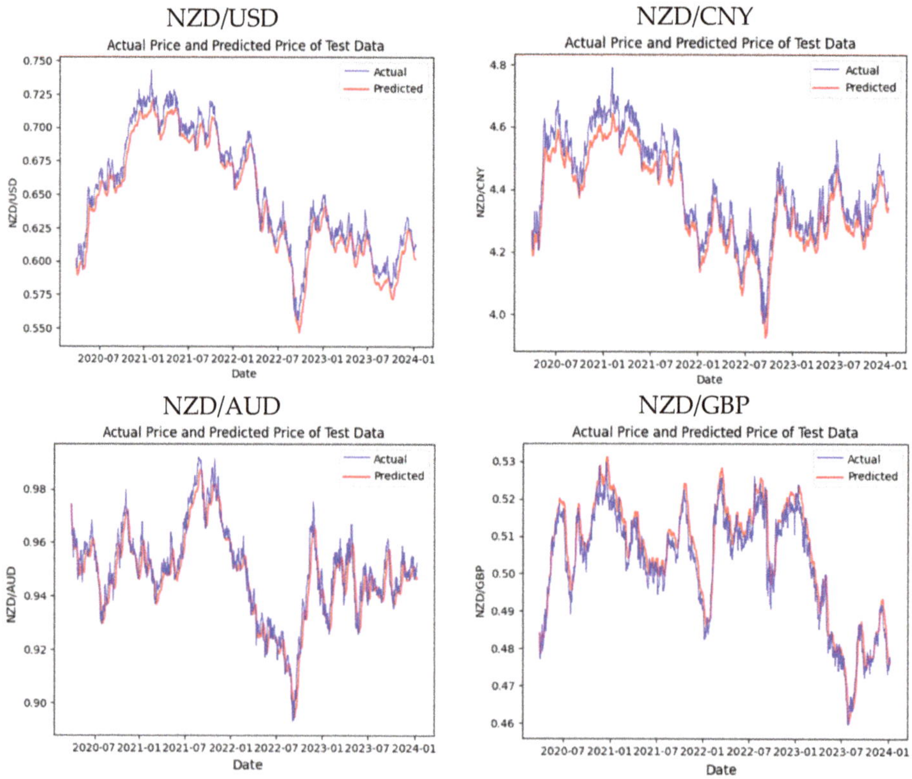

Figure 2. The predictive results of each dataset by using Transformer.

By evaluating the model with four different indicators, we notice that in the training and prediction of the Transformer model based on the four datasets, NZD/USD exhibits remarkably high precision and reliability. The very low RMSE and MAE values show that the forecast values are extraordinarily close to the actual values. Furthermore, the low MAPE value 0.0141 verifies that the error percentage is minor, representing an ideal outcome in currency prediction. In comparison, an R^2 value close to 0.94 indicates that the model has strong predictive power and a high degree of explanatory capability regarding the fluctuating exchange rate trends.

Although the MAPE values are relatively low in the NZD/CNY and NZD/AUD predictions, at 0.0113 and 0.0048, respectively, the increased RMSE and MAE indicate that the model faces more significant challenges in forecasting these currency pairs. Possible reasons may include higher market volatility, differences in trading volume, or the characteristics of these datasets. Nevertheless, the R^2 values for both currency pairs exceed 0.85, reflecting the Transformer's powerful capability to capture essential information and trends.

Compared to other results, NZD/GBP has the lowest RMSE and MAE, implying that the model is able to generate highly accurate predictions with minimal error for this currency pair. An R^2 value 0.8841 demonstrates a satisfactory model fit, and though slightly lower than NZD/USD, it is still an excellent result, given the complexity of the currency market.

The strong performance of the Transformer model partly derives from its self-attention mechanism, which allows it to fully consider the influence of other points in time when predicting the exchange rate at any given moment.

In summary, the Transformer performs outstandingly across all four datasets, especially in NZD/USD predictions, where it achieves a very high level of accuracy as shown in Figure 3.

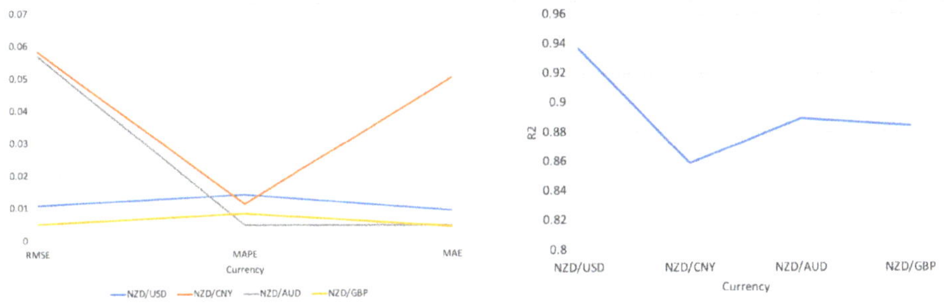

Figure 3. Visualization of the experimental results on Transformer.

3.2. Experimental Results of Informer

The second model we conducted in this experiment was the Informer, an advancement based on the Transformer framework. The prediction trend in Figure 4 is as follows through the training and prediction of four datasets.

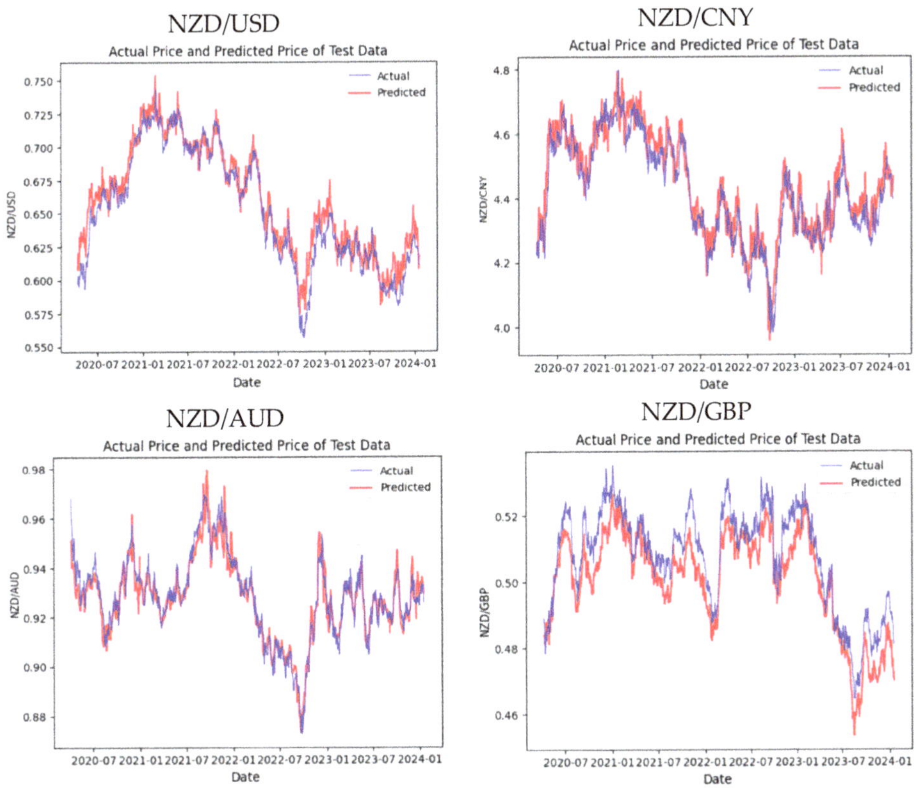

Figure 4. The predictive results of each dataset performed by using Informer.

From the prediction trend in Figure 5, the actual and predicted values of NZD/USD are roughly similar, especially at the peaks and troughs. However, between July 2022 and January 2023, there is a relatively large gap between the predicted and actual lines. As for NZD/CNY, the overall prediction for this currency pair also maintained synchronicity, but the deviation at the beginning of 2023 was more extensive than that of NZD/USD. Similar to NZD/USD and NZD/AUD, where the prediction curve of this currency pair closely matches the actual price curve most of the time. Likewise, in a number of intervals, the prediction failed to capture the rapid changes in the exact exchange rate. Slightly different from the trend results of the other three, the trend of NZD/GBP did not match as well as the others, but it also captured the trend of the exchange rate. Table 2 illustrates the results based on the four evaluation metrics.

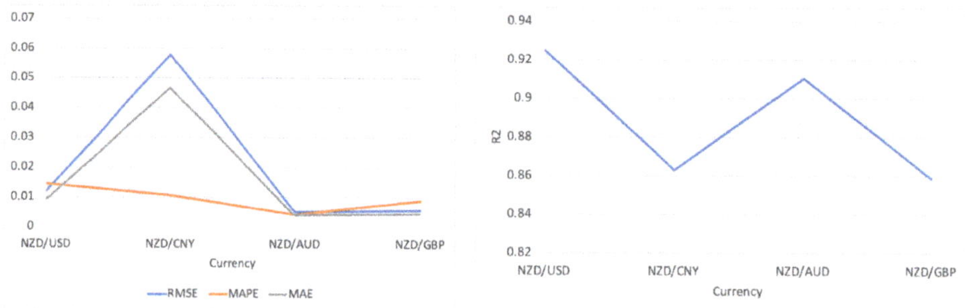

Figure 5. Visualization of the experimental results on Informer.

Table 2. The parameter settings of Transformer.

Parameters	Settings
input_window	7
batch_size	100
learning_rate	0.0005
epochs	150

In the NZD/USD results, the Informer model achieved a high level of precision, specifically reflected in the low RMSE value 0.012. At the same time, the low MAPE and MAE values 0.0144 and 0.0092, respectively, also demonstrate that the forecast errors are relatively minor. An R^2 value 0.925 further indicates that the Informer can broadly explain fluctuations in the exchange rate.

In the NZD/CNY results, despite the low MAPE value 0.0105, which explains a certain degree of accuracy, the higher RMSE and MAE values reveal the challenges faced by the Informer in predicting this currency pair. Nevertheless, an R^2 value exceeding 0.85 means that the Informer can still fit the data reasonably well despite the difficulties.

Regarding NZD/AUD and NZD/GBP, the Informer performed exceptionally well, especially in NZD/AUD, where the very low RMSE and MAE values reflect the superior performance of the Informer model in terms of prediction accuracy. The MAPE value is nearly zero, almost achieving a perfect prediction effect. This shows that the Informer can accurately predict the exchange rate movements of these two currency pairs, even in the face of fluctuations in exchange rates.

Overall, the Informer model demonstrates adaptability and accuracy under different market conditions in handling the exchange rate predictions of these four datasets. Particularly in predicting NZD/AUD and NZD/USD, it illustrates the advantages of being an improved model based on the Transformer. Although there are challenges in the NZD/CNY predictions, the model can still effectively capture and predict the dynamics of exchange rate changes.

3.3. Experimental Results of TFT

Our third trained model is the TFT, an enhancement of the Transformer model that specializes in processing time series data. Figure 6 exhibits the TFT's prediction trends for the four test sets.

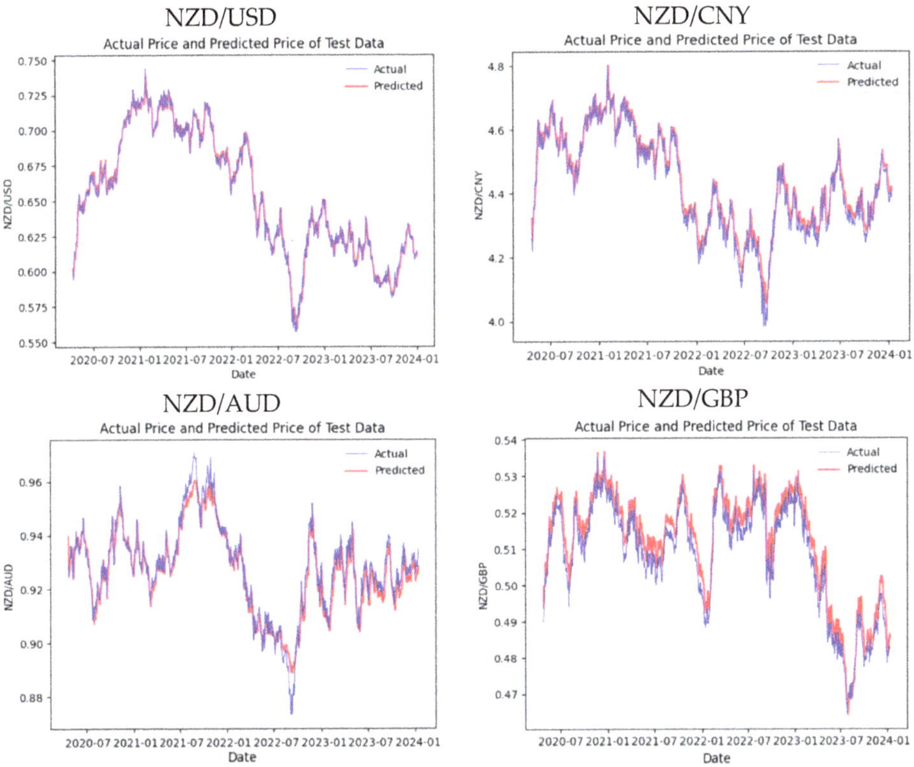

Figure 6. The predictive results of each dataset performed on TFT.

From the trend chart of NZD/USD, the prediction curve closely follows the actual price curve most of the time, demonstrating the solid predictive capability of the TFT model for this currency pair, particularly in adapting quickly during significant trend changes. As for the trend charts of the other three currency pairs, we observe the lag or deviation at critical turning points. Nevertheless, the TFT model generally follows the actual trends well. Table 3 shows the result by using evaluation metrics.

Table 3. The parameter settings of Informer.

Parameters	Settings
sequence_length	64
predict_length	5
batch_size	128
learning_rate	5×10^{-5}
epochs	60

The assessment results in Table 3 show that the predictions for NZD/USD are the best, with shallow RMSE, MAPE and MAE values 0.0045, 0.0055 and 0.0035, respectively, revealing that the predicted values are very close to the actual values. The high R^2 value additionally confirms the nearness between the predicted and actual trends of exchange rate fluctuations for this currency pair.

As for the results of NZD/CNY, though the MAPE remains at a low level 0.0056, a relatively higher RMSE suggests significant deviations between the predicted and actual values at specific time points. However, the high R^2 value 0.96 indicates that the TFT model can still capture most exchange rate changes.

In the predictions for NZD/AUD, even though the R^2 value is slightly lower than that of NZD/USD, the remarkably low errors indicate the high accuracy of the TFT on this test set.

Although NZD/GBP has the highest MAE among all the currency pairs at 0.0075, this does not mean that the overall performance of this model is poor. An R^2 value 0.9122 points out that the model successfully captures most of the dynamics of the pound's exchange rate changes, with a slight decrease in predictive accuracy, possibly due to the complexity of market fluctuations during specific periods.

The TFT model performs reasonably well across all four test sets, especially in predicting NZD/USD and NZD/AUD, showing high accuracy and reliability. Despite the drop in predictive precision for NZD/CNY and NZD/GBP, the R^2 values still demonstrate that the model's predictions are pretty reliable for these currency pairs as shown in Figure 7.

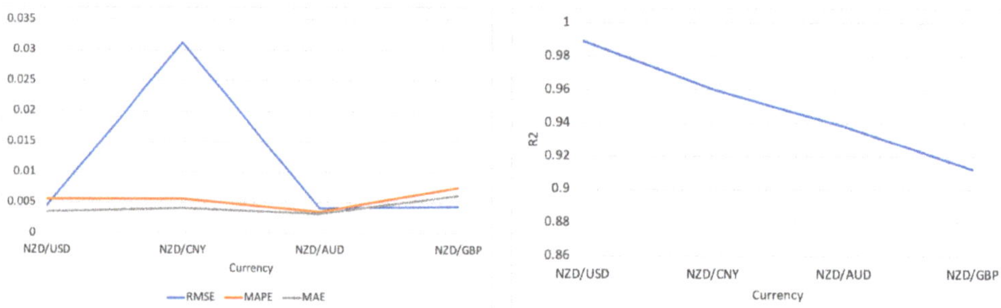

Figure 7. Visualization of the experimental results on TFT.

4. Analysis and Discussion

To compare the performance of these three models more thoroughly—Transformer, Informer, and TFT, we summarized the evaluation results of each model for the four test sets, taking the average for each evaluation criterion. The results are presented in Table 4.

Table 4. The parameters setting of TFT.

Parameters	Settings
learning_rate	0.001
hidden_size	32
attention_head_size	1
output_size	8
batch_size	128
epochs	150

In Table 5, it is evident that the Transformer model has relatively high RMSE and MAE values. Nevertheless, an R^2 value 0.8922 indicates a reasonable correlation between the predictions and actual values. Its explanatory power is slightly weaker compared to the other two models. As an improved version of the Transformer, the Informer has lower RMSE and MAE values in Table 6, at 0.0201 and 0.016, respectively, while its MAPE is 0.0095 and R^2 is 0.8893. This suggests that the Informer performs better than the original Transformer, especially when dealing with time series data with high volatility. Lastly, the TFT exhibits the best performance among all the models in Table 7, with an RMSE of only 0.0111, a MAPE 0.0055, an MAE 0.0043, and the highest R^2 value 0.9499. The TFT model integrates various methods for time series forecasting, including time attention mechanisms and interpretable features, enabling it to excel across all evaluation metrics in Table 8.

Table 5. The experimental results with four datasets using Transformer.

Currency	RMSE	MAPE	MAE	R^2
NZD/USD	0.011	0.0141	0.0092	0.9369
NZD/CNY	0.0585	0.0113	0.0502	0.8589
NZD/AUD	0.0571	0.0048	0.0046	0.8891
NZD/GBP	0.0051	0.0084	0.0042	0.8841

Table 6. The experimental results with four datasets by using Informer.

Currency	RMSE	MAPE	MAE	R^2
NZD/USD	0.011	0.0141	0.0092	0.9369
NZD/CNY	0.0585	0.0113	0.0502	0.8589
NZD/AUD	0.0571	0.0048	0.0046	0.8891
NZD/GBP	0.0051	0.0084	0.0042	0.8841

Table 7. The TFT experiment results with four datasets.

Currency	RMSE	MAPE	MAE	R^2
NZD/USD	0.0045	0.0055	0.0035	0.9892
NZD/CNY	0.0312	0.0056	0.0041	0.96
NZD/AUD	0.0041	0.0035	0.0032	0.9381
NZD/GBP	0.0044	0.0075	0.0062	0.9122

Table 8. The evaluation results of each model based on the test set.

Model	RMSE	MAPE	MAE	R^2
Transformer	0.0329	0.0097	0.0171	0.8922
Informer	0.0201	0.0095	0.016	0.8893
TFT	0.0111	0.0055	0.0043	0.9499

As shown in Figure 8, these results imply that the TFT performs best in handling the currency exchange rate prediction, possibly because it was designed to capture complex patterns in time series. The Informer and Transformer also perform well but cannot achieve outstanding results like the TFT for this specific task. The differences may derive from the special treatment of the time dimension in its model architecture and its ability to capture and integrate various factors affecting the predictive variables.

Additionally, from the perspective of training time and model convergence speed, the Informer is able to reach stable and accurate predictions within a relatively few 60 epochs, which might make it more efficient than the traditional Transformer and the TFT. However, by considering the performance after model training, the TFT has demonstrated the highest R^2 value in currency exchange rate predictions. Although the TFT might require a more complex training process, its return on investment in model performance is optimal.

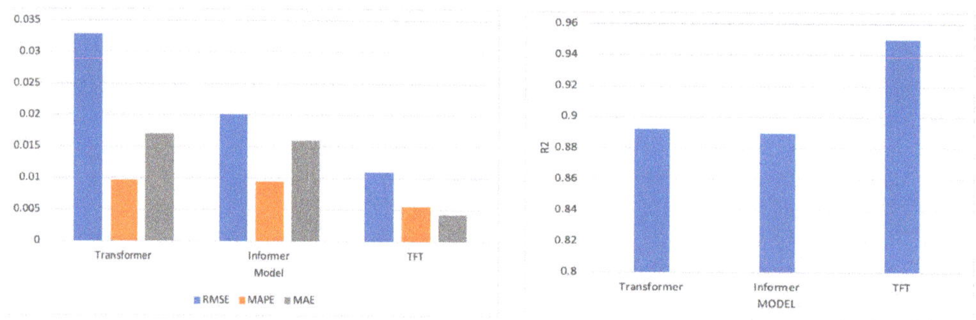

Figure 8. The visualization result of the three models' performance.

5. Conclusions

This paper aims to analyze and discuss the accuracy and performance of models through exchange rate predictions. This paper makes use of three models: Transformer and its advanced versions, Informer and TFT. We collected four exchange rate datasets, namely, NZD/USD, NZD/CNY, NZD/GBP and NZD/AUD, and applied them to the three models for training and validation. Our experiments were conducted on the Google Colab platform, four evaluation criteria were utilized to analyze and compare the performance of the three models.

All three models achieved satisfactory prediction effects on the four datasets. However, comparisons indicated that the TFT model offered the best performance in exchange rate prediction, especially regarding accuracy and capturing trends in data changes. The Informer balanced efficiency and accuracy, demonstrating excellent predictive capabilities in fewer epochs. This is due to its sparse attention mechanism, which reduces computational complexity. Among the three models, the Transformer performed the least ideally, with relatively higher RMSE and MAE values and the lowest R^2 value.

The limitations of this paper mainly fall into three parts. Firstly, the variables selected for this project are limited, only including primary exchange rate data. However, exchange rate trends are influenced by other complex factors, such as national policies, inflation rates, and investor psychological expectations. Thus, the lack of comprehensive feature selection will inevitably lead to unavoidable errors in prediction. Based on this, it is possible to consider incorporating more factors that affect exchange rates in the data selection process. Secondly, due to limited time, each model's selection of parameters and functions was primarily based on relevant literature and materials, which may introduce subjectivity and randomness. Therefore, further research and experimentation are needed to select the optimal parameters. Thirdly, the experiments in this paper are all based on the Transformer model's framework. It is vital to conduct experimental comparisons with other cutting-edge models to comprehensively analyze and determine the best model for predicting exchange rates.

Although this paper has made great progress in exchange rate prediction, numerous shortages and issues still require further investigation. Therefore, our future research work will be conducted in the following aspects. To enhance the accuracy of our models in predicting exchange rates, it is necessary to include more economic indicators and other relevant factors influencing exchange rates in the data collection process. Hence, further research work and experimental validation are required to optimize model parameters. In addition, we plan to expand the experimental data by using currencies from other representative countries as benchmarks for exchange rate prediction. We will also explore and compare more recent models to further enhance the effectiveness and accuracy of exchange rate forecasting, thereby providing valuable reference recommendations for the financial markets.

Author Contributions: Conceptualization, L.Z.; methodology, L.Z.; software, L.Z.; validation, L.Z.; formal analysis, L.Z.; investigation, L.Z.; resources, L.Z. and W.Q.Y.; data collection, L.Z.; writing—original draft preparation, L.Z.; writing—review and editing, L.Z.; supervision, W.Q.Y.; project administration W.Q.Y. All authors have read and agreed to the published version of the manuscript.

Funding: This research project has no external funding.

Data Availability Statement: Data are contained within the article.

Conflicts of Interest: The authors declare no conflicts of interest.

References

Bi, Jiarui, Zengliang Zhu, and Qinglong Meng. 2021. Transformer in computer vision. Paper presented at 2021 IEEE International Conference on Computer Science, Electronic Information Engineering and Intelligent Control Technology (CEI), Fuzhou, China, September 24–26.

Fayer, Geane, Larissa Lima, Felix Miranda, Jussara Santos, Renan Campos, Vinícius Bignoto, Marcel Andrade, Marconi Moraes, Celso Ribeiro, Priscila Capriles, and et al. 2023. A temporal fusion transformer deep learning model for long-term streamflow forecasting: A case study in the funil reservoir. *Southeast Brazil. Knowledge-Based Engineering and Sciences* 4: 73–88.

Gong, Mingju, Yin Zhao, Jiawang Sun, Cuitian Han, Guannan Sun, and Bo Yan. 2022. Load forecasting of district heating system based on Informer. *Energy* 253: 124179. [CrossRef]

Han, Kai, Yunhe Wang, Hanting Chen, Xinghao Chen, Jianyuan Guo, Zhenhua Liu, Yehui Tang, An Xiao, Chunjing Xu, Yixing Xu, and et al. 2022. A survey on vision transformer. *IEEE Transactions on Pattern Analysis and Machine Intelligence* 45: 87–110. [CrossRef] [PubMed]

Hu, Zexin, Yiqi Zhao, and Matloob Khushi. 2021. A survey of forex and stock price prediction using deep learning. *Applied System Innovation* 4: 9. [CrossRef]

Khashei, Mehdi, and Mehdi Bijari. 2011. A novel hybridization of artificial neural networks and ARIMA models for time series forecasting. *Applied Soft Computing* 11: 2664–75. [CrossRef]

Lai, Guokun, Wei-Cheng Chang, Yiming Yang, and Hanxiao Liu. 2018. Modeling long-and short-term temporal patterns with deep neural networks. Paper presented at 41st International ACM SIGIR Conference on Research & Development in Information Retrieval, Ann Arbor, MI, USA, July 8–12; pp. 95–104.

Lara-Benítez, Pedro, Luis Gallego-Ledesma, Manuel Carranza-García, and José M. Luna-Romera. 2021. Evaluation of the transformer architecture for univariate time series forecasting. Paper presented at 19th Conference of the Spanish Association for Artificial Intelligence, CAEPIA 2020/2021, Málaga, Spain, September 22–24.

Li, Shuai, Wanqing Li, Chris Cook, Ce Zhu, and Yanbo Gao. 2018. Independently recurrent neural network (indrnn): Building a longer and deeper RNN. Paper presented at IEEE Conference on Computer Vision and Pattern Recognition, Salt Lake City, UT, USA, June 18–22.

Lim, Bryan, Sercan Ö. Arık, Nicolas Loeff, and Tomas Pfister. 2021. Temporal fusion transformers for interpretable multi-horizon time series forecasting. *International Journal of Forecasting* 37: 1748–64. [CrossRef]

Niu, Hongli, and Lin Zhang. 2017. Nonlinear multiscale entropy and recurrence quantification analysis of foreign exchange markets efficiency. *Entropy* 20: 17. [CrossRef] [PubMed]

Pirani, Muskaan, Paurav Thakkar, Pranay Jivrani, Mohammed Husain Bohara, and Dweepna Garg. 2022. A comparative analysis of ARIMA, GRU, LSTM and BiLSTM on financial time series forecasting. Paper presented at IEEE International Conference on Distributed Computing and Electrical Circuits and Electronics (ICDCECE), Ballari, India, April 23–24.

Pradeepkumar, Dadabada, and Vadlamani Ravi. 2018. Soft computing hybrids for FOREX rate prediction: A comprehensive review. *Computers & Operations Research* 99: 262–84.

Rout, Ajit Kumar, Pradiptaishore Kishore Dash, Rajashree Dash, and Ranjeeta Bisoi. 2017. Forecasting financial time series using a low complexity recurrent neural network and evolutionary learning approach. *Journal of King Saud University-Computer and Information Sciences* 29: 536–52. [CrossRef]

Sridhar, Sashank, and Sowmya Sanagavarapu. 2021. Multi-head self-attention transformer for dogecoin price prediction. Paper presented at International Conference on Human System Interaction (HSI), Gdańsk, Poland, July 8–10.

Sun, Yuzhen, Lu Hou, Zhengquan Lv, and Daogang Peng. 2022. Informer-based intrusion detection method for network attack of integrated energy system. *IEEE Journal of Radio Frequency Identification* 6: 748–52. [CrossRef]

Tay, Yi, Mostafa Dehghani, Dara Bahri, and Donald Metzler. 2022. Efficient transformers: A survey. *ACM Computing Surveys* 55: 1–28. [CrossRef]

Vaswani, Ashish, Noam Shazeer, Niki Parmar, Jakob Uszkoreit, Llion Jones, Aidan N. Gomez, Łukasz Kaiser, and Illia Polosukhin. 2017. Attention is all you need. Paper presented at Advances in Neural Information Processing Systems 30., Long Beach, CA, USA, December 4–9.

Wang, Xixuan, Dechang Pi, Xiangyan Zhang, Hao Liu, and Chang Guo. 2022. Variational transformer-based anomaly detection approach for multivariate time series. *Measurement* 191: 110791. [CrossRef]

Wen, Qingsong, Tian Zhou, Chaoli Zhang, Weiqi Chen, Ziqing Ma, Junchi Yan, and Liang Sun. 2023. Transformers in time series: A survey. Paper presented at Thirty-Second International Joint Conference on Artificial Intelligence, Macao, China, August 19–25; pp. 6778–86.

Wu, Haixu, Jiehui Xu, Jianmin Wang, and Mingsheng Long. 2021. Autoformer: Decomposition transformers with auto-correlation for long-term series forecasting. *Advances in Neural Information Processing Systems* 34: 22419–30.

Xu, Yang, Liyan Han, Li Wan, and Libo Yin. 2019. Dynamic link between oil prices and exchange rates: A non-linear approach. *Energy Economics* 84: 104488. [CrossRef]

Yamak, Peter T., Li Yujian, and Pius K. Gadosey. 2019. A comparison between arima, lstm, and GRU for time series forecasting. Paper presented at International Conference on Algorithms, Computing and Artificial Intelligence, Sanya, China, December 20–22.

Yıldıran, Cenk Ufuk, and Abdurrahman Fettahoğlu. 2017. Forecasting USDTRY rate by ARIMA method. *Cogent Economics & Finance* 5: 1335968.

Zhang, Hao, Yajie Zou, Xiaoxue Yang, and Hang Yang. 2022. A temporal fusion transformer for short-term freeway traffic speed multistep prediction. *Neurocomputing* 500: 329–40. [CrossRef]

Zhou, Haoyi, Shanghang Zhang, Jieqi Peng, Shuai Zhang, Jianxin Li, Hui Xiong, and Wancai Zhang. 2021. Informer: Beyond efficient transformer for long sequence time-series forecasting. Paper presented at AAAI Conference on Artificial Intelligence, Virtually, February 2–9.

Journal of
Risk and Financial Management

MDPI

Article

Does ICT Investment Affect Market Share and Customer Acquisition Cost? A Comparative Analysis of Domestic and Foreign Banks Operating in India

Gulam Goush Ansari and Rajorshi Sen Gupta *

Department of Economics and Finance, BITS Pilani, K K Birla Goa Campus, Zuarinagar 403726, India; p20200019@goa.bits-pilani.ac.in
* Correspondence: rajorshis@goa.bits-pilani.ac.in

Abstract: Competitive banks aggressively invest in information and communication technologies (ICT) to enhance their market share and reduce Customer Acquisition Costs (CAC). This study examines the impact of *cumulative stock* of ICT investment on (a) deposit and loan market share and (b) CAC of banks operating in India. The analysis uses a longitudinal dataset of 84 domestic and 70 foreign banks from 2000 to 2020, employing a two-step system Generalized Method of Moment (GMM). It is found that ICT investment adversely affects the market share of domestic banks, indicating a need for these banks to strategically invest more in CAC. Conversely, foreign banks are able to increase their market share through ICT investment and reduced CAC, thereby demonstrating greater efficiency in utilizing ICT. The study underscores the strategic importance of cumulative stock of ICT investment for banks. Nonetheless, it is emphasized that ICT investment must be complemented with innovative marketing strategies to enhance customer experience, reduce CAC, and increase market share. Overall, while foreign banks are able to leverage ICT to boost efficiency, domestic banks must leverage ICT to implement targeted marketing strategies and strive to enhance their customer service.

Keywords: ICT investment; deposit and loan market share; banks; customer acquisition cost

1. Introduction

In the context of emerging economies, competitive interaction between domestic and foreign banks can have important ramifications. Overall, such competition is expected to enhance the efficiency of the banks in terms of providing financial services. Nevertheless, foreign banks might also engage in poaching the relatively safe borrowers and depositors away from domestic banks (Giannetti and Ongena 2012). Thus, the foreign banks would essentially be competing with the domestic banks in terms of deposit and loan market shares. It is expected that the entry of foreign banks would lead to increased competition in a given market. This would create opportunities and incentives for the domestic banks to introduce cost efficiency. Such cost reduction might occur through the assimilation of superior banking technologies and practices of the foreign banks (Claessens et al. 2001).

It is also well known that the banking sector in emerging markets is characterized by large asymmetric information (Dell'Ariccia 2001). In such markets, information and communication technology (ICT) is expected to play an instrumental role, both for domestic and foreign banks, in the game of acquiring market share. Technological changes have indeed led to enhanced competition in the banking sector.

In an emerging economy like India, the knowledge-intensive service sector plays a crucial role. Not surprisingly, ICT has become indispensable for the service sector. As a general-purpose technology, it complements innovative activities and augments firms' productive capacity. The Internet revolution and Industry 4.0 regime have made ICT indispensable for the growth of the financial services sector. Such events have facilitated unprecedented innovations in financial services. Consequently, the financial services sector has emerged as one of the most intensive users of ICT (Scott et al. 2017). Essentially, ICT leads to *information acquisition*, which has important practical implications for the banking sector (Arabyat and Aziz 2022).

In recent years, ICT has brought about a paradigm shift in banking services. It determines the effectiveness of a bank's core banking system. Unlike brick-and-mortar banking, technology-enabled banking follows a multi-channel approach, such as internet banking, automated teller machines (ATM), and mobile banking. This transformation has led the world into a different spectrum of banking by making modern banking time- and place-independent. Empowered with ICT, banks are technically able to collect, process, analyze, and optimally use information obtained from their customers to design customized products and services for them. For instance, customized loans, pre-approved credit and debit cards, incentive offers, and privileges (e.g., airport lounge access, flight vouchers, and exclusive memberships) are provided on the basis of the observable credit history of the customers. Banks are able to verify the credentials of their customers by using technology-enabled electronic know-your-customer (KYC) systems. Much of the erstwhile labor-intensive, time-consuming operations are being automated. All of these factors have supposedly led to a favorable impact on the cost of providing banking services. In order to further enrich the customer experience, banks have made significant advances in Artificial Intelligence (AI), machine learning, business analytics, cloud computing, and blockchain technology. The diffusion of these technologies in banking has enabled round-the-clock access to core banking services.

Banks have implemented technology to provide a one-stop solution for most of the customer needs. The radical transformation in banking has eliminated the need to visit banks to avail themselves of relevant services. Customers can open accounts from their homes, apply for digital loans in real-time, and make cardless withdrawals from multiple digital platforms. Digital transformation has helped banks build, sustain, and expand customer relationships, leading to a persistent market share. Banks today resort to user-friendly interfaces like websites, mobile interfaces, and social media to render many services. Unified Payment Interface (UPI), banking applications, contactless lending platforms, WhatsApp banking, voice know-your-customer (VKYC), and other technology-enabled services have added new dimensions to modern banking. For customers' convenience, Indian banks have made their websites available in multiple languages. Indian banks incorporated UPI Lite in January 2022, following the Reserve Bank of India's (RBI) offline transaction framework. This interface uses Near-Field Communication (NFC) technology to facilitate real-time small-value transactions. The interface also ensures successful payments irrespective of low or no Internet connectivity. UPI thus accounts for the largest share of transactions in terms of volume in India. The success of UPI Lite has paved the way for RBI to launch UPI Lite X, Tap & Pay, and conversational payment interfaces in 2023. These innovations are further expected to enable banks to render hassle-free services to the customers.

Notwithstanding such ICT innovations being introduced, very little is known about the relevance of ICT on market shares and customer acquisition efforts of competing banks operating in emerging markets. This paper seeks to address such important, understudied issues in the context of domestic and foreign banks operating in India.

There is a strand of the literature that emphasizes the impact of ICT on financial indicators, especially profitability, return on assets (ROA), and return on equity (ROE) (Ghose and Maji 2022; Sharma 2023). Nonetheless, the extant studies indicate that the effect of ICT investment on the profitability of banks is, at best, equivocal. For instance, some studies have found a *positive* impact of ICT on a bank's profitability, efficiency, and productivity (Ghose and Maji 2022). Yet another branch of the literature demonstrated an *ambiguous* effect of ICT on the performance indicators of Indian banks (Sharma 2023). Such inconsistent and mixed findings preclude a clear understanding of the impact of ICT on bank performance as measured by the usual financial indicators. Given such an inconclusive verdict on the impact of ICT on the typical financial metrics of banks, this paper contributes to the literature along the following four aspects.

First, it is evident that the outcome of ICT investment is not likely to be instantaneous (Beccalli 2007; Hernando and Nieto 2007; Scott et al. 2017). The authors have postulated that the benefits of ICT investment accrue over an extended period. To realize positive outcomes, it becomes imperative for banks to invest consistently in the latest technologies. Consequently, it is imperative to measure the effect of *cumulative* ICT investment on appropriately chosen metrics of bank performance. Cumulative ICT investment is a bank's total expenditure over a specific period to acquire and maintain ICT assets and capabilities. Consistent investment in ICT equips a bank with a resilient technological infrastructure. It facilitates cost minimization and improves operational efficiency. The literature lacks empirical studies examining the impact of cumulative ICT investment on the performance of banks in India. This study contributes to the literature by examining the possible link between cumulative ICT investment, bank market share, and customer acquisition cost (CAC).

Second, the impact of ICT has been analyzed mostly within the context of profitability and ROA and ROE metrics. The volume of deposits and loans reflects a bank's efficiency in attracting deposits and utilizing loanable funds to produce additional profits (Baker et al. 2023; Nguyen et al. 2021). This process improves its financial position. A bank's market share also indicates its reputation and trustworthiness among retail customers and firms. For this reason, the market share of deposits and loans are important indicators of bank performance and resilience.

It is important to justify the *economic rationale* behind focusing on market share in this study. Deposit market share (DMS) is defined as the ratio of each bank's deposits to total deposits of all banks in a given year. Similarly, loan market share (LMS) is defined as the ratio of each bank's loans to the total loans of all banks in a given year. Attracting deposits is one of the most important goals and a competitive tool for a bank. Enhanced market share is expected to lead to higher market power. There is a strong association between market share and profitability indices. Thus, the second novelty of this study comes from the analysis of how cumulative ICT investment affects alternative performance metrics, specifically market share and CAC.

Third, this study performs a comparative examination of how ICT investment affects the performance of domestic and foreign banks operating in an emerging market like India. The rationale for this approach stems from the fundamental premises of the *home field advantage hypothesis* vis-à-vis the *global advantage hypothesis*. Berger et al. (2000) proposed these hypotheses while examining the effect of foreign ownership on bank performance. According to the home field advantage hypothesis, domestic banks tend to demonstrate greater efficiency in providing financial services. Foreign banks would have to incur higher costs of rendering financial services due to cross-border disadvantages emanating from distance, language, and cultural barriers. In contrast, the global advantage hypothesis holds that foreign banks tend to possess higher efficiency. Superior managerial skills and the use of advanced technologies would give a comparative advantage to the foreign banks. Consequently, foreign banks might be able to perform better in comparison to domestic banks. The extant literature supports both of these competing theories (Berger et al. 2000; Lensink and Naaborg 2007). In the context of domestic and foreign banks operating in India, the applicability of these theories has not been tested. This is the third differentiator of the current paper.

Fourth, unlike most of the extant literature, the analysis is conducted for the years 2000–2020. It is important to note that prior to 2000, the level of ICT investment in the banking sector was quite low. Although automation of some of the banking activities had started during the 1990s, even computerization of basic banking operations did not occur until the end of the decade. Essentially, these two decades capture the most important phases of ICT evolution in the Indian banking sector. The major technological and policy initiatives that occurred during this period are Internet banking (2000), the IT Act (2000), and the launch of centralized payment systems (CPS) in 2004–2005. These events were followed by the promotion of mobile banking (2011) and the launch of UPI (2016). Such significant events have altered the dynamics of banking in India. Hence, the 2000–2020 time period helps us to capture the learning and adjustment effects associated with the adoption of new technologies in emerging markets. Moreover, the Indian economy started to liberalize during 1991–1992. Due to liberalized Foreign Direct Investment (FDI) norms, entry of foreign banks became relatively easier during the late 1990s. Thus, the chosen time period, 2000–2020, also enables us to analyze the competition between the domestic and foreign banks.

Based on the gaps identified in the extant literature, there are three specific research questions of this study:

1. What has been the impact of ICT investment on the deposit and loan market share of banks operating in India?
2. What is the effect of ICT investment on Customer Acquisition Costs of banks operating in India?
3. Is there any differential impact of ICT investment on the market share and Customer Acquisition Costs of domestic and foreign banks?

This paper is structured as follows. Section 2 builds a theoretical framework, followed by a review of the literature and hypotheses formulation in Section 3. The methodology adopted in the study is discussed in Section 4. Econometric results are reported in Section 5, followed by a discussion of major findings in Section 6. Section 7 provides the managerial implications and Section 8 concludes.

2. Conceptual Framework

The relationship between ICT investment and market share of banks is conceptualized as a sequential process described below.

Stage 1: Both domestic and foreign banks invest in ICT. Such investment increases the *stock* of ICT capital of each of the banks.

Stage 2: The *stock* of ICT increases the efficiency of banking operations by reducing transaction costs for both customers and bank employees.

Stage 3: Notwithstanding the investment in ICT, only a subset of the banks can provide improved services to their customers. Such improved services may be attributed to various non-ICT factors (like foreign or domestic bank status, interest rates, the governance of banks).

Stage 4: Both existing and new customers would respond favorably to the signals provided by their preferred banks. This, in turn, would have a favorable impact on market shares of a subset of banks. The other set of banks, whose customer service has not improved, would experience an adverse impact on their market share.

Stage 5: As a response to declining market share, a subset of banks would optimally respond by increasing their marketing and Customer Acquisition Costs. In contrast, the other subset of banks with increasing market share would have the ability to reduce marketing and Customer Acquisition Costs.

With the conceptual background described above, the testable hypotheses of this study are formulated as follows.

3. Literature Review and Hypotheses Formulation

In the context of this paper, a survey of prior studies pertaining to the relevance of ICT on banks and their customers is warranted. These are summarized as follows.

3.1. Impact of ICT on Banks

The usage of ICT helps to improve competitive advantage by increasing the customer base (Kim and Davidson 2004). Technology-intensive banks experience larger economies of scale (DeYoung 2005), which gives them a cost advantage. According to Chen (2020),

Claessens et al. (2001), DeYoung (2001), and DeYoung (2005), banks can shift their cost advantage to customers by either lowering interest on loans or increasing deposit interest. The authors have identified the effectiveness of this approach in attracting customers without affecting bank earnings. ICT has made banking operations more cost-efficient and enabled banks to maintain stability in their financial performance (DeYoung et al. 2007; Ho and Mallick 2010). Thus, investment in ICT has become a strategic necessity and an operational requirement for banks (Beccalli 2007; DeYoung et al. 2007; Ho and Mallick 2010).

Banking has become increasingly agile, secure, and convenient, fostering more robust customer relationships as a result of its inclination towards technology (Banker and Kauffman 1988; DeYoung et al. 2007). Customers demonstrate an increased willingness to purchase additional deposit services (DeYoung et al. 2007). Banks using technology also fare better in advancing loans (Kim and Davidson 2004; Sheng 2021). Technology assists banks in monitoring borrowers' credit history, thereby reducing *information asymmetry*. The digital lending channel quickens loan advancement, lowers lending rates, and increases bank lending.

Market share plays an important role in determining a bank's profit. Banks' core functions of deposit acceptance and lending are significantly affected by their market share. Banks are able to influence their market share through the acquisition and retention of customers. In one of the earlier studies, authors have identified the strategic contribution of ICT. By investing in ATM, banks were found to improve the deposit market share of their branches (Banker and Kauffman 1988). Arabyat and Aziz (2022) analyzed how profits are affected by IT investment in the context of Jordanian banks. They found that IT investment affected the market share of Jordanian banks, which moved the banking system away from an efficient equilibrium.

3.2. *Impact of ICT on Customers*

ICT has also favorably affected bank customers in various tangible ways. For instance, by accessing ATMs, customers are able to reduce the opportunity costs of standing in long queues. Most of the banking services can now be conducted by using a computer or smartphone. This is particularly important for business owners whose opportunity cost of time of visiting a bank used to be quite high. In a competitive environment, banks are aggressively using ICT to offer pre-approved, instant loans to businesses. Such innovative products and services are expected to affect businesses in a favorable way. This, in turn, is expected to have important effects on the market shares of domestic and foreign banks operating in India.

3.3. *Hypotheses of the Study*

3.3.1. Foreign vs. Domestic Banks

In a competitive market, banks ought to differentiate themselves from their peers in terms of service provision. Therefore, they need to *continuously* innovate in terms of the service they provide. In other words, competition fosters financial innovation among banks to attract new and retain existing customers. In the context of banking services, it may be argued that a sustained ICT investment can foster the introduction of innovative products and services. ICT has proved to be an important tool to introduce such innovations. For instance, ICT has facilitated the development of electronic banking services. Market share has also been recognized as the cause of innovation and ICT investment by banks. The application of ICT tools by banks is likely to improve their banking services.

Nevertheless, the relationship between ICT and the market share of banks need not be straightforward. It is possible that in spite of investing in ICT, some banks do not experience any improvement or even reduction in their market share. This is plausible when such banks consistently fail to enhance their services, which dissuades customers away from them. Which of the above theories holds well in the context of the banks operating in India? This is an empirical question that is addressed in this paper.

Prashad (2020) found evidence of regulatory arbitrage, which explains the presence of foreign banks in India. Foreign banks operating in India were among the early adopters of technology (Sensarma 2006). These banks introduced modern banking technologies and innovative banking practices in India. Foreign banks are also highly specialized in offering banking products like derivatives, advisory services, and trade finance. Hence, technological leadership and product innovation would have provided a long-term competitive advantage to the foreign banks. In contrast, the old private and public sector banks emerged as late bloomers in technology adoption (Rishi and Saxena 2004). The technological gap has been instrumental in augmenting the operational efficiency of foreign banks. Moreover, it is the quality of banking services that determines the market share of domestic and foreign banks. Although both the categories of banks would have invested in ICT, ceteris paribus, it is the quality and persistence of customer service that would ultimately determine their market shares. This is one important aspect where the foreign banks seem to have fared better in comparison to the domestic banks. Thus, it is expected that foreign banks would experience a favorable impact of ICT on their market share. This argument leads us to the following hypotheses.

H1a: *Cumulative ICT investment is expected to have an adverse impact on the deposit and loan market share of the domestic banks.*

H1b: *Cumulative ICT investment is likely to have a favorable impact on the deposit and loan market share of foreign banks.*

3.3.2. ICT and Customer Acquisition Cost

CAC is a key metric of advertising and marketing strategies adopted by the banks. Targeted marketing by the banks can attract more customers at lower costs, which boosts their competitiveness (Cao and Gruca 2005). ICT has given a stimulus to banks' customer outreach programs through various digital platforms. Integrating technology into banking operations is more likely to make banks efficient in customer acquisition. For instance, DeYoung (2001) examined the financial performance of "Internet banks" in the US. He found that by adopting Internet banking, it is possible to address the problem of high marketing costs for banks. Subsequent studies by Hernando and Nieto (2007) and Mithas et al. (2012) also support this finding. Modern banking is, therefore, expected to be more cost-efficient in acquiring new customers than traditional brick-and-mortar banking. Banks' technology-enabled systems have effectively automated various facets of customer acquisition. CRM (customer relationship management) systems, for instance, through emails and phone calls, automate the tracking of customer interactions. This process has a crucial implication for targeted marketing by banks, consequently reducing unnecessary marketing expenses. Banks' multi-channel approach offers a multitude of banking services that are time- and place-independent. This approach becomes an effective conduit for more robust marketing. Mithas et al. (2012) observed that using multiple channels allows banks to connect to a more extensive customer base at a lower cost.

Technological advancements and product and process innovations are expected to empower foreign banks to expand their customer base in India. Foreign banks typically enter host market(s) with enhanced operational competencies and superior customer services. Such technological advantages and differentiated services are likely to lead to cost-effective customer acquisition for foreign banks. Domestic banks, on the other hand, due to slower technology diffusion may exhibit highly inefficient customer acquisition practices. Thus, the following hypotheses are formulated.

H2a: *The domestic banks are not able to enhance their market share through cumulative ICT investment. Consequently, the domestic banks would strategically respond to such reduced market share by increasing their Customer Acquisition Costs.*

H2b: *Cumulative ICT investment will lead to enhanced market share of foreign banks. Consequently, the foreign banks are expected to have reduced Customer Acquisition Costs.*

To address the issue of omitted variable bias, it is important to control for the effect of bank-specific factors like age, size, interest on loans, interest on deposits, and deposits. This would allow us to analyze the impact of such non-ICT factors that might also affect the deposit and advance market share of a bank.

3.3.3. Bank Size

The log of total assets is taken as a proxy for bank size in the literature (Świtała et al. 2020; Ünvan and Yakubu 2020). The relatively large-sized banks would be able to undertake technological advancements to minimize operating costs and render better services. Larger banks may offer diversified services to customers that can attract a larger customer base and enhance market share (Kim and Davidson 2004; Ünvan and Yakubu 2020). Bank size also influences its efficiency in mobilizing loanable funds. Larger banks are willing to endure the potential risks associated with lending. Hence, large banks demonstrate higher ability to increase lending (Sheng 2021; Świtała et al. 2020). Customers might also consider governance related factors while determining with which bank they would prefer to conduct their financial transactions. In the context of India, customers seem to prefer the relatively larger (and older) banks that are perceived to have better governance mechanisms in comparison to the mid-sized and smaller banks.

The size of operations is an important determinant of interest margin (Maudos and de Guevara 2004). It may be argued that ICT makes legacy technologies obsolete. This would increase the turnover and market share of the larger banks, who are typically the first movers in terms of adopting such technologies. Consequently, the larger banks would be able to charge lower interest rates. Thus, the following is hypothesized:

H3: *The larger banks are expected to have more loanable funds and, hence, have a greater ability to offer lower interest rates. Moreover, in comparison to smaller banks, large-size banks are expected to have a greater ability to support a continuous increase in the latest ICT. Thus, the size of a bank is expected to have a favorable impact on deposit and loan market share. This is applicable to both domestic and foreign banks.*

3.3.4. Bank Age

The age of a bank reflects its years of operation since its inception. The effect of the age of a bank on its market share can be understood in terms of two opposing forces. The relatively older banks would have the benefit of the trust of the customers that is being accumulated over longer years of operation. The number of years the bank has rendered services determines the strength of its customer relationship. The older banks would also exhibit strong Arrow's "learning by doing" effect and, hence, enjoy more market power over the younger banks. This significantly impacts a bank's brand image and reputation. Older banks have more expertise that can facilitate innovation, the formulation of marketing strategies, and the evaluation of customer needs. All of these endeavors are likely to build a loyal customer base for banks. Hence, the conventional wisdom goes that banks already operating successfully are less likely to lose their incumbent customers (Banker and Kauffman 1988; Berger and Dick 2007). This would affect their market share in a favorable way.

In contrast, it may also be argued that in comparison to the order banks, the relatively newer banks would have a higher propensity to invest in ICT. Anecdotally, the older banks have demonstrated inertia in terms of investing in the latest digital technologies. Such banks are stuck with legacy systems which are outdated and inefficient. The older banks may face organizational resistance to risky projects (Alshwayat et al. 2023). Younger banks may demonstrate their willingness to take risks for an aggressive market share expansion. Such banks are also more receptive to new ideas and more agile in adopting new technology (Malhotra and Singh 2007). By leveraging the new-age ICT, the newer banks are expected to increase their market share. Thus, it is essential to consider the potential non-linear relationship between these two variables. Therefore, the following is hypothesized:

H4: *There is an ambiguous relationship between age and market share of the domestic and foreign banks.*

3.3.5. Deposits

A large volume of deposits can significantly impact a bank's lending capacity and, therefore, its loan market share (Yitayaw 2021). A bank with a higher deposit base would be able to meet the credit requirements of individuals and firms. The volume of deposits of a bank is a key indicator of its financial stability and reliability. Thus, the following is hypothesized:

H5: *The volume of deposits is expected to have a favorable impact on the loan market share of domestic and foreign banks.*

3.3.6. Interest on Deposits

Interest-on-deposits banks play a crucial role in determining the extent of deposit mobilization. A significant motivation for individuals to deposit their funds with banks emanates from the attractive interest offered by the banks. When banks provide higher interest rates, the opportunity cost of holding money would increase. Consequently, higher interest rates incentivize individuals to deposit more with banks.

Additionally, a bank can differentiate itself from others by offering various deposit products with varying interest rates. This differentiation strategy allows the bank to cater to a broader range of customers. In essence, interest on deposits empowers banks to gain a competitive advantage by acquiring and retaining customers. Consequently, the following is hypothesized:

H6: *An increase in interest on deposits is expected to have a favorable impact on the deposit market share of domestic and foreign banks.*

3.3.7. Interest on Loans

Banks play an instrumental role in financial deepening through deposit mobilization and supplying loanable funds. Providing credit on flexible terms and competitive interest will enhance customer satisfaction. Loan interest should neither be too low nor too high (Yitayaw 2021). A low interest rate undoubtedly attracts borrowers, but at the cost of the bank's financial stability. On the other hand, high interest negatively affects the public's credit demand (Yitayaw 2021). Hence, a competitive interest rate is pivotal for banks to gain competitive advantage, manage risk, and foster lending relationships. Therefore, the following is hypothesized:

H7: *An increase in interest on loans is expected to have an unfavorable impact on the loan market share of domestic banks and foreign banks.*

3.3.8. Public vs. Private Ownership

During the post-1991 economic liberalization phase of the Indian economy, several important initiatives were undertaken to make the banking sector more competitive and efficient. Such liberalization led to the operational efficiency of the Indian banking system, largely comprising of the public banks (Bhattacharyya et al. 1997; Patra et al. 2023; Sathye 2003). Historically, the public sector banks have dominated the industry (Sensarma 2006). The public sector banks in India had already established a strong foothold in deposits and loan market share. Thus, it is plausible that the customers would *perceive* the public banks to be more trustworthy than the private banks. They would try to maintain their business with the more familiar, government-backed public banks instead of the private banks. Nonetheless, post liberalization, the competition between public and private banks started to intensify. The private banks honed their operational skills in retail banking and better customer service. For instance, George and Chattopadhyay (2012) and Singh and Sirohi (2014) found that private banks started offering better-quality and user-friendly Internet banking services than public sector banks. This may be attributed to the better customer relationship management practices and technological focus of the private banks. Consequently, the following is hypothesized:

H8: *The impact of ownership on the market share of banks is ambiguous. The public banks may be able to increase their market share due to perceived trustworthiness among the historically well-established customer base. In contrast, it is also plausible that private banks would be able to increase their market share due to better customer relationship management practices and technological superiority in comparison to public banks.*

4. Data and Methodology

4.1. Sample Description

The sample consists of 154 banking firms in India, out of which 84 are domestic and 70 are foreign banks. The data were extracted from the Centre for Monitoring Indian Economy (CMIE) Prowess database from 2000 to 2020.

4.2. Econometric Specification

Customers' banking relations are generally enduring. Building relationships with new banks involves high transaction and information costs for customers (Clemes et al. 2010). This enduring relationship makes banks' market share persist for a long time. Likewise, marketing expenses incurred by banks in the past are likely to affect customer acquisition costs in the subsequent years. To capture the underlying *persistence* of bank share and Customer Acquisition Costs, using a dynamic panel data approach becomes more appropriate. By controlling for the persistence of the dependent variable, it provides consistent estimates of regression coefficients (Horobet et al. 2021). The two-step system GMM is also effective in tackling the issues of omitted variable bias, autocorrelation, and heteroscedasticity (Chattopadhyay et al. 2022). The method is considered to be more efficient and provides robust standard errors (Rego et al. 2013). The models to be estimated are specified as follows:

$$lnDMS_{it} = \alpha_0 + \alpha_1 lnDMS_{i,t-1} + \alpha_2 lnCum\_ICT_{it} + \Sigma controls_{it} + Year\_FE_t + \varepsilon_{it} \quad (1)$$

$$lnLMS_{it} = \beta_0 + \beta_1 lnLMS_{i,t-1} + \beta_2 lnCum\_ICT_{it} + \Sigma controls_{it} + Year\_FE_t + \varepsilon_{it} \quad (2)$$

$$lnCAC_{it} = \gamma_0 + \gamma_1 lnCAC_{i,t-1} + \gamma_2 lnCum\_ICT_{it} + \Sigma controls_{it} + Year\_FE_t + \varepsilon_{it} \quad (3)$$

The variables $lnDMS_{it}$, $lnLMS_{it}$, and $lnCAC_{it}$ denote deposit market share, loan market share, and customer acquisition cost of bank i at time t. ε_{it} is the disturbance term. Control variables used in Equation (1) are lnAge, $lnAge^2$, lnAssets, and lnInterest_deposits. Likewise, in Equation (2), we control for effect of lnAge, $lnAge^2$, lnAssets, and lnInterest_loans. lnAge, $lnAge^2$, lnAssets, and lnDeposits are controlled in Equation (3). $Year\_FE_t$ denotes year-fixed effects. A concise description of the underlying variables is presented in Table 1.

Table 1. Description of variables.

Symbol	Variable	Description
lnDMS	Log of deposit market share	The ratio of each bank's deposits to total deposits of all banks at a given time period t
lnLMS	Log of loan market share	The ratio of each bank's loans and advances to total loans and advances of all banks at a given time period t
lnCAC	Log of customer acquisition cost	The sum of a bank's advertising and marketing expenses (Rupees in millions)
lnCum_ICT	Log cumulative ICT investment	The cumulative sum of net expenses towards software, net expenditure on computers and IT systems, communication equipment, and IT-enabled service charges in the preceding years, i.e., 2000, 2001, 2002, . . .till the year at time period t (Rupees in Million)
lnInterest_Deposits	Log on interest on deposits	Interest paid on time deposits, savings deposits, recurring deposits, current deposits, demand deposits, or other kinds of interest-bearing deposits (Rupees in million)
lnInterest_loans	Log of interest on loans and advances	Interest on all types of loans and advances (Rupees in million)
lnDeposits	Log of bank deposits	Total amount of deposits collected by banks (Rupees in million)
lnAge	Log of bank's age	Difference between the year of observation and year of incorporation
Size	Log of total assets	Size of bank (Rupees in million)
Ownership_Dummy	Dummy variable	Public Limited bank = 1 Private Limited bank = 0

Source: authors' preparation.

4.3. Descriptive Statistics

The summary statistics of the variables used in the study are presented in Table 2. As expected, considerable difference is observed between the domestic and foreign banks in terms of the mean values of the underlying variables like DMS, LMS, cumulative ICT investment, and CAC. The larger market share of domestic banks may be attributed to their sizable presence in rural and semi-urban areas. On the other hand, foreign banks have typically limited their operations to major cities and metropolitan areas in India. Most importantly, it is important to note that, on average, the domestic banks have been spending more on ICT investment as well as CAC in comparison to their foreign counterparts. The mean values of size, age, deposits and interest on loans are also found to be higher for domestic banks. In contrast, the interest on deposits is higher for foreign banks.

Table 2. Descriptive statistics.

	Domestic Banks					Foreign Banks				
Variable	**Observations**	**Mean**	**Std. Dev.**	**Minimum**	**Maximum**	**Observations**	**Mean**	**Std. Dev.**	**Minimum**	**Maximum**
lnDMS	941	−5.014	2.26	−20.88	−0.36	519	−8.88	2.79	−20.28	−4.029
lnLMS	1198	−5.68	2.92	−20.69	−1.42	740	−8.54	2.5	−18.99	−4.01
lnCAC	995	2.95	2.85	−2.3	10.38	840	2.82	2.89	−2.3	10.16
lnCumulative ICT	1191	10.04	3.57	−1.6	13.62	739	8.48	4.23	−1.2	13.61
lnAge	1541	3.63	1.15	0	5.04	1080	3.26	1.21	0	5.11
Size	1214	12.17	2.56	−0.69	17.49	747	9.95	2.07	5.42	14.6
lnDeposits	941	12.6	2.25	−2.3	17.29	519	9.06	2.81	−2.3	14.27
lnInterest_deposits	988	7.99	3.11	−2.3	14.15	840	8.03	2.88	−2.3	14.2
lnInterest_loans	996	8.34	2.89	−2.3	14.29	843	8.21	2.85	−2.3	14.4
Ownership_Dummy	1786	0.75	0.43	0	1					

Source: authors' calculations. Note: DMS denotes deposit market share, LMS denotes loan market share, CAC denotes Customer Acquisition Costs, ICT denotes information and communication technology.

5. Results

The econometric analyses were conducted by using STATA version 17. Tables 3 and 4 report the results of the two-step system GMM analysis conducted for domestic and foreign banks, respectively.

Table 3. Two-step system GMM results for domestic banks.

	(1)	(2)	(3)	(4)
Variables	**lnDMS**	**lnDMS**	**lnLMS**	**lnLMS**
L.lnDMS	−0.351 ***	−0.336 ***		
	(0.107)	(0.105)		
L.lnLMS			0.585 ***	0.595 ***
			(0.154)	(0.164)
lnCum_ICT	−0.0711 **	−0.0987 ***	−0.0301	−0.0459 **
	(0.0353)	(0.0380)	(0.0201)	(0.0224)
lnAge	−0.117	−0.219	−0.377 **	−0.472 **
	(0.255)	(0.242)	(0.186)	(0.195)
$lnAge^2$	0.0403	0.0563	0.0469 *	0.0629 **
	(0.0365)	(0.0354)	(0.0260)	(0.0277)
Size	1.461 ***	1.477 ***	0.201 *	0.255 **
	(0.117)	(0.121)	(0.112)	(0.114)
lnInterest_deposits	−0.00486	−0.00370		
	(0.0147)	(0.0135)		
lnInterest_loans			0.00743	0.00837
			(0.0111)	(0.00965)
lnDeposits			0.279	0.239
			(0.207)	(0.223)
Ownership_dummy		−0.151 **		−0.0950 **
		(0.0642)		(0.0428)
Constant	−26.56 ***	−26.27 ***	−7.695 ***	−7.574 **
	(2.212)	(2.181)	(2.904)	(3.113)
Observations	240	240	273	273
Number of banks	56	56	61	61
AR(1) (*p*-value)	0.001	0.045	0.018	0.000
AR(2) (*p*-value)	0.450	0.444	0.549	0.577
Hansen Test (*p*-value)	0.466	0.551	0.349	0.293
No. of Instruments	31	32	31	31
Year FE	Yes	Yes	Yes	Yes

Source: authors' calculations. Note: standard errors in parentheses, *** $p < 0.01$, ** $p < 0.05$, * $p < 0.1$. DMS denotes deposit market share, LMS denotes loan market share, CAC denotes Customer Acquisition Costs, ICT denotes information and communication technology.

Table 4. Two-step system GMM results for foreign banks.

	(1)	(2)	(3)	(4)
Variables	lnDMS	lnDMS	lnLMS	lnLMS
L.lnDMS	0.930 ***	0.203		
	(0.238)	(0.150)		
L.lnLMS			0.874 ***	0.654 ***
			(0.0285)	(0.0716)
lnCum_ICT	0.0197	0.200 **	0.243 ***	0.725 **
	(0.0704)	(0.0897)	(0.0911)	(0.313)
lnAge	−0.774 ***	−0.213	2.291	0.321 **
	(0.284)	(0.874)	(2.989)	(0.128)
$lnAge^2$	0.108 **	0.0183	−4.671 *	−0.0632 ***
	(0.0424)	(0.119)	(2.488)	(0.0185)
Size	0.0224	0.827 ***	1.018 ***	0.451 **
	(0.284)	(0.160)	(0.0959)	(0.200)
lnInterest_deposits		−0.0182		
		(0.0226)		
lnInterest_loans				0.0256 *
				(0.0141)
lnDeposits				0.293 ***
				(0.0542)
Constant	0.729	−16.47 ***	1.729	−7.685 ***
	(5.533)	(4.182)	(3.854)	(1.440)
Observations	387	136	519	129
Number of banks	43	33	50	33
AR(1) (*p*-value)	0.025	0.000	0.022	0.030
AR(2) (*p*-value)	0.802	0.258	0.763	0.433
Hansen Test (*p*-value)	0.624	0.634	0.247	0.136
No. of Instruments	27	31	51	36
Year FE	Yes	Yes	Yes	Yes

Source: authors' calculations. Note: standard errors in parentheses, *** $p < 0.01$, ** $p < 0.05$, * $p < 0.1$. DMS denotes deposit market share, LMS denotes loan market share, CAC denotes Customer Acquisition Costs, ICT denotes information and communication technology.

Given the main research objective of this paper, the most important result relates to the impact of cumulative ICT investment on the DMS and LMS of the banks. From the results reported in Table 3, it is observed that cumulative ICT has a statistically significant, *negative* impact on the DMS and LMS of domestic banks. In stark contrast, as reported in Table 4, cumulative ICT is found to have a *positive* impact on the DMS and LMS of foreign banks. Moreover, the impact is significant in three specifications. Thus, hypothesis H1a is supported for the domestic banks across all of the model specifications. For the foreign banks, hypothesis H1b is supported in three out of four specifications.

Bank size is found to have a positive, significant effect on LMS and DMS for both the categories of banks. Therefore, hypothesis H3 is supported for both domestic and foreign banks.

In Table 3, the effect of age on the DMS of domestic banks is found to be non-linear but insignificant. However, there exists a U-shaped and significant relationship between age and LMS of domestic banks.

As reported in Table 4, for the foreign banks, the effect of age on DMS is U-shaped. This effect, however, is significant only in specification (1). The relationship between age and LMS is found to be inverted-U shaped and significant in specification (3) and (4). The graphical representations of the relationship between age, DMS, and LMS are provided in Figures 1 and 2.

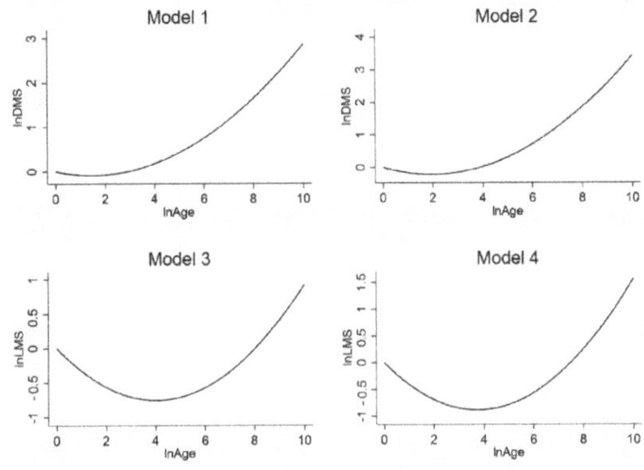

Figure 1. Effect of age on DMS and LMS of domestic banks.

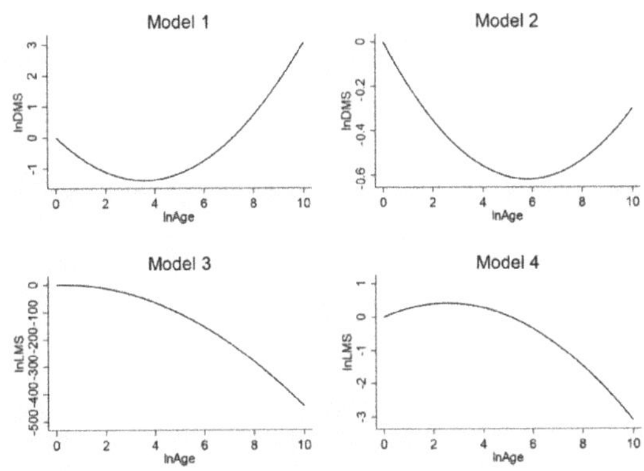

Figure 2. Effect of age on DMS and LMS of foreign banks.

In accordance with hypothesis H5, bank deposit is found to have a positive effect on the LMS of both domestic and foreign banks. However, this effect is significant only for the foreign banks.

The effect of interest on deposits on DMS is found to be negative and insignificant for both domestic and foreign banks. Hence, hypothesis H6 is not being supported.

Contrary to the expectation, interest on loans has a positive effect on the LMS of both categories of banks. This effect is significant for foreign banks. Thus, hypothesis H7 is not supported.

From Table 3, it is found that for the domestic banks, the coefficient of the ownership dummy variable is negative. It is statistically significant for DMS but not for LMS. The results indicate that in comparison to the private banks (base category), there is an unfavorable impact on the market share of public banks. Thus, private banks are found to be relatively better positioned in terms of increasing their market share. Hence, hypothesis H8 is validated in favor of the private banks.

Finally, given the important finding that ICT has a *differential* impact on the market share of domestic and foreign banks, what is the implication on the *strategic* variable, CAC of the banks? Table 5 reports the findings of this investigation.

Table 5. Impact of cumulative ICT on customer acquisition cost.

	(1)	(2)	(3)	(4)
	Domestic	Domestic	Foreign	Foreign
Variables	lnCAC	lnCAC	lnCAC	lnCAC
L.lnCAC	−0.310 **	−0.230 **	−0.131 *	−0.190 **
	(0.133)	(0.112)	(0.0743)	(0.0815)
lnCum_ICT	0.678 **	1.874 *	−0.787	−1.502 *
	(0.343)	(1.044)	(0.487)	(0.787)
lnAge		3.904		−0.229
		(3.947)		(1.233)
$lnAge^2$		−0.438		−0.0699
		(0.548)		(0.204)
lnAssets		−1.204		1.525 ***
		(1.215)		(0.493)
lnDeposits		−1.243		0.289
		(0.832)		(0.283)
Ownership_dummy		1.219 *		
		(0.653)		
Constant	−0.570	13.75 **	5.302 ***	−1.578
	(2.577)	(6.769)	(1.907)	(4.739)
Observations	377	309	261	162
Number of banks	72	64	58	43
AR(1) (p-value)	0.003	0.001	0.005	0.009
AR(2) (p-value)	0.121	0.192	0.678	0.455
Hansen Test (p-value)	0.100	0.316	0.336	0.286
No. of Instruments	36	43	40	44
Year FE	Yes	Yes	Yes	Yes

Source: authors' calculations. Note: standard errors in parentheses, *** $p < 0.01$, ** $p < 0.05$, * $p < 0.1$. DMS denotes deposit market share, LMS denotes loan market share, CAC denotes Customer Acquisition Costs, ICT denotes information and communication technology.

One of the practical issues faced by banks pertains to the relevance of ICT on their Customer Acquisition Costs. Specifically, it is important to understand how ICT affects CAC for domestic and foreign banks. From Table 3, it is evident that ICT investment is found to have an *adverse* impact on the market share of domestic banks. Consequently, the domestic banks would need to strategically spend more on CAC. This explains the positive, significant coefficient of CAC in specifications (1) and (2) of Table 5. In contrast, results from Table 4 indicate that ICT investment leads to a *favorable* impact on the market share of foreign banks. Consequently, the foreign banks would be able to reduce their CAC. This explains the negative coefficient of CAC in specifications (3) and (4) of Table 5. Consequently, both hypotheses H2a and H2b are supported.

Validity of Methodology

As explained in Section 4.2, the dependent variables under consideration (DMS, LMS, and CAC) are expected to depend on their values in previous periods. This underlying logic justifies the use of dynamic panel specification. Consistent estimators are obtained by using the Arellano-Bond system GMM method, where appropriate lags of the regressors are used as instruments (Roodman 2009; Cameron and Trivedi 2010).

The validity of the system GMM methodology relies on two important conditions (Roodman 2009; Baltagi 2021). First, there must be the absence of serial correlation in the original error term. The null hypothesis is the absence of serial correlation in the first differenced errors, $cov(\Delta\varepsilon_{it}, \Delta\varepsilon_{i,t-k}) = 0$. If ε_{it} are serially uncorrelated, then the null hypothesis should be rejected at order 1 but not at order 2. As reported in Tables 3–5, the p-values corresponding to AR(1) indicate that the null hypothesis is rejected, i.e., AR(1) is significant at 5%. Additionally, the p-values corresponding to AR(2) indicate that the null hypothesis cannot be rejected, i.e., AR(2) is not significant at 10%. The absence of serial correlation in the original error term is ensured in all model specifications. Consequently, the parameter estimates are consistent.

Second, the instruments must be exogenous, i.e., uncorrelated with the error term. This condition is examined by using the Hansen test of overidentifying restrictions. As reported in Tables 3–5, the p-values associated with the Hansen test statistic indicate that the null hypothesis (overidentifying restrictions are valid) cannot be rejected at 10%. Thus, it is ensured that the instruments are uncorrelated with the error term.

6. Discussion

One of the most important findings of this paper relates to the *differential* impact of ICT investment on the market shares of domestic and foreign banks operating in India. Specifically, it has been found that cumulative ICT investment has a significant, negative effect on the deposit and loan market share of domestic banks. It is plausible that the domestic banks are less efficient in utilizing ICT. In spite of investments in ICT, these banks are not able to enhance their customer service, which, in turn, explains the adverse impact on their market share. In contrast, there is a statistically positive, significant impact of cumulative ICT on deposits and loan market share of foreign banks. Thus, the foreign banks operating in India tend to exhibit greater efficiency in ICT utilization. This result corroborates with the *global advantage hypothesis* (Berger et al. 2000). This theory postulates that advanced technologies make foreign banks more efficient than domestic banks (Lensink and Naaborg 2007). Investment in state-of-the-art technology enhances foreign banks' operational efficiency, customer service, and risk-management capabilities. Another explanation for the favorable relationship between ICT investment on market share comes from the *resource-based view*. This theory contends that the unique resource endowment of a firm gives it a competitive advantage. The theory also holds that firms undertaking innovative activities and efficiently leveraging technology tend to perform better. Foreign banks have not only capitalized on technological efficiency but also benefited from the *first-mover advantage* of technology adoption. As early adopters, foreign banks introduced innovative technologies (like ATM) to the Indian banking system, thereby establishing technological leadership. This has played a crucial role in enabling foreign banks to have a favorable impact on market share.

In contrast, the slower technology diffusion among the domestic banks resulted in operational inefficiencies and limited customer engagement. It is interesting to note how the entry of foreign banks changed the dynamics of the Indian banking system. Heavy technology usage by foreign banks exerted competitive pressure on Indian banks to invest in ICT. The big push for technology adoption also came from the government in the early 1990s (Rishi and Saxena 2004). Indian banks, however, were reluctant to pivot away from their conventional banking operations. Organizational resistance to technological change has been a major obstacle to technology diffusion among Indian banks. For instance, HSBC introduced India's first ATM in 1987. However, it took almost two decades for ATMs to be adopted by domestic banks. Therefore, the slow diffusion and inefficient use of ICT would have an adverse impact on the overall performance of domestic banks. The finding that ICT has a negative impact on the market share of domestic banks also seems to corroborate with Solow's technological *productivity paradox* doctrine (Brynjolfsson and Hitt 1998; Malhotra and Singh 2007; Sharma 2023).

The impact of age on the DMS and LMS of domestic banks is found to be U-shaped. Such a non-linear relationship between age and market shares indicates that during the initial years of operation, new banks tend to face severe competition from the incumbent banks. However, as banks mature, they eventually gain improved market share. Banks that have consistently offered superior quality service over a long period are able to develop trust and goodwill. Customers are more likely to transact with those banks with which they have an enduring relationship. As a result, older banks have the potential to leverage their expertise, brand, and reputation to expand their market share. Long-term banking relationships lead to greater trust and goodwill, which is expected to have a favorable impact on a bank's market share.

A U-shaped relationship is also found between age and DMS of foreign banks. Initially, foreign banks are likely to face challenges such as cultural differences, regulatory uncertainties in the host country, and intense competition from domestic banks. However, with increasing years of operation and *continuous* investment in ICT, these banks are able to collect more information about an erstwhile unknown market. Along with more information, the perceived superior customer service of the foreign banks leads to a snowballing effect. Thus, foreign banks are able to enhance their deposit market share by utilizing the benefits of ICT. In light of the results of this study, foreign banks ought to be patient in terms of their years of operation in host countries. They also need to put *persistent* efforts toward introducing innovative financial products and enhanced customer service in host countries.

The relationship between age and foreign banks' LMS is found to be inverted U-shaped. The non-linear relationship between age and LMS suggests that foreign banks would have a larger share of the credit market in their initial years. Subsequently, with increased years of operation, their loan market share diminishes. The *resource-based view* and *dynamic capability* theory can account for such a relationship. According to the *resource-based view*, younger banks' unique resources give them a competitive edge. Such banks are more agile in adopting technology, undertaking innovation and, thus, gain a larger market share. However, with maturity, they might face problems due to strategic transformation (Thornhill and Amit 2003). The *dynamic capability* theory postulates that a firm's ability to augment its competencies to align with the changing business environment would determine its competitive advantage. Hence, persistence in market share would depend on the bank's dynamic capabilities. It is plausible that younger banks are able to respond quickly to changes in the business environment. In contrast, the possible mismatch between the capabilities of older banks and the prevailing competitive environment might lead to customer disengagement (Denrell and Powell 2016).

The effect of bank size is found to be positive and significant on the market share of both domestic and foreign banks. This finding corroborates with previous studies (Kim and Davidson 2004; Sheng 2021; Świtała et al. 2020; Ünvan and Yakubu 2020). Nonetheless, a word of caution is necessary. The larger banks should not remain complacent with their extant market shares. This paper underscores the importance of *continuous* investment in ICT, even among the big players in the market.

The result related to the insignificant relationship between interest on deposits and banks' DMS is intriguing and warrants an explanation. While it is expected that interest on deposits would have a favorable impact on the DMS of banks, the counterintuitive finding can be explained as follows. Over the last few years, cash-surplus customers have been routing their investments to equity, stocks, and mutual funds, which tend to provide higher net returns than bank deposits. Indeed, the banks have been facing increased competition from these alternative investment channels. Therefore, it might not be sufficient just to increase deposit rates to entice the customers. Apart from interest rates, factors such as enhanced customer service and building long-term trustworthiness among customers through technological advancements are expected to play an important role in maintaining the market share of banks.

The effect of interest on loans on LMS is positive for both domestic and foreign banks but significant for only the latter. This counterintuitive result may be attributed to the market segmentation practiced by foreign banks. Foreign banks in India engage in 'cream skimming' (Gormley 2010; Sarma and Prashad 2016), where they tend to extend credit to the most profitable entities. Foreign banks would focus on individuals and entities that are less price-sensitive and value service quality over the cost of borrowing.

The results reported in Tables 3 and 4 indicate a positive impact of deposits on the loan market share of both domestic and foreign banks. Banks are able to seek new, profitable lending opportunities due to expansion in their deposit base. This result corroborates with the extant literature that deposits have a positive impact on the loans extended by banks (Kashyap and Stein 1995; Genay 2000; Yitayaw 2021).

The results reported in Table 5 indicate that banks incurring high (low) CAC in the past would have to spend less (more) on CAC in subsequent periods. One plausible explanation might be that acquiring new customers is costlier than customer retention (Filiatrault and Lapierre 1997). Hence, banks that have previously acquired customers would focus on retaining their incumbent customers. It is also important to note that cumulative ICT investment is found to *increase* the CAC of domestic banks. This result highlights the strategic response of domestic banks to enhance their market share. In contrast, foreign banks are able to increase their market share by leveraging ICT. This enables them to *reduce* CAC in the Indian market.

There are certain limitations of this study which must be addressed. Future research is warranted on these important issues. First, the ICT data used in this study capture traditional forms of technologies like hardware, equipment, and software. They do not include investment in modern digital technologies that are currently being used by the banks. Digital marketing indeed plays a crucial role in augmenting a bank's customer reach and providing a competitive advantage. It also facilitates cost-effective customer acquisition. Another limitation of this study emanates from the lack of CAC data for several foreign banks. Thus, in comparison to the domestic banks, the sample size of foreign banks is less. Future studies comprising a larger sample of banks are warranted.

Second, the analysis of this paper has been conducted at the bank level, but not the branch level. This is predominantly due to the lack of coherent longitudinal data for all the underlying variables at the branch level. For instance, it is plausible that both CAC and market share would be determined by the location of a branch. It would be interesting to examine whether branches located in urban areas tend to outperform the rural branches.

Third, due to data availability constraints, the study is unable to incorporate some of the important variables that would presumably affect ICT investment strategies and market shares of the banks. For instance, the size and characteristics of the Board of Directors are expected to have an impact on investment strategies and bank performance (de Andres and Vallelado 2008; Belkhir 2009). Bank-specific internal factors, like impaired loans or gross interest margin, can also affect the performance of banks (Lamothe et al. 2024). In the context of the banks operating in India, detailed micro-data on these important variables is sparse. Given such practical limitations due to data constraints, the results should be carefully interpreted. It is stressed that the system GMM is an effective method in tackling the issues of omitted variable bias (Chattopadhyay et al. 2022). Future studies are warranted to take some of these variables into consideration, wherever feasible.

It is plausible that during the COVID-19 years, i.e., 2020–2022, the ICT investment of the banks might have been adversely affected. However, the pandemic also drastically altered consumer behavior and banking operations in *favorable* ways. This is particularly relevant in the post-pandemic era, wherein customers were more acquainted with digital technologies like mobile banking and WhatsApp banking. It may be argued that the pandemic has actually incentivized customers to shift more toward digital and online banking operations. The banks have also taken the signal and resorted to additional investment in modern ICT technologies that would facilitate digital banking operations at a larger scale. Therefore, in *cumulative* terms, it is expected that ICT investment by the banks would have registered an upward trend after the pandemic ended. In the present study, the COVID-19 years are excluded primarily due to the unavailability of consistent data related to the underlying variables for all the banks. Nevertheless, future studies are warranted to analyze the effect during the pandemic years and the rebounding effect, if any, during the post-pandemic years.

7. Managerial Implications

The findings of this paper have several important implications for bank management. First, the domestic banks must re-evaluate their ICT investment strategies, given the adverse impact of ICT investment on their market share. Evidently, ICT investment is not sufficient. The management should continuously invest in quality training programs that would enhance the adoption of novel ICT tools among the bank employees. Such strategies would enhance the *quality of service* provided by the banks and, consequently, their market shares.

Second, investment in ICT should not be considered a one-shot game. Given the statistical significance of *cumulative* ICT, banks ought to update the software and equipment to the latest versions so that they can remain ahead of the competition. For instance, given the changing consumer preferences toward digital transactions, the banks must continuously differentiate themselves from their peers. In order to gain further market share, the banks would be better off introducing innovative products like digital wallets and, thus, have additional sources of revenue. Overall, the banks would need to enhance customer experience and convenience by introducing innovative products and services. *Continuous* investment in ICT is an important tool for achieving these goals.

Third, the impact of ICT is found to differ among domestic and foreign banks operating in India. It may be argued that both categories of banks would have access to similar, non-differentiable ICT tools. Almost all banks are vigorously using technology (like ICT) along with human capital (like Relationship Managers) to increase their customer acquisition. The banks are using the latest information technologies and advanced analytics to target new customers. Banks have also established dedicated customer acquisition centers that collect, process, and utilize customer-centric data. Nonetheless, the impact of ICT on market shares of domestic and foreign banks is found to differ. What is the economic explanation behind such an intriguing result? This may be attributed to the differentiation of *service* provided by the banks as perceived by the customers. The domestic and foreign banks seem to differ in terms of their ability to utilize ICT to create innovative products and provide improved services. The results indicate that domestic banks are relatively inefficient in terms of ICT usage and, therefore, would have to increase their CAC. Consequently, domestic banks should focus on leveraging ICT for targeted marketing strategies and cost-effective customer acquisition. The management must re-examine the efficacy of their currently deployed marketing strategies and the effectiveness of their Relationship Managers.

The study also provides important insights pertaining to the foreign banks. As reported in Table 4, cumulative ICT has a positive and significant impact on their market shares. Thus, foreign banks ought to maintain their ICT investment in a *sustained* manner. Since the lagged dependent variables (DMS and LMS) are found to be positive and statistically significant, it is important for foreign banks to sustain their high level of customer service. This underscores the strategic importance of sustained investment in ICT to offer enhanced customer service. Also, it is found that deposits have a significant, positive impact on the LMS of foreign banks. Consequently, foreign banks might consider offering higher interest rates in order to remain competitive in the Indian market.

8. Conclusions

This paper focuses on the differential impact of ICT investment on domestic and foreign banks operating in India. Specifically, the study examines the impact of stock of ICT investment on the market share and Customer Acquisition Costs of domestic and foreign banks. Market shares of the banks are considered to be a proxy for their market power. Sustained investment in ICT can be the right tool to enhance market power, albeit only when complemented with prudent customer service and management strategies.

The impact of ICT is found to differ among domestic and foreign banks operating in India. Since ICT is found to have an adverse impact on the market share of domestic banks, they need to strategically invest more in Customer Acquisition Costs. In contrast, since foreign firms are found to increase their market share by investing in ICT, they have the ability to reduce their Customer Acquisition Costs. Thus, foreign banks are found to be relatively more efficient than domestic banks in utilizing ICT. The differential impact of ICT can be attributed to the differentiation of the *service* provided by foreign banks from the viewpoint of the customers. Consequently, it is important for banks to re-examine the effectiveness of their extant marketing techniques and implement appropriate strategies to enhance customer service by utilizing the information acquired through ICT investment.

Author Contributions: Conceptualization, G.G.A. and R.S.G.; methodology, G.G.A. and R.S.G.; validation, R.S.G.; formal analysis, G.G.A.; original draft writing, G.G.A. and R.S.G.; supervision, R.S.G. All authors have read and agreed to the published version of the manuscript.

Funding: This research received no external funding. The financial support received from BITS Pilani KK Birla Goa Campus is gratefully acknowledged.

Data Availability Statement: The data were collected from CMIE Prowess database available from https://prowess.cmie.com/.

Conflicts of Interest: The authors declare no conflicts of interest.

References

Alshwayat, Dana, Hamzah Elrehail, Esam Shehadeh, Nidal Alsalhi, Mohamed Dawood Shamout, and Shafique Ur Rehman. 2023. An exploratory examination of the barriers to innovation and change as perceived by senior management. *International Journal of Innovation Studies* 7: 159–70. [CrossRef]

Arabyat, Yaser Ahmed, and Omar G. Aziz. 2022. Dynamics of Information Acquisition: Does Investment in Information Technology Matter? *Global Journal of Emerging Market Economies* 14: 348–65. [CrossRef]

Baker, Hafez, Thair A. Kaddumi, Mahmoud Daoud Nassar, and Riham Suleiman Muqattash. 2023. Impact of financial technology on improvement of banks' financial performance. *Journal of Risk and Financial Management* 16: 230. [CrossRef]

Baltagi, Badi H. 2021. *Econometric Analysis of Panel Data*. Berlin/Heidelberg: Springer.

Banker, Rajiv D., and Robert J. Kauffman. 1988. Strategic contributions of information technology: An empirical study of ATM networks. Paper presented at 9th International Conference on Information Systems 1988, Minneapolis, MN, USA, December 5–7.

Beccalli, Elena. 2007. Does IT investment improve bank performance? Evidence from Europe. *Journal of Banking & Finance* 31: 2205–30.

Belkhir, Mohamed. 2009. Board of directors' size and performance in the banking industry. *International Journal of Managerial Finance* 5: 201–21. [CrossRef]

Berger, Allen N., and Astrid A. Dick. 2007. Entry into banking markets and the early-mover advantage. *Journal of Money, Credit and Banking* 39: 775–807. [CrossRef]

Berger, Allen N., Robert DeYoung, Hesna Genay, and Gregory F. Udell. 2000. Globalization of financial institutions: Evidence from cross-border banking performance. *Brookings-Wharton Papers on Financial Services* 1: 23–120. [CrossRef]

Bhattacharyya, Arunava, C. A. Knox Lovell, and Pankaj Sahay. 1997. The impact of liberalization on the productive efficiency of Indian commercial banks. *European Journal of Operational Research* 98: 332–45. [CrossRef]

Brynjolfsson, Erik, and Lorin M. Hitt. 1998. Beyond the productivity paradox. *Communications of the ACM* 41: 49–55. [CrossRef]

Cameron, Adrian Colin, and Pravin K. Trivedi. 2010. *Microeconometrics Using STATA*. College Station: STATA Press.

Cao, Yong, and Thomas S. Gruca. 2005. Reducing adverse selection through customer relationship management. *Journal of Marketing* 69: 219–29. [CrossRef]

Chattopadhyay, Arup Kumar, Debdas Rakshit, Payel Chatterjee, and Ananya Paul. 2022. Trends and Determinants of FDI with Implications of COVID-19 in BRICS. *Global Journal of Emerging Market Economies* 14: 43–59. [CrossRef]

Chen, Kuan-Chieh. 2020. Implications of Fintech developments for traditional banks. *International Journal of Economics and Financial Issues* 10: 227. [CrossRef]

Claessens, Stijn, Aslı Demirgüç-Kunt, and Harry Huizinga. 2001. How does foreign entry affect domestic banking markets? *Journal of Banking & Finance* 25: 891–911.

Clemes, Michael D., Christopher Gan, and Dongmei Zhang. 2010. Customer switching behaviour in the Chinese retail banking industry. *International Journal of Bank Marketing* 28: 519–46. [CrossRef]

de Andres, Pablo, and Eleuterio Vallelado. 2008. Corporate governance in banking: The role of the board of directors. *Journal of Banking & Finance* 32: 2570–80.

Dell'Ariccia, Giovanni. 2001. Asymmetric information and the structure of the banking industry. *European Economic Review* 45: 1957–80. [CrossRef]

Denrell, Jerker, and Thomas C. Powell. 2016. Dynamic Capability as a Theory of Competitive Advantage: Contributions and Scope Conditions. In *The Oxford Handbook of Dynamic Capabilities*. Edited by David J. Teece and Sohvi Heaton. Oxford: Oxford University Press. [CrossRef]

DeYoung, Robert. 2001. The financial performance of pure play Internet banks. *Economic Perspectives-Federal Reserve Bank of Chicago* 25: 60–73.

DeYoung, Robert. 2005. The performance of Internet-based business models: Evidence from the banking industry. *The Journal of Business* 78: 893–948. [CrossRef]

DeYoung, Robert, William W. Lang, and Daniel L. Nolle. 2007. How the Internet affects output and performance at community banks. *Journal of Banking & Finance* 31: 1033–60.

Filiatrault, Pierre, and Jozée Lapierre. 1997. Managing business-to-business marketing relationships in consulting engineering firms. *Industrial Marketing Management* 26: 213–22. [CrossRef]

Genay, Hesna. 2000. *Recent Trends in Deposit and Loan Growth: Implications for Small and Large Banks*. Chicago: The Federal Reserve Bank of Chicago, No. 160.

George, Sajeev Abraham, and Nilanjan Chattopadhyay. 2012. An investigative study of operational performance and service quality of Indian public sector banks. *International Journal of Business Performance Management* 13: 408–25. [CrossRef]

Ghose, Biswajit, and Santi Gopal Maji. 2022. Internet banking intensity and bank profitability: Evidence from emerging Indian economy. *Managerial Finance* 48: 1607–26. [CrossRef]

Giannetti, Mariassunta, and Steven Ongena. 2012. "Lending by example": Direct and indirect effects of foreign banks in emerging markets. *Journal of International Economics* 86: 167–80. [CrossRef]

Gormley, Todd A. 2010. The impact of foreign bank entry in emerging markets: Evidence from India. *Journal of Financial Intermediation* 19: 26–51. [CrossRef]

Hernando, Ignacio, and María J. Nieto. 2007. Is the Internet delivery channel changing banks' performance? The case of Spanish banks. *Journal of Banking & Finance* 31: 1083–99.

Horobet, Alexandra, Magdalena Radulescu, Lucian Belascu, and Sandra Maria Dita. 2021. Determinants of bank profitability in CEE countries: Evidence from GMM panel data estimates. *Journal of Risk and Financial Management* 14: 307. [CrossRef]

Ho, Shirley J., and Sushanta Kumar Mallick. 2010. The impact of information technology on the banking industry. *Journal of the Operational Research Society* 61: 211–21. [CrossRef]

Kashyap, Anil K., and Jeremy C. Stein. 1995. The impact of monetary policy on bank balance sheets. *Carnegie-Rochester Series on Public Policy* 42: 151–95. [CrossRef]

Kim, Chang-Soo, and Lewis F. Davidson. 2004. The effects of IT expenditures on banks' business performance: Using a balanced scorecard approach. *Managerial Finance* 30: 28–45. [CrossRef]

Lamothe, Prosper, Enrique Delgado, Miguel A. Solanlamo, and Sergio M. Fernández. 2024. A global analysis of bank profitability factors. *Humanities and Social Sciences Communications* 11: 124. [CrossRef]

Lensink, Robert, and Ilko Naaborg. 2007. Does foreign ownership foster bank performance? *Applied Financial Economics* 17: 881–85. [CrossRef]

Malhotra, Pooja, and Balwinder Singh. 2007. Determinants of internet banking adoption by banks in India. *Internet Research* 17: 323–39. [CrossRef]

Maudos, Joaquín, and Juan Fernández de Guevara. 2004. Factors explaining the interest margin in the banking sectors of the European Union. *Journal of Banking and Finance* 28: 2259–81. [CrossRef]

Mithas, Sunil, Ali Tafti, Indranil Bardhan, and Jie Mein Goh. 2012. Information technology and firm profitability: Mechanisms and empirical evidence. *MIS Quarterly* 36: 205–24. [CrossRef]

Nguyen, James, Parsons Richard, and Argyle Bronson. 2021. An examination of diversification on bank profitability and insolvency risk in 28 financially liberalized markets. *Journal of Behavioral and Experimental Finance* 29: 100416. [CrossRef]

Patra, Biswajit, Purna Chandra Padhan, and Puja Padhi. 2023. Efficiency of Indian Banks–private versus public sector banks: A two-stage analysis. *Cogent Economics & Finance* 11: 2163081.

Prashad, Anjali. 2020. Regulatory Arbitrage and Presence of Foreign Banks: Evidence from the Indian Banking Sector. *Global Journal of Emerging Market Economies* 12: 303–34. [CrossRef]

Rego, Lopo L., Neil A. Morgan, and Claes Fornell. 2013. Re-examining the market share–customer satisfaction relationship. *Journal of Marketing* 77: 1–20. [CrossRef]

Rishi, Meenakshi, and Sweta C. Saxena. 2004. Technological innovations in the Indian banking industry: The late bloomer. *Accounting, Business & Financial History* 14: 339–53.

Roodman, David. 2009. How to do xtabond2: An introduction to difference and system GMM in Stata. *The Stata Journal* 9: 86–136. [CrossRef]

Sarma, Mandira, and Anjali Prashad. 2016. Do Foreign Banks in India Indulge in 'Cream Skimming'? *Economic and Political Weekly* 51: 120–25.

Sathye, Milind. 2003. Efficiency of banks in a developing economy: The case of India. *European Journal of Operational Research* 148: 662–71. [CrossRef]

Scott, Susan V., John Van Reenen, and Markos Zachariadis. 2017. The long-term effect of digital innovation on bank performance: An empirical study of SWIFT adoption in financial services. *Research Policy* 46: 984–1004. [CrossRef]

Sensarma, Rudra. 2006. Are foreign banks always the best? Comparison of state-owned, private and foreign banks in India. *Economic Modelling* 23: 717–35. [CrossRef]

Sharma, Shweta. 2023. E-banking services and bank performance: Perspective from India. *International Journal of Electronic Finance* 12: 176–91. [CrossRef]

Sheng, Tianxiang. 2021. The effect of fintech on banks' credit provision to SMEs: Evidence from China. *Finance Research Letters* 39: 101558. [CrossRef]

Singh, Shamsher, and Naveen J. Sirohi. 2014. Internet banking services as tool of CRM: A study of customer satisfaction in the national capital region, Delhi. *International Journal of Electronic Customer Relationship Management* 8: 101–18. [CrossRef]

Świtała, Filip, Iwona Kowalska, and Karolina Malajkat. 2020. Size of banks as a factor which impacts the efficiency of the bank lending channel. *Financial Internet Quarterly* 16: 36–44. [CrossRef]

Thornhill, Stewart, and Raphael Amit. 2003. Learning about failure: Bankruptcy, firm age, and the resource-based view. *Organization Science* 14: 497–509. [CrossRef]

Ünvan, Yüksel Akay, and Ibrahim Nandom Yakubu. 2020. Do bank-specific factors drive bank deposits in Ghana? *Journal of Computational and Applied Mathematics* 376: 112827. [CrossRef]

Yitayaw, Mekonnen. 2021. Firm-specific, industry-specific and macroeconomic determinants of commercial banks' lending in Ethiopia: Panel data approach. *Cogent Economics & Finance* 9: 1952718.

MDPI AG
Grosspeteranlage 5
4052 Basel
Switzerland
Tel.: +41 61 683 77 34

Journal of Risk and Financial Management Editorial Office
E-mail: jrfm@mdpi.com
www.mdpi.com/journal/jrfm

www.ingramcontent.com/pod-product-compliance
Lightning Source LLC
Chambersburg PA
CBHW061835210926
51850CB00006B/893